Millennial Capitalism and the Culture of Neoliberalism

A MILLENNIAL QUARTET BOOK

ALTERNATIVE MODERNITIES,
edited by Dilip Parameshwar Gaonkar

GLOBALIZATION, *edited by Arjun Appadurai*

MILLENNIAL CAPITALISM AND THE
CULTURE OF NEOLIBERALISM, *edited
by Jean Comaroff & John L. Comaroff*

COSMOPOLITANISM, *edited by
Carol A. Breckenridge, Sheldon Pollock,
Homi K. Bhabha, & Dipesh Chakrabarty*

PUBLIC CULTURE BOOKS

Millennial Capitalism and the Culture of Neoliberalism

Edited by Jean Comaroff and John L. Comaroff

DUKE UNIVERSITY PRESS * DURHAM & LONDON 2001

Contents

Millennial Capitalism and the Culture of Neoliberalism

Millennial Capitalism:

First Thoughts on a Second Coming

Jean Comaroff and John L. Comaroff

We live in difficult times, in times of monstrous chimeras and evil dreams and criminal follies. — Joseph Conrad, *Under Western Eyes*

The global triumph of capitalism at the millennium, its Second Coming, raises a number of conundrums for our understanding of history at the end of the century. Some of its corollaries — "plagues of the 'new world order,'" Jacques Derrida (1994: 91) calls them, unable to resist apocalyptic imagery — have been the subject of clamorous debate. Others receive less mention. Thus, for example, populist polemics have dwelt on the planetary conjuncture, for good or ill, of "homogenization and difference" (e.g., Barber 1992); on the simultaneous, synergistic spiraling of wealth and poverty; on the rise of a "new feudalism," a phoenix disfigured, of worldwide proportions (cf. Connelly and Kennedy 1994).[1] For its part, scholarly debate has focused on the confounding effects of rampant liberalization: on whether it engenders truly global flows of capital or concentrates circulation to a few major sites (Hirst and Thompson 1996); on whether it undermines, sustains, or reinvents the sovereignty of nation-states (Sassen 1996); on whether it frees up, curbs, or compartmentalizes the movement of labor (see the Geschiere and Nyamnjoh essay in this volume); on whether the current fixation with democracy, its resurrection in so many places, implies a measure of mass empowerment or an "emptying out of [its] meaning," its reduction "to paper" (Negri 1999: 9; Comaroff and Comaroff 1997).[2] Equally in question is why the present infatuation with civil society has been accompanied by alarming increases in civic strife, by an escalation of civil war, and by reports of the dramatic growth in many countries of domestic violence, rape, child abuse, prison populations, and most dramatically of all, criminal "phantom-states" (Derrida 1994: 83; Blaney and Pasha 1993). And why, in a like vein, the politics of consumerism, human rights, and entitlement have been shown to coincide with puzzling new patterns of exclusion, patterns that inflect older lines of gender, sexuality, race, and class in ways both strange and familiar (Gal 1997; Yúdice 1995). Ironies, here, all the way down; ironies, with apologies to Jean-Paul Sartre, in the very soul of the Millennial Age.

Other features of our present predicament are less remarked, debated, questioned. Among them are the odd coupling, the binary complementarity, of the legalistic with the libertarian; constitutionality with deregulation; hyperrationalization with the exuberant spread of innovative occult practices and money magic, pyramid schemes and prosperity gospels; the enchantments, that is, of a decidedly *neo*liberal economy whose ever more inscrutable speculations seem to call up fresh specters in their wake. Note that, unlike others who have discussed the "new spectral reality" of that economy (Negri 1999: 9; Sprinker 1999), we do not talk here in metaphorical terms. We seek, instead, to draw attention to, to interrogate, the distinctly pragmatic qualities of the messianic, millennial capitalism of the moment: a capitalism that presents itself as a gospel of salvation; a capitalism that, if rightly harnessed, is invested with the capacity wholly to transform the universe of the marginalized and disempowered (Comaroff and Comaroff 1999b).

All this points to another, even more fundamental question. Could it be that these characteristics of millennial capitalism—by which we mean *both* capitalism at the millennium and capitalism in its messianic, salvific, even magical manifestations—are connected, by cause or correlation or copresence, with other, more mundane features of the contemporary historical moment? Like the increasing relevance of consumption, alike to citizens of the world and to its scholarly cadres, in shaping selfhood, society, identity, even epi-stemic reality? Like the concomitant eclipse of such modernist categories as social class? Like the "crises," widely observed across the globe, of reproduction and community, youth and masculinity? Like the burgeoning importance of generation, race, and gender as principles of difference, identity, and mobilization? The point of this essay lies in exploring the possibility of their interconnection; even more, in laying the ground of an argument for it.

As this suggests, our intent in this selection of essays from *Public*

Culture is to animate further debate on the enigmatic nature of millennial capitalism, and also on its implications for theorizing history and society at the start of the twenty-first century. However we wish to characterize our current moment — as an age of death (of ideology, politics, the subject) or rebirth (of the spirit of Marx, Weber, the two Adams, Ferguson and Smith) — ours are perplexing times: "Times of monstrous chimeras" in which the conjuncture of the strange and the familiar, of stasis and metamorphosis, plays tricks on our perceptions, our positions, our praxis. These conjunctures appear at once to endorse and to erode our understanding of the lineaments of modernity and its postponements. Here, plainly, we can do no more than offer preliminary observations and opening lines of argument on a topic whose full extent can only be glimpsed at present.

Let us, then, cut to the heart of the matter: to the ontological conditions-of-being under millennial capitalism. This begins for us — as it did for the "fathers" of modernist social theory — with epochal shifts in the constitutive relationship of production to consumption, and hence of labor to capital. This requires, in turn, that we consider the meaning of social class under prevailing political and economic conditions, conditions that place growing stress on generation, gender, and race as indices of identity, affect, and political action. In light of these reflections we go on to explore three corollaries, three critical faces of the millennial moment: the shifting provenance of the nation-state and its fetishes, the rise of new forms of enchantment, and the explosion of neoliberal discourses of civil society.

First, however, back to basics.

CAPITALISM AT THE MILLENNIUM, MILLENNIAL CAPITALISM

The political history of capital [is] a sequence of attempts by capital to withdraw from the class relationship; at a higher level we can now see it as the history of the successive attempts of the capitalist class to emancipate itself from the working class. — Mario Tronti, "The Strategy of Refusal" (Tronti's emphasis)

Specters, Speculation: Of Cons and Pros Consumption, recall, was the hallmark disease of the eighteenth and nineteenth centuries, of the First Coming of Industrial Capitalism, of a time when the ecological conditions of production, its consuming passions (Sontag 1978; cf.

Jean Comaroff 1997a), ate up the bodies of producers.[3] Now, at the end of the twenty-first century, semiotically transposed, it is often said to be the "hallmark of modernity" (van Binsbergen and Geschiere n.d.: 3), the measure of its wealth, health, and vitality. An overgeneralization, maybe, yet the claim captures popular imaginings and their representation across the earth. It also resonates with the growing Euro-cultural truism that the (post)modern person is a subject made with objects. Nor is this surprising. Consumption, in its ideological guise — as "consumer*ism*" — refers to a material sensibility actively cultivated, for the common good, by Western states and commercial interests, particularly since World War II. It has even been cultivated by some non-capitalist regimes: In the early 1990s, Deng Xiaoping advocated "consumption as a motor force of production" (Dirlik 1996: 194).

In social theory, as well, consumption has become a prime mover (van Binsbergen and Geschiere n.d.: 3). Increasingly, it is *the* factor, *the* principle, held to determine definitions of value, the construction of identities, and even the shape of the global "ecumene."[4] As such, tellingly, it is the invisible hand, or the Gucci-gloved fist, that animates the political impulses, the material imperatives, and the social forms of the Second Coming of Capitalism — of capitalism in its neoliberal, global manifestation. Note the image: the invisible hand. It evokes the ghost of crises past, when liberal political economy first discerned the movements of the market beneath swirling economic waters, of "free" enterprise behind the commonweal. Gone is the deus ex machina, a figure altogether too concrete, too industrial for the "virtualism" (Carrier and Miller 1998) of the post-Fordist era.

As consumption became the moving spirit of the late twentieth century, so there was a concomitant eclipse of production; an eclipse, at least, of its *perceived* salience for the wealth of nations. This heralded a shift, across the world, in ordinary understandings of the nature of capitalism. The workplace and labor, especially work-and-place securely rooted in a stable local context, are no longer prime sites for the creation of value or identity (Sennett 1998). The factory and the shop, far from secure centers of fabrication and family income, are increasingly experienced by virtue of their erasure: either by their removal to an elsewhere — where labor is cheaper, less assertive, less taxed, more feminized, less protected by states and unions — or by their replacement at the hands of nonhuman or "nonstandard" means of manufacture.

Which, in turn, has left behind, for ever more people, a legacy of irregular piecework, of menial "workfare," of relatively insecure, transient, gainless occupation. Hence the paradox, in many Western economies, of high official employment rates amidst stark deindustrialization and joblessness.[5] In the upshot, production appears to have been superseded, as the *fons et origo* of wealth, by less tangible ways of generating value: by control over such things as the provision of services, the means of communication, and above all, the flow of finance capital. In short, by the market and by speculation.

Symptomatic in this respect are the changing historical fortunes of gambling. The latter, of course, makes manifest a mechanism integral to market enterprise: It puts the adventure into venture capital. Financial risk has always been crucial to the growth of capitalism; it has, from the first, been held to warrant its own due return. But, removed from the dignifying nexus of the market, it was until recently treated by Protestant ethics and populist morality alike as a "pariah" practice. Casinos were set apart from the workaday world. They were situated at resorts, on reservations and riverboats: liminal places of leisure and/or the haunts of those (aristocrats, profligates, "chancers") above and beyond honest toil. Living off the proceeds of this form of speculation was, normatively speaking, the epitome of immoral accumulation: the wager stood to the wage, the bet to personal betterment, as sin to virtue. There have, self-evidently, always been different cultures and mores of betting. However, the activity—whether it be a "flutter" on the horses or a domestic card game, on a sporting contest or an office pool—has generally been placed outside the domain of work and earning, at best in the ambiguous, nether space between virtue and its transgression. Over a generation, gambling, in its marked form, has changed moral valence and invaded everyday life across the world.[6] It has been routinized in a widespread infatuation with, and popular participation in, high-risk dealings in stocks, bonds, and funds whose fortunes are governed largely by chance. It also expresses itself in a fascination with "futures" and their downmarket counterpart, the lottery. Here the mundane meets the millennial: "Not A LOT TO TOMAR, OW!" proclaims an ironic inner-city mural in Chicago (see "Millennial Transitions" in this volume), large hands grasping a seductive pile of casino chips, beside which nestles a newborn, motherless babe.[7] This at a moment when "gambling [is] the fastest growing industry in the US," when it is "tightly woven into the national fabric," when it is increasingly "operated and promoted" by government.[8]

Life itself has become the object of bookmaking; it is no longer the sole preserve of the "respectable" insurance industry, of its abstract argot of longevity statistics and probability quotients. A recent article in *Newsweek* sports the headline "Capital Gains: The Lottery on Lives": "In America's *fin de siècle* casino culture, no wager seems *outré*. So how about betting on how long a stranger is likely to live? You can buy part or all of his or her insurance policy, becoming a beneficiary. Your gamble: that death will come soon enough to yield a high return on the money you put up. The Viatical Association of America says that $1 billion worth of coverage went into play last year."[9] A much better bet, this, than the sale of the Savior for thirty pieces of silver. Inflation notwithstanding.

In the era of millennial capitalism, securing instant returns *is* often a matter of life and death. The failure to win the weekly draw was linked with more than one suicide in Britain in the wake of the introduction of national lottery in 1994; in 1999, the *India Tribune* reported that one of the biggest central Indian States, Madya Pradesh, was "caught in the vortex of lottery mania," which had claimed several lives.[10] Witnesses described "extreme enthusiasm among the jobless youth towards trying their luck to make a fast buck," precisely the kind of fatal ecstasy classically associated with cargo cults and chiliastic movements (Cohn 1957). More mundanely, efforts to enlist divine help in tipping the odds, from the Taiwanese countryside to the Kalahari fringe, have become a regular feature of what Weller (in this volume) terms "fee-for-service" religions (Comaroff and Comaroff 1999b). These are locally nuanced fantasies of abundance without effort, of beating capitalism at its own game by drawing a winning number at the behest of unseen forces. Once again, that invisible hand.

The change in the moral valence of gambling also has a public dimension. In a neoliberal climate where taxes are anathema to the majoritarian political center, lotteries and gaming levies have become a favored means of filling national coffers, of generating cultural and social assets, of finding soft monies in times of tough cutbacks. The defunct machinery of a growing number of welfare states, to be sure, is being turned by the wheel of fortune. With more and more governments and political parties depending on this source for quick revenue fixes, betting, says

George Will, has "been transformed from a social disease"—subjected, not so long ago, to scrutiny at the hands of Harvard Medical School— "into social policy."[11] Once a dangerous sign of moral turpitude, "it is now marketed almost as a 'patriotic duty.'"[12]

Put these things together—the explosion of popular gambling, its legitimate incorporation to the fiscal heart of the nation-state, the global expansion of highly speculative market "investment," and changes in the moral vectors of the wager—and what has happened? "The world," answers a reflective Fidel Castro, has "become a huge casino." Because the value of stock markets has lost all grounding in materiality, he says—anticipating a point to which we shall return—their workings have finally realized the dream of medieval alchemy: "Paper has been turned into gold."[13] This evokes Susan Strange (1986: 1–3; cf. Harvey 1989: 332; Tomasic and Pentony 1991), who, in likening the Western fiscal order to an immense game of luck, was among the first to speak specifically of "casino capitalism": "Something rather radical has happened to the international financial system to make it so much like a gambling hall. . . . [It] has made inveterate, and largely involuntary, gamblers of us all." Insofar as the growth of globalized markets, electronic media, and finance capital have opened up the potential for venture enterprise, the gaming room has actually become iconic of capital: of its "natural" capacity to yield value without human input (Hardt 1995: 39), to grow and expand of its own accord, to reward speculation.

And yet crisis after crisis in the global economy, and growing income disparities on a planetary scale, make it painfully plain that there is no such thing as capitalism sans production, that the neoliberal stress on consumption as the prime source of value is palpably problematic. If scholars have been slow to reflect on this fact, people all over the world—not least those in places where there have been sudden infusions of commodities, of new forms of wealth—have not. Many have been quick to give voice, albeit in different registers, to their perplexity at the enigma of this wealth: of its sources and the capriciousness of its distribution, of the mysterious forms it takes, of its slipperiness, of the opaque relations between means and ends embodied in it. Our concern here grows directly out of these perplexities, these imaginings: out of worldwide speculation, in both senses of the term, provoked by the shifting conditions of material existence at the turn of the twentieth century.

We seek, here, to interrogate the *experiential* contradictions at the core of neoliberal capitalism, of capitalism in its millennial manifestation: the fact that it appears both to include and to marginalize in unanticipated ways; to produce desire and expectation on a global scale (Trouillot 1999), yet to decrease the certainty of work or the security of persons; to magnify class differences but to undercut class consciousness; above all, to offer up vast, almost instantaneous riches to those who master its spectral technologies — and, simultaneously, to threaten the very existence of those who do not. Elsewhere (1999c) we have argued that these contradictions, while worldwide in effect, are most visible in so-called postrevolutionary societies — especially those societies that, having been set free by the events of 1989 and their aftermath, entered the global arena with distinct structural disadvantages.[14] A good deal is to be learned about the historical implications of the current moment by eavesdropping on the popular anxieties to be heard in such places. How do we interpret the mounting disenchantment, in these "liberated zones," with the effects of hard-won democracy? Why the perceptible nostalgia for the security of past regimes, some of them immeasurably repressive? Why the accompanying upsurge of assertions of identity and autochthony? How might they be linked to widespread fears, in many parts of Eastern Europe and Africa alike, about the preternatural production of wealth?

The end of the Cold War, like the death of apartheid, fired utopian imaginations. But liberation under neoliberal conditions has been marred by a disconcerting upsurge of violence, crime, and disorder. The quest for democracy, the rule of law, prosperity, and civility threatens to dissolve into strife and recrimination, even political chaos, amidst the oft-mouthed plaint that "the poor cannot eat votes or live on a good Constitution."[15] Everywhere there is evidence of an uneasy fusion of enfranchisement and exclusion; of xenophobia at the prospect of world citizenship without the old protectionisms of nationhood; of the effort to realize modern utopias by decidedly postmodern means. Gone is any official-speak of egalitarian futures, work for all, or the paternal government envisioned by the various freedom movements. These ideals have given way to a spirit of deregulation, with its taunting mix of emancipation and limitation. Individual citizens, a lot of them marooned by a rudderless ship of state, try to clamber aboard the good ship Enterprise. But in so doing, they find themselves battling the eccentric currents of the "new" world order, which short-circuit received ways and means. Caught up in these currents, many of them come face to face with the most fundamental metamorphosis wrought by the neoliberal turn: the labile role of labor in the elusive equation connecting production to consumption, the pro to the con of capitalism.[16]

Which brings us back to the problematic status of production at the turn of the new century.

Labor's Pain: Producing the Class of 2000   The emergence of consumption as a privileged site for the fabrication of self and society, of culture and identity, is closely tied to the changing status of work under contemporary conditions. For some, the economic order of our times represents a completion of the intrinsic "project" of capital: namely, the evolution of a social formation that, as Mario Tronti (1980: 32) puts it, "does not look to labor as its dynamic foundation" (cf. Hardt 1995: 39). Others see the present moment in radically different terms. Scott Lash and John Urry (1987: 232–33), for instance, declare that we are seeing not the denouement but the demise of organized capitalism, of a system in which corporate institutions could secure compromises between management and workers by making appeals to the national interest. The internationalization of market forces, they claim, has not merely eroded the capacity of states to control national economies. It has led to a decline in the importance of domestic production in many once industrialized countries—which, along with the worldwide rise of the service sector and the feminization of the workforce, has dispersed class relations, alliances, and antinomies across the four corners of the earth. It has also put such distances between sites of production and consumption that their articulation becomes all but unfathomable, save in fantasy.

Not that Fordist fabrication has disappeared. There is a larger absolute number of industrial workers in the world today than ever before (Kellogg 1987). Neither is the mutation of the labor market altogether unprecedented. For one thing, Marx (1967: 635) observed, the development of capitalism has always conduced to the cumulative replacement of "skilled laborers by less skilled, mature laborers by immature, male by female"—also "living" labor by "dead." As David Harvey (1989: 192–93) reminds us, the devaluation of labor power has been a traditional response to falling profits and periodic crises of commodity production. What is more, the growth of global markets in commodities and services has *not* been accompanied by a correspondingly unrestricted flow of workers; most nation-states still try to regulate their movement to a greater or lesser extent. The simultaneous "freeing" and compartmentalizing of labor, Peter Geschiere and Francis Nyamnjoh (in this volume) point out, is a tension long endemic to capitalism.

Nonetheless, Harvey insists, if not in quite the same terms as Lash and Urry (1987), that the current moment *is* different: that it evinces features that set it apart, fracturing the continuing history of capital — a history, Engels once said, that "remain[s] the same and yet [is] constantly changing" (quoted by Andre Gunder Frank [1971: 36]). Above all, the explosion of new markets and monetary instruments, aided by sophisticated means of planetary coordination and space-time compression, have given the financial order a degree of autonomy from "real production" unmatched in the annals of political economy (cf. Turner n.d.: 18). The consequences are tangible: "Driven by the imperative to replicate money," writes David Korten (1996: 13; cf. McMichael 1998: 98), "the [new global] system treats people as a source of inefficiency": ever more disposable. The spiraling virtuality of fiscal circulation, of the accumulation of wealth purely through exchange, exacerbates this tendency: it enables the speculative side of capitalism to act as if it were entirely independent of human manufacture. The market and its masters, an "electronic herd" (Friedman 1999) of nomadic, deterritorialized investors, appear less and less constrained by the costs or moral economy of concrete labor.

If capital strives to become autonomous of labor, if the spatial and temporal coordinates of modernist political economy have been sundered, if the ontological connection between production and consumption has come into question, what has happened to the linchpin of capitalism: the concept formerly known as class?

Denunciations of the concept, Fredric Jameson (1999: 46–47) laments, have become "obligatory." Even for Marxists. This in spite of the fact that class names an "ongoing social reality," a persistently active dimension of "post-Cold War maps of the world system." He is, moreover, unconvinced by claims that it no longer makes sense of the transnational division of labor; nor is he persuaded that gender, race, and ethnicity are more constitutive of concrete experience in the contemporary moment. For Jameson, gender and race are too easily reconciled with the demands of liberal ideology, with its solutions to social problems, with the sorts of politics it proffers. Class, finally, remains more intractable and more fundamental. Thus Tom Lewis (1999: 151): the failure to recognize it as "the most effective subject position" through which to organize against racism and sexism is "particularly regrettable."

But surely the matter runs deeper than this? Subject positions are multiply determined, shaped less by political expediency than by the compelling truths of sense and perception. As Jameson himself notes (1999: 49), "Nothing is more complexly allegorical than the play of class connotations across the . . . social field." Our task, surely, is to examine how consciousness, sentiment, and attachment are constituted under prevailing conditions; why class has become a less plausible basis for self-recognition and action when growing disparities of wealth and power would point to the inverse (cf. Storper, in this volume); why gender, race, ethnicity, and generation have become such compelling idioms of identification, mobilizing people, both within and across nation-states, in ways often opposed to reigning hegemonies.

Once again, this problem is hardly new. There has long been debate about the two big questions at the nub of the historical sociology of class: Why do social classes seem so seldom to have acted for themselves (*für sich*)? And why have explicit forms of class consciousness arisen relatively infrequently, even under the worst of Fordist conditions (see, e.g., Wallerstein 1972: 173; Comaroff and Comaroff 1987)? Complex, poetically rich, culturally informed imaginings have always come between structural conditions and subjective perceptions — imaginings that have multiplied and waxed more ethereal, more fantastic, as capitalist economies have enlarged in scale. Neither the absolute increase in industrial workers across the globe nor the fact that 70 percent of the population in advanced capitalist societies "structurally belong to the working class" (Lewis 1999: 150–51) dictates that people will experience the world, or act upon it, in classic proletarian terms.

Quite the opposite. As we have already said, the labile relation of labor to capital may have intensified existing structures of inequality, but it is also eroding the conditions that give rise to class opposition as an idiom of identity and/or interest. Key here is the dramatic transnationalization of primary production (this by contrast to trade in raw materials and finished products, which has long crossed sovereign borders; see Dicken 1986: 3). A world-historical process, it is having profound effects on the configuration, and the cognition, of social relations of production everywhere: (1) By undermining the capacity of states to sustain economies in which "production, plant, firm and industry were essentially national phenomena" (Hobsbawm 1979: 313), it renders obsolete the old system of bargaining in which labor and capital could negotiate wages and conditions within an enclaved territory (Lash and Urry 1987: 232–33; see above); (2) by subverting domestic production in industrialized countries, it encourages the cutting of labor costs through casualization, outsourcing, and the hiring of discounted (female, immigrant, racinated) workers, thereby either making blue-collar employees redundant or forcing them into the menial end of the service sector; (3) by widening the gulf between rich and poor regions, it makes the latter—via the export of labor or the hosting of sweatshops and maquiladoras—into the working class of the former; and (4) by reducing proletarians everywhere to the lowest common denominator, it compels them to compete with little protection against the most exploitative modes of manufacture on the planet.

To the extent, then, that the nation-state is, as Aijaz Ahmad (1992: 318) says, "the terrain on which actual class conflicts take place," it follows that the global dispersal of manufacture is likely to fragment modernist forms of class consciousness, class alliance, and class antinomies at an exponential rate. It is also likely to dissolve the ground on which proletarian culture once took shape and to disrupt any sense of rootedness within organically conceived structures of production. Already, in many places, there has been a palpable erosion of the conventional bases of worker identity. Thus, while it is possible to argue, with Terence Turner (n.d.: 25; cf. Cox 1987: 271), that transnational flows of capital and labor have replicated "internal" class divisions on an international scale, existing relations among labor, place, and social reproduction—and, with them, the terms of class conflict itself—have been thoroughly unsettled for now.

While the contours of the global proletariat are ghostly at best—and while middle classes seem everywhere to be facing a loss of socioeconomic security, their center ground ever shakier (cf. Storper, in this volume)—a transnational capitalist class is taking more and more tangible shape. Here, again, there are questions of nuance about the old and the new: international bourgeoisies are, arguably, as old as capitalism itself. Dependency theorists have long insisted that they were a critical element in the making of modern European states and their national economies; also that their exploitation of colonial wealth was indispensable to the development of the Western metropoles. The new transnational capitalist elite—its frequent-flier executives, financiers, bureaucrats, professionals, and media moguls—may appear to be the planetary version of those older cosmopolitan bourgeoisies, its cadres centered in the imperial capitals of the world. But, as Leslie Sklair (1998: 136–37) argues, this new elite is distinctive in several ways. Above all, its interests are vested primarily in globalizing forms of capital: capital whose shareholder-driven imperatives are related to any particular local enterprise, metropolitan or colonial. Hence, while its business ventures might loop into and out of national economies, this does not, as Saskia Sassen (n.d.) stresses, make them "national" enterprises. The entrepreneurial activities of this class are conceived in terms of markets, monetary transactions, and modes of manufacture that transcend national borders. They seek to disengage from parochial loyalties and jurisdictions, thus to minimize the effects of legal regulations, environmental constraints, taxation, and labor demands.[17]

Decontextualization, the distantiation from place and its sociomoral pressures, is an autonomic impulse of capitalism at the millennium;[18] crucial, in fact, to its ways and means of discounting labor by abstracting itself from direct confrontation or civic obligation. The poor are no longer at the gates; bosses live in enclaved communities a world away, beyond political or legal reach. Capital and its workforce become more and more remote from each other. Here is the harsh underside of the culture of neoliberalism. It is a culture that, to return to our opening comment, re-visions persons not as producers from a particular community, but as consumers in a planetary marketplace: persons as ensembles of identity that owe less to history or society than to organically conceived human qualities.

This logos does not go uncontested, of course—neither by popular nationalisms nor by social movements of various stripes, left and right, North and South, especially among the marginal (Sklair 1998: 137; Turner n.d.). But, as Žižek (1997: 127) suggests, marginalities of different kinds do not, for obdurate structural reasons, often come together in enduring "rainbow coalitions." To be sure, the gospel of laissez-faire is a potent presence in contemporary capitalist societies, its axioms reinforced by quotidian experience and its truths instilled in its subjects by the remorseless commodification of ever more finely targeted areas of everyday life. Witness the following interpolation: "You are at one with the world. . . . The real world where time treads with a leisure measure. You express your commitment to the new age . . . in the way you think, the way you talk, the way you dress. Leisure time dressing is YOU." This off-the-peg call to postproletarian identity comes from a label attached to a pair of women's shorts marketed in a climate of "patriotic capitalism" by a South African chain store.[19] The thickening hegemony to which it speaks is borne also by the global communicative media, themselves seeking to construct a planetary "ecumene," whose satellite signals and fiber-optic nerves reach the widest possible audience. Those signals are designed to evade control exercised by states over flows of images and information—flows once integral to the creation of political communities and national "publics" (cf. Anderson 1983: 63).

For all their transformative power, as anthropologists have repeatedly insisted, these material and cultural forces do not have simple, homogenizing effects. They are, in some measure, refracted, redeployed, domesticated, or resisted wherever they come to rest. What we call globalism is a vast ensemble of dialectical processes, processes that cannot occur without the grounded, socially embedded human beings from whom they draw value. Nor can these processes occur without the concrete, culturally occupied locales—villages, towns, regions, countries, subcontinents—in which they come to rest, however fleetingly. Still, they are re-forming the salience of locality, place, and community in ways that often bypass the state. Hence the proliferation of attachments at once more particular and more universal than citizenship (Turner n.d.: 8)—from those based on gender, sex, race, and age through those organized around issues such as environmentalism and human rights to those, like the Nation of Islam or the hip-hop nation, that conjure with nationhood itself.

The paradox of class at the millennium, in sum, must be understood in these terms. Neoliberalism aspires, in its ideology and practice, to intensify the abstractions inherent in capitalism itself: to separate labor power from its human context, to replace society with the market, to build a universe out of aggregated transactions. While it can never fully succeed, its advance over the "long" twentieth century has profoundly altered, if unevenly in space and time, the phenomenology of being in the world. Formative experiences—like the nature of work and the reproduction of self, culture, and community—have shifted. Once-legible processes—the workings of power, the distribution of wealth, the meaning of politics and national belonging—have become opaque, even spectral. The contours of "society" blur, its organic solidarity disperses. Out of its shadows emerges a more radically individuated sense of personhood, of a subject built up of traits set against a universal backdrop of likeness and difference. In its place, to invert the old Durkheimean telos, arise collectivities erected on a form of mechanical solidarity in which *me* is generalized into *we*.

In this vocabulary, it is not just that the personal is political. The personal is the only politics there is, the only politics with a tangible referent or emotional valence. By extension, *inter*personal relations—above all, sexuality, from the peccadillos of presidents to the global specter of AIDS—come to stand, metonymically, for the inchoate forces that threaten the world as we know it. It is in these privatized terms that action is organized, that the experience of inequity and antagonism takes meaningful shape. In this sense, Jameson (1999: 47) is correct. There is no autonomous discourse of class. Certainly not now, if ever. Oppositions of gender and race, even if not in themselves explicit vehicles for that discourse, are frequently "reinvested" with its practical dynamics and express its stark antagonisms. This is inevitable. Reigning hegemonies, both popular and academic, may separate the construction of identity from the antinomies of class. But the market has always made capital out of human difference and difference out of capital, cultivating exploitable categories of workers and consumers, identifying pariahs, and seeking to isolate enemies of established enterprise (Wright, in this volume). As lived reality, then, social class is a multiply refracted gestalt. Its contrasts are mobilized in a host of displaced registers, its distinctions carried in a myriad of charged, locally modulated signs and objects—from the canons of taste and desire to the niceties of language use, the subtle discriminations of advertising to the carnal conflict of sport.

In short, as neoliberal conditions render ever more obscure the rooting of inequality in structures of production, as work gives way to the mechanical solidarities of "identity" in constructing selfhood and social being, class comes to be understood, in both popular and scholarly discourse, as yet another personal trait or lifestyle choice. Which is why it, like citizenship, is measured increasingly by the capacity to transact and consume; why politics is treated as a matter of individual or group entitlement; why social wrongs are transposed into an issue of "rights"; why diffuse concerns about cultural integrity and communal survival are vested in "private" anxieties about sexuality, procreation, or family values; why the fetus, neoliberal subject par excellence, becomes the focus of a macabre nativity play, in which, "vexed to nightmare by a rocking cradle," moral antagonists lock in mortal battle over the right to life (Jean Comaroff 1997a; Berlant 1997). Analytically, of course, it is imperative for us *not* to take these things at face value. The problem, rather, is to explain why, in the millennial age, class has become displaced and refracted in the way that it has. Which is why, finally, its reduction, to the mere "experience of inferiority," as Jameson (1999: 47) would have it, is insufficient. The concept of class so reduced captures neither the complex construction of contemporary experience nor the crises of social reproduction in which much of the world appears to be caught.

Generating Futures: Youth in the Age of Incivility   That sense of physical, social, and moral crisis congeals, perhaps more than anywhere else, in the contemporary predicament of youth, now widely under scrutiny (Comaroff and Comaroff forthcoming). Generation, in fact, seems to be an especially fertile site into which class anxieties are displaced. Perhaps that much is overdetermined: it is on the backs of the pubescent that concerns about social reproduction — about the viability of the continuing present — have almost always been saddled. Nonetheless, generation as a principle of distinction, consciousness, and struggle has long been neglected, or taken for granted, by theorists of political economy. This will no longer do: The growing pertinence of juveniles — or, more accurately, their impertinence — is an ineluctable feature of the present moment, from Chicago to Cape Town, Calcutta to Caracas. Preadulthood, of course, is a historically constructed category: While, in much of the late-twentieth-century English-speaking world, young white persons are *teenagers,* their black counterparts are *youth,* adolescents with attitude. And most often, if not always, male.

There are startling similarities in the current situation of youth the world over, similarities that appear to arise out of the workings of neoliberal capitalism and the changing planetary order of which we have spoken. These similarities seem to be founded on a doubling, on simultaneous inclusion and exclusion. On one hand is their much remarked exclusion from local economies, especially from shrinking, mutating blue-collar sectors. As the expansion of the free market runs up against the demise of the welfare state, the modernist ideal in which each generation does better than its predecessor is mocked by conditions that disenfranchise the unskilled young of the inner city and the countryside (cf. Abdullah 1998). Denied full, waged citizenship in the nation-state, many of them take to the streets, often the only place where, in an era of privatization, a lumpen public can be seen and heard (cf. Appadurai 2000). The profile of these populations reflects also the feminization of post-Fordist labor, which further disrupts gender relations and domestic reproduction among working people, creating a concomitant "crisis of masculinity": a crisis as audible in U.S. gangsta rap as in South African gang rape, as visible in the parodic castration of *The Full Monty* as in the deadly machismo of soccer violence or the echoing corridors of Columbine High. This crisis is not confined to youth or workers, of course — world cinema has made that point cogently in recent years — but it is magnified among them.

On the other hand is the recent rise of assertive, global youth cultures of desire, self-expression, and representation; in some places, too, of potent, if unconventional, forms of politicization. Pre-adults have long been at the frontiers of the transnational: the waxing U.S. economy in the 1950s was marked by the emergence of "teens" as a consumer category with its own distinctive, internationally marketable culture. This, however, intensified immeasurably during the 1980s and 1990s. To a greater extent than ever before, generation became a concrete principle of mobilization, inflecting other dimensions of difference, not least class, in whose displacements it is closely entailed (cf. Corrigan and Frith 1976). Youth activism, clearly, has been hugely facilitated by the flow of information, styles, and currencies across old sovereign boundaries. The signifying practices on which it is based appear to flourish, more than most things, with space-time compression.

This is not to imply that the young form a "homogeneous, sociological category of people which thinks, organizes and acts" in coherent ways (Seekings 1993: xiv). The fact that youth culture is increasingly capacious in its reach does not mean that the situation of "kids," or the nature of their social experience, is everywhere the same. But it *is* to say that, in recent times, this segment of the population has gained unprecedented autonomy as a social category *an und für sich,* both in and for itself; this in spite, or maybe because, of its relative marginalization from the normative world of work and wage. In many Western contexts they, along with other disenfranchised persons (notably the homeless and the unemployed), constitute a kind of counternation: a virtual citizenry with its own twilight economies, its own spaces of production and recreation, its own modalities of politics with which to address the economic and political conditions that determine its plight (Venkatesh 1997).

As a consequence, youth tend everywhere to occupy the innovative, uncharted borderlands along which the global meets the local. This is often made manifest in the elaboration of creolized argots, of streetspeak and cybertalk, that give voice to imaginative worlds very different from those of the parental generation. But these borderlands are also sites of tension, particularly for disadvantaged young people from postrevolutionary societies, from inner cities, and from other terrors incognita who seek to make good on the promises of the free market; also for anyone who jostles against the incivilities, illegalities, and importunities of these precocious entrepreneurs. At the opening of the new century, the image of youth-as-trouble has gained an advanced capitalist twist as impatient adolescents "take the waiting out of wanting" by developing remarkably diverse forms of illicit enterprise[20] — from drug trafficking and computer hacking in the urban United States, through the "bush" economies of West and Central Africa, which trade diamonds and dollars, guns and gasoline over long distances (Roitman 1999; De Boeck 1999), to the supply of services both legal and lethal. In this they try to link the poles of consumption and production and to break into the cycle of accumulation, often by flouting received rules and conventions. The young have felt their power, power born partly of the sheer weight of numbers, partly of a growing inclination and capacity to turn to the use of force, partly of a willingness to hold polite society to ransom.

Bill Buford (1993: 264–65) has suggested that British soccer fans experience a compelling sense of community in moments of concerted violence. Others have said the same of gangland wars in North American cities, witch burning in the northerly provinces of South Africa, and cognate social practices elsewhere. Is it surprising, then, that so many juveniles see themselves as ironic, mutant citizens of a new world order? Or that the standardized nightmare of the genteel mainstream is an increasingly universal image of the adolescent, a larger-than-life figure wearing absurdly expensive sports shoes, headphones blaring gangsta rap, beeper tied to a global underground economy—in short, a sinister caricature of the corporate mogul? Is this not a dramatic embodiment of the dark side of consumerism, of a riotous return of the repressed, of a parallel politics of class, social reproduction, and civil society?

Precisely because of its fusion of monstrosity, energy, and creativity, this figure also subsumes some of the more complex aspects of millennial capitalism, if in the manner of a grotesque: its tendency to spark the pursuit of new ways and means for the production of wealth; its ambivalent, contradictory engagement with the nation-state; its play on the presence and absence of civil society. It is to these three faces of the "rough beast, its hour come round at last," that we now turn.

THREE FACES OF MILLENNIAL CAPITALISM

Liberal democracy . . . has never been . . . in such a state of dysfunction. . . . Life is not only distorted, as was always the case, by a great number of socio-economic mechanisms, but it is exercised with more and more difficulty in a public space profoundly upset by techno-tele-media apparatuses and by new rhythms of information and communication, . . . by the new modes of appropriation they put to work, by the new structure of the event and its spectrality.—Jacques Derrida, *Specters of Marx*

Occult Economies and New Religious Movements: Privatizing the Millennium A striking corollary of the dawning Age of Millennial Capitalism has been the global proliferation of "occult economies."[21] These economies have two dimensions: a material aspect founded on the effort to conjure wealth—or to account for its accumulation—by appeal to techniques that defy explanation in the conventional terms of practical reason; and an ethical aspect grounded in the moral discourses and (re)actions sparked by the real or imagined production of value through such "magical" means. It is difficult, of course, to quantify the presence of the occult—and, therefore, to make any claim to its increase. As we note above, finance capital has always had its spectral enchantments, its modes of speculation based on less than rational connections between means and ends. Both its underside (the pariah forms of gambling of which we spoke a moment ago) and its upper side (a fiscal industry, embracing everything from insurance to stock markets) have been rooted, from the first, in two inscrutables: a faith in probability (itself a notoriously poor way of predicting the future from the past) and a monetary system that depends for its existence on "confidence," a chimera knowable, tautologically, only by its effects. Wherein, then, lies the claim that occult economies are presently on the rise?

In the specific context of South Africa, we have demonstrated (1999b, 1999c) that there has been an explosion of occult-related activity—much of it violent, arising out of accusations of ritual killing, witchcraft, and zombie conjuring—since the late apartheid years. These also include fantastic Ponzi schemes, the sale of body parts for "magical" purposes, satanic practices, tourism based on the sighting of fabulous monsters, and the like. Here middle-class magazines run "dial-a-diviner" advertisements, national papers carry headline articles on medicine murders, prime-time television broadcasts dramas of sorcery, and more than one "witchcraft summit" has been held. Patently, even here we cannot be sure that the brute quantum of occult activity exceeds that of times past. But what *is* clear is that their reported incidence, written about by the mainstream press in more prosaic, less exoticizing terms than ever before (Fordred 1999), has forced itself upon the public sphere, rupturing the flow of mediated "news." It is this rupture—this focus of popular attention on the place of the arcane in the everyday production of value—to which we refer when we speak of a global proliferation of occult economies.

It is not difficult to catalogue the presence of occult economies in different parts of the world. In West Africa, for example, Peter Geschiere (1997), among others, has shown how zombie conjuring is becoming an endemic feature of everyday life, how sorcery and witchcraft have entered into the postcolonial political economy as an integral element of a thriving alternative modernity, how magic has become as much an aspect of mundane survival strategies as it is indispensable to the ambitions of the powerful (see also Bastian 1993). Nor is all of this based in rural situations or among poor people. In South Africa a recent case involved a well-known physician: she was "turned into a zombie" by a "Nigerian devil-worshipper," who, having rendered her insensate, took a large sum of money from her bank account.[22] By labeling the accused a Nigerian devil worshipper, the report ties the menace of the satanic to the flow of immigrants across national borders.

Nor is this only an African phenomenon. In various parts of Asia occult economies thrive, often taking surprising turns (see Morris, in this volume). In Thailand—where fortune-telling has been transformed by global technology and e-mail divination has taken off—one "traditional" seer, auspiciously named Madam Luk, reports that her clients nowadays ask three questions to the exclusion of all others: " 'Is my company going broke?' 'Am I going to lose my job?' and 'Will I find another job?' " [23] In the United States, too, the fallout of neoliberal capitalism is having its impact on magical practice. There is, for instance, a growing use ("seeping into the grassroots" of the U.S. heartland and taking its place beside other millennial pursuits) of tarot readings as a respectable form of therapy—described by the director of the Trends Research Institute as a low-cost "shrink in the box." [24] By these means are psychology, spirituality, and fortune-telling fused.

Sometimes dealings in the occult take on a more visceral, darker form. Throughout Latin America in the 1990s, as in Africa and Asia, there have been mass panics about the clandestine theft and sale of the organs of young people, usually by unscrupulous expatriates (Scheper-Hughes 1996). Violence against children has become metonymic of threats to social reproduction in many ethnic and national contexts, the dead (or missing) child having emerged as the standardized nightmare of a world out of control (Jean Comaroff 1997a). There, and in other parts of the globe, this commerce—like international adoptions, mail-order marriage, and indentured domestic labor—is seen as a new form of imperialism, the affluent North siphoning off the essence of poorer "others" by mysterious means for nefarious ends. All of which gives evidence, to those at the nether end of the global distribution of wealth, of the workings of insidious forces, of potent magical technologies and modes of accumulation.

That evidence reaches into the heart of Europe itself. Hence the recent scares, in several countries, about the sexual and satanic abuse of children (La Fontaine 1997); about the kidnapping and murder of street "urchins," most recently in Germany by "Russian gangs," for purposes of organ harvest and export; about the alleged "trafficking in women [especially] from . . . nations of the former Soviet bloc" for prostitution, labor, and other "personal services" in Western Europe, the Americas,

Japan, and China.[25] Again, the United States is not exempt from anxieties over the pilfering of human bodies and body parts for profit. Note, for just one extreme instance, the urban myth that traversed the Internet in 1997 about the secret excision of kidneys, by apparently incredible means, from business travelers.[26]

In other contexts, the occult concentrates itself in purely financial dealings. Thus there seems to have been an extraordinary intensification of pyramid schemes lately, many of them tied to the electronic media. These schemes, and a host of scams allied with them—a few legal, many illegal, some alegal—are hardly new. But their recent mushrooming across the world has drawn a great deal of attention—partly because of their sheer scale and partly because, by crossing national borders and/or registering at addresses far from the site of their local operation, they insinuate themselves into the slipstream of the global economy, thereby escaping control. Recall the ten or so whose crash sparked the Albanian revolution early in 1997, several of which took on almost miraculous dimensions for poor investors. One pyramid manager in Albania, according to the *New York Times,* was "a gypsy fortune teller, complete with crystal ball, who claimed to know the future." [27] Even in the tightly regulated stock markets of the United States, there has been a rise in illegal operations that owe their logic, if not their precise operation, to pyramids: another *New York Times* report attributes this to the fact that investors are presently "predisposed to throw dollars at get-rich-quick schemes." Six billion dollars were lost to scams on the New York Stock Exchange in 1996.[28] These scams also bring to mind others that arise from a promiscuous mix of scarcity and deregulation, among them, the notorious Nigerian-based "419," a truly transnational con that regularly traps foreign businessmen into signing over major assets and abets large-scale, amazingly intricate forms of fraud (Apter 1999); also the Foundation for New Era Philanthropy, a U.S. pyramid created "to change the world for the glory of God." On the basis of a promise to double their money in six months, its founder, John Benett, persuaded five hundred nonprofit organizations, Christian colleges, and Ivy League universities to invest $354 million.[29] The line between Ponzi schemes and evangelical prosperity gospels is very thin indeed.[30]

All of these things have a single common denominator: the allure of accruing wealth from nothing. In this respect, they are born of the same animating spirit as casino capitalism; indeed, perhaps they *are* casino capitalism for those who lack the fiscal or cultural capital—or who, for one or another reason, are reluctant—to gamble on more conventional markets. Like the cunning that made straw into gold (Schneider 1989), these alchemic techniques defy reason in promising unnaturally large profits—to yield wealth without production, value without effort. Here, again, is the specter, the distinctive spirit, of neoliberal capitalism in its triumphal hour. So much for the demise of disenchantment.

Speaking of the neoliberal spirit, occult economies have close parallels in the spread of new religious movements across the planet. To wit, the latter may be seen as holy-owned subsidiaries of the former. These movements take on a wide variety of guises. In the case of the Vissariontsi, "disenchanted Soviet intellectuals" who follow a traffic warden-turned-messiah, members exchange their earthly wealth for life in the City of Sun, a congregation in Siberia that recalls a communist farm. The Second Coming here, led by a man with a sense of both history and irony—a City of *Sun,* in Siberia? A career in Russian *traffic* management for the Son of God?—envisages a future in the past, a hereafter (or therebefore?) that recaptures the glories of a socialist commune.[31] But the renunciatory orientation of the Vissariontsi is not usual among new religious movements at the millennium. Much closer to the global mood of the moment are fee-for-service, consumer-cult, prosperity-gospel denominations. These creeds are well exemplified by any number of neo-Pentecostal sects, best perhaps by the Universal Church of the Kingdom of God (*Igreja Universal do Reino de Deus*), a denomination of Brazilian origin which, true to its name, has opened up outposts in many parts of the world (Kramer 1999).

The Universal Church reforms the Protestant ethic with enterprise and urbanity, fulsomely embracing the material world. It owns a major television network in Brazil, has an elaborate Web site, and, above all, promises swift payback to those who embrace Christ, denounce Satan, and "make their faith practical" by "sacrificing" all they can to the movement.[32] Here Pentecostalism meets neoliberal enterprise. In its African churches, most of them (literally) storefronts, prayer meetings respond to frankly mercenary desires, offering everything from cures for depression through financial advice to remedies for unemployment; casual passersby, clients really, select the services they require. Bold color advertisements for BMWs and lottery winnings adorn altars; tabloids pasted to walls and windows carry testimonials by followers whose membership was rewarded by a rush of wealth and/or an astonishing recovery of health. The ability to deliver in the here and now, itself a potent form of space-time compression, is offered as the measure of a genuinely global God, just as it is taken to explain the power of satanism (Comaroff and Comaroff 1999b); both have the instant efficacy of the magical and the millennial. As Kramer (1999: 35) says of Brazilian neo-Pentecostals, "Inner-worldly asceticism has been replaced with a concern for the pragmatics of material gain and the immediacy of desire. . . . The return on capital has suddenly become more spiritually compelling and imminent . . . than the return of Christ." This shift has been endemic to many of the new religious movements of the late twentieth century. For them, and for their millions of members, the Second Coming evokes not a Jesus who saves, but one who pays dividends. Or, more accurately, one who promises a miraculous return on a limited spiritual investment.

Why? How—to put the matter more generally—are we to account for the current spread of occult economies and prosperity cults?

To the degree that millennial capitalism fuses the modern and the postmodern, hope and hopelessness, utility and futility, the world created in its image presents itself as a mass of contradictions: as a world, simultaneously, of possibility and impossibility. This is precisely the juxtaposition associated with cargo cults and chiliastic movements in other times and places (Worsley 1957; Cohn 1957). But, as the growth of prosperity gospels and fee-for-service movements illustrates, in a neoliberal age the chiliastic urge emphasizes a privatized millennium, a personalized rather than a communal sense of rebirth; in this, the messianic meets the magical. At the turn of the twenty-first century, the cargo, glimpsed in large part through television, takes the form of huge concentrations of wealth that accrue, legitimately or otherwise, to the rich of the global economy—especially the enigmatic new wealth derived from financial investment and management, from intellectual property and other rights, from cyberspace, from transport and its cognate operations, and from the supply of various post-Fordist services. All of which points to the fact that the mysterious mechanisms of a changing market, not to mention abstruse technological and informational expertise, hold the key to hitherto unimaginable fortunes amassed by the ever more rapid flow of value, across time and space, into the fluid coordinates of the local and the global; to the much mass-mediated mantra that the gap between the affluent and the indigent is growing at an exponential rate; and to the strange convolutions in the structural conditions of labor, discussed above, that seem at once to reduce and produce joblessness by altering conventional terms of employment, by feminizing the workforce, and by deterritorializing proletariats.

This, of course, is the flip side of the coin: the sense of impossibility, even despair, that comes from being left out of the promise of prosperity, from having to look in on the global economy of desire from its immiserated exteriors. Whether it be in post-Soviet Central Europe or postcolonial Africa, in Thatcherite Britain or the neoliberal United States, in a China edging toward capitalism or neo-Pentecostal Latin America, the world-historical process that came to be symbolized by the events of 1989 held out the prospect that everyone would be set free to accumulate and speculate, to consume, and to indulge repressed cravings in a universe of less government, greater privatization, more opulence, infinite enterprise. For the vast majority, however, the millennial moment passed without visible enrichment.

The implication? That, in these times — the late modernist age when, according to Weber and Marx, enchantment would wither away — more and more ordinary people see arcane forces intervening in the production of value, diverting its flow toward a new elect: those masters of the market who comprehend and control the production of wealth under contemporary conditions. They also attribute to these arcane forces their feelings of erasure and loss: an erasure in many places of community and family, exacerbated by the destabilization of labor, the translocalization of management, and the death of retail trade; a loss of human integrity, experienced in the spreading commodification of persons, bodies, cultures, and histories, in the substitution of quantity for quality, abstraction for substance.[33] None of these perceptions is new, as we have said. Balzac (1847: 418, 117) described them for France in the 1840s, as did Conrad (1911) for prerevolutionary Russia; Gluckman (1959), moreover, spoke of the "magic of despair" that arose in similarly dislocated colonial situations in Africa. Nonetheless, to reiterate, such disruptions are widely *experienced* throughout the world as intensifying at a frightening rate at present. That is why the ethical dimensions of occult economies are so prominent; why the mass panics of our times tend to be moral in tone; why these panics so often express themselves in religious movements that pursue instant material returns and yet condemn those who enrich themselves in nontraditional ways. To be sure, occult economies frequently have this bipolar character: At one level, they consist in the constant quest for new, magical means for otherwise unattainable ends; at another, they vocalize a desire to sanction, to demonize and even eradicate, people held to have accumulated assets by those very means. The salvific and the satanic are conditions of each other's possibility.

Occult economies, then, are a response to a world gone awry, yet again: a world in which the only way to create real wealth seems to lie in forms of power/knowledge that transgress the conventional, the rational, the moral—thus to multiply available techniques of producing value, fair or foul. In their cultural aspect, they bespeak a resolute effort to come to terms with that power/knowledge, to account for the inexplicable phenomena to which it gives rise, and to plumb its secrets. The unprecedented manifestation of zombies in the South African countryside, for instance, has grown in direct proportion to the shrinking labor market for young men. The former provides a partial explanation for the latter: The living dead are commonly said to be killed and raised up by older people, witches of wealth, to toil for them (Comaroff and Comaroff 1999b), thereby rendering rural youth jobless. There are, in this era of flexitime employment, even part-time zombies, a virtual working class—of pure, abstract labor power—that slaves away at night for its masters. In this context, furthermore, the angry dramas during which ritual murderers are identified often become sites of public divination. As they unfold, the accusers discuss, attribute cause, and give voice to their understanding of the forces that make the postcolony such an inhospitable place for them. This is an extreme situation, obviously. But in less stark circumstances, too, these economies tend to spawn simultaneous strivings to garner wealth *and* to put a stop to those who do so by allegedly misbegotten means.

As all this suggests, appeals to the occult in pursuit of the secrets of capital generally rely on local cultural technologies: on vernacular modes of divination or oracular consultation, spirit possession or ancestral invocation, sorcery busting or forensic legal procedures, witch beliefs or prayer. But the use of these technologies does not imply an iteration of, a retreat into, "tradition." On the contrary, their deployment in such circumstances is frequently a means of fashioning new techniques to preserve older values by retooling culturally familiar signs and practices. As in cargo cults of old, this typically involves the mimicking of powerful new means of producing wealth.

In short, the rise of occult economies — amidst and alongside more conventional modes of economic practice that shade into the murky domains of crime and corruption — seems overdetermined. This, after all, is an age in which the extravagant promises of millennial capitalism run up against an increasingly nihilistic, thoroughly postmodern pessimism; in which the will to consume outstrips the opportunity to earn; in which, relatively speaking, there is a much higher velocity of exchange than there is of production. As the connections between means and ends become more opaque, more distended, more mysterious, the occult becomes an ever more appropriate, semantically saturated metaphor for our times. Not only has it become commonplace to pepper media parlance, science-speak, psychobabble, and technologese with the language of enchantment; even the drear argot of the law is showing traces of the same thing.[34] And we all remember voodoo economics, that Reagan-era insult to the rationality of Caribbean ritual practice. But, we insist, occult economies are not reducible to the symbolic, the figurative, or the allegorical. Magic is, everywhere, the science of the concrete, aimed at making sense of and acting upon the world — especially, but not only, among those who feel themselves disempowered, emasculated, disadvantaged. The fact that the turn to enchantment is not unprecedented, that it has precursors in earlier times, makes it no less significant to those for whom it has become an integral part of everyday reality. Maybe, too, all this describes a fleeting phase in the long, unfinished history of capitalism. But that makes it no less momentous.

Of all the enchantments that accompanied the First Coming of Capitalism, perhaps the most perduring was nationalism. And the nation-state, a political community — conjured always out of difference, often against indifference — that gave the Durkheimean conscience collective a distinctive, effervescent twist. Recently, as everyone knows, there has been much talk of its death, especially with the end of the Age of Empire, the close of the Cold War, and the onset of the postcolonial era; it is as if the Treaty of Westphalia has finally given way to the Failure of the West. We shall consider this view, and the articulate dissent it has provoked, in a moment. What *is* beyond question, however, is that the Second Coming, the dawning Age of Millennial Capitalism, has had complex, controversial effects on the present and future of the nation-state.

Alien-Nation, Hyphen-Nation, Desti-Nation: The Future of the Nation-State and the Fetishism of Law   In its broad outlines, the scholarly debate over the current condition of *the* nation-state — the definite, singular article — has become something of a cliché. The thesis that the hyphenated modernist polity is being dramatically subverted, doomed even, has been rehearsed ad infinitum, with varying degrees of nuance; aspects of it have been foreshadowed in what we have already said.

Nation-states, from this vantage, have been rendered irrelevant by world market forces (1) because capital has become uncontrollable and keeps moving, at its own velocity, to sites of optimum advantage; (2) because the global workforce has become ever more mobile as job seekers, increasingly managed by private agencies, migrate ever farther in pursuit of even the most menial of jobs, under even the most feudal of conditions;[35] and (3) because these human flows seem, in varying proportions, to elude surveillance, despite the highly repressive mechanisms often put into place to monitor national frontiers. Under such conditions, state regulation of both capital and labor becomes obsolete, impossible; so, too, do fiscal designs that run counter to the mechanisms of global markets and/or the imperatives of global corporations. Stakes, it is said, "can no longer independently affect the levels of economic activity or employment within their territories. . . . [Their] job is to provide the infrastructure and public goods needed at the lowest possible cost" (Hirst and Thompson 1996: 175–76).

In its historical framing, this thesis sees the leitmotif of the twentieth century as the "battle between government and the marketplace" (Yergin and Stanislaw 1998), the latter winning out to the point that "public sectors are shrinking, deregulation is everyone's priority, state companies are being auctioned off to private investors, and Wall Street is the most powerful influence on economies everywhere" (Garten 1998: 7). As Sassen (n.d.: 4–5) notes, this perspective casts the strength of the nation-state in a zero-sum opposition to the global economy — note, not to neoliberal capitalism, nor globalization *tout court,* but to the global *economy.* Where one gains, the other must lose. Thus, says Robert Ross (1990: 206–7, 218), until recently the regulatory role of national governments expanded progressively. Now, however, corporations are able to prevail on states "to restrain regulations, cut taxes, and allocate more public funds toward subsidizing production costs," which puts "global capital in a position to *demand* changes in state policy" (211; emphasis ours). Taken together, this adds up to the prognosis that, "in the long run, the power of the state, of centralized government, will weaken everywhere, an inevitability which will change profoundly the very texture of history" (Lukacs 1993: 157).

In all this, as will be clear, it is the workings of transnational corporations, and especially the mobility of their productive operations, that are held accountable for the imminent demise of the nation-state. Others have also laid causal stress on the fiscal mechanics of the world economy, in particular on their technological transformations. Joel Kurtzman (1993), for example, holds that the growth of a global electronic economy — based on an "electronic commons" in which virtual money and commodities may be exchanged instantly via an unregulated world network of computers — has shattered the integrity of sovereign polities (85–86, 214–15): It has eroded their monopolistic control over the money supply, their capacity to contain wealth within borders, and even their ability to tax citizens or corporations. From this perspective, the emergence of a global economy is said to be undermining the nation-state by deconstructing currency, credit, and customs boundaries — which formerly gave governments a major means of control over the wealth of their nations — by creating mobile markets across the planet, thus dispersing the production and circulation of value. Which is why, it is so commonly said, many states are finding it impossible to meet the material demands placed upon them by their citizenry or to carry out effective economic development policies; why few can adequately house, feed, school, and ensure the health of their populations; why even fewer can see their way clear to settling their national debt or reducing their deficits; why only a handful can be confident about the replacement of infrastructure over the medium term; why almost none have any great capacity to control their money supply, let alone flows of goods and people; and why a growing number have shown a startling inability to regulate violence.

The thesis has also been argued in terms other than the simply economic, of course. The eroding boundedness of the nation-state, its loss of sovereignty as a commonwealth of signs, has been variously attributed to the impact of planetary cultural flows and electronic media (see, e.g., Appadurai 1990; Hannerz 1989: 69–70; Moore 1989; Foster 1991); to the assertive spread of transnational communities, social movements, and identities; to the universalization of many aspects of the law (if not of justice; Silbey 1997: 209), the expansion of tribunals that subject national jurisdictions to supranational ones (Darian-Smith 1995, 1999), and the rise of an intercontinental commercial arbitration establishment (Garth and Dezalay 1996); to "worldkill," the commodification of violence that makes it possible for corporations, political blocs, shadow states, or nations to rent soldiers on the Internet, to arrange for the application of force in breach of sovereign borders, even to buy a coup from a multinational company (John L. Comaroff 1996);[36] to the shift in dominant patterns of warfare from confrontations between countries to civil conflicts that tend to translocalize themselves, to kill higher proportions of civilians than ever before, and to feed an arms industry that has metamorphosed from a highly regulated import-export business to a global trade in illicit gun-running;[37] to the assimilation of many of the traditional functions of government either into the private sector or into supranational combinations.

As Peregrine Worsthorne noted, in an essay tellingly entitled "Farewell to England's Nation State," the "only area where [the country] remains independent and sovereign is sport." On which Patriotic Front, he adds laconically, "miserable results say all that needs to be said." Even here, labor has become a mobile commodity as citizens-of-convenience take the field in acquired ("naturalized") colors; although it is true that this is perhaps the most significant, sentiment-inspiring, trauma-inducing site of national effervescence in many parts of the world.[38] In every other domain, Worsthorne continues, English institutions, all of them dysfunctional, have been replaced by more effective international or global ones. "But who cares?" he asks. "It is time to change our thinking."[39] This from a notable public intellectual, in Britain's most widely read conservative newspaper, about *England*, self-appointed cradle of modernity, democracy, and the state—not some struggling postcolony still trying to throw off the effects of the Age of Empire.

Some do care—and are not prepared to give up so easily on the salience of the nation-state. It is not yet time, says Khachig Tölölyan (1991: 5), "to write [its] . . . obituary." Turner (n.d.: 25), for one, argues that the "development of the global capitalist system" has "not led to any withering away of the state" at all. Quite the opposite, the relevance of "[nation-]state boundaries" has been heightened; contemporary states, especially successful ones, still "attempt to regulate, encourage or obstruct flows of workers, capital and commodities across their borders" (25). In stark contrast to the likes of Kurtzman (1993), Turner also speaks of the perceived "need for national economies to remain competitive under global conditions" (23–24); a far cry, this, from the notion that there no longer is any such thing. Similarly Hirst and Thompson (1996: 17): "The globalization of production," they hold, "has been exaggerated." Companies, of which few are truly transnational (*see above*), are "tethered to their home economies and are likely to remain so" (2). Also overstated are claims for "the dominance of world markets and their ungovernability" (6); in point of fact, financial flows and trade are concentrated in the "triad" of North America, Europe, and Japan (2). Here, in a nutshell, is the countercase.

This antithetical position has a nontrivial political dimension for its advocates, especially those on the left. To the degree that globalization dissolves the sovereign nation-state into a sea of planetary economic forces and legal jurisdictions, it would appear to negate any real prospect of progressive or proletarian politics — be they international or intranational — as they would have no terrain on which to occur, no concrete object in terms of which to frame themselves, no obvious target against which to act (cf. Hirst and Thompson 1996: 1; Ahmad 1992: 317).[40] We share the concern. As it is, there is a strong argument to be made that neoliberal capitalism, in its millennial moment, portends the death of politics by hiding its own ideological underpinnings in the dictates of economic efficiency: in the fetishism of the free market, in the inexorable, expanding "needs" of business, in the imperatives of science and technology. Or, if it does not conduce to the death of politics, it tends to reduce them to the pursuit of pure interest, individual or collective — or to struggles over issues (the environment, abortion, health care, child welfare, human rights) that, important though they may be, are often, pace Jameson (1999: 47), dissociated from anything beyond themselves. It is here that the analytic case for the sustained salience of the modernist polity merges into the normative case for its desirability.

A parenthetic comment here. There are those who would muddy the argument by pointing out that the notion of a strong nation-state has always been something of a fantasy. This on three grounds: the state, the nation, and the hyphen. Recall, in respect of the first, Philip Abrams

(1988: 75–77), for whom the state was always "the distinctive collective *mis*representation of capitalist societies": an "essentially imaginative construction," it was, at once, a "triumph of concealment" and an ongoing "ideological project." Even more extreme is Ralph Miliband's (1969: 49) famous claim that "the 'state' . . . does not, as such, exist." Shades here of things written long ago. Philip Corrigan and Derek Sayer (1985: 7) remind us that Marx (1967) believed the state to be "in an important sense an illusion . . . : [It] is at most a message of domination — an ideological artifact attributing unity, structure and independence to the disunited, structureless and dependent workings of the practice of government." For Weber (1946: 78), too, it was "a *claim* to legitimacy, a means by which politically organized subjection is simultaneously accomplished and concealed, and it is constituted in large part by the activities of institutions of government themselves" (Corrigan and Sayer, 1985: 7). A truly curious force of history, this: at once an illusion, a potent claim to authority, a cultural artifact, a present absence and an absent presence, a principle of unity masking institutional disarticulation. But nothing like the kind of essentialized "thing" that much of the current debate treats either as alive or dead. Likewise the nation: the enormous literature on the topic — both before and after *Imagined Communities* (Anderson 1983) — makes it abundantly clear that neither at its dawn nor in its high modernist phase was this polity homogeneous, that even its European exemplars were as different as they were alike. What is more, their capacity to regulate boundaries and to control flows — of capital and cultural property, communications and currencies, persons and information — was invariably incomplete in the face of transnational pressures and incentives. So, too, was their hold over the loyalty of their citizens and subjects. Indeed, the nation-state has always and everywhere been a work in progress, nowhere a fully realized accomplishment. The same may be said, by extension, of its hyphennation: of the articulation of state to nation. Polities across the planet vary hugely in both the extent to which, and the manner in which, nation and state are conjoined in them, of which more shortly.

In part, it is just such complexities that have led to reformulations of the argument from both sides — and to the opening up of a middle ground. Even those who have made the case most forcibly for the continuing relevance of the nation-state do not deny that it is undergoing transformation or that it has been weakened in some respects in the face of global capitalism (see, e.g., Hirst and Thompson 1996: 170–71). The problem, of course, is to specify *how* it has changed. For some, its metamorphosis is captured in an aphoristic shift, an apt metaphor for the millennial moment: Philip McMichael (1998: 113), for one, speaks of the substitution of the "citizen state" by the "consumer state." This is a polity, adds Susan Hegeman (1991: 72–73), in which identity, at all levels, is defined not merely by the consumption of objects, but also by the consumption of the past (89–91). Echoes, here, of Jean Baudrillard (1998); also of the language of national charters, in which the protection of consumers takes precedence over the protection of workers and citizens are redefined as "stakeholders."

More substantively, synthetic positions typically begin by deconstructing the zero-sum opposition between globalization and the autonomous functioning of nation-states. Few would continue to deny that the sovereign independence of the latter *has* contracted, not least in the realms of economic management, defense, and communications; that, for all their efforts to regulate the flow of labor, their hold over the mobility of people, inward or outward, *has* been more or less undermined; that their parliamentary politics *are* devoted, in increasing proportion, to safeguarding the operations of the market, to providing stable and secure environments for transnational corporations, and to attracting overseas investment. In this respect, add Hirst and Thompson (1996: 179), it is also true that, without international warfare and conventional enemies, the state *does* become less immediately significant to its citizens; "national efficiency" (in such things as industrial growth, education, health care, welfare, and the provision of infrastructure) *does* diminish; and solidarity, save for sporting allegiances, *does* pale. At the same time and in counterpoint, Sassen (n.d.: 6–9) observes, "Most global processes materialize in national territories, [largely] through national institutional arrangements, from legislative acts to firms." These may be transformed in the process, but they remain perceptibly national in their location and operation. To be sure, Sassen continues, states often participate actively in setting up those fiscal and legal frameworks through which the global economy works, and without whose specialized instruments it could not exist — they are not just inert objects on which that economy impacts. Nor are they inert objects in the face of the emergence of regional economic spheres that breach their frontiers — whether these be officially constituted, like the Oresund Region in Scandinavia (Peebles n.d.), or spaces of unregulated activity dominated by armed factions, like the Chad Basin in West Africa. With regard to the latter, in fact, Janet Roitman (1998) demonstrates that, far from proclaiming the demise of the nation-state, these transnational networks exist in complicated, mutually perpetuating, often complicitous relations with it; this notwithstanding the fact that those who control the networks — often very powerful armed factions — compete with government for financial and regulatory ascendancy. In doing so, they depend on the very national frontiers they transgress and the institutions of the state in order to produce wealth; conversely, the state establishes its own legitimacy, and justifies its own existence, by doing battle with these armed factions.

It is also the case, as we have intimated, that not all nation-states submit to the demands of the global economy without some mediation or intervention; few administrations would survive if they did. Take postcolonial South Africa again: Although the African National Congress (ANC) government is unreservedly committed to participating in the global capitalist economy, its new labor laws seek to protect workers in ways that do not simply serve the interests of transnational business; quite the opposite, employers have protested these laws for that very reason. Whether or not they will survive, and what their effects will be over the long run, is still very much in question. But the general point of which this is an exemplary instance — that nation-states *do* seek to hold a measure of control over the terms on which their citizens engage with the market — will be clear. So, too, will the fact that the processes by which millennial capitalism is taking shape do not reduce to a simple narrative according to which the nation-state either lives or dies, ebbs or flourishes. Its impact is much more complicated, more polyphonous and dispersed, and most immediately felt in the everyday contexts of work and labor, of domesticity and consumption, of street life and media-gazing.

This brings us back full circle to the relationship between the nation-state and millennial capitalism — which, we reiterate, is not synonymous with globalism, although globalization is an inherent part of it. Rounding off the dialectics of the argument we have just outlined, we would like to make a few points about this relationship. All flow from things already said.

Let us begin with the most basic. There is an anomaly at the heart of the contemporary history of the modernist polity. On one hand, there is no such thing, save at very high levels of abstraction, as "*the* nation-state." Self-evidently, the sociology of the polities that exist under its sign varies dramatically. It is difficult to establish any terms in which, say, Germany and Guinea, Bhutan and Belgium, Uganda and the United States, England and Eritrea may be held to belong to anything but the most polythetic of categories. Nor are the substantive differences among them — differences that are *growing* as a result of their engagement with global capitalism — satisfactorily captured by resort to vapid oppositions, to conventional contrasts like rich versus poor, North versus South, successful versus unsuccessful countries. In some places, as we all know, the state can hardly be said to perdure at all, or to perdure purely as a private resource, a family business, a convenient fiction; in others, the nation, as imagined community, is little more than a rhetorical figure of speech, the color of a soccer stripe, an airline without aircraft, a university rarely open. More complicatedly, there are many postcolonial, postrevolutionary polities, not least but not only in Africa and the former Soviet Union, in which there have developed deep fissures between state and government, this being a corollary of the transition from old to new regimes, in which, as often as not, the power brokers, bureaucrats, and administrative personnel of the past are either left in situ or succeed in finding less visible ways to keep their hands on the levers of authority. Almost invariably, this sets in motion a struggle into which neoliberal capitalist enterprise inserts itself, often with decisive effects. On occasion, too, as in Russia (Ries 1999), organized crime seizes on that struggle to fashion itself into a spectral, underground para-state, providing civic amenities and policing on a fee-for-service basis (cf. Derrida 1994: 83). This, in turn, leads to the popular impression that government has retreated, that order has evaporated, that the nation-state is no longer.

On the other hand, despite this variability in their political sociology, nation-states *appear,* at least in their exterior forms, to be more similar than ever before, converging on the same notions of the rule of law, enacting similar constitutions, speaking more and more English, borrowing from a single stock of signs and symbols, worshipping together at the altar of Adam Smith, and, yes, all alike dealing with the impact of the global economy—as well as the sense of crisis, real or imagined, to which its implosion has given rise. Even the strongest, for reasons we have spelled out, find themselves hard put to sustain past levels of public expenditure and/or the costs of infrastructural reproduction. Many of them, moreover, have been witness both to calls for "less government" and to a widening rupture in their hyphen-nation; in the disarticulation, that is, between nation and state. Indeed, the assertion of civil society *against* the state, itself a burgeoning global phenomenon, is just one symptom of that disarticulation. Of, so to speak, alien-nation. Again, none of this is unprecedented. Throughout their history, states have suffered legitimation crises, been held to account for excessive public spending, and had to deal with threats to the integrity of the political community. That, however, does not diminish their significance in the white heat of the millennial moment.

The millennial moment.

As the term suggests, it is out of the current sense of change and crisis, especially in its impact on the hyphen-nation of the modernist polity, that the millennial dimensions of millennial capitalism reenter our narrative—in two ways.

First, it is striking that almost everywhere that occult economies have arisen, the perceived need to resort to magical means of producing wealth is blamed, in one way or another, on the inability of the state to assure its national citizens a regular income: to protect them from destitution as productive employment migrates away across its borders; to stop the inflow of immigrants and others who divert the commonweal away from autochthons; to incarcerate criminals, witches, and other nefarious characters who spoil the world for upright, hardworking people. The state is also held culpable for failing to safeguard those upright people from violence. To wit, when communal action is taken—in the name of informal justice, cultural policing, or whatever—against those who ply the immoral economy, it is often in the millennial hope of restoring coherence and control in a world run amok, of filling the void left by the withdrawal of the state and making good on its sundered obligation to the nation.

Second, in the face of the same rupture, there is a strong tendency for states to appeal to new or intensified magicalities and fetishes in order to heal fissures and breaches in the fabric of the polity. Here, again, an interpolation: Recall our comments on the question of identity. For rea-

sons alluded to earlier (and explored *in extenso* elsewhere; John L. Comaroff 1996), one of the most notable corollaries of the changing face
of nationhood in the neoliberal age, and especially after 1989, has been
an explosion of identity politics. Under these conditions, imagining
the nation rarely presumes a "deep horizontal fraternity" any longer,
not even in what once regarded themselves as the most undifferentiated of polities. While the vast majority continue to live as citizens *in*
nation-states, they tend to be only conditionally, partially, and situa-
tionally citizens *of* nation-states. Ethnic struggles, ranging from polite
altercations over resources to genocidal combat, seem immanent almost everywhere as membership is claimed on the double front of innate substance and primordial sentiment, as culture becomes intellectual property (Coombe 1998), as indigenous knowledge becomes an
object of commerce, as aboriginal spirituality becomes the site of a consumerist quest (Povinelli, in this volume), as self-imaginings, visual representations, even genes become copyright incarnate.[41] In the event,
homogeneity—as "national fantasy" (Berlant 1991), national aspiration
(Anderson 1983), national imperative—is giving way rapidly to a recognition of the irreducibility of difference. All of which puts even greater
stress on hyphen-nation; all of which presses even more the necessity
of finding its millennial key. The more diverse nation-states become in
their political sociology, the higher the level of abstraction at which *"the*
nation-state" exists, the greater the imperative to find that key. By their
very nature, as David Harvey (1989: 108) notes, modernist states had
always "to construct a . . . sense of community . . . based on [more than]
money," and, hence, to conjure up definition of public interests over
and above the [bourgeois] class and sectarian interests" they served.
They still have to fabricate that sense of community. But, with the displacement of class, the interests that they have now to encompass lie in
cultural and other forms of identity.

That states rely on magical means to succeed in the work of hyphen-
nation, of articulating nationhood, is a point made by Michael Taussig
(1997) and Fernando Coronil (1997), each in his own way. A resort to
mass-mediated ritual both to produce state power and national unity
and to persuade citizens of their reality is epidemic in the age of millennial capitalism—in rough proportion, perhaps, to populist perceptions of crisis, to the inability of governments to sustain their monopoly
over the means of violence and the flow of wealth, and to the alien-

nation of their subjects. Thus, suggests Eric Worby (1998: 560), in those parts of Africa where the hold of ruling cadres is tenuous at best, executive authority has become dependent on the performance of quotidian ceremonial, extravagant in its dramaturgy and improvisational content alike, to ensure the collusion of citizen-subjects. The latter, he goes on (562; after Mbembe 1992a: 3–4), live with the state in a promiscuous hybrid of accommodation and refusal, power and parody, embodiment and detachment. This, in turn, tends to rob "the public" of its vitality and, reciprocally, vulgarizes the political—with it, nationhood as well—reducing it to a chimera, which creates the need for yet more magic.

Here, it seems, lies the key to the magicality of the state in the age of millennial capitalism. It is not just that ruling regimes resort to theatrical display or to illusion to conjure up the present and future of the political community, its destination; this has always been true, from Elizabethan royal progresses (cf. Geertz 1977) to the trumped-up rites of colonial regimes (cf. Fields 1985). It is, rather, that they become caught up in cycles of ritual excess in which ceremonial enactments of hyphen-nation, alike in electronic space and real time, stand as alibis for realpolitik—which recedes ever farther as its surfaces are visible primarily through the glassy essence of television, the tidal swirl of radio waves, the fine print of the press. By constantly narrating hyphennation, moreover, these ceremonial enactments tend to draw attention to its fragility, to the ineluctable differences on which the body politic is built, to the divergence of interests that it must embrace. State ritual itself, then, becomes something of a pyramid scheme: The more it is indulged, the more it is required. Hence its cyclicity, its excess, its millennial qualities.

But it is not only in the register of ritual that nation-states engage with the millennial. Another crucial dimension is the fetishism of the law, of the capacity of constitutionalism and contract, rights and legal remedies, to accomplish order, civility, justice, empowerment. Like all fetishes, the chimerical quality of this one lies in an enchanted displacement, in the notion that legal instruments have the capacity to orchestrate social harmony. This misses a point once cogently made, in prose fiction, by Carlos Fuentes (1992), namely that power produces rights, not rights power; that law in practice, by extension, is a social product, not a prime mover in constructing social worlds. Still, like many fetishes—including the "free" market itself—this one continues to survive its repeated demystification.

The modernist nation-state has, from the first, been grounded in a culture of legality. Its spirit, with a nod to Montesquieu, has always been the spirit of the law. Globalization and the growth of neoliberal capitalism intensify this by an order of magnitude: the latter, because of its contractarian conception of human relations, property relations, and exchange relations, its commodification of almost everything, and its celebration of deregulated private exchange, all of which are heavily invested in a culture of legality;[42] the former, because of the way in which it demands new institutional modes of regulation and arbitration to deal with new forms of property, practice, and possession—as well as with the abrogation of old jurisdictional lines and limits (cf. Jacobson 1996; Salacuse 1991; Shapiro 1993). But the fetishism of the law goes way beyond this.

In situations of ruptured hyphen-nation, situations in which the world is constructed out of apparently irreducible difference, the language of the law affords an ostensibly neutral medium for people of difference—different cultural worlds, different social endowments, different material circumstances, differently constructed identities—to make claims on each other and the polity, to enter into contractual relations, to transact unlike values, and to deal with their conflicts. In so doing, it forges the impression of consonance amidst contrast, of the existence of universal standards that, like money, facilitate the negotiation of incommensurables across otherwise intransitive boundaries.[43] Hence its capacity, especially under conditions of moral and cultural disarticulation, to make one thing out of many, illocutionary force out of illusion, concrete realities out of often fragile fictions. Hence, too, its hegemony, despite the fact that it is hardly a guarantor of equity. As an instrument of governance, it allows the state to represent itself as the custodian of civility against disorder: as having a mandate to conjure moral community by exercising the monopoly of which Harvey (1989: 108) spoke—a monopoly over the construction of a commonweal out of inimical, fractious diversities of interest. This, in large part, is reflected in the rash of new constitutions written since the late 1980s. If law underpins the *langue* of neoliberalism, constitutionalism has become the *parole* of universal human rights, a global argot that individuates the citizen and, by making cultural identity a private asset rather than a collective claim, transmutes difference into likeness. It is an open question whether or not these constitutions yield any empowerment at all. (Interestingly, the celebrated South African one has been dubbed a Tower of Babel: it is utterly incomprehensible in the vernaculars of those whom it was supposed to enfranchise.) [44] After all, as we have said, not one of these instruments actually speaks of an entitlement to the means of survival. They do not guarantee the right to earn or to produce, only to possess, to signify, to consume, to choose. This is consistent not only with the neoliberal mood of the millennium but also with another of its panaceas: the renaissance of procedural democracy, a "universal human right" that transposes freedom into choice by offering empowerment through the ballot—the black box that reduces politics to the rough equivalent of a quinquennial shopping spree—all in the name of the rule of law, of its magical capacity to promise new beginnings.

But cultures of legality, constitutionality, right, and democracy speak primarily to the question of hyphen-nation, to moral community and citizenship, from the discursive vantage of the state and its functionaries. From the other side of the hyphen, from the side of "society *against* the state," there has emerged another, complementary discourse of populist, millennial optimism: civil society.

Postnative, Posthuman, Postscript: Civil Society in Pursuit of the Millennium   More than any other sign, perhaps, civil society has surfaced as the Big Idea of the Millennial Moment [45]—indeed, as an all-purpose panacea for the postmodern, postpolitical, postnative, even "posthuman" condition.[46] Its genealogy, before and after 1989, is too well known to detain us here (see, e.g., Walzer 1992; Cohen and Arato 1994; Krygier 1997), save to say that the more of a global obsession it has become, the less clear it is what the term might actually *mean*— as a concrete object(ive), as an abstract concept, or as a political practice. Civil society, it seems, is known primarily by its absence, its elusiveness, its incompleteness, from the traces left by struggles conducted in its name. More aspiration than achievement, it retreats before the scrutinizing gaze. For all those, like Václav Havel (n.d.), who seek a way *Toward a Civil Society,* there are others who deny the point of so doing. Why? Some, like Michael Hardt (1995: 27), argue that we are already in the "postcivil society" era, an era incapable of producing the conditions of its possibility. Others simply dismiss it as an inherently polymorphous, inchoate, unspecifiable signifier. Worse yet, it is said to conflate an analytic construct with an ideological trope, thus rendering the former promiscuous and the latter vacuous (Comaroff and Comaroff 1999a).

In spite of this, *civil society* has served as a remarkably potent battle cry across the world. During inhospitable times, it reanimates the optimistic spirit of modernity, providing scholars, public figures, poets, and ordinary people alike a language with which to talk about democracy, moral community, justice, and populist politics; with which, furthermore, to breathe life back into "society," declared dead almost twenty years ago by the powerful magi of the Second Coming, especially Maggie Thatcher. Amidst fin de siècle cynicism and retrospection, protagonists of civil society look bravely toward a new world. True, their idyll has been disparaged for its excessive Eurocentrism, for its naive liberalism, for re-presenting old-style imperialism in a seductive new garb, and for the manner of its export by such latter-day evangelists as nongovernmental organizations. True, too, it has been downsized, localized, tailored to the neoliberal age—purged, in short, of global historical visions and grand emancipatory dreams (cf. Cohen and Arato 1994: xii). But, notwithstanding the skepticism, the Idea—the fetish— has worked its magic, kindling a reformist spirit all over the place as it promises rescue from the political vacuum of postmodern nihilism.

What is it, then, about civil society that so fires the moral imagination? What makes it such a trenchant trope for these millennial times? An answer is to be found in the parallels between the history of the here and now and the history of the First Coming of the Idea in the late eighteenth century; the post-Enlightenment age in Europe, that is, that spawned the hyphenated nation-state, the concepts of political economy, culture, the civil, civility, civilization—and the distinction between "the state" and something that came to know itself as "society" (cf. Keane 1988a: 15).

It is common cause that the world-historical conditions of the late eighteenth century embraced philosophers and everypersons alike in a phenomenology of uncertainty (Becker 1994: xii—xiv): a sense of unease occasioned by the intersection of epochs, at which time the generic nature of humanity, of sociality, of selfhood and its abstraction in labor, property, and rights, of the value of things, of received means and ends was under reconstruction. Though they could not have known it, they were living at the front end of an Age of Revolution (Hobsbawm 1962), an age that posed profound issues of practical epistemology. Those issues were formulated, in the first instance, in political terms: they grew out of a malaise of governance, of populist opposition to absolutist rule and monarchial despotism (see, e.g., Woods 1992: 79; Keane 1988b: 65).

But behind the surfaces of the political were working much more fundamental processes of reconstruction: those attendant upon the advance of capitalism and commodity relations; upon the birth of the right-bearing citizen-subject; upon the empowerment of the bourgeoisie and the emergence of a public "with its own opinion[s]" and "interests" (Taylor 1990: 108; cf. Habermas 1989); upon the dawn of modernist nationhood; upon the rise of what Crawford Macpherson (1962) was famously to dub "possessive individualism." In light of these processes, the problem of "the social" presented itself with particular force. How, given the erosion of old ways of being and knowing—not to mention the expanding scale and cumulative abstraction of human relations— was the present and future of "society" to be grasped? Wherein lay its moral, material, and regulatory moorings? It became imperative, says Tester (1992: 7), to "explain how society was [even] possible" in a world in which "time-honoured answers were collapsing through mixtures of political crisis, intellectual enlightenment, technological development and the . . . rapid urbanization of social life"; in which new, national divisions of labor were taking root amidst the encroachment on everything of finance; in which the sanctity of the family was seen to be at risk; in which people, things, and nature (cf. Coronil, in this volume) were being objectified in an altogether unprecedented manner. In which the prospect of Adam Smith's faceless "society of strangers" stalked disturbingly close to hand—novel specters of a haunted gothic fiction dramatized the strangeness of what had become real (Clery 1995: 174).

It is not hard to see why, at the time, discourses of civil society, in both their analytic and utopic registers, should have focused on the issues that they did: on the relationship between state (or, more generally, political authority) and society; on the posited existence, in the space between the citizen and the sovereign polity, of an interpolated public with its own will; on the role of voluntary associations in providing alternative loci for the achievement of the commonweal; on a democratizing image of self-generating moral community, whose elemental atom was the Christian family; on the significance of the free market in underwriting the prosperity of that community; on the capacity of commerce to inscribe civility in a new civics. Foreshadowing here of Hegel, Simmel, Durkheim, Habermas.

The parallels with the present are more than obvious; indeed, they knit together all the various strands of our portrait of the Age of Millennial Capitalism. Now, as then, the call for civil society typically presents itself as an emancipatory reaction to a familiar doubling: on one hand, to the greater opacity, intrusiveness, and monopolistic tendencies of government; on the other, to its diminishing capacity "to satisfy even minimally the political and economic aspirations" of its component publics (Haynes 1997: 16), to guarantee the commonweal, or to meet the needs of its citizenry. Thus, for example, in Central Europe the pursuit of the Idea, which took on millennial features from the first, is said to have arisen in response to increasingly repressive communist rule—and in postcolonial times, to have been sustained by the memory of Soviet excesses (see, e.g., Rupnik 1988; Krygier 1997). In the West, a cause for it has been found in burgeoning corporatism of the state (Taylor 1990: 95–96) and a disenchantment with politics *tout court*. And in Africa it is ascribed to the rise of antistatist, promarket populism occasioned by the collapse of totalitarian regimes (Young 1994: 36), whose "politics of the belly" (Bayart 1993) and vulgar spectacles of power (Mbembe 1992b) persuaded citizens that governments no longer "champion society's collective interests" (Haynes 1997: 2).

But this, too, speaks purely to surfaces. Now, as then, the roots of the process lie deeper: in the interiors, and the animating forces, of the Age of Millennial Capitalism—in particular, in its impulse to displace political sovereignty with the sovereignty of "*the* market," as if the latter had a mind and a morality of its own; to reorder the relationship of production to consumption; to reconstruct the essence of labor, identity, and subjectivity; to disarticulate the nation from the state; to reduce difference to sameness by recourse to the language of legality; to elevate to first causes "value-free" technological necessity and the ostensibly neutral demands of economy; to treat government as immanently undesirable, except insofar as it deregulates or protects "market forces"; to fetishize "the law" as a universal standard in terms of which incommensurable sorts of value—of relationship, rights, and claims—may be mediated; to encourage the rapid movement of persons and goods, and sites of fabrication, thus calling into question existing forms of community; to equate freedom with choice, especially to consume, to fashion the self, to conjure with identities; to give free reign to the "forces" of hyperrationalization; to parse human beings into free-floating labor units, commodities, clients, stakeholders, strangers, their subjectivity distilled into ever more objectified ensembles of interests, entitlements, appetites, desires, purchasing "power." And so to raise the most fundamental question of all: In what consists the social? Society? Moral community?

Here, then, is our point. As in the late eighteenth century, and in strikingly similar fashion, the Idea of Civil Society makes its appearance in the late twentieth century just as the fabric of the social, the possibility of society, the ontological core of humanity, the nature of social distinction, and the essence of identity are being dramatically challenged; just as we experience an epochal metamorphosis in the organization of production, labor, and the market, in technology and its sociocultural implications, in the constitutive connections between economy and polity, nation and state, culture and place, person, family, and community; just as we find it impossible to sustain the dominant terms of modernist sociology-as-lived, of received anthropologies of knowledge, of our geographical grasp of an increasingly four-dimensional world (see Harvey, in this volume). Amid populist moral panics, mass-mediated alienation, crises of representation, and scholarly perplexity, Civil Society, in its Second Coming, once more becomes especially "good to think," to signify with, to act upon. The less substance it has, the emptier its referents, the more this is so, which is why its very polyvalence, its unfixability, is intrinsic to its power as panacea. It is the ultimate magic bullet in the Age of Millennial Capitalism. For it promises to conjure up the most fundamental thing of all: a meaningful social existence. And, thereby, to lay to rest—for now at least—Adam Smith's ghostly phantasm: the Society of Strangers.

We have argued that many of the enigmatic features of economy and society circa 2000—be they the allegorical transfiguration of the nation-state, the assertive stridency of racinated adolescence, the crisis of masculinity, the apotheosis of consumption, the fetishism of civil society, the enchantments of everyday life—are concrete, historically specific outworkings of millennial capitalism and the culture of neoliberalism. For all their apparent polysemy and disarticulation, these things are closely interrelated, all at once rooted in the past and new in the present. Together, they point to the fact that we inhabit an age that is revolutionary and yet is also an ongoing chapter in the story of capital, a story that, in Theodor Adorno's (1981: 96) phrase, "sound[s] so old, and yet [is] so new." Despite the proclamations of neoliberal prophets, history has not come to an end. Nor will it soon. As Felipe Fernandez-Armesto (1999) puts it, "Millenarianism will survive the millennium." Today's apocalypse will become tomorrow's mundane reality, laying down the terms of a dialectic out of which human beings will struggle to make sense of the world, to make livelihoods, politics, communities.

Already there are signs of altered configurations, of fresh efforts to challenge the triumphal reign of the market, to turn aside the sweeping consequences of transnational economic pressures. In the wake of fragmenting national identities, Turner (n.d.) observes, newly assertive social movements have begun to pursue common cause on a world scale, forging an alternative, critical "global civil society." It is too early, patently, to take the measure of their success. But their "passionate intensity," to invoke the spirit of Yeats one last time, might yet kindle the mature politics of a new age; "the worst" might yet become the best. There are also signs that organized labor is seeking expansive ways and means to deal with the emergent economic order. Thus a leading unionist: "The end of the century is the starting point of . . . an international labor fightback. . . . Global unionism is born." [47]

We can only hope. History, of course, will determine the substance of the politics of the twenty-first century. For our part, we find it unimaginable that innovative forms of emancipatory practice will not emerge to address the excesses of neoliberal capitalism. But that is in the future. For now, in introducing the rich array of essays in this volume, we seek to stress the epistemic importance of critical distance. Of a refusal, that is, to be seduced into treating the ideological tropes and surface forms of the culture of neoliberalism — its self-representations and subjective practices, identities and utilities — as analytic constructs. Life, under millennial capitalism, is neither a game nor a repertoire of rational choices. It is irreducible to the utilitarian pragmatics of law and economy or to methodological individualisms of one kind or another.

Indeed, these and other theoretical discourses are part of the problem. Critical disbelief, in pursuit of a reinvigorated praxis, is the beginning of a solution.

NOTES

Our thanks go to Carol Breckenridge, Arjun Appadurai, and the editorial committee of *Public Culture* for persuading us first to undertake this project. Caitrin Lynch, managing editor of that journal, has been a model of creative encouragement and help, not least in the preparation of this book. We owe her a debt of gratitude. Our research assistant, Maureen Anderson, has, as usual, gone far beyond the call of duty, identifying closely with the project and bringing her own special insights to bear on it.

1 New feudalism is Flourishing in an English country garden, *Guardian* (London), 26 August 1995, 37. See also the series on The downsizing of America, *New York Times*, 3–9 March 1996.

2 Tham Moyo and Christine Chiweshe-Adewal, Why we hate South Africa, *Mail and Guardian* (Johannesburg), 29 October–4 November 1999, 32.

3 The following paragraphs closely follow ideas developed in the opening section of Comaroff and Comaroff 1999c.

4 "Ecumene" refers to a region of "persistent cultural interaction and exchange" (Kopytoff 1987: 10; cf. Hannerz 1989: 66).

5 The following joke did the rounds in the United States in the late 1990s: "Sure, there are plenty of jobs to be had. At the moment I have three, and I still can't afford to eat!"

6 On the moral valence of gambling, see, for example, George F. Will, Hooked on gambling: Other comment, *International Herald Tribune*, 26–27 June 1999, 8; also Michael Tackett and Ted Gregory, Gambling's lure still a divisive issue, *Chicago Tribune*, 20 May 1998, 3.

7 By Jeffrey A. Zimmermann, the mural in the next essay, "Paid Programming," captures superbly the poignant, mundane millennialism that we allude to here. It is painted alongside an American flag-turned-bar-code. The artist told us that he used "Spenglish" in the work to address the local Chicano population.

8 Will, Hooked on gambling.

9 Jane Bryant Quinn, Capital gains: The lottery on lives, *Newsweek*, 15 March 1999, 55. "Viaticals" are insurance policies bought from the terminally ill, especially those in the late stages of AIDS.

10 Lottery mania grips Madya Pradesh, many commit suicide, *India Tribune* (Chicago), 2 January 1999, 8. We thank Arjun Appadurai for alerting us to this material.

11 Will, Hooked on gambling. On the Harvard Medical School study, see Brett Pulley, Compulsion to gamble seen growing, *New York Times*, 7 December 1997, 22.

12 Tackett and Gregory, Gambling's lure still a divisive issue, 3; the words quoted are those of James Dobson, president of Focus on the Family, a Christian media ministry. They echo observations made by a range of witnesses for the U.S. National Gaming Impact Study Commission, set up in 1996 to study the effects of gambling.

13 Fidel Castro, Castro: World has become a huge casino, *Sunday Independent* (Johannesburg), 6 September 1998, 4; the article is a transcript of a speech given to the South African Parliament.

14 By "postrevolutionary" societies we mean societies—such as those of the former Soviet Union—that have recently witnessed a dramatic metamorphosis of their political, material, social, and cultural structures, largely as a result of the end of the Cold War and the growth of the global market economy.

15 Ebrahim Harvey, Spectre of capitalism haunts ANC, *Mail and Guardian* (Johannesburg), 29 October–4 November 1999, 43.

16 All this, pace the simplifying optimism of Francis Fukuyama (1999), who claims that the "Great Disruption" that beset the industrialized world from the mid-1960s to the early 1990s—a result of the rise of the "postindustrial economy" and the "information age"—is coming to an end.

17 It is a matter of note, in this respect, that neither the chartered companies nor the imperial enterprises operated by old international bourgeoisies globalized production itself in the way that transnational corporations now do (Dicken 1986: 57).

18 As this implies, we see the progressive abstraction entailed in processes of decontextualization as part of the evolving logic of capitalism—a point made by Marxian theories of reification, whose salience endures. To suggest, as Daniel Miller (1999: 212; Carrier and Miller 1998) does, that "virtualism," one manifestation of these processes, may be a "replacement for 'capitalism' " in comprehending the current moment—or that it may provide a "new political economy"—is to confuse cause and effect.

19 On "patriotic capitalism," see the press announcement for the annual general conference of the South African Black Management Forum, 18–20 November 1999, on Patriotic Capitalism: The Dilemma of the New Millennium, which was published in, among other places, *Sowetan,* 2 November 1999, 29.

20 The phrase "take the waiting out of wanting" was the advertising slogan of a major British credit card in the 1970s. The "twilight" economies at issue here are seldom entirely in the hands of the young. The drug trade, for instance, is a vast transnational business that conforms with brutal clarity to the principles of capitalist enterprise. As Sudhir Venkatesh (1997) shows, black youth on U.S. city streets depend on bosses on whose account they take large risks for small profit.

21 This section owes much to an earlier essay (1999b), in which we explored the rise of occult economies in South Africa.

22 Mzilikazi Wa Afrika, "I was turned into a Zombie": Doctor says she endured eight days of torment after a devil-worshipper lured her into a trap, *Sunday Times* (Johannesburg) [Extra], 11 July 1999, 1.

23 Uli Schmetzer, Letter from Bangkok: Thai seers dealt reversal of fortune, *Chicago Tribune,* 18 November 1997, 4.

24 Connie Lauerman, "Got a problem? Pick a card: Tarot has moved out of the occult realm—to become the low-cost "Shrink in a box," *Chicago Tribune,* Tempo Section, 4 December 1997, 1, 13.

25 There have been countless stories in British tabloids about the sexual and satanic

abuse of children. For an especially vivid one, see Brian Radford, Satanic ghouls in baby sacrifice horror, *News of the World* (London), 24 August 1997, 30–31. Its two subtitles—Cult is cover for pedophile sex monsters and They breed tots to use at occult rites—reflect well the moral panic to which they speak. On the kidnapping of German children for these purposes, see Children killed for their organs, *Sunday World* (Johannesburg), 31 October 1999, 10; the report, based on German secret service documents from Berlin, originated with Reuters. The quotation about the trafficking in women is in Vladimir Isachenkov, Enslaving women from former Soviet bloc is widespread, *Santa Barbara News-Press*, 8 November 1997, A8; see also Denis Staunton, Couple on trial for child torture offer, *Guardian* (London), 8 August 1997, 13.

26 According to this urban myth, the telling of which is always accompanied by authenticating detail, the victim is offered a drink at an airport—New Orleans appears to be a favorite—and awakes in a hotel bath, body submerged in ice. A note taped to the wall warns him not to move, but to call 911. He is asked, by the operator, to feel carefully for a tube protruding from his back. When he finds one, he is instructed to remain still until paramedics arrive: His kidneys have been harvested.

27 Edmund L. Andrews, Behind the scams: Desperate people, easily duped, *New York Times,* 29 January 1997, 3. See also Celestine Bohlen, Albanian parties trade charges in the pyramid scandal, *New York Times,* 29 January 1997, 3.

28 See Leslie Eaton, Investment fraud is soaring along with the stock market, *New York Times,* 30 November 1997, 1, 24. Eaton also notes that these scams have been facilitated "by the rise of low cost telecommunications and . . . the internet."

29 Charity pyramid schemer sentenced to 12 years, *Chicago Tribune,* 23 September 1997, 6.

30 Large-scale scams have occurred in Russia, Romania, Bulgaria, Serbia, and other former communist countries; see Andrews, Behind the scams. They are also common in Africa (Comaroff and Comaroff 1999b).

31 Tom Whitehouse, Messiah on the make in Sun City, *Observer* (London), 30 May 1999, 26.

32 The phrases in quotes were uttered to us in 1997 by a Universal Church pastor in Mafikeng, South Africa, where the denomination is growing fast: it has two storefront chapels, several rural centers, and a much-watched daily program on the local television channel.

33 This progressive sense of loss, it hardly needs saying, was a touchstone of the culture industry throughout the 1990s: Consider such "condition of England" films as *The Full Monty* and *Brassed Off,* their European parallels (*The Dreamlife of Angels,* for example), and innumerable non-Western counterparts.

34 We were struck by one recent instance that resonates so obviously with our concerns here: Michael Metelits, speaking of labor legislation in the "new" South Africa, referred to it as a "tricky, not to say occult business." See his "Toiling masses and honest capitalists," *Work to Rule: A Focus on Labour Legislation,* supplement to *Mail and Guardian* (Johannesburg), 15–21 October 1999, 11.

35 A striking example of the management of the global workforce by private agen-

cies is Staff Solutions, a U.K. company that recruits foreigners—producing them "like magic"—to toil in British agriculture for a pittance under "new feudal conditions" that the U.K. government has refused to regulate, preferring to allow neoliberal enterprise free reign. New feudalism is flourishing, 37.

36 See, for example, Doug Brooks, SA private armies can supply peacekeepers to DRC, *Star* (Johannesburg), 3 November 1999, 10.

37 See, for example, Richard Norton-Taylor and Owen Bowcott, Deadly cost of new global warfare, *Mail and Guardian* (Johannesburg), 29 October–4 November 1999, 20.

38 See The high price of defeat, *Mail and Guardian* (Johannesburg), 5–11 November 1999, 21, in which it is noted that losses by national teams may cause the fall of governments. In New Zealand, a defeat in the Rugby World Cup had such a "shattering" effect on the "national psyche" that a local "university is offering grief counselling." See Blues counselling for all black fans, *Star* (Johannesburg), 5 November 1999, 1.

39 Peregrine Worsthorne, Farewell to England's nation state, *Daily Telegraph* (London), 29 June 1988, 14.

40 This is not to say that there have not been efforts to create new forms of politics. Derrida 1994, for example, posits the possibility of a "new International," the formulation of which, however, has drawn much criticism, most notably from Aijaz Ahmad (1999: 104–5).

41 Even those considered, by popular stereotype, to be anything but "modern" have taken to asserting legal rights over their mass-mediated image. The !Xoo, a San group in Namibia, are suing for the use of pictures of themselves on postcards and in an airline magazine advertisement, claiming financial compensation. Bobby Jordan, San people in legal action over "insulting" ad, *Sunday Times* (Johannesburg), 31 October 1999, 9.

42 Hence the affinity between neoliberal economics and the work of the "law and economics" school of legal theory that is closely associated with the University of Chicago Law School. Almost any recent text emanating from that school will serve to substantiate the point.

43 We have made a parallel argument for the salience of law to colonial states—which, in this respect, foreshadowed the situation we describe here; see John L. Comaroff 1998.

44 Goloa Moiloa, Constitutional Tower of Babel, *Sunday World* (Johannesburg), 31 October 1999, 16.

45 The topics discussed in this section are dealt with in extenso in Comaroff and Comaroff 1999a.

46 *Postnative* is used by Geertz (1995: 6) to describe Obeyesekere's subject position in his debate with Sahlins over the death of Captain Cook, but it applies as well to the generic subject in the age of neoliberal capitalism. *Posthuman* appears for the first time, to our knowledge, in Hayles 1999.

47 Frank Nxumalo, Global capital can bank on worldwide resistance, *Sunday Independent* (Johannesburg), 7 November 1999, Business Report, 1. The unionist is John Maitland, president of the International Chemical Energy Mining and General Workers Union, which represents 20 million workers.

REFERENCES

Abdullah, Ibrahim. 1998. Bush path to destruction: The origin and character of the Revolutionary United Front/Sierra Leone. *Journal of Modern African Studies* 36, no. 2: 203–35.

Abrams, Philip. 1988. Notes on the difficulty of studying the state (1977). *Journal of Historical Sociology* 1, no. 1: 58–89.

Adorno, Theodor W. 1981. *In search of Wagner,* translated by R. Livingstone. London: New Left Books.

Ahmad, Aijaz. 1992. *In theory: Classes, nations, literatures.* New York: Verso.

———. 1999. Reconciling Derrida: "Specters of Marx" and deconstructive politics. In Sprinker 1999.

Anderson, Benedict. 1983. *Imagined communities: Reflections on the origin and spread of nationalism.* London: Verso.

Appadurai, Arjun. 1990. Disjuncture and difference in the global cultural economy. *Public Culture* 2: 1–24.

———. 2000. Spectral housing and urban cleansing: Notes on millennial Mumbai. *Cosmopolitanism,* special issue, *Public Culture* 12 (1): 1–19.

Apter, Andrew. 1999. IBB = 419: Nigerian democracy and the politics of illusion. In *Civil society and the political imagination in Africa: Critical perspectives,* edited by John L. and Jean Comaroff. Chicago: University of Chicago Press.

Balzac, Honoré de. 1965 [1847]. *Poor relations,* Part 1, *Cousin Bette,* translated by Marion Ayton Crawford. Harmondsworth, U.K.: Penguin.

Barber, Benjamin R. 1992. Jihad vs. McWorld. *Atlantic Monthly,* March: 53–65.

Bastian, Misty L. 1993. "Bloodhounds who have no friends": Witchcraft and locality in the Nigerian popular press. In *Modernity and its malcontents: Ritual and power in postcolonial Africa,* edited by Jean and John L. Comaroff. Chicago: University of Chicago Press.

Baudrillard, Jean. 1998. *The consumer society: Myths and structures.* Newbury Park, Calif.: Sage.

Bayart, Jean-François. 1993. *The state in Africa: Politics of the belly.* New York: Longman.

Becker, Marvin B. 1994. *The emergence of civil society in the eighteenth century: A privileged moment in the history of England, Scotland, and France.* Bloomington: Indiana University Press.

Berlant, Lauren G. 1991. *The anatomy of national fantasy: Hawthorne, utopia, and everyday life.* Chicago: University of Chicago Press.

———. 1997. *The queen of America goes to Washington city: Essays on sex and citizenship.* Durham, N.C.: Duke University Press.

Blaney, David L., and Mustapha Kamal Pasha. 1993. Civil society and democracy in the Third World: Ambiguities and historical possibilities. *Studies in Comparative International Development* 28, no. 1: 3–24.

Buford, Bill. 1993. *Among the thugs.* New York: Vintage Departures.

Carrier, James G., and Daniel Miller, eds. 1998. *Virtualism: A new political economy.* Oxford: Berg.

Clery, E. J. 1995. *The rise of supernatural fiction, 1762–1800*. Cambridge: Cambridge University Press.

Cohen, Jean, and Andrew Arato. 1994. *Civil society and political theory*. Cambridge: MIT Press.

Cohn, Norman Rufus Colin. 1957. *The pursuit of the millennium: Revolutionary millenarians and mystical anarchists of the middle ages*. London: Secker and Warburg.

Comaroff, Jean. 1997a. Consuming passions: Nightmares of the global village. In *Body and self in a post-colonial world*, edited by E. Badone, special issue, *Culture* 17, no. 1-2: 7–19.

———. 1997b. Portrait of an unknown South African: Identity in a global age. *Macalaster International* 4 (spring): 119–43; and *Novos Estudos* 49: 65–83.

———. 1999a. Introduction. In *Civil society and the political imagination in Africa: Critical perspectives*, edited by John L. and Jean Comaroff. Chicago: University of Chicago Press.

———. 1999b. Occult economies and the violence of abstraction: Notes from the South African postcolony. *American Ethnologist* 26: 279–301.

———. 1999c. Alien-nation: Zombies, immigrants, and millennial capitalism. *CODESRIA Bulletin*, 3/4: 17–28.

———. Forthcoming. Reflections on youth, from the past to the postcolony. *Politique africaine*, special edition on youth in Africa (2001).

Comaroff, John L. 1996. Ethnicity, nationalism and the politics of difference in an age of revolution. In *The politics of difference: Ethnic premises in a world of power*, edited by P. MacAllister and E. Wilmsen. Chicago: University of Chicago Press.

———. 1998. Reflections on the colonial state, in South Africa and elsewhere: Fragments, factions, facts, and fictions. *Social Identities* 4, no. 3: 321–61.

Comaroff, John L., and Jean Comaroff. 1987. The madman and the migrant: Work and labor in the historical consciousness of a South African people. *American Ethnologist* 14: 191–209.

———. 1997. Postcolonial politics and discourses of democracy in southern Africa: An anthropological reflection on African political modernities. *Journal of Anthropological Research*, 53 no. 2: 123–46.

Connelly, Matthew, and Paul Kennedy. 1994. Must it be the rest against the West? *Atlantic Monthly*, December: 61–84.

Conrad, Joseph. 1957 [1911]. *Under Western eyes*. Harmondsworth, U.K.: Penguin.

Coombe, Rosemary J. 1998. *The cultural life of intellectual properties: Authorship, appropriation, and the law*. Durham, N.C.: Duke University Press.

Coronil, Fernando. 1997. *The magical state: Nature, money, and modernity in Venezuela*. Chicago: University of Chicago Press.

Corrigan, Paul, and Simon Frith. 1976. The politics of youth culture. In *Resistance through rituals: Youth subcultures in post-war Britain*, edited by S. Hall and T. Jefferson. London: Hutchinson.

Corrigan, Philip, and Derek Sayer. 1985. *The great arch: English state formation as cultural revolution*. Oxford: Basil Blackwell.

Cox, Robert W. 1987. *Production, power, and world order: Social forces in the making of history*. New York: Columbia University Press.

Darian-Smith, Eve. 1995. Law in place: Legal mediations of national identity and state territory in Europe. In *Nationalism, racism, and the rule of law*, edited by P. Fitzpatrick. Brookfield, Vt.: Dartmouth.

———. 1999. *Bridging divides: The Channel Tunnel and English legal identity in the new Europe*. Berkeley: University of California Press.

De Boeck, Filip. 1999. Borderland Breccia: The historical imagination of a central African frontier. Paper presented at The Black West: Reinventing History, Reinterpreting Media conference, San Diego, Calif., April.

Derrida, Jacques. 1994. *Specters of Marx: The state of debt, the work of mourning, and the new international*, translated by Peggy Kamuf. New York: Routledge.

Dicken, Peter. 1986. *Global shift: Industrial change in a turbulent world*. London: Harper and Row.

Dirlik, Arif. 1996. Looking backwards in an age of global capital: Thoughts on history in Third World cultural criticism. In *Pursuit of contemporary East Asian culture*, edited by X. Tang and S. Snyder. Boulder, Colo.: Westview Press.

Fernandez-Armesto, Felipe. 1999. *Millennium: A history of our last 1000 years*. New York: Random House.

Fields, Karen E. 1985. *Revival and rebellion in colonial central Africa*. Princeton, N.J.: Princeton University Press.

Fordred, Lesley. 1999. Narrative, conflict, and change: Journalism in the new South Africa. Ph.D. diss., University of Cape Town.

Foster, Robert J. 1991. Making national cultures in the global ecumene. *Annual Review of Anthropology* 20: 235–60.

Frank, Andre Gunder. 1971. *Capitalism and underdevelopment in Latin America: Historical studies of Chile and Brazil*. Harmondsworth, U.K.: Penguin.

Friedman, Thomas L. 1999. *The Lexus and the olive tree*. New York: Farrar, Straus and Giroux.

Fuentes, Carlos. 1992. *The campaign*, translated by A. M. Adam. New York: Harper-Collins.

Fukuyama, Francis. 1999. *The great disruption: Human nature and the reconstitution of social order*. New York: Free Press.

Gal, Susan. 1997. Feminism and civil society. In *Transitions, environments, translations*, edited by J. Scott, C. Kaplan, and D. Keats. New York: Routledge.

Garten, Jeffrey E. 1998. The gradual revolution. *New York Times Book Review*, 8 February, 7.

Garth, Bryant G., and Yves Dezalay. 1996. *Dealing in virtue: International commercial arbitration and the construction of a transnational legal order*. Chicago: University of Chicago Press.

Geertz, Clifford. 1977. Centers, kings, and charisma: Reflections on the symbolics of power. In *Culture and its creators: Essays in honor of Edward Shils*, edited by J. Ben-David and T. Nichols Clark. Chicago: University of Chicago Press.

———. 1995. Culture war. *New York Review of Books*, 30 November, 4–6.

Geschiere, Peter. 1997. *The modernity of witchcraft: Politics and the occult in postcolonial Africa.* Charlottesville: University of Virginia Press.

Gluckman, Max. 1959. The magic of despair. *The Listener,* 29 April. Republished in *Order and rebellion in tribal Africa.* London: Cohen and West, 1963.

Habermas, Jürgen. 1989. *The structural transformation of the public sphere,* translated by T. Burger and F. Lawrence. Cambridge: MIT Press.

Hannerz, Ulf. 1989. Notes on the global ecumene. *Public Culture* 1: 66–75.

Hardt, Michael. 1995. The withering of civil society. *Social Text,* no. 45: 27–44.

Harvey, David. 1989. *The condition of postmodernity: An enquiry into the origins of cultural change.* Oxford: Blackwell.

Havel, Václav. n.d. *Toward a civil society: Selected speeches and writings 1990–1994,* translated by Paul Wilson et al. Prague: Lidové Noviny Publishing House.

Hayles, N. Katherine. 1999. *How we became posthuman: Virtual bodies in cybernetics, literature, and informatics.* Chicago: University of Chicago Press.

Haynes, Jeff. 1997. *Democracy and civil society in the Third World: Politics and new political movements.* Cambridge: Polity Press.

Hegeman, Susan. 1991. Shopping for identities: "A nation of nations" and the weak ethnicity of objects. *Public Culture* 3: 71–92.

Hirst, Paul, and Grahame F. Thompson. 1996. *Globalization in question: The international economy and the possibilities of governance.* Cambridge: Polity Press.

Hobsbawm, Eric J. 1962. *The age of revolution, 1789–1848.* New York: New American Library (Mentor Book).

———. 1979. The development of the world economy. *Cambridge Journal of Economics* 3: 305–18.

Jacobson, David. 1996. *Rights across borders.* Baltimore, Md.: Johns Hopkins University Press.

Jameson, Fredric. 1999. Marx's purloined letter. In Sprinker 1999.

Keane, John. 1988a. Introduction. In *Civil society and the state: New European perspectives,* edited by J. Keane. New York: Verso.

———. 1988b. Despotism and democracy: The origins and development of the distinction between civil society and the state, 1750–1859. In *Civil society and the state: New European perspectives,* edited by J. Keane. New York: Verso.

Kellogg, P. 1987. Goodbye to the working class? *International Socialism* 2, no. 36: 105–12.

Kopytoff, Igor. 1987. The internal African frontier: The making of African culture. In *The African frontier,* edited by I. Kopytoff. Bloomington: Indiana University Press.

Korten, David. 1996. *When corporations rule the world.* East Hartford, Conn.: Kumarian Press.

Kramer, Eric. 1999. Possessing faith: Commodification, religious subjectivity, and community in a Brazilian neo-Pentecostal church. Ph.D. diss., University of Chicago.

Krygier, Martin. 1997. *Between fear and hope: Hybrid thoughts on public values.* Sydney: ABC Books.

Kurtzman, Joel. 1993. *The death of money: How the electronic economy has destabilized the world's markets and created financial chaos.* New York: Simon and Schuster.

La Fontaine, Jean S. 1997. *Speak of the devil: Allegations of satanic child abuse in contemporary England.* Cambridge: Cambridge University Press.

Lash, Scott, and John Urry. 1987. *The end of organized capitalism.* Madison: University of Wisconsin Press.

Lewis, Tom. 1999. The politics of "hauntology" in Derrida's *Specters of Marx.* In Sprinker 1999.

Lukacs, John. 1993. *The end of the twentieth century and the end of the modern age.* New York: Ticknor and Fields.

Macpherson, Crawford Brough. 1962. *The political theory of possessive individualism: Hobbes to Locke.* Oxford: Oxford University Press.

Marx, Karl. 1967. [1867]. *Capital: A critique of political economy,* vol. 1. New York: International Publishers.

Mbembe, Achille. 1992a. Provisional notes on the postcolony. *Africa* 62, no. 1: 3–37.

———. 1992b. The banality of power and the aesthetics of vulgarity in the postcolony. *Public Culture* 4: 1–30.

McMichael, Philip. 1998. Development and structural adjustment. In Carrier and Miller 1998.

Miliband, Ralph. 1969. *The state in capitalist society.* London: Weidenfeld and Nicholson.

Miller, Daniel. 1999. Conclusion: A theory of virtualism. In Carrier and Miller 1998.

Moore, Sally Falk. 1989. The production of cultural pluralism as a process. *Public Culture* 1: 26–48.

Negri, Antonio. 1999. The specter's smile. In Sprinker 1999.

Peebles, Gustav. n.d. Bills and boundaries: Contestations of money, space, and future in the new Europe. Doctoral research proposal, Department of Anthropology, University of Chicago, 1998.

Ries, Nancy. 1999. Mafia as a symbol of power and redemption in post-Soviet Russia. Paper presented at workshop on Transparency and Conspiracy: Power Revealed and Concealed in the Global Village, London School of Economics, May.

Roitman, Janet. 1998. The Garison-Entrepôt. *Cahiers d'Études africaines* 150–152, 28, nos. 2–4: 297–329.

———. 1999. Unsanctioned wealth, or the productivity of debt in the Chad Basin. Paper presented at conference on Commodification and Identities—The Social Life of Things Revisited, Amsterdam, 10–14 June.

Ross, Robert J. S. 1990. The relative decline of relative autonomy: Global capitalism and the political economy of state change. In *Changes in the state: Causes and consequences,* edited by E. S. Greenberg and T. F. Mayer. Newbury Park, Calif.: Sage.

Rupnik, Jacques. 1988. Totalitarianism revisited. In *Civil society and the state: New European perspectives,* edited by John Keane. New York: Verso.

Salacuse, Jeswald W. 1991. *Making global deals: Negotiating in the international marketplace.* Boston: Houghton Mifflin.

Sassen, Saskia. 1996. *Losing control? Sovereignty in an age of globalization.* New York: Columbia University Press.

———. n.d. Cracked casings: Notes towards an analytics for studying transnational processes. Manuscript.

Scheper-Hughes, Nancy. 1996. Theft of life: The globalization of organ stealing rumors. *Anthropology Today* 12, no. 3: 3–11.

Schneider, Jane. 1989. Rumpelstiltskin's bargain: Folklore and the merchant capitalist intensification of linen manufacture in early modern Europe. In *Cloth and human experience,* edited by A. Weiner and J. Schneider. Washington: Smithsonian Institution Press.

Seekings, Jeremy. 1993. *Heroes or villains? Youth politics in the 1980's.* Johannesburg: Ravan Press.

Sennett, Richard. 1998. *The corrosion of character: The personal consequences of work in the new capitalism.* New York: W. W. Norton.

Shapiro, Martin. 1993. The globalization of law. *Indiana Journal of Global Legal Studies* 1 (fall): 37–64.

Silbey, Susan S. 1997. "Let them eat cake": Globalization, postmodern colonialism, and the possibilities of justice. *Law and Society Review* 31, no. 2: 207–35.

Sklair, Leslie. 1998. The transnational capitalist class. In Carrier and Miller 1998.

Sontag, Susan. 1978. *Illness as metaphor.* New York: Farrar, Straus and Giroux.

Sprinker, Michael, ed. 1999. *Ghostly demarcations: A symposium of Jacques Derrida's Specters of Marx.* London: Verso.

Strange, Susan. 1986. *Casino capitalism.* Oxford: Blackwell.

Taussig, Michael T. 1997. *The magic of the state.* New York: Routledge.

Taylor, Charles. 1990. Modes of civil society. *Public Culture* 3: 95–118.

Tester, Keith. 1992. *Civil society.* London: Routledge.

Tölölyan, Khachig. 1991. The nation-state and its others: In lieu of a preface. *Diaspora* (spring): 3–7.

Tomasic, Roman, and Brendan Petony. 1991. *Casino capitalism? Insider trading in Australia.* Canberra: Australian Institute of Criminology.

Tronti, Mario. 1980. The strategy of refusal. *Semiotext(e)* 3: 28–36.

Trouillot, Michel-Rolph. 1999. Close encounters of the deceptive kind: The anthropology of the state in the age of globalization. Paper presented on the occasion of the fiftieth anniversary of the founding of anthropology at Stanford University, 9–10 April.

Turner, Terence. n.d. Globalization, the state, and social consciousness in the late twentieth century. Manuscript.

Van Binsbergen, Wim, and Peter Geschiere. n.d. Call for papers for an international conference on Commodification and Identities — *The Social Life of Things* Revisited, Amsterdam, 10–14 June 1999.

Venkatesh, Sudhir. 1997. American project: An historical ethnography of Chicago's Robert Taylor Homes, 1962–1995. Ph.D. diss., University of Chicago.

Wallerstein, Immanuel. 1972. Social conflict in post-independence black Africa: The concepts of race and status group reconsidered. In *Racial tensions in national identity,* edited by E. Campbell. Nashville, Tenn.: Vanderbilt University Press. Reprinted in *The capitalist world economy,* by I. Wallerstein. Cambridge: Cambridge University Press, 1979.

Walzer, Michael. 1992. The civil society argument. In *Dimensions of radical democracy: Pluralism, citizenship, community,* edited by Chantal Mouffe. New York: Verso.

Weber, Max. 1946. *From Max Weber: Essays in Sociology,* edited and translated by H. H. Gerth and C. Wright Mills. New York: Oxford University Press.

Woods, Dwayne. 1992. Civil society in Europe and Africa: Limiting state power through a public sphere. *African Studies Review* 95, no. 2: 77–100.

Worby, Eric. 1998. Tyranny, parody, and ethnic polarity: Ritual engagements with the state in Northwestern Zambia. *Journal of Southern African Studies* 24: 561–78.

Worsley, Peter M. 1957. *The trumpet shall sound: A study of "cargo" cults in Melanesia.* London: Macgibbon and Kee.

Yergin, Daniel, and Joseph Stanislaw. 1998. *The commanding heights: The battle between government and the marketplace that is remaking the modern world.* New York: Simon & Schuster.

Young, Crawford. 1994. In search of civil society. In *Civil society and the state in Africa,* edited by J. W. Harbeson, D. Rothchild, and N. Chazan. Boulder, Colo.: Lynne Rienner.

Yúdice, George. 1995. Civil society, consumption, and governmentality in an age of global reconstruction. *Social Text,* no. 45: 1–25.

Žižek, Slavoj. 1997. *The Plague of Fantasies.* London: Verso.

Millennial Transitions

Irene Stengs, Hylton White, Caitrin Lynch,

and Jeffrey A. Zimmermann

HAPPY

NEW

YEAR

Wishing you

a lot of wealth

ขอให้รวย

mon•ey \ ˈmə-nē \ *n*

In the steady repertoire of auspicious
Thai New Year cards that carry por-
traits of royalty and holy monks, a
new type of card appeared in 1998.
The images on these cards are 100-,
500-, or 1000-baht banknotes complete
with the currency's small portrait of
the present king. The accompanying
texts plainly wish the receiver "a lot
of wealth" (*kho haj ruaj*). The 1997
collapse of the Asian economies has
boosted the hope of many Thai that
the king's moral and spiritual powers
can lead them into a new period of
prosperity. — Irene Stengs

Mfanefile, KwaZulu Natal Province, South Africa, 1997. © *Hylton White*

bride·wealth \ 'brīd-welth \ *n*

Using money to purchase cattle, or even to stand for
them in the context of bridewealth exchange, made
it possible for marriage to proceed in the southern
African countryside despite the collapse of pastoral
autonomy under colonialism. But it also meant that
social reproduction came to depend on the wages
remitted by migrant workers. In order to make her
more marriageable, this man adorns his only
daughter with money and clothes that represent her
value as a future wife and mother. — Hylton White

A Christmas Bonanza, Kandy, Sri Lanka, December 1995. © Caitrin Lynch

¹lot•tery \ ˈlä-tə-rē \ *n*

The globalization of the Christian holiday of Christmas has accompanied economic liberalization. In Sri Lanka, this global capitalist holiday has been appropriated by non-Christians: The Christmas season has become the buying season, with the main icon Santa Claus, not Jesus Christ. When the government introduced its economic liberalization package in 1977, it also introduced *Sevana,* the nation's first lottery. Twenty years later, many of the numerous lotteries are run by the state, which has "refigured wagering as an act of charity"—proceeds are directed toward government projects for housing, development, and education.* Nearly two millennia after Jesus's birth, when hopeful consumers purchased these *Sevana* Christmas lottery tickets in 1995, their money would also go toward building houses for the poor—the Christmas season of charity refigured in the act of wagering. — Caitrin Lynch

*Steven Kemper, "The Nation Consumed: Buying and Believing in Sri Lanka," *Public Culture* 5 (1993): 386.

"Paid Programming," a mural by Jeffrey A. Zimmermann, Honore Street at North Avenue, Bucktown, Chicago 1999. © Jeffrey A. Zimmermann

²**lot•tery** \ ˈlä-tə-rē \ *n*

"Not A LOT TO TOMAR, OW!" and "Cash ola," details from "Paid Programming" mural, Chicago.
© *Jeffrey A. Zimmermann*

Toward a Critique of Globalcentrism:
Speculations on Capitalism's Nature

Fernando Coronil

The end of a millennium is a time that invites speculations about the future as well as reckonings with the past. In his *Confessions,* Saint Augustine suggested that it is only at the end of a life that one can apprehend its meaning. The current fashionable talk about the end of History, of socialism, even of capitalism — or at least the long-announced demise of its familiar industrial form and the birth of an era defined by the dominance of information and services rather than material production — suggests that the close of the millennium has generated fantasies inspired by a similar belief. In a striking coincidence, the end of the millennium has also marked the victory of capitalism over socialism after a protracted confrontation that polarized humanity during much of the twentieth century. Its triumph at this time makes capitalism appear as the only valid social horizon, granting it a sacralized sense of finality that conjures up what Sylvia Thrupp identified as the millennial expectation of a "perfect age to come" (1970: 12).

As an expression of this millennial fantasy, corporate discourses of globalization evoke with particular force the advent of a new epoch free from the limitations of the past. Their image of globalization offers the promise of a unified humanity no longer divided by East and West, North and South, Europe and its Others, the rich and the poor. As if they were underwritten by the desire to erase the scars of a conflictual past or to bring it to a harmonious end, these discourses set in motion the belief that the separate histories, geographies, and cultures that have divided humanity are now being brought together by the warm embrace of globalization, understood as a progressive process of planetary integration.[1]

Needless to say, discourses of globalization are multiple and far from homogeneous. Scholarly accounts generally contest the stereotypical image of an emerging global village popularized by the corporations and the media. These accounts suggest that globalization, rather than being new, is the intensified manifestation of an old process of transcontinental trade, capitalist expansion, colonization, worldwide migrations, and transcultural exchanges, and that its current neoliberal modality polarizes, excludes, and differentiates even as it generates certain configurations of translocal integration and cultural homogenization. For its critics, neoliberal globalization is implosive rather than expansive: it connects powerful centers to subordinate peripheries, its mode of integration is fragmentary rather than total, it builds commonalities upon asymmetries. In short, it unites by dividing. From different perspectives and with different emphases, these critics offer not the comforting image of a global village, but rather the disturbing view of a fractured world sharply divided by reconfigured relations of domination.[2]

Although I, too, am drawn by the desire to make sense of capitalism's history at the millennium's end, I will explore its life not so much by chronicling its biography from the vantage point of the present, as Saint Augustine suggests, but by discerning its present configuration and speculating about its future in light of its dark colonial past. My brief sketch of capitalism will be highly selective, drawing on certain features in order to paint, with broad strokes, a rough image of its changing dynamics at this time. To bring forth this image as I see it emerging at the turn of millennium, I will trace some links between the colonial past within which capitalism evolved and the imperial present within which neoliberal globalization has gained hegemony. Needless to say, there is a risk in referring to capitalism by a single word (and in the singular) and attributing to it features that may give the impression that it is a bounded or self-willed entity, rather than a complex, contradictory, and heterogeneous process mobilized by the actions of innumerable social agents. Against the opposite danger of missing the forest (or forests!) for the trees, I opt for the risk of producing what may be no more than a caricature of the capitalist jungle, in the hope that it can help us recognize defining features of its evolving configuration.

NATURE, GLOBALIZATION, AND OCCIDENTALISM

Our familiar geopolitical map of modern world—defined by such classificatory devices as the three-worlds scheme, the division between the West and the non-West, and the opposition between capitalist and socialist nations — is being redrawn by a number of processes associated with the hegemony of neoliberal globalization. These include (1) the recomposition of temporal and spatial relations through new forms of communication and production, (2) the increasing tension between the national basis of states and the international connections of national economies, and (3) the growing polarization of social sectors both within and among nations, together with the concentration of power in transnational networks. As a result of these changes, peoples and natural resources that have been treated as external domains to be colonized by capital increasingly appear as internal to it, subjected to its hegemonic control. In accordance with the *Communist Manifesto*'s famous anticipation, capital, mobilized by its relentless and tireless dynamics, seems to be melting all solid barriers that have stood in its way, expanding its reach over our familiar material world, propelling it toward ever more immaterial domains, and subjecting all realms under its power to ever more abstract forms of control. My aim is to catch an image of capital's expansive dynamics throughout planet Earth as well as into cyberspace in order to explore the significance of its expansion for the organization and representation of cultural differences.

Inspired by the speculative spirit of millennial thinking, I wish to suggest that the current phase of neoliberal globalization involves a significant reordering and redefinition of geohistorical units. Dominant discourses of globalization recast the centrality of the West/Other opposition that has characterized Eurocentric representations of cultural difference. Previous Occidentalist modalities of representation have been structured by a binary opposition between the Occident and its others. As I argue elsewhere, Occidentalist constructs obscure the mutual constitution of "Europe" and its colonies, as well as of the "West" and its postcolonies, through representational practices that separate the world's components into bounded units, disaggregate their relational histories, turn difference into hierarchy, and thus help reproduce asymmetrical power relations (Coronil 1996: 57).

My argument in this essay is that dominant discourses of globalization constitute a circuitous modality of Occidentalism that operates through the occlusion rather than the affirmation of the radical difference between the West and its others. In contrast to the Western bias or Eurocentrism of previous Occidentalisms, what I call the globalcentrism of dominant globalization discourses expresses the ongoing dominance of the West by a number of representational operations that include: the dissolution of the "West" into the market and its crystallization in less visible transnational nodules of concentrated financial and political power; the attenuation of cultural antagonisms through the integration of distant cultures into a common global space; and a shift from alterity to subalternity as a dominant modality for constituting cultural difference. These changes entail a consolidation of the economy as the neoliberal age's "cultural dominant," which I see, building on Fredric Jameson, as a structuring principle that counters notions of random difference while allowing "for the presence and coexistence of very different, yet subordinate features" (Jameson 1991: 4–6). As an "economic" cultural dominant, discourses of neoliberal globalization coexist with celebratory discourses of cultural diversity, as well as with warnings concerning the coming "clash of civilizations"; they subsume the world's multiple cultures, and competing discourses about them, as subordinate elements within an encompassing, planetary economic culture.

At a time when capitalism parades as most universal and independent of its material foundations, I hope to show that a focus on its relation to nature helps to render visible an emerging imperial cartography of modernity occluded by increasingly abstract modalities of domination.

NATURE, CAPITALISM, AND COLONIALISM

A central dimension of post-Enlightenment discourses of modernity has been the establishment of a radical separation between "culture" and "nature." These discourses of historical progress typically assert the primacy of time over space and of culture over nature. The separation of history from geography and the supremacy of time over space has the effect of producing images of society cut off from their material environments. Dominant views take for granted the natural world upon which societies depend. Despite the significant work of geographers, feminists, and ecologists who have examined the intimate relation between the social and natural domains, nature is insufficiently theorized in the discussion of capitalism.

Among Western theoreticians of capitalism, Adam Smith, David Ricardo, and Karl Marx were exceptional in the detailed theoretical attention they paid to the social significance of the natural foundations of social production. Building on Smith's and Ricardo's insights, Marx employed the category "land/rent" as a way of conceptualizing the role of socially mediated natural powers in the construction of capitalism. Yet his analysis of capitalism tended to privilege the capital/labor relation and to assume that "land" (by which he meant all the socially mediated power of nature) would be absorbed by capital. In critical dialogue with liberal and Marxist discussions of natural resources, I have suggested that a fuller recognition of nature's role in the making of capitalism expands and modifies the temporal and geographical referents that have framed dominant narratives of modernity (Coronil 1997). I present a brief version of this critique now in order to frame my examination of the role of nature during the present phase of neoliberal globalization.

Marx claimed that the relationship among capital-profit, labor-wages, and land-ground rent "holds in itself all the mysteries of the social production process" (1981: 953). As if wishing to evoke simultaneously a celestial mystery and its earthly resolution, he called this relationship "the trinity form." Yet few analysts, Marx included, have seriously applied this formula to resolve the enigma of the role of "land" in the making of capitalism. Looking at capitalism from a European standpoint, Henry Lefebvre is unusual in both noting this neglect and suggesting ways of examining the role of the social agents associated with land, including the state, in the making of European capitalism (1974).[3] Lefebvre, however, confined his vision to Europe, and did not see the implications of his insight for recasting the relationship between capitalism and colonialism.

Given the importance of the (post)colonies as providers of natural resources that continue to be essential for the development of capitalism, a view of capitalism from the (post)colonies helps modify conventional understandings of capitalism's dynamics and history in two respects.

First, it helps theorize more fully the role of nature as a constitutive dimension of modern wealth, rather than simply as a form of "natural" capital—as is the common view among liberal economists—or as capital's necessary condition of existence, a limitation to its growth, or a source of entropy—as some Marxists have argued (see O'Connor 1994). Even thinkers like Marx, who recognize nature's role in the formation of wealth, often forget their own insight in their analysis of capitalist production. Drawing from William Petty (and reproducing a common identification of culture with man and nature with woman), Marx argues that wealth must be seen as the union of labor ("the father") and nature ("the mother") (1967: 43). Yet in an influential section of *Capital,* Marx argues that the physical properties of commodities have "nothing to do with their existence as commodities" (1967: 72). In his effort to demonstrate that labor power is the only source of value and therefore that a commodity's value resides in the inscription, not in the object, Marx neglects his own insight that labor inscribes value through a material medium, and that wealth is the joint result of labor and nature. This neglect of nature by capitalism's major critic has obscured the dynamics of capitalist wealth formation. A recognition that a commodity is inseparable from its physical materiality, and that as a unit of wealth it embodies both its natural and its value form, presents a different view of capitalism. This perspective makes it possible to view the specific mechanisms through which capitalist exploitation extracts surplus labor from workers as well as natural riches from the earth under different historical conditions. It also makes it possible to see lines of continuity and change between modes of appropriating nature under colonial and neoliberal regimes of domination.

Second, a "grounded" view that complements the recognized importance of labor with the neglected but no less fundamental significance of nature in capitalism's formation reinforces works that have sought to counter Eurocentric conceptions that identify modernity with Europe and relegate the periphery to a premodern primitivity. By bringing out a neglected structuring principle of capitalist development, this perspective helps us to see capitalism as a global process rather than as a European phenomenon.[4] Since for Marx *land* stands for *nature* in its socialized materiality rather than in its independent material existence, "bringing nature back in" recasts the social actors directly associated with it. Instead of restricting these agents to vanishing feudal lords or declining landowners (the emphasis in *Capital*), they may be expanded to encompass the social agents that since colonial times have been involved in the commodification of what I have called "rent-capturing" or "nature-intensive" commodities, to distinguish them from commodities whose exchange value predominantly reflects labor power rather than ground-rent. In (post)colonial nations, these agents include the states and social classes that directly own natural resources or regulate their production and commercialization (Coronil 1997). Deciphering the mystery of the "trinity form" involves seeing the dialectical play among capital, labor, and land in specific historical situations.

A perspective that recognizes the triadic dialectic among labor, capital, and land leads to a fuller understanding of the economic, cultural, and political processes entailed in the mutual constitution of Europe and its colonies, processes that continue to define the relation between postcolonial and imperial states.[5] It helps to specify the operations through which Europe's colonies, first in America and then in Africa and Asia, provided it with cultural and material resources with which it fashioned itself as the standard of humanity—the bearer of a superior religion, reason, and civilization embodied in European selves. As the Spanish notion of "purity of blood" gave way in the Americas to distinctions between superior and inferior races, this superiority became variously incarnated in biological distinctions that have been essential in the self-fashioning of European colonizers and continue to inform contemporary racisms.[6] Just as the colonial plantations in the Americas, worked by African slave labor, functioned as protoindustrial factories that preceded those established in Manchester or Liverpool with "free" European labor (Mintz 1985), the American colonies prefigured those established in Africa and Asia during the age of high imperialism. Colonial "primitive accumulation," far from being a precondition of capitalist development, has been an indispensable element of its ongoing dynamic. "Free wage labor" in Europe constitutes not the exclusive condition of capitalism but its dominant productive modality, one historically conditioned by "unfree labor" elsewhere, much as the "productive" labor of wageworkers depends on the ongoing "unproductive" domestic labor of women at home. Instead of viewing nature and women's labor as "gifts" to capital (for a critique of this view, see Salleh 1994: 113), they should be seen as confiscations by capital, as part of its colonized others, as its dark side. If colonialism is the dark side of European capitalism, what is the dark side of globalization?

There has been much discussion about globalization, its origins, its various phases, and its current characteristics. There seems to be agreement that what distinguishes the present phase of globalization is not the volume of transnational trade and capital flows, for these have occurred in similar proportions in other periods, particularly during the three decades preceding World War I (Hoogvelt 1997; Weiss 1998). What seems significantly new since the 1970s is that a transformation in the volume, character, and concentration of financial flows (enabled by new technologies of production and communication) has led to a contradictory combination of new patterns of global integration and a heightened social polarization within and among nations.

I will use two remarkable accounts of globalization to discuss these changes. I have chosen them because they are public statements, grounded in scholarly research, that address globalization in terms of its political effects from opposite political positions. Perhaps inspired by millennial numerological spiritualism, each one of these documents uses seven subheadings to present its image of globalization.

The first is a (1997) report of the United Nations Conference on Trade and Development (UNCTAD) that documents rising worldwide inequalities. The report analyzes in detail seven "troublesome features" of the contemporary global economy and argues that they pose a serious threat of a political backlash against globalization. I will identify these features briefly, without summarizing the evidence that supports them:

1. Global economic growth rates have slowed.
2. The gap between the developed and developing countries, as well as within countries, is widening steadily [As supporting evidence, the report offers a revealing statistic: in 1965 the average GNP per capita for the top 20 percent of the world's population was thirty times that of the poorest 20 percent; by 1990, it had doubled to sixty times].
3. The rich have gained everywhere, and not just in relation to the poorest sections of society, but also in relation to a hallowed middle class.
4. Finance has gained an upper hand over industry, and rentiers over investors.
5. Capital's share of income has increased over that assigned to labor.

6. Employment and income insecurity are spreading worldwide.
7. The growing gap between skilled and unskilled labor is becoming a global problem.

The second document, titled "The Fourth World War Has Begun," is an article written from the mountains of Chiapas, Mexico, by Subcomandante Marcos, the leader of the indigenous Zapatista movement EZLN (Ejército Zapatista de Liberación Nacional), and published in *Le Monde Diplomatique* (1997). Since Marcos's argument is both more complex and less familiar than the one presented in the UNCTAD report, I will summarize it more extensively.

According to Marcos, neoliberal globalization must be understood "for what it is," that is, as "a new war of conquest of territories." He thus creates a new typology of twentieth-century world wars that decenters metropolitan conceptions of contemporary history. Marcos renames the Cold War "the Third World War," both in the sense that it was a third global war and because it was fought in the Third World. For the Third World, the so-called Cold War was really a hot war, made up of 149 localized wars that claimed 23 million deaths.[7] The Fourth World War is the current neoliberal globalization that, according to Marcos, is claiming the lives of vast numbers of people subjected to increasing poverty and marginalization. While World War III was waged between capitalism and socialism with varying degrees of intensity in dispersed localized territories in the Third World, World War IV involves a conflict between metropolitan financial centers and the world's majorities, taking place with constant intensity on a global scale.

According to Marcos, World War IV has fractured the world into multiple pieces. He selects seven of these broken pieces in order to put together what he calls the *rompecabezas* (puzzle) of neoliberal globalization. I will briefly list them — some of the titles are self-explanatory — omitting most of the data he offers to support his claims.

1. "Concentration of wealth and distribution of poverty," which synthesizes well-known information concerning the extent to which global wealth is being polarized among and within nations.
2. "The globalization of exploitation," which discusses how this polarization goes hand in hand with the increasing power of capital over labor worldwide.
3. "Migration as an errant nightmare," which reveals not only the ex-

pansion of migratory flows forced by unemployment in the Third World, but also by local wars that have multiplied the number of refugees (from 2 million in 1975 to over 27 million in 1995, according to United Nations figures).

4. "Globalization of finances and generalization of crime," which shows the growing complicity between megabanks, financial corruption, and hot money coming from the illegal traffic in drugs and arms.

5. "The legitimate violence of an illegitimate power?" which answers this question by arguing that the "striptease" of the state and the elimination of its welfare functions have reduced the state in many countries to an agent of social repression, transforming it into an illegitimate protection agency at the service of megaenterprises.

6. "Megapolitics and Dwarfs," which argues that strategies directed at eliminating trade frontiers and at uniting nations lead to the multiplication of social frontiers and the fragmentation of nations, turning politics into a conflict between "giants" and "dwarfs," that is, between the megapolitics of financial empires and the national policies of weak states.

7. "Pockets of resistance," which claims that in response to the pockets of concentrated wealth and political power, multiple and multiplying pockets of resistance are emerging—ones whose richness and power reside, in contrast, in their diversity and dispersion.

Despite their contrasting perspectives, both accounts view neoliberal globalization as a process driven by increasingly unregulated and mobile market forces that polarize social differences among and within nations. While the gap between rich and poor nations—as well as between the rich and the poor—is widening everywhere, global wealth is concentrating in fewer hands, and these few include those of subaltern elites. In this reconfigured global landscape, the "rich" cannot be identified exclusively with metropolitan nations; nor can the "poor" be identified exclusively with the Third and Second Worlds. The closer worldwide interconnection of ruling sectors and the marginalization of subordinate majorities has undermined the cohesiveness of these geopolitical units. Although it also has had an impact on metropolitan nations, this weakening of collective bonds more severely undermines Third World countries as well as the ex-socialist countries of the mori-

bund Second World (China requires separate attention).[8] Particularly in
the less populated or less resourceful countries, the polarizing effects of
neoliberalism are heightened by a steady process of capital expatriation,
denationalization of industries and services, brain drain, and the intensification of migratory flows. The privatization of the economy and of
public services, or what Marcos calls the "striptease" of the state, has led
not only to the reduction of bureaucratic inefficiency and in some cases
to increased competitiveness and productivity, but also to the demise of
projects of national integration and the erosion or at least the redefinition of collective attachments to the nation. The social tensions resulting from these processes often lead to a racialization of social conflict
and the rise of ethnicities (Amin 1997).

For example, in Venezuela the repression of the 1989 riots against
the imposition of an IMF (International Monetary Fund) program was
justified in terms of a discourse of civilization that revealed the submerged presence of racist prejudices in a country that defines itself as
a racial democracy (Coronil and Skurski 1991). Since then the ideal of
racial equality has been eroded by intensified practices of segregation
and discrimination, including apparently trivial ones that show how
racial boundaries are being redrawn (such as the exclusion of darker-
skinned Venezuelans from upper-middle-class discotheques). The same
polarizing process, with similar racialized expressions, is taking place
in other Latin American countries, such as Peru, where the Supreme
Court recently judged in favor of the right of a club that had excluded
dark-skinned Peruvians.

As has occurred in many Third World countries, neoliberal globalization may promote economic "growth" and yet erode a sense of
national belonging. In Argentina, the privatization of the national
petroleum company led to massive layoffs (from 5,000 workers down
to 500) as well as to a significant increase in profitability (from losses
of $6 billion between 1982 and 1990 to profits of $9 million in 1996).
This typical combination of economic growth that benefits a few private
(often foreign) pockets and economic dread that covers large domestic sectors has transformed the way many Argentinians relate to their
country. In January 1998, the *New York Times* reported that one of the
workers who was fired from the oil company now feels alienated from a
nation that offers him few opportunities: "I used to go and camp or fish,

but now I hear that Ted Turner is here, Rambo there, the Terminator somewhere else. And I say, no, this is not my Argentina."

Subordinate sectors commonly respond to their marginalization from the globalized market with a deepening involvement in an "informal" local economy, which in its speculative aspects recalls the unproductive dynamics of what Susan Strange calls "casino capitalism" (1986). The proliferation of schemes and scams intended to make money with money as well as the commodification of anything that can be sold have become not just regular economic practices but agonistic survival strategies. For many who find themselves at the mercy of market forces and yet have little to sell, the "market" takes the form of drug trade, black markets, sex work, and the trade in stolen goods or even in body parts. This anomic capitalism is often accompanied by discourses of "crisis," the spread of moral panics, and the deployment of magical means to make money in "occult" economies (Comaroff and Comaroff 1999; Verdery 1996). Although the increasingly unruly commodification of social life offers possibilities for some people, it turns the world into a risky and threatening environment for vast majorities.

In contrast, for the corporate sectors whose business is to make money out of risks, the unregulated expansion of the market turns the world into a "landscape of opportunity." Corporate control of highly sophisticated technologies permits companies to intensify the commodification of nature and to capture for the market such elements as genetic materials or medicinal plants. From a global corporate perspective, some countries of the world are seen as sources of cheap labor and natural resources.

A striking example illustrates how new technologies make it possible to deepen the appropriation of nature in tropical areas for an ever more exclusive market. In Gabon, through a blimp-and-raft device used to scour the treetops of rain forests, Givaudan and Roure, one of the leading corporations in the "big business" of fragrances and tastes, appropriates natural aromas and sells their components to companies such as Balmain, Christian Dior, and Armani. "As nature in cooler climates has been fully explored, the search for new molecules has moved to the tropics" (Simons 1999: 59).[9] Advanced technologies can also be used not just to discover natural products, but to create new ones, changing nature into what Arturo Escobar calls "technonature" (1997). While these humanmade natural products blur the distinction between the natural and the cultural, they also extend the significance of nature as a market resource.

For many nations, the integration of their economies to the free global market has led to a heightened reliance on nature-dependent activities and to the erosion of projects of state-promoted national development. Nature, in the form of traditional or new natural resources and of ecotourism as nature-dependent tourism, has become their most secure comparative advantage. The growth of sex tourism as a source of foreign exchange and of prostitution as a strategy of individual survival reveals a link between the naturalization of market rationality and the perverse commodification of human beings through the transformation of what are generally considered "natural" functions or private activities into a marketed form of labor power. As Chile's "success" story demonstrates, even when natural resources become the foundation of a neoliberal model of development based on the expansion of related industries and services, the price — despite relatively high rates of economic growth — is social polarization and denationalization (Moulian 1997).

In some respects we could view this process of reprimarization (as a return to a reliance on primary export products) as a regression to older forms of colonial control. Yet this process is unfolding within a technological and geopolitical framework that transforms the mode of exploiting nature. If under "colonial globalization" (by which I mean the mode of integration of colonies to the global economy), direct political control was needed to organize primary commodity production and trade within restricted markets, then under neoliberal globalization, the unregulated production and free circulation of primary commodities in the open market requires a significant dismantling of state controls previously oriented toward the protection of national industries. Before, the exploitation of primary commodities took place through the visible hand of politics; now it is organized by the ostensibly invisible hand of the market in combination with the less prominent, but no less necessary, helping hand of the state (for an argument concerning the ongoing centrality of the state, see Weiss 1998).

Prior to this period of neoliberal globalization, postcolonial states sought to regulate the production of primary commodities. During the post–World War II period of state-promoted economic growth (roughly the 1940s to 1970s), many Third World nations used the foreign exchange obtained from the sale of their primary products to diversify their productive structures. Primary production, often defined as a "basic" national activity, was carefully regulated and brought under domestic control. As the market has become the dominant organizing principle of economic life, however, it has imposed its rationality on society, naturalizing economic activity and turning commodities into narrowly "economic" things, stripped of their symbolic and political significance. In countries such as Argentina or Venezuela, there is increasing pressure to turn resources like oil, previously defined as a national patrimony, into mere commodities subject to the free play of market forces.

WEALTH AND NEOLIBERAL GLOBALIZATION

A telling symptom of the growing dominance of market rationality is the tendency not just to treat all forms of wealth as capital in practice, but to conceptualize them as such in theory. For example, while the World Bank has in the past followed conventional practice in defining "produced assets" as the "traditional measure of wealth," it now suggests that we also include "natural capital" and "human resources" as the constituent elements of wealth. In two recent books, *Monitoring Environmental Progress* (1995) and *Expanding the Measure of Wealth: Indicators of Environmentally Sustainable Development* (1997), the World Bank proposes that this reconceptualization be seen as a paradigm shift in the measurement of the wealth of nations and the definition of development objectives. According to the World Bank, expanding the measure of wealth entails a new "paradigm of economic development." Now development objectives are to be met by the management of portfolios whose constituents are natural resources, produced assets, and human resources (1997: v, 1–3). Ironically, as nature is being privatized and held in fewer hands, it is being redefined as the "natural capital" of denationalized nations ruled by the rationality of the global market.

It could be argued that this new "paradigm" only rephrases an older conception according to which land, labor, and capital are the factors of production. In my view, what seems significantly new is the attempt by leading financial institutions to homogenize these factors, to treat natural resources, produced assets, and human resources directly as capital. By disregarding their differences and subsuming them under the abstract category of "capital," these resources are treated as equivalent constituents of a "portfolio." The treatment of people as capital leads to their valorization strictly as a source of wealth. In effect, the second report's opening line emphasizes this: "Natural resources count, but people count even more. This is the main lesson from the new estimates of the wealth of nations contained in this report" (1997: 1). Yet people may "count more" or "less" than natural resources only in terms of a perspective that equates them; the value of people can be compared to the value of things only because both are reduced to capital. The definition of people as capital means that they are to be treated as capital — taken into account insofar as they contribute to the expansion of wealth, and marginalized if they do not. The same criteria apply to the treatment of "natural resources" as capital. They are valued as sources of profit. As human beings and nature are defined as capital, the logic of capital comes to define their identity as "assets."

The notion of *portfolio* already entails the requirement to maximize profits: development objectives are to be met by the management of portfolios by experts, rather than through an inherently political process involving social contests over the definition of collective values. Market technique replaces politics. The World Bank's current development "paradigm" posits development agents as investment brokers and development as a kind of gamble in risky markets rather than as a predominantly political concern and moral imperative.[10]

This redefinition of wealth as a portfolio of various forms of "capital" acquires new significance in the context of the neoliberal global market. In an insightful book that examines the joint evolution of the market and the theater in England from the sixteenth to the eighteenth centuries, Jean C. Agnew (1986) argues that the "market" evolved during this period from a place to a process — from fixed locations in the interstices of feudal society to fluid transactions dispersed throughout the world. In this shift from place to process, the market remained placed, as it were, within the limits of really existing geographic space.

Analysts of globalization have noted how its contemporary forms result not in the extension of the market in geographic space, but instead in its concentration in social space. As international capital becomes more mobile and grows detached from its previous institutional locations, Ankie Hoogvelt argues, "core-periphery is becoming a social relationship, and no longer a geographic one" (1997: 145). This shift from a geographically expanding capitalism to an economically imploding one is propelled by "financial deepening," that is, the growth but also the concentration of financial transactions and their dominance over trade in material goods (1997: 122).

Confirming this analysis, the February 1999 *New York Times* set of articles on globalization also highlights the significance of the growing detachment of financial transactions from the trade of real goods. As one of these articles pointed out, "In a typical day the total amount of money changing hands in the world's foreign exchange markets alone is $1.5 trillion — an eightfold increase since 1986, an almost incomprehensible sum, equivalent to total world trade for four months." The article quotes a Hong Kong banker: "It is no longer the real economy driving the financial markets, but the financial markets driving the real economy." According to the article, the amount of investment capital has "exploded": in 1995 institutional investors controlled $20 trillion, ten times more than in 1980. As a result, "the global economy is no longer dominated by trade in cars and steel and wheat, but by trade in stocks, bonds, and currencies." This wealth is increasingly stateless, as national capital markets are merging into a global capital market. It is significant that these investments are channeled through derivatives that have grown exponentially: In 1997 they were traded at a value of $360 trillion, a figure equivalent to a dozen times the size of the entire global economy (Kristof 1999: A10).

In my view, financial deepening implies a significant transformation of the market: not just its concentration in social space and its ever larger control over material space both at the geographical and subatomic levels, but its extension in time. Now capital travels beyond the constraints of existing geographical boundaries into cyberspace — that is, in time. This temporal expansion of the market, or if you prefer, its extension into cyberspace — perhaps a further development of what David Harvey and others describe as the transformation of time into space — gives new significance to the redefinition of nature as capital. Thus, it is not just that fewer private hands, largely unconstrained by public controls, hold more wealth, but that in these hands wealth is being transformed through a process of growing homogenization and abstraction.

I have come to think of this process as the transmaterialization of wealth. By this I do not mean the "dematerialization of production," that is, a purported decline in the intensity of raw material use (Kouznetsov 1988: 70; for an alternative view, see Bunker 1989), but the transfiguration of wealth through the ever more abstract commodification of its elements across time and space. An article from *Time* magazine on the future of money highlights the significance of both new forms of wealth and new ways of thinking about them (Ramo 1998). Wealth, according to this article, is increasingly treated by investors and bankers not as tangible commodities but as risks assumed on them, such as derivatives. The Magna Carta of this new form of conceptualizing wealth, the author suggests, is a speech delivered in 1993 by Charles Sanford, then CEO of Bankers Trust.

In this impressive document, titled "Financial Markets in 2020," Sanford recognizes the novel complexity of the present situation. Although acknowledging that reality is moving faster than our categories, he self-confidently proclaims that through a combination of art and science the corporate world, including its own universities, will produce theories capable of accounting for the changes that are now taking place in the world. He uses the number 2020 to express his expectation of perfect vision and the estimated date when it will be achieved. Despite the blurred vision of the present, Sanford anticipates that this perfect vision will entail a radical shift in perspective: "We are beginning from a Newtonian view, which operates at the level of tangible objects (summarized by dimension and mass) to a perspective more in line with the nonlinear and chaotic world of quantum physics and molecular biology." Building on this analogy with quantum physics and modern biology, he calls this theoretical reconceptualization "particle finance" (Sanford 1994: 6).

Particle finance will allow financial institutions to consolidate all wealth and investments into "wealth accounts," and to break down these accounts into particles of risk derived from the original investment, which can be sold as bundles in a global, computerized network. To help us visualize the nature of the change, Sanford says: "We have always had transportation—people walked, eventually they rode donkeys—but the automobile was a break from everything that came before it. Risk management will do that to finance. It's a total break" (cited in Ramo 1998: 55). Echoing Sanford, the author of the *Time* article observes that derivatives, one of the main modes of managing risk, "have changed the rules of the game forever" (Ramo 1998: 55).

In order to imagine the new game, he asks us "to think of the world as a landscape of opportunity—everything from distressed Japanese real estate to Russian oil futures—marketed and packed by giant banks like Bankamerica or by fund companies like Fidelity Investments and the Vanguard Group" (Ramo 1998: 55). The examples of "distressed Japanese real estate" and "Russian oil futures" are general tropes—they could represent as well Gabon aroma futures, Cuban tourism, Nigerian foreign debt, or any thing, fragment, or aroma of a thing that can be turned into a commodity. Echoing Sanford, *Time*'s Joshua Cooper Ramo states that "E-(lectronic) cash, wealth accounts, and consumer derivatives will have made these firms as essential as cash itself once was." These changes will make these capitalist firms so indispensable as to render them eternal: "If business immortality can be purchased," the article concludes, "these are the people who will figure out how to finance it. And they will be doing so with your money" (Ramo 1998: 58).

A UTOPIAN CRITIQUE OF GLOBALCENTRISM
FOR THE COMING MILLENNIUM

While this corporate vision may be hyperbolic and reflect the changes it wishes to bring about from a partisan perspective, it helps visualize the transformations in global power I have discussed so far. In my view, two related processes are shifting the commanding heights of imperial power from a location in "Europe" or "the West" to a less identifiable position on the "globe." On the one hand, neoliberal globalization has homogenized and abstracted diverse forms of "wealth," including nature, which has become for many nations their most secure comparative advantage and source of foreign exchange. On the other hand, the deterritorialization of Europe or the West has entailed its invisible reterritorialization in the elusive figure of the globe, which conceals the socially concentrated but more geographically diffuse transnational financial and political networks that integrate metropolitan and peripheral dominant social sectors. As the West disappears into the market, it melts and solidifies at once. The ascent of Euroland should not obscure its close articulation with Dollarland through financial circuits that link dominant sectors from both "lands." As many critics have noted, the "transparency" demanded by proponents of the free market does not include making visible and accountable the new commanding heights of global economic and political power.

These two interrelated processes are linked to a host of cultural and political transformations that redefine the relations between the West and its others. The image of a unified globe dispenses with the notion of an outside. It displaces the locus of cultural difference from highly Orientalized others located outside metropolitan centers to diffuse populations dispersed across the globe. Nations have become increasingly open to the flow of capital, even as they remain closed to the movement of the poor. Although the elites of these nations are increasingly integrated in transnational circuits of work, study, leisure, and even residence, their impoverished majorities are increasingly excluded from the domestic economy and abandoned by their states.

It is likely that, even under these conditions, nations will remain fundamental political units and sources of communal imaginings in the years to come (particularly metropolitan nations), but supranational and nonnational "cultural" criteria are already playing an increasingly large role as markers and makers of collective identities. In poorer nations, the emergence of ethnic movements is the expression not only of their growing strength, but also of the weakness of integrationist nationalist projects. At stake is the redefinition of the nation-state, rather than its decline. Central American nations are being reconceptualized as multiethnic communities both by their states and by international financial institutions. In some cases, states that have engaged in a "striptease" are being forced to put on new clothes by the pressure of discontented subjects or the threat of political upheaval. Growing concern with the political effects of global poverty at the highest level of the international system, as expressed in the UNCTAD report and in the recent meetings of the World Bank, IMF, and G7, may yet give states a renewed role as central agents in the construction of national imaginaries.

Since the conquest of the Americas, projects of Christianization, colonization, civilization, modernization, and development have shaped the relationship between Europe and its colonies in terms of a sharp opposition between a superior West and its inferior others. In contrast, neoliberal globalization conjures up the image of an undifferentiated process without clearly demarcated geopolitical agents or target populations; it conceals the highly concentrated sources of power from which it emanates and fragments the majorities on which it impacts. Although neoliberal globalization entails the subjection of non-Western peoples, their subjection, like the subjection of subordinate populations within the West, appears as a market effect, rather than as the consequence of a Western political project.

Unlike other Occidentalist strategies of representation that highlight the difference between the West and its others, discourses of neoliberal globalization evoke the potential equality and uniformity of all peoples and cultures. Insofar as globalization works by reinscribing social hierarchies and standardizing cultures and habits, it is a particularly pernicious imperialist modality of domination. But insofar as it decenters the West, effaces differences between centers and margins, and postulates, at least in principle, the fundamental equality of all cultures, globalization promotes diversity and represents a form of universality that may prefigure its fuller realization. Just as the formal proclamation of human equality during the French Revolution was taken at its word by Haitian slaves and given fuller content by their actions, forcing the abolition of slavery and expanding the meaning of freedom (Dubois 1998), globalization's professed ideals of equality and diversity may open spaces for liberatory struggles (just as they may give rise to conservative reactions). In social spaces organized under neoliberal global conditions, collective identities are being constructed in unprecedented ways through a complex articulation of such sources of identification as religion, territoriality, race, class, ethnicity, gender, and nationality, but now informed by universal discourses of human rights, international law, ecology, feminism, cultural rights, and other means of respecting difference within equality (Sassen 1998; Alvarez, Dagnino, and Escobar 1998).

The current modality of globalization is unsettling not just geographical and political boundaries, but also disciplinary protocols and theoretical categories, rendering obsolete approaches polarized in terms of oppositions between the material and the discursive, political economy and culture, wholes and fragments. More than ever, just as so-called local phenomena cannot be understood outside the global conditions under which they unfold, global phenomena are unintelligible when the local forces that sustain them are not accounted for.

We can hope that the effort to make sense of the relationship between localization and globalization in the context of globalized conditions of knowledge production will decenter Western epistemologies and lead to more enabling visions of humanity.[11]

If the critique of globalcentrism is to be a response to the connection between colonial and postcolonial violence, it must address the new forms of subjection of postcolonial empires. While the critique of Eurocentrism has sought to provincialize Europe and to question its professed universality, the critique of globalcentrism should seek to differentiate the globe and show its highly uneven distribution of power and immense cultural complexity. A critique that demystifies globalization's universalistic claims but recognizes its liberatory potential may make less tolerable capitalism's destruction of nature and degradation of human lives and, in the same breath, expand the spaces where alternative visions of humanity are imagined, whether in "pockets of resistance" to capital, in places still free from its hegemony, or within its own contradictory locations.

NOTES

I would like to express my deep gratitude to the members of my graduate seminar, Globalization and Occidentalism, winter 1999, for their helpful comments on this essay and stimulating discussions throughout the semester. I greatly appreciate the detailed comments by Genese Sodikoff, Elizabeth Ferry, and María González. My thanks also to Julie Skurski and David Pederson for their keen observations, and to the editorial committee of *Public Culture* that, through Jean and John Comaroff, offered me valuable suggestions. An earlier draft of this essay benefited from discussions at the Coloniality Working Group at SUNY Binghamton.

1 The mass media have been a major avenue for celebratory discourses of globalization, from corporate advertisements to songs. This trend gained currency with the expansion of multinational corporations in the 1960s and was intensified by the breakdown of the socialist world and the ensuing hegemony of neoliberalism.

2 It is impossible to do justice to the vast scholarly literature on globalization. Although not all authors agree on what characterizes it or on its newness, most are critical of the celebratory discourses on globalization and suggest different ways in which the processes commonly identified by this term are conflictive or exclusionary. For examples, see Amin 1997 and 1998; Appadurai 1996; Arrighi 1994; Corbridge, Martin, and Thrift 1994; Dussel 1995; Greider 1997; Harvey 1989; Henwood 1997; Hirst and Thompson 1996; Hoogvelt 1997; López Segrera 1998; Massey 1999; Quijano and Wallerstein 1992; Robertson 1992; Sassen 1998; and Weiss 1998.

3 Some Marxists, however, have noted the significance of ground rent with respect to certain aspects of capitalism, such as urban real estate, but few have used it to recon-

ceptualize the development of capitalism. Reflecting on Marxist theorizing on ground rent, Jean-Claude Debeir, Jean-Paul Deléage, and Daniel Hémery have noted that the relationship "society/nature was considered only in the framework of purely economic theory, that of ground rent" (1991: xiii). Their own effort is directed at seeing this relationship in terms of a more general conceptualization of energy use. In my view, "land-ground rent" (just as labor-wages and capital-profit) should not be reduced to "purely economic theory." A holistic analysis of ground rent would reveal its many dimensions, which include, as they have shown in their work, historical transformations in energy use but also the formation of the historical agents involved in the production of "land" as an economic category.

4 For example, Ortiz 1995, Dussel 1995, Mignolo 1995, and Quijano 1993. My use of the word *grounded* is influenced by the conference Touching Ground: Descent into the Material/Cultural Divide, organized by the students in the doctoral program in anthropology and history, University of Michigan, 2 April 1999. The conference sought to overcome, as its statement of purpose indicates, a "pre-existing habit of dividing the analysis of the cultural from the economic and the symbolic from the material. Textual and discursive analyses, even when invoking a material context for readings of cultural content, still tend to avoid engaging directly with the study and theorization of such phenomena as work, the structure and practice of political domination and economic exploitation, and the material organization of patriarchy."

5 Within anthropology, the works of Sidney Mintz (1985) and Eric Wolf (1982) have significantly contributed to illuminating the role of colonial primary commodities in the making of the modern world. I have sought to develop this perspective by building upon the work of Fernando Ortiz (Coronil 1995, 1997).

6 Numerous theorists have examined the relationship between colonialism and racialization. These comments draw in particular on the work of Anibal Quijano (1993), Walter Mignolo (1999), and Ann Stoler (1995).

7 The category *Third World* emerged out of the process of decolonization connected with World War II, as a result of which the Third World became the military and ideological battleground between the capitalist First World and the socialist Second World. Now that this contest is over for all practical purposes, the countries of what used to be called the Third World are no longer the prized objects of competing political powers, but struggling actors in a competitive world market. For an illuminating discussion of the three-world schema, see Pletsch 1981.

8 The two reports on globalization I examine here present evidence that shows the existence of a growing gap between the rich and the poor in metropolitan nations. A revealing response to this polarization is Reich 1991, which argues for the need to integrate the internationalized and the domestic sectors of the U.S. population.

9 My thanks to Genese Sodikoff for sharing this article.

10 I am grateful to Genese Sodikoff for these formulations.

11 There is always the risk that "localization" and "globalization" will be seen as a reified binary rather than as a dialectical relationship. For a critique of the local/global binary, see Briggs 1999, Eiss 1999, and Pederson 1999.

REFERENCES

Agnew, Jean Christophe. 1986. *Worlds apart: The market and the theater in Anglo-American thought, 1550–1750.* Cambridge: Cambridge University Press.

Alvarez, Sonia E., Evelina Dagnino, and Arturo Escobar. 1998. *Culture of politics, politics of cultures.* Boulder, Colo.: Westview Press.

Amin, Samir. 1997. *Capitalism in the age of globalization: The management of contemporary society.* London: Zed Books.

———. 1998. *Spectres of capitalism: A critique of current intellectual fashions.* New York: Monthly Review Press.

Appadurai, Arjun. 1996. *Modernity at large: Cultural dimensions of globalization.* Minneapolis: University of Minnesota Press.

Arrighi, Giovanni. 1994. *The long twentieth century.* London: Verso.

Briggs, Charles. 1999. Globalization, petroleum, and the shifting politics of race, nation, and citizenship on the margins of Venezuela. Paper presented at the 99th annual meeting of the American Anthropological Association, Chicago, 17–21 November.

Bunker, Stephen G. 1989. Staples, links, and poles in the construction of regional development theories. *Sociological Forum* 4: 589–610.

Comaroff, Jean, and John L. Comaroff. 1999. Occult economies and the violence of abstraction: Notes from the South African postcolony. *American Ethnologist* 26: 279–301.

Corbridge, Stuart, Ron Martin, and Nigel Thrift, eds. 1994. *Money, power, and space.* Oxford: Blackwell.

Coronil, Fernando. 1995. Transculturation and the politics of theory: Countering the center, Cuban counterpoint. Introduction to Ortiz 1995.

———. 1996. Beyond Occidentalism: Towards non-imperial geohistorical categories. *Cultural Anthropology* 1, no. 1: 51—87.

———. 1997. *The magical state: Nature, money, and modernity in Venezuela.* Chicago: University of Chicago Press.

Coronil, Fernando, and Julie Skurski. 1991. Dismembering and remembering the nation: The semantics of political violence in Venezuela. *Comparative Studies in Society and History* 33: 288–337.

Debeir, Jean-Claude, Jean-Paul Deléage, and Daniel Hémery, eds. 1991. *In the servitude of power: Energy and civilization through the ages.* London: Zed Books.

Dubois, Laurent. 1998. *Les Esclaves de la République: L' Histoire oubliée de la première émancipation, 1789–1794.* Paris: Calman-Lévy.

Dussel, Enrique. 1995. *El encubrimiento del otro: Hacia el orígen del mito de la modernidad.* Madrid: Nueva Utopía.

Eiss, Paul. 1999. The world is not no-place: Some reflections on the globe as utopia. Paper presented at the 99th annual meeting of the American Anthropological Association, Chicago, 17–21 November.

Escobar, Arturo. 1997. Cultural politics and biological diversity: State, capital, and social movements on the Pacific coast of Colombia. In *The politics of culture in the shadow of capital,* edited by Lisa Lowe and David Lloyd. Durham, N.C.: Duke University Press.

Greider, William. 1997. *One world, ready or not: The manic logic of global capitalism*. New York: Simon & Schuster.

Harvey, David. 1989. *The condition of postmodernity*. Oxford: Blackwell.

Henwood, Doug. 1997. *Wall Street: How it works and for whom*. London: Verso.

Hirst, Paul, and Grahame Thompson. 1996. *The globalization in question: The international economy and the possibilities of governance*. Cambridge, U.K.: Polity Press.

Hoogvelt, Ankie. 1997. *Globalization and the postcolonial world: The new political economy of development*. Baltimore, Md.: Johns Hopkins University Press.

Jameson, Fredric. 1991. *Postmodernism, or the cultural logic of late capitalism*. Durham, N.C.: Duke University Press.

Kouznetsov, Alexander. 1988. Materials technology and trade implications. In *Advance technology alert system*, issue 5, *Material technology and development*. New York: United Nations, 67–71.

Kristof, Nicholas D. 1999. Who went under in the world's sea of cash: Global contagion, a narrative (first of four articles). *New York Times*, 15 February, A1, A10–11.

Lefebvre, Henry. 1974. *La Production de l'espace*. Paris: Anthropos.

López Segrera, Francisco, ed. 1998. *Los retos de la globalización*. Caracas: UNESCO.

Marcos, Subcomandante. 1997. La 4e Guerre Mondiale a commencé. *Le Monde diplomatique*, August 1, 4–5.

Marx, Karl. 1967 [1867]. *Capital*, vol. 1. New York: International Publishers.

———. 1981 [1894]. *Capital*, vol. 3. New York: Vintage Books.

Massey, Doreen. 1999. Imagining globalization: Power-geometries of time-space. In *Global futures: Migration, environment, and globalization*, edited by Avtar Brah, Mary J. Hickman, and Maírtín Mac an Ghaille. New York: St. Martin's Press.

Mignolo, Walter. 1995. *The darker side of the Renaissance: Literacy, territoriality, and colonization*. Ann Arbor: University of Michigan Press.

———. 1999. Coloniality of power and the colonial difference. Paper presented at the Second Annual Conference of the Coloniality Working Group at SUNY Binghamton, 23 April.

Mintz, Sidney. 1985. *Sweetness and power: The place of sugar in modern history*. New York: Penguin Books.

Moulian, Tomás. 1997. *Chile actual: Anatomía de un mito*. Santiago: ARCIS.

O'Connor, Martin. 1994. *Is capitalism sustainable? Political economy and the politics of ecology*. New York: Guilford Press.

Ortiz, Fernando. 1995. *Cuban counterpoint: Tobacco and sugar*. Durham, N.C.: Duke University Press.

Pederson, David E. 1999. American value(s): Services and subsistence in El Salvador and the United States. Paper presented at the 99th annual meeting of the American Anthropological Association, Chicago, 17 – 21 November.

Pletsch, Carl. 1981. The three worlds, or the division of social scientific labor, circa 1950–1975. *Comparative Studies in Society and History* 23: 565–90.

Quijano, Anibal. 1993. *José Carlos Mariátegui and Europe: The other aspect of the discovery*. Lima: Editorial Amauta.

Quijano, Anibal, and Immanuel Wallerstein. 1992. Americanity as a concept, or the

Americas in the modern world-system. *International Social Sciences Journal* 44: 549–558.

Ramo, Joshua Cooper. 1998. The big bank theory: What it says about the future of money. *Time,* 27 April, 47—58.

Reich, Robert. 1991. *The work of nations: Preparing ourselves for twenty-first century capitalism.* New York: Knopf.

Robertson, Roland. 1992. *Globalization: Social theory and global culture.* London: Sage Publications.

Salleh, Ariel. 1994. Nature, woman, labor, capital: Living the deepest contradiction. In *Is capitalism sustainable? Political economy and the politics of ecology,* edited by Martin O'Connor. New York: Guilford Press.

Sanford, Charles. 1994. Financial markets in 2020. *Federal Reserve Bank of Kansas City, first quarter,* 1–10.

Sassen, Saskia. 1998. *Globalization and its discontents.* New York: New Press.

Simons, Marlene. 1999. Eau de rain forest. *New York Times Magazine,* 2 May, 57–62.

Stoler, Ann. 1995. *Race and the education of desire.* Durham, N.C.: Duke University Press.

Strange, Susan. 1986. *Casino capitalism.* Oxford: Blackwell.

Thrupp, Sylvia, ed. 1970. *Millennial dreams in action: Studies in revolutionary religious movements.* New York: Schocken Books.

United Nations. 1997. *Trade and development report, 1997.* New York: United Nations.

Verdery, Katherine. 1996. *What was socialism and what comes next?* Princeton, N.J.: Princeton University Press.

Weiss, Linda. 1998. *The myth of the powerless state.* Ithaca, N.Y.: Cornell University Press.

Wolf, Eric R. 1982. *Europe and the people without history.* Berkeley: University of California Press.

World Bank. 1995. *Monitoring environmental progress. A report on work in progress.* Washington: World Bank.

———. 1997. *Expanding the measure of wealth: Indicators of environmentally sustainable development.* Washington: World Bank.

Lived Effects of the Contemporary Economy: Globalization, Inequality, and Consumer Society

Michael Storper

It is now commonplace to refer to such diverse phenomena as globalization, increases in economic inequality, the decline of class-based societies, the intensification of consumerism, and global cultural homogenization as though they were all part of the same problematic. Indeed, all these elements seem in various ways to characterize our experience of the current era. Yet their connections remain obscure. There is little consensus about how significant the recent increases in income inequality are, and even less over their relationship to globalization. Beyond this, those who call attention to growing inequality have a difficult time explaining the absence of organized discontent in the political and cultural spheres. Those who associate globalization with a loss of diversity — a deepening massification of Western culture — are at a loss to account for the stunning new variety and rapid change in the outputs of knowledge-based capitalism.

It is difficult to confront these associations in any structured way because the phenomena they refer to remain the preserves of specialized academic fields. Each such field documents a piece of the bigger picture, and as a result we remain unable to account for seemingly contradictory aspects of the contemporary experience. If our standard for the analysis of growing income inequality is limited to the distribution of money income, for example, we will find it difficult to understand why, in the real world, people do not seem very upset about it.

One way to understand the connections between what economists say about the economy and how the rest of us feel and act in relation to it is provided by the concept of consumption and its corollary in the cultural sphere, consumerism. Many of the political effects of globalization — what is regretted, what is celebrated, what meets with passivity — that seem contradictory when viewed in either exclusively cultural or economic terms can be understood in terms of the relationship between globalization and the evolution of consumer societies. But beyond this, I will argue, the rise of consumerist identities helps explain the economic processes of globalization — most notably, the diffusion of labor-saving technologies — which in turn are responsible for much of the recent rise in inequality. These linkages do not appear in standard analyses.

This essay's reasoning is drawn primarily from economics, with elements from other disciplines brought in as needed. Although I have made every effort to keep technical language to a minimum, I have found it helpful in places to situate my analysis within this well-developed literature in order to identify the mechanisms that can link globalization and inequality.

INCOME INEQUALITY AND GLOBALIZATION

Increasing Inequality   Income inequality has increased in most of the major industrial countries of Western Europe and North America, as well as in most of the middle-income developing countries, over the last twenty years, a period that has also witnessed unprecedented growth in world trade. The degree of inequality increase has shown some variation: highest in the United States and Britain, lower in most of the economies of continental Europe, still lower in Scandinavia (Crafts 1998; Johnson and Webb 1993). Whether measured by the Gini coefficient or by the ratio of the income of the lowest 20 percent to that of the highest 20 percent, the trend is similar (Krugman 1992; Krugman and Lawrence 1993; Hanson and Harrison 1994; Katz, Loveman, and Blanchflower 1995).

In virtually all the major developed economies, moreover, a major component of growth in income inequality is the extraordinary growth of income at the top. We can summarize the facts roughly as follows: the top 20 percent or so of the population has seen very rapid growth in its real incomes and shares of total income. Within this group, the income share of the top 1 percent of U.S. earners has more than doubled since 1979 (Frank and Cook 1995). In 1979, the ninety-fifth percentile earner received ten times as much as the fifth, but in 1995, the corresponding ratio was more than twenty-five. As a result, the worth of the rich and superrich, both absolutely and proportionately, has grown considerably (Frank 1999). The middle 60 percent or so had also enjoyed growth in real household income from the late 1970s through the 1980s, though at a rate much lower than that of the top 20 percent.[1] In the 1990s, however, the results have been quite different; the median household actually lost 2 percent of its income in real terms (Frank 1999). There is considerable debate among economists about the character of middle-class incomes. Some claim that what appears to be relative stability is attributable to the increasing presence of two-earner households.[2] Others, however, maintain that average wages have continued to rise in most countries, albeit at a much slower rate than for most of the post–World War II period. But it is indisputable that the *share* of this group in total income has declined. In other words, a great deal of income — the proportion that would have been accrued had the group's rate of growth but remained constant — has in fact been foregone by its members.

The bottom 20 percent seems to offer a more complex story. In 1996, the percentage of the total population living in poverty (defined by the Organization for Economic Cooperation and Development [OECD] as subsistence on family or individual income amounting to less than 50 percent of the national median) was about 14 percent in France and the United States. The poverty rate is slightly lower in Germany and the Nordic countries, and higher in the United Kingdom (ca. 22 percent in 2000). Except in the case of Britain — where it exploded under Thatcher — the poverty rate in most countries has risen slightly, if at all, over the last twenty years and is still well below its postwar peak, which was attained in most countries in the 1950s and 1960s (Jencks 1992).

Given that overall absolute income has been rising, it follows that at least some of the people in the bottom 20 percent, including some officially defined as poor, might also have experienced real income increases over the past twenty years. Yet about a third of the poor became more poor in absolute terms (5 to 10 percent of the population) (Jencks 1992). This proportion is similar to that of the urban ghetto population in the United States. Thus, while most of the population is enjoying higher absolute real incomes, and some part of those living below the poverty line is also better off in absolute terms, there remains a group suffering ever harder and deeper poverty (Jencks 1992; Wilson 1987).

To sum up: The general picture in Western Europe, North America, and a number of middle-income developing countries is a combination of decline and stagnation at the bottom, moderate growth and relative loss in the middle, and big growth at the top.

Wages and Occupations: The Globalization Hypothesis in Economics
Explaining this increase in inequality, however, turns out to be difficult. Some of the standard explanations for the increase attribute it directly to globalization. In economics, the approach is to examine the impact of international trade in goods and services on the domestic labor market in terms of labor demand and wages. According to trade theory going back as far as David Ricardo — and adapted for modern use as the Heckscher-Ohlin model — international trade cannot affect domestic wages directly, but does so indirectly through the domestic prices of imported goods. If imports come from an area with lower wages, then under competitive conditions their price should decline. Either the domestic labor market meets the labor prices of the foreign country, or the domestic firms are pushed out of the market. In the latter, more likely case, the workers so released will have to find other things to do. In the short run, such fixed skills as they can offer are now in oversupply. In most of the literature, low-skilled, manual manufacturing workers are considered to belong to this category. Oversupply means that workers become unemployed and then often accept jobs at lower wages, because the above-mentioned price effects of trade create new and lower equilibrium prices for the products concerned. In other words, the effects of trade on relative domestic product prices are reflected in a new set of interindustry wage differentials.

This process, known as *factor price equalization,* is formalized in the Stolper-Samuelson extension of Heckscher-Ohlin trade theory: for a given factor, trade gradually brings about a convergence of the factor's prices to the world level. This model provides a compelling explanation for income loss among those low-skilled workers in industrialized countries whose outputs can be made in the developing world. But key to this line of analysis — as I will demonstrate later on — is the notion that technologies of production are fixed. In the Stolper-Samuelson model, there is a fixed relationship between the outputs of goods and the inputs of factors. This implies a similarly fixed relationship between the prices of goods and the wages of factors. The model does not take into account any difference in production functions in, say, the clothing industries of the United States and Mexico. What varies is where the factors are used and how the location of industries affects domestic factor demands and prices.

But this is only the starting point for economists analyzing the possible effects of globalization on wages and incomes. The next step is to proceed to investigations of the complex interactions between such sectoral labor market effects and the labor markets of other industries, their product prices, and their output levels. These are known as *partial* or *general equilibrium approaches.* They generally posit that a wealthy economy faced with import competition will move up the product chain into more sophisticated intermediate and final goods and services. According to equilibrium theories, clothing and shoe production may go offshore, for example, but in compensation, more high-tech and advanced goods and services will be developed and exported. In the highly developed economy, then, there is a shift to different goods and to more of them—a global "filtering" of activities into a new geographical pattern. Labor demand shifts with this change in specialization. Thus, the shock of trade liberalization could lead initially to declining wages in import-sensitive sectors and rising relative wages in export-oriented sectors.

> For example, if the United States imported 10 additional children's toys, which could be produced by American workers, the effective supply of unskilled workers would increase by five (or alternatively, domestic demand for such workers would fall by five) compared with the alternative in which those 10 toys were produced domestically. This five-worker shift in the supply-demand balance would put pressure on unskilled wages to fall, causing those wages to fall in accord with the relevant elasticity. Any trade-balancing flow of exports would, contrarily, reduce the effective endowment of skilled workers (raise their demand) and thus increase their pay. (Freeman 1995: 23)

Most general equilibrium theories predict a full absorption of labor initially displaced by imports. Once this is achieved, there is no further change—the ratio of prices between import and export sectors remains constant (Richardson 1995). Ongoing trade under conditions of openness will not affect relative factor prices because an economy in equilibrium moving from one endogenous state to another (along a given "production possibility frontier") has no mechanism to change relative factor rewards.

Empirical research on the topic is quite difficult in terms of methods and data and has turned up very mixed results (see Bound and Johnson 1992; Freeman 1995; Nickell and Bell 1995; Katz and Murphy 1992; Katz, Loveman, and Blanchflower 1995). In attempting to measure the factor content of imports to determine whether they are dominated by low-wage, low-skill labor, economists have found very modest contributions to American income inequality (Lawrence and Slaughter 1994; Borjas, Freeman, and Katz 1992). When the prices of imports are measured to see if they are falling relative to domestically produced goods, the conclusion is that there is an effect but that it is rather small (Sachs and Schatz 1994; Feenstra and Hanson 1996).[3] In contrast with these findings, Berman, Bound, and Griliches (1994) find that the negative effect on unskilled wages applies to all sectors, not just import-heavy ones. All in all, William Cline (1997), in an attempt to synthesize the evidence, suggests that somewhere between 5 and 15 percent of the observed increase in inequality has to do with import competition from low-wage countries. Most estimates are that at maximum, there has been a 5 percent reduction of unskilled labor demand in the United States attributable to low-wage import substitutes. Manufactured imports from low-wage countries accounted for only 3 percent of American GDP in 1990, and this is concentrated in certain highly visible consumer sectors such as clothing (Cline 1997). Studies such as these have led to the mainstream conclusion that it is impossible for the "tail" of low-wage imports to wag the "dog" of labor markets.

There are dissenters from this position, however. Adrian Wood (1994, 1995) claims that in most of the empirical research, the equality-inducing effects of North-South trade are underestimated by a factor of up to four. This discrepancy is rooted in different ways of calculating how much labor is displaced when production moves abroad. He goes on to argue that the static picture of technology as presented in standard theory is incorrect. A common reaction to low-wage competition on the part of firms in developed countries has been precisely to search for new methods of production that economize on unskilled labor. With this argument, Wood abandons a key element of standard general equilibrium models.

A few general equilibrium economists have come to the same conclusion via a different route. They hold that the sectors that expand as a result of trade should take in resources from the rest of the economy, but will nevertheless be unable to absorb workers likely to be released from other sectors by the initial opening to trade unless wages fall (Leamer 1994, 1995). Unlike in the Stolper-Samuelson model, these falling wages have effects on the production techniques of the remaining sectors. For example, the developed economy's expanding sectors might substitute more labor for capital because of the fresh availability of cheap labor, and though this would absorb some displaced labor, it would also widen intersectoral productivity gaps and hence maintain wage inequality in spite of a return to full employment.

Furthermore, none of the standard work takes into account what might be the most important impact of trade on wages. Production is increasingly "disintegrated" into geographically separated tasks and "shared" among countries. Robert Feenstra describes this global outsourcing through the example of the Barbie Doll:

> The raw materials for the doll are obtained from Taiwan and Japan. . . . the molds themselves come from the United States, as do additional paints used in decorating the dolls. Other than labor, China supplies only the cotton cloth used for dresses. Of the $2 export value for the dolls when they leave Hong Kong for the United States, about 35 cents covers Chinese labor, 65 cents the cost of materials, and the remainder covers transportation and overhead. . . . The majority of value-added is from US activity. (Feenstra 1998: 35)

In other words, in many U.S.-made goods there are large foreign components with potentially big effects on U.S. labor demand and wages. Measuring only final products from each country is likely to mask these effects, which are upstream in the value chain.

Finally, Wood calls attention to the large probable impact of traded services on the wages of unskilled workers, none of which are taken into account by the standard calculations that are based only on manufacturing. All in all, Wood claims that a 20 percent decline in the demand for skilled labor could be accounted for by North-South trade, not the 5 percent of the standard approaches.

The bigger picture of inequality presents other problems. Although the efforts discussed above help describe the drop in relative wages at the very bottom, they do not explain what has happened to everyone else. Three additional issues can be identified here.

First, absolute and relative incomes have grown rapidly at the top of the distribution—not just among the superrich, but among the college-educated classes in general (Mishel, Bernstein, and Schmitt 1998). Yet many of the "advanced product" sectors, in which developed countries are coming to specialize in the face of global trade and which employ the college educated, have occupational and wage compositions that are changing rapidly. There are indications that some jobs are being downskilled. More important, the supply of highly skilled, or college-educated, labor has expanded rapidly, and this increase should have pushed down relative wages in these jobs. For the moment, however, this does not appear to have occurred.

Second, between the unskilled who are affected by imports and these highly skilled college graduates there would seem to be a vast middle ground of semiskilled labor. There are many industries, or parts of industries, in which semiskilled labor is prominent, and these people seem to have lost out in the last couple of decades. But most of the standard approaches suggest that their wages should have risen with trade and relocation. This is because in the kinds of industries that traditionally employ semiskilled labor (for instance, capital-intensive manufacturing of consumer durables), the assembly processes, which employ unskilled labor, have been relocated to less developed areas, but the "intermediate goods" portions remain largely in the developed countries. These intermediate or upstream parts of the industries now export more than they did previously, and economists argue that this should be reflected in a rising relative demand for semiskilled labor in these sectors and correspondingly rising rewards. Empirical research does not bear this out.

Third, interoccupational wage differentials are not the only ones that have changed. Even more dramatic has been the shift of wages *within* occupational categories. In many occupations, the spread of wages has risen over the past decade, so that there has been an individualization of remunerations provided to people performing the same type of work, even within the same firms (Gottschalk and Moffitt 1994; Kramarz, Lolliver, and Pele 1994). It is unclear whether and how this could be related to globalization.

Technological Change as the Source of Increasing Inequality   Trade-based explanations for increasing inequality are generally set against the "technological change hypothesis," which holds that it is automation and organizational change that shift labor demand away from the less skilled and toward the more skilled, thereby widening the gap in their incomes. This argument focuses on factoral or occupational as opposed to sectoral skill differences. This can have a powerful effect on relative sectoral output prices (and hence wages), but such developments are seen as the result of variable rates of technological change *between* sectors. There are two versions of this story. What might be called the empirical version simply tracks the elasticities of labor demand. But such commonsense reasoning is rejected by most economists as being insufficiently theoretical. They turn to more complex equilibrium-based models of intersectoral adjustments. These models rephrase the technology effect as differential rates of total factor productivity (TFP) change between sectors, leading to durable differences in factor rewards (Richardson 1995). The factor rewards of skilled workers are increasing relative to those of unskilled workers in those sectors in which advanced economies are coming to specialize (high-technology manufacturing, capital goods, advanced services, high-quality goods), because their productivity is rising faster than those sectors with a high proportion of unskilled workers.

Most of the literature favors this general perspective, whether in its factoral or its sectoral focus, over the global-trade-based explanation of increasing inequality (as noted in the review by Freeman 1995). But, as seen above, there are observers such as Edward Leamer (1994, 1995), Feenstra (1998), and Wood (1994, 1995) who see technological change and globalization as intimately related. This is a theme to which I will return shortly.

The Four Tiers of Globalization   I want to argue that certain causes of inequality can be understood only through a combination of the technological change and globalization explanations. These approaches combined allow us to take into account two lacunae: (1) the broad category of semiskilled—as opposed to unskilled—workers, and (2) the effects of trade among developed countries as well as between the North and the South.[4] This combined approach will in turn yield the basis for a consideration of the role of consumerism in globalization and technological change.

Before considering this alternative explanation of inequality, however, it might be helpful to present a broad-brush portrait of sectors in the industrialized West in the age of globalization. At the top of a contemporary industrialized economy are activities that are globalized because they are rooted in scarce, unevenly distributed skills. There are certain sectors in which the highest-quality products enjoy global markets. The market may be accessible to them at very low or zero marginal cost thanks to the increasing reach of communications and infrastructure; alternatively, the supply of the product or service in question may be extremely limited, so that, in the absence of a substitute, supplemental costs to market are not an issue. The high-powered corporate attorney, the film or television star, and the internationally known medical specialist are examples of this internationalization of labor services. The providers of such services have earnings levels that are very high relative to the average in their occupational categories. Though such privileged individuals constitute a very small percentage of the total, their absolute numbers and absolute and relative earnings have been increasing rapidly in recent years. When a sports star, recording artist, international lawyer, or top executive gets fabulous compensation, it is because her or his services now have worldwide markets. Some of the reshaping of income distribution toward the top is a result of this "winner-take-all" phenomenon (Frank and Cook 1995).

Another part of this first economic tier also feeds the top end of the labor market. Most industrialized economies have certain sectors in which they specialize; they display high concentrations of certain industries (as reflected in a variety of indicators such as high location quotients). This uneven distribution of activities is due to the uneven supply of the individual or collective skills on which they depend. Examples include aerospace (United States, United Kingdom, France), high-quality shoes (Italy), machine tools (Germany, Japan), Hollywood films (United States), specialized financial products (United States, United Kingdom), and civil engineering services (France, United States) (for France, Italy, and United States, see Storper and Salais 1997; for a broader picture, see Porter 1990). These sectors are generally more labor intensive and higher waged than the economy as a whole. It is the higher overall wages in these sectors, along with earnings of the winner-take-all class, that drive the previously mentioned college/noncollege educated wage gap in economies where the favored industries are science- and engineering-intensive (for example, the United States). The college/noncollege educated gap is less important in places such as

Italy, Germany, or Denmark, owing to the medium-tech composition of the industries emphasized by these economies. In these cases, there is increasing income inequality within manufacturing occupations or sectors (Hanson and Harrison 1994; Maskell et al. 1998). Nevertheless, in spite of the wage gap, it can generally be said that these world-serving industrial specialties represent the "good" side of globalization for any country.

In the second tier of the economy are found the industries that can be relocated to low-skill, cheap-labor areas, and which are therefore the focus of most anxiety about globalization. Average wages and income shares have been dropping for workers in these industries in the developed countries. But, as noted above, they probably account for no more than 5 percent of total labor demand in the rich economies and a maximum of 10 to 15 percent of the change in income shares (in the United States) or unemployment (in Europe). The industries concerned are generally consumer nondurables (such as clothing and shoes) or the assembly phases of durable goods (such as electrical and electronic goods). Most of the intermediate goods (for example, production equipment, conception, marketing services) are still produced in the richer nations. This is globalization as depicted in the Stolper-Samuelson model.

The third tier of industries consists of services that are partly or completely nontradable. Fast food has to be prepared close to the point of consumption, so it cannot be offshored; dry cleaning and car repair must be located close to the customer. It is not possible to relocate these activities to low-wage countries. Nonetheless, because such jobs have few educational requirements, and because there is little tradition of unionization in many of the countries under consideration, they often pay very low wages. European countries have tried to raise wages in these sectors through minimum wage policy, but the principal effect of this has been to make services more automated than in the United States. The jobs that do remain are at the low end of the wage spectrum. Identifying a reason for the decline in relative wages in this tier is difficult. Is it due to increasing competition from low-skilled workers shed from the import-sensitive tradable manufacturing sectors? Or is it due to immigration, which swells the labor pool?

The fourth tier is traditionally associated with the middle of the income distribution. It consists of sectors using semiskilled labor in routine manufacturing (for instance, consumer durables) and certain services that have not been or cannot be offshored to low-wage countries. These are the sectors upon which the postwar middle-class miracle was largely built. But it is fairly well accepted that in most cases, their recent employment growth has been inferior to their productivity growth (Mishel, Bernstein, and Schmitt 1998). A steep decline in relative demand for their labor has resulted in a weakening position for semiskilled workers in the labor market. Their real wages have suffered stagnation, as in Europe, or outright decline, as in the United States. And while trade and foreign direct investment have been rising in these sectors, the kind of globalization this represents is altogether different from that characterizing the industries discussed above. In general, in this tier, only a few phases in the commodity chain (for instance, assembly) are relocated to developing countries. The great mass of value-added remains in the high-wage countries. Globalization as it emerges here essentially concerns cross-investment among countries with high wages, most of it transatlantic, and imports of manufactured goods from Japan to the West. Much of this is motivated by the rationalization of intermediate inputs and product differentiation. Hence it takes the form of rapidly growing intraindustry (and sometimes intrafirm) trade.[5]

This decline in the real wages of semiskilled, as opposed to unskilled, labor is thus characteristic of a broad swath of industries, to some degree globalized but still primarily concentrated within the developed countries. This phenomenon is a major cause of increasing income inequality.[6] In this context, the plight of semiskilled workers poses the debate with its major unsolved question. It is unlikely that their wages have fallen because of a decline in their relative productivity, since their jobs are disappearing precisely because of productivity-enhancing technical change. In this light, the argument made by Leamer (1994, 1995) seems to apply to certain "traditional" import-competing sectors, but not to many capital-intensive industries. For the semiskilled occupations, then, declining relative wages are consistent with declining labor demand but inconsistent with rising productivity.

Technological Change: A Result of Globalization by Ideas   Why has technological change continued to reduce demand for semiskilled labor, even though the combined productivity and wage effects should have leveled off the rate of change? A key to answering this question comes by considering the process by which such technological change might have come about. Most critically, why and how did such technological changes occur in so many different countries at roughly the same time (Berman, Bound, and Machin 1997)? There are three possible responses. One would be to attribute change to pressures from global financial capital; but there are strong doubts about the validity of such an explanation, because investors are interested in overall results, not in detailed management of production processes. A second would claim that countries with similar price levels should display similar production techniques. It is conceivable that all the developed economies, because they face similar developmental forces, have moved together from one envelope of feasible production possibilities (known as PPF, or "production possibility frontier") to another. But in this case, there is no reason for relative factor rewards to change (the formal model for this widely accepted point is presented in Richardson 1995). Moreover, virtually all of the detailed historical studies of industrial technology go against this notion of a "spontaneous" convergence of technologies, showing rather that convergence happens because of the spatial and temporal diffusion of such technologies, which have local origins (Hounshell 1974; Scranton 1997).

The third hypothesis can be introduced with the following points:

1. Many economic sectors are undergoing a global diffusion of certain labor-saving, capital-augmenting production techniques.
2. Producers implement new technologies *defensively*, because they fear loss of markets to foreign competitors if they do not. In this sense, technological change and globalization are not mutually exclusive, but two sides of the same process. In other words, I am suggesting that Wood's argument about technological change due to low-wage import competition can also be applied to North-North global competition (Western Europe, North America, Japan, and a few other places), and in different sectors or parts of sectors than for the North-South case. Such technological change may be considered neutral across sectors, but biased against unskilled workers in virtually every sector it affects.
3. Globalization—relocation and trade—makes such defensiveness rational. Even though industrialized countries, prior to trade lib-

eralization, may have had roughly similar factor costs and limited productivity differentials, there are still big differences in their products and the ways they organize their firms and production systems, which could pose mutual threats.[7] But these differences fall largely outside the purview of standard models.

4. It cannot be known whether all forms of defensive technological change among advanced economies augment total factor productivity and hence whether they fit within standard economic thinking.[8] My guess is that they do not, but instead represent a process of mutual imitation across international borders, or what I will call "globalization by ideas."

An Example of Globalization by Ideas In order to see what this theoretical explanation means, consider the evolution of the American car industry in the context of rising U.S.-Japan trade from the mid-1970s until the present. In the United States, car companies underwent a productivity slowdown and profitability crunch in the early 1970s and were strongly shaken by Japanese imports. The American story is thus in a sense one of import competition, not from a cheap or unregulated labor country, but from a high-wage country where new productivity techniques and resulting prices and product qualities outcompeted the American producers. The managerial elites in the United States initially did not understand the import threat in manufacturing and simply let their markets be flooded with better products from Japan in the late 1970s and early 1980s (Tolliday and Zeitlin 1992; Abernathy, Clark, and Kantrow 1992). Later on, they did try to stem the tide with voluntary import restrictions and misguided attempts at restructuring their firms, but the damage was already done. The American producers finally responded to the new techniques in the late 1980s. There was no longer any possibility of sticking with the old strategies for the American two-thirds of the domestic market, because consumer loyalties were being eroded.

A very interesting geographical process took place behind this sequence of events: the large-scale, long-distance diffusion and mastery of a set of labor-saving and productivity-heightening production techniques that align American quality, productivity, and price norms with those of their Japanese competitors (Abernathy, Clark, and Kantrow

1992). This phenomenon falls well into the standard trade theory notion that trade is a vehicle of knowledge diffusion (Eaton and Kortum 1995; Bernstein and Mohnen 1994; Park 1995).

This experience may not be the most common. The more typical case may be that of Western Europe, which is made up of countries that are on average three to four times more open to foreign trade than the United States. In most of the Western European car markets, Japanese competition has not had a strong direct influence. Today in France, for example, Japanese car imports are less than 3 percent of the total; and virtually all other imports of cars come from other Western European countries that have similar labor laws and wage levels often higher than those of France. Yet the Japanization of techniques, product qualities, and price levels has assuredly taken place in Western Europe. It would be hard to apply here the explanation advanced above for the U.S.-Japan case—there isn't (yet) enough actual trade to claim that Japanization in Europe is a way to reclaim lost market shares. Rather, it is clearly a defensive, anticipatory strategy.

Moreover, this implementation of techniques that carry a powerful labor-saving bias is taking place in countries with strong labor laws and labor movements, and where until recently there were substantial formal or informal restrictions on non-European trade. In light of these circumstances, why shouldn't firms and workers in these countries be able to shelter themselves from such techniques, with their extreme labor-saving and flexibility bias, and thereby preserve labor demand, maintain wage shares, and resist the inequality that would otherwise ensue? In other words, why do these countries' distinctive institutional structures not keep their staffing, wage, and skill levels in a different configuration from that typically brought about by diffusion of the new technologies? What alternative form of globalization is it that has permitted this worldwide diffusion of labor-saving technologies?[9]

In the European cases, workers did indeed resist these techniques, and even management did not show much interest in them in the beginning (Tolliday and Zeitlin 1992). Some national governments also resisted them because of the unemployment costs they would incur under the existing labor-law regimes there. And yet, in retrospect, their march forward seems to have been inexorable. In France, for example, both Peugeot and Renault dramatically increased the quality of their cars, their design, their reliability, the range of models; they adapted models more quickly to market changes by the late 1980s, and real prices declined when adjusted for quality. This story is not unusual; the real prices for many goods and services — sometimes in absolute terms as well as in quality-adjusted terms — have dropped over the past fifteen years in the United States and Western Europe (Lebergott 1993, 1996; Schor 1999; Gordon 1990). This is merely a way of stating the concrete consequences of what is assumed in every theory of expanding world trade and specialization: by reducing the internal prices of consumption goods relative to investment goods, expenditures are shifted toward consumption.

In this view, moreover, the vehicle of the current globalization process can be thought of as being quite different from what occurred earlier in the twentieth century. Instead of concentrating on direct, or trade-based, globalization, economists should also take into account a non-trade-based process of globalization that develops via flows of knowledge and ideas. Even in markets characterized by relatively modest shares of foreign goods — and this is frequently the case — it may be these global idea flows that call the shots. This suggests the advisability of a reorientation in how we think about the economics of globalization this time around.[10]

CONSUMPTION AND CONSUMERISM

The account given above is about strategies that take place within a large-scale collective action process — the conventional interaction between producers and consumers. On the producer side, there is learning to engage in defensive technological innovation as a way to head off potential loss of market share.[11] On the consumer side, there is a diffusion of calculating, internationally informed, and consciously comparative consumer behavior. This space- and time-sensitive interaction between production norms and consumption norms has not been well studied, to my knowledge. I believe that it holds the key to many dimensions of what might be called industrial hypermodernity — the ever more frantic race for product quality, variety, rapidity of adjustment, and cheapness — at the end of the twentieth century.

In markets, supply and demand transform each other through a sort of back-and-forth movement between the two, a kind of dance between the producer and the consumer.[12] Given that the current rapid rise in trade began around 1973, one can surmise that in cases such as the automobile industry examined above, consumers began to be heavily exposed to the prices and qualities of imported goods in the 1980s. This exposure was accelerated by increased global advertising. Domestic producers responded by imitating the prices and qualities of foreign goods that were taking away, or were poised to take away, their market shares. In this way, over the 1980s and early 1990s, consumer expectations about the relationship between price and quality of many products changed. Though consumers were unaware of it, their expectations now depended on methods of production using the new labor-saving and quality-improving techniques. A new demand structure, rooted in these consumer expectations, has now made it much more difficult — if not impossible — for any country to use local institutional structures, such as labor market structure or protectionism, to enforce local technical norms that might deviate from world productivity standards for a given product.

This demand structure provides a starting point for understanding the diffusion of such production techniques, in that firms in countries with strong labor laws and institutions may not initially have intended to go head-to-head with those strong social forces. Instead, they typically found themselves unable to adapt to changing market conditions in the 1970s and early 1980s. The story unfolded in different ways in different places, but three elements may be identified as consistent factors: (1) the commitment of producers to the new techniques in relation to the labor market rules and institutions as referred to above; (2) the degree to which producers supported open markets; and (3) consumer society's impact in the form of consumption norms and conventions.

In contrast with the United States, in most of the rest of the developed world, the identity of "consumer" is a very recent one — if by that word is understood a social category openly and favorably acknowledged by firms, politicians, the media, and indeed by individuals describing themselves (Cross 1993; Lynn 1971; Lury 1996; Slater 1997). Of course, it is difficult to say exactly how and why this shift from "producerist" identities to "consumerist" identities has happened in the Western European countries. But it might be proposed that in the early days of the rapid growth of trade (the late 1970s through the mid-1980s), the selective and limited importation of goods served as a vehicle of diffusion of new standards of prices and quality that subsequently became assimilated as

104 * MICHAEL STORPER

expectations by consumers. Increasingly, firms appeal directly to consumers in order to bring about technological changes that sometimes have damaging effects on the incomes of those very same people.

The Strengthening of Consumerism and Consumer Identities   Of course, one could argue that consumerism is nothing new, especially in the United States. But a strong case can be made that consumerism has become markedly more pervasive in the United States since the 1970s, when the current trade expansion began, and that it became culturally dominant for the first time in Western Europe during this period. Psychological and economic as well as institutional and organizational factors can all point to this conclusion.

Consumerism has long existed as an institutional field, in the sense of a set of routinized social practices anchored in structured relationships between organizations (Powell and DiMaggio 1992). There is abundant reason to believe that this field has been expanding in many areas of the world, including not only the developed countries, but many developing areas as well. Evidence of this includes the following: the explicit education of consumers by firms about the ways that they improve their goods and services; the massive increase in brand-name advertising as a percentage of overall firm expenditures; the rapid rise in the number of consumer associations; and the nearly tenfold increase in the number of new products introduced yearly in the United States between the 1970s and the mid-1990s (Madrick 1996; Schor 1999). Mention must also be made of the shopping experience itself, long exoticized for the upper classes and now presented as "experiential" for wide swaths of middle-class consumption as well—while at the same time reaching peaks of pure price- and quantity-oriented massification, such as the spread of discounting (Miller 1998).

What is the result of these institutional practices in terms of the behavior of people and the ways in which they define their interests and identify themselves in the world? There is little hard or quantifiable data regarding these complex intangibles. In my view, it would be a mistake to hold that consumption is simply "pushed" on people, that they are duped into it by powerful institutional forces such as advertising. A more plausible interpretation is that consumerism, however it begins, ultimately sustains itself by becoming an intimate part of the action frameworks of individuals, how they see themselves and define their interests, how they approach the world, and how they present themselves to others (see Goffman 1956; Douglas and Isherwood 1996; Rauscher 1993; Slater 1997, Chao and Schor 1994; Lury 1996). Such a model of the institutional field of consumerism would consist of a set of conventions that link and coordinate the behaviors of producers and consumers.

The notion that people might become hooked on consuming has a firm basis in psychology. There is now a considerable body of research in social psychology on the fundamental attractions of arousal (versus boredom), pleasure (versus comfort), and comfort (versus discomfort), and the human strategies for getting from less desirable to more desirable states. Key among these are material means, and in today's world, material means are usually consumed rather than self-produced (see Scitovsky 1976, chaps. 2–4). Pleasure is apt to be induced by seduction — *l'appétit vient en mangeant* — and this is the psychological target for the institutional field mentioned above. Humans also have a tendency to become addicted to certain forms of pleasure or arousal. One of the chief ways this addiction can be maintained is through novelty, since pleasure diminishes rapidly due to habituation, and arousal peaks, declines, and must be reignited again (Scitovsky 1976).

Psychology can provide a suggestive departure for an inquiry into the desire to consume. But what are the dynamics of the interests that come into play when consumers meet producers? The classical economic approaches to this question stressed a presumed relationship between rising affluence and consumerism, often linked to the idea that affluence frees up time. Consumption thus becomes a leisure activity that is strongly linked to status differentiation (Veblen 1976; Tawney 1952; Galbraith 1958). More recently, however, a central premise of these analyses has been questioned, for it is now widely recognized that increasing affluence does not generate increases in free time. Indeed, the prevailing trend seems to be in the opposite direction (Hochschild 1997; Schor 1991; Hirschman 1973; Cross 1993).

In light of this discrepancy, Juliet Schor (1999) suggests that the fundamental assumptions of mainstream economics with respect to consumption are fundamentally wrong. Economics has long assumed that what we consume is necessarily an expression of what we want — that it is the objective expression of our subjective preferences. The two assumptions behind this are "worker sovereignty" and "consumer sovereignty." The former term refers to the idea that workers actually choose how much to work and how much to earn, and competition ensures that what they want will be available in the labor market. The latter refers to the premise that consumers choose the basket of goods and services that maximize their satisfaction, and competition ensures that what they want will be available for sale. If these twin sovereignties hold, then consumers consume to the point of optimal satisfaction. But if, for example, workers cannot in reality trade off consumption for leisure, the reasoning falls apart. And considerable empirical evidence is available to discredit this notion of worker choice (Kahneman, Slovic, and Tversky 1979).

Such studies enable Schor to argue that because workers cannot choose their hours of work, the current trade-off between leisure, income, and spending is not free and optimal. Rather, since workers cannot increase their leisure time, they consume with the income they do earn. The literature on the "time bind" supports the idea that in an affluent society, we consume because it is our only realistic choice. As we spend our higher incomes, habit formation takes over and leads to a sort of cumulative effect of consumption (endogenous preference adjustment). These are the structural reasons consumerism and consumer society have found such fertile ground in contemporary developed economies. When combined with the psychological motivations and institutional forces noted above, the case appears quite powerful.

The Lived Effects of Income Inequality: Consumption and Consumer Surplus Economics has a concept, usually deployed as an efficiency measure, that can help explain one of the lived dimensions of changes in absolute and relative income levels. *Consumer surplus* is the term for the gains consumers receive when lower production costs are passed on in the form of cheaper goods. If consumer surplus is growing, then, at a given income level, it is possible for the absolute material standard of living to increase.

Thus, in order to understand the lived effects of income distribution changes, the evolution of the absolute material standards of living of those affected must be considered. The evidence in this regard gives a somewhat different picture from that provided by income distribution figures alone. In Western Europe, North America, and Japan, real material standards of living have continued to rise for a very high percentage of the population, perhaps 90 percent or more, through the last 25 years (Lebergott 1993, 1996). This is all the more remarkable because productivity growth for these economies in the same period has averaged only 2 percent per year, in contrast with the postwar average of about 5 percent per year up to 1970. Virtually every quality-of-life indicator corresponds to this view: housing size and quality; the use of durable and nondurable consumer goods; travel and leisure; health; and even schooling (Lebergott 1993; Burtless 1996). As discussed above, the same phenomenon that has caused income stagnation for much of the labor force—dramatic labor-saving technological change resulting in a drop in relative demand for the semiskilled—has also cheapened and improved most consumer goods and services. This is reflected in real consumer prices (Gordon 1990) and is experienced as a dramatic increase in consumer surplus. Even for that part of the population whose wages are most negatively affected by globalization—the unskilled—it is estimated that in the United States, a 3 percent direct decline in real wages has been compensated for by a 3 percent consumer surplus (Cline 1997).

There are, however, more disquieting signs for a hard-core group of the poor that was never eliminated in the United States but that almost disappeared in Western Europe in the early 1970s.[13] It appears that the production of public goods (roads, schools, and so forth) has declined in some countries due to policies that reduce the transfer of income from private to public hands, and this has undoubtedly had a greater impact on the poor than on the rich. Increases are also indicated in certain negative externalities disproportionately suffered by the poor (such as pollution, violence). Still, the overall picture is not one of decline in absolute material standards of living, but of increases for the vast majority. This forces us to think very differently about how the effects of income distribution changes are actually felt by the majority.

This raises a collective action problem similar to the one referred to in the previous section. There, I hypothesized that consumer interests and identities have played an increasing role in many countries in permitting producers to implement productivity strategies that run up against powerful organized interests—unions in particular, or wageworkers in general. One of the reasons there may have been less protest over the emerging income distribution than might have been expected from a straight reading of the income figures is this: many of those who are losing in relative — and even in absolute — terms as workers, are still gaining in absolute, material terms as consumers.

The Lived Effects of Income Inequality: Positionality   Still, one might ask, if consumer surplus is growing, sustaining higher material consumption, why do so many people feel dissatisfied? Why is there a widespread impression of decline or inadequate progress in the standard of living in so many countries? An answer to these questions might include three elements.

Many of our expectations about standards of living are derived from observation of the generation that precedes us. In the postwar period, up until the early 1970s, there was a very rapid and sustained increase in the standard of living in the industrialized world. Since then, the much lower rate of productivity growth, from about 5 percent per year to half of that, represents an enormous overall loss in output — whether experienced as income or consumer surplus — from what would have been obtained had overall growth continued at the previous rate (Madrick 1996).

As a second reason for widespread dissatisfaction, it can be proposed that there is a big difference between the overall effects of technological and organizational change on income in the economy and their experiential effects on given individuals. Behind the fact that absolute average incomes for low- and semiskilled people have declined or stagnated is a great deal of individual turbulence. Many individuals have seen what they considered to be secure jobs, with certain income expectations, disappear, and they have found themselves unemployed or reclassified downward in terms of skill and income (Mishel, Bernstein, and Schmitt 1998). This is an important corrective to the use of averages in the standard analyses.

The third reason is less apparent and has to do with the *shape* of consumption. The malaise of the middle classes goes beyond the experience of individuals who have been the victims of labor-market displacement. It affects many members of the middle class who have actually benefited from the consumer surpluses alluded to above without incurring the negative wage effects. And to these may even be added the people at the top, who are benefiting from increases in both income and consumer surplus. Yet empirical research on subjective well-being in relation to real income has long confirmed that once basic needs are met, satisfaction fails to increase. Robert Frank (1999: 72), quoting results from the National Opinion Research Center, shows that real per capita GDP in the United States rose by 37 percent between 1972 and 1991, but the percentage of respondents reporting themselves to be "very happy" never exceeded 40 percent—its 1973 level. Ruut Veenhoven (1993), in a study of Japan from 1961 to 1987, shows that although per capita income grew fourfold, the average level of reported happiness stayed flat (see also Kahneman 1998). Indeed, this is an old theme in the critique of consumer society (Tawney 1952; Galbraith 1958; Sen 1987), although it is now easier to confirm and to theorize (Easterlin 1995; Duncan 1975–76).

But surely the people at the top are happier as they consume away? The appearance of greater numbers of high-income earners has altered consumption patterns. At the very top, the winners in winner-take-all markets constitute, in terms of their purchasing power and habits, something like a new aristocracy (Frank 1999). Below this top 3 percent are another 17 percent or so whose purchasing power now permits them to acquire very large quantities of fine goods and services (Frank 1999; Frank and Cook 1995; Schor 1999). One explanation that has been offered for the stagnation in subjective well-being comes from the social psychologists' notion of a fixed hierarchy of needs (Maslow 1954): a ladder up which people move as they get richer in absolute terms. The implication is that richer people will be more satisfied, and everyone else will be less satisfied. But empirical research does not strongly bear this out. Frank (1999: 114) shows that the relationship between well-being and income is quite noisy; there is a great deal of individual variation at all income levels. Factors other than income are important, many of them nonmaterial.

A more powerful explanation for the stagnation of satisfaction, on average and at the top, comes from the notion of *positionality* in economics. A portion of the satisfaction we get from certain kinds of goods or services has been shown to depend on their position in a hierarchy of quality and status, and not on their absolute qualities. There are two ways in which many consumer goods fit this pattern. First, they have status attributes and not simply use-values. The enjoyment that comes from them has to do in part with how they compare to what we know is available. As noted above, one of the principal psychological dimensions of consumerism (and some of the other pleasures in life) is that the pleasure effect wears off with familiarity, and change heightens it again. This is true also of the pleasures of status-seeking: jockeying for position eventually yields to familiarity, and the position itself is objectively changed when others catch up. Both lead to reduction of pleasure and renewal of the search for status. Psychological research suggests that status-seeking may have addictive properties (discussed in Hunt 1996).

In addition, the absolute qualities of certain goods change with position.[14] This is the case for some of the most important collective goods, such as schools or transportation. If everyone goes to public schools, they have a certain range of qualities. If richer or better-prepared children go to private schools, then not only do public schools change in relative status, but their absolute qualities may be changed as a result of the withdrawal of privileged students to private schools.

All of these are examples of a condition that violates one of the fundamental precepts of the way the pursuit of satisfaction is viewed in standard economics: that each person's preferences are independent, severable expressions of their wants, which they can combine and transform optimally. The present analysis suggests that preferences are interdependent (Tomes 1986). Considerations of status-seeking behavior (Duesenberry 1949; Bearden and Etzel 1982; Chao and Schor 1994; Frank 1999, 1985; Rauscher 1993) and of the real relationship of absolute to relative quality (Alessie and Kapteyn 1991; Easterlin 1995) can both be deployed in support of this more recent view.

Thus, along with the considerable decreases in price and increases in quality offered by producers as a result of the new production paradigms and their global price norms, there has also been an increase in positionality. The dissatisfaction of the middle classes has to do in part with this flip side of globalization—their stagnating money incomes and positionality in consumption are not entirely offset by the cheapening of many goods. They are consuming more but still losing out in critical ways. These are not optical illusions or the psychological hangups of spoiled people from wealthy countries. They are objective, real effects. It follows, of course, that the people at the bottom of the income distribution suffer even more egregiously from the new positional inequality in consumption.

Public Goods and Positionality: The Prisoner's Dilemma   One of the biggest differences between most Western European economies and the United States is the percentage of total economic output that goes to public expenditure. There is a variation of almost 20 percent between the United States (around 30 percent) and most of the high-public-expenditure continental countries (around 50 percent). Considering that military expenditures account for a relatively high percentage of U.S. public expenditure and that large amounts of these funds end as private-sector procurement expenses, there are big differences in the quantities of public goods provided to the citizens of these nations. Public goods tend to be less positional than private goods, although they are certainly not immune from positionality effects (this depends largely on how they are produced and distributed). But public goods are more frequently nonstatus goods than private goods; although many desirable private goods (such as savings, some forms of education, hobbies, and conviviality) do not have status qualities (Frank 1999). Public goods are often distributed so as to equalize access to certain kinds of necessities, and thus some of the positionality effects of status consumption should be offset.

Another way in which most Western European economies (as well as Japan's) differ from the United States is in the degree of wage dispersion. The multiple of average occupational wages in the highly remunerated occupations to the lower-paid ones is much higher in the United States than elsewhere (Crafts 1998).[15] In Europe, the effect of winner-take-all labor markets has not been as prominent, in part because of the different sectoral specializations of European economies — less high-tech, for example. (The United Kingdom is something of an exception, with the City of London and its corporate management stratum featuring wage structures that are closer to those of the United States than of continental Europe.) Positionality effects seem to be growing mildly in Western Europe as the occupational wage structure comes to be influenced more by international trends, aided by policy changes in many countries.

One of the most worrisome aspects of positionality, in the face of growing income inequality, is that it may tend to crowd out nonstatus goods in general and public goods in particular. If status consumption is insatiable, it will eat up much income that might otherwise go to nonstatus goods, even where absolute incomes are rising. This is the pattern at work in the seeming paradox of people getting richer and still wanting to pay lower taxes. The only way to slow down status consumption is collectively, with mechanisms that simultaneously limit what our status competitors are doing.

The classic example of this sort of scenario, in which rational individual choices lead to collective outcomes that most would not prefer, is known as the "prisoner's dilemma." Two accused prisoners in different cells agree to confess when promised a lower sentence in return for revealing their partner's crime. Both will go free if neither one says anything, whereas if either one confesses in order to obtain a lower sentence, they will both remain imprisoned. In spite of abundant private wealth in the United States, it is very difficult to persuade even members of the increasingly prosperous upper middle class to reallocate more of their income to public goods, because most of them do not feel confident that others will do the same. In Europe, with lower absolute growth, more modest average incomes, and less inequality, it is easier to do so—for the time being.

In sum, the consumption experience at the start of a new century reflects a tug-of-war between a number of forces. The lower price of many goods and services creates consumer surplus, but there are in addition national forces—customs, education (supply effects), and regulations—that powerfully shape the ways in which wage inequality due to globalization and technological change actually affects individual experience. These include the degree and shape of positionality in consumption, as well as the split between private and collective consumption.

Homogenization and Diversity   Contradictory claims are frequently made about the nature of contemporary material culture. A commonly heard complaint is that there are so many options for material purchases, services, and cultural events that material and cultural life has become excessively fragmented. Others celebrate this apparently dizzying variety of possibilities (Miller 1998; Lury 1996). Both advocates and detractors generally recognize that contemporary capitalism has greatly increased its capacity to support a diversified material culture with much greater variety than ever before.

Some examples: Many more consumer products are introduced each year today than in the 1970s—perhaps six to ten times more (Frank and Weiland 1997). The rate of product changeover in many fashion and seasonal industries is now so rapid that it is often said that the fashion business has gone from four to nine seasons per year. In many markets, there are more versions of competing products that meet a given type of function (cars of similar horsepower and size, for instance) than ever before. Even the number of specialized culture festivals in the United States has risen more than tenfold since the 1970s. Much of the management and industrial economics literature is consistent with this view of things: Managers are concerned to cope with increased risks of market shifts, and industrial economics has become preoccupied with product and process innovation and continuous "learning" (Porter 1990; Lundvall 1996).

Just as frequently, however, we hear lamentations about the loss of diversity—about a world that seems more and more homogeneous—that echo the longstanding postwar concern with mass consumer culture (Scitovsky 1976). For the purposes of the present analysis of globalization, there appear to be two relevant dimensions to this phenomenon, which are quite often confused with each other.

The first has to do with the geographical rescaling and integration of consumer capitalism. Throughout the advanced economies, and in the biggest cities of the rest of the world, there has been a considerable diffusion of certain similar dimensions of mass culture: fast food, films, youth fashion, and shopping centers come immediately to mind. Whether we go to a jazz club in Greenwich Village or Paris, to a gay disco in San Francisco or London, or to a big rock concert or standard symphony hall, high-culture event anywhere, the venues resemble each other; in the latter instances, they might not only present the same acts, they are often organized by the same people. To be sure, beyond such internationalized aspects of consumerism, great local differences remain; but there is a definite convergence in certain kinds of consumerism and corresponding ways of life for certain social classes. This is even true of vacationing, which has traditionally been the activity by which we pursue the different or exotic: the average beach resort in Mexico looks a lot like the average beach resort in Tunisia or the Costa Brava, with its chains of hotels, restaurants, shops, and nightclubs (Urry 1995).

Many smaller U.S. cities now typically feature a variety of ethnic and specialty restaurants, touring theater companies, and even art films. These places have become at once more internally diversified and more like their metropolitan counterparts. The loss of "authentic" local culture in these places is a constant lament. But on the other hand, for the residents of such places—or of Paris, Columbus, or Belo Horizonte, for that matter—there has been an undeniable increase in the variety of material, service, and cultural outputs. In short, the perceived loss of diversity would appear to be attributable to a certain rescaling of territories: from a world of more internally homogeneous localities where diversity was to be found by traveling between places with significantly different material cultures to a world where one travels between more similar places but finds increasing variety within them.

The prevailing condition is not marked just by variety, however; there are forces that pull in the other direction. For example, advances in communications and information processing have made it possible to manage large service-delivery organizations with a great diversity of products and frequent changeovers. Such scope used to be reserved to the most gigantic companies, and even they used to be limited to relatively stable markets, but this is no longer the case.

To cite an upper-middle-class example: In U.S. cities, it is now possible to find many cafés serving specialty coffees, often many kinds in the same café. But at the same time, we find the same chain—Starbucks—in thousands of locations across the country, often every few blocks in the same city. In California, the joke today is that in the gentrified urban neighborhoods that are supposed to feature the most diversified specialty consumption, the most profitable specialists have simply crowded everything else out, resulting in a familiar cluster of corporate logos to be repeated every few blocks: Starbucks–Banana Republic–Noah's Bagels–Gap–Barnes & Noble. This is simply massification with a different, more small-scale look. The material context of consumption—the places where we do it—gives us an impression of sameness, even as we are confronted with a plethora of product choices. And lest it be thought that this is only a characteristic of upper-income areas, it might also be mentioned that chain stores have been taking over food marketing in heavily Latino East Los Angeles, where the big competition is between the Mexican chain *Gigante* and local chains started by ethnic entrepreneurs, to the detriment of independent, locally owned shops (Rosenberg 1999).

It is true that straightforward economies of scale in managing organizations, which can now extend and replicate themselves over wider territories, are part of the story. In other words, to be huge, Wal-Mart is only one, and perhaps not the most important, model today. Hugeness can come through numerous widely scattered outlets rather than a smaller number of huge outlets. This is the point at which marketing and management can usually wrap up their happy story about how the consumer can now be served a huge variety of high-quality and specialized products with all the benefits of both scale and proximity to the consumer.

But there is another force at work in certain markets that encourages a loss of diversity *tout court*. This is a concept known to economists as *Hotelling's duopoly*. It concerns the parable of a beach, four kilometers long, with two ice cream vendors. If the vendors were to choose their locations with an eye to providing optimal service to the sunbathers spread equally along the four kilometers, they would take up position at kilometers 1 and 3. No bather would be more than a kilometer away from ice cream, and only a small number, positioned right at kilometer 2, would ever shift loyalties. But that isn't what happens. When the two vendors compete, they shift positions to cut into each other's markets. After several rounds of moving toward kilometer 2 in order to grab some of the other's customers, they both end up clustered around kilometer 2, so they each get half the customers for the entire length of the beach. The sunbathers at either end of the strip lose out, because they have to go much farther to get ice cream. The result is bad for everybody, but it's the outcome of rational competitive behavior.

This is a locational metaphor for a broader economic phenomenon. In certain product markets, a small number of producers will act in a duopolistic way, effectively reducing the range of outputs to cluster around the middle of the demand structure. Major Hollywood film studios, for example, have figured out that they can make a lot more money by producing middle-taste or formula films. Filmgoers may see films that feature different stars and some slight variations on a common theme, but as far as the decision makers in the industry are concerned, they could be rolling out installments in a series. Moreover, the price of making and distributing a successful formula film has risen geometrically, reducing the amount of studio capital available for other kinds of films. The result is that producers aim their products increasingly toward the middle of the market.

This is often incorrectly described as oligopolistic market control, but the markets are in fact highly competitive.[16] Such convergence, characteristic of many contemporary markets, helps to explain the sense on the part of consumers that many products — most notably cultural products such as films and music, but also even certain kinds of manufactured goods — lack variety. A fantastic number of options, colors, and certain kinds of functional differences may be available, but middle-of-the-road marketing criteria nevertheless dominate the selection.

There are exceptions, one might protest. There is a proliferation of independent films; you can find specialty manufactured products in specialty stores if you know where to look. For the latter, however, price premiums must be paid (Scitovsky 1976); for the former, almost insuperable barriers exist to the high-level financing prerequisite for the technical sophistication that has become the norm for the mass market. U.S. journalism, both print and broadcast, displays the characteristics of Hotelling dynamics, with fierce competition focusing on the coverage of material whose newsworthiness is defined by a seldom contested middlebrow attitude. Evidently, there is a very complex real mixture of variety-enhancing and variety-reducing changes occurring in the markets of even the richest economies. Our apparently contradictory impressions may very well be entirely accurate. The point is that these contradictory effects have to do with globalization in two ways: the rescaling of markets, and Hotelling dynamics within enlarged and deepened markets.

BY WAY OF CONCLUSION

The argument here has ranged widely across issues often dealt with in separate academic fields, so it may be helpful to draw the threads together. I began by exploring a paradox at the heart of economic globalization: Why have "producerist" countries (as represented by the social democracies of Western Europe) essentially restructured their industries along the same lines as the "nonlaborist" Americans, incorporating labor-saving and inequality-promoting changes in production techniques? I investigated how consumer society has been mobilized in favor of such changes, thereby reinforcing the ability of firms to implement defensive technological changes. In this way, I hope to have shown the relationship between globalization and increasing income inequality to be broader than it is represented in many economic analyses.

An inquiry into why increasing inequality has stimulated only minor social protest identified effects on material consumption and real standards of living that offset some of the income lost by certain groups due to contemporary economic restructuring. The contemporary citizen at times acts as a consumer, at other times as a producer. His or her behaviors seem inconsistent if evaluated only in terms of standard class or income (producerist) criteria.

Yet overall satisfaction levels in the advanced economies have not increased with growing material wealth. My third point was, therefore, that even as consumerism has been widened and deepened and its logic extended farther down the social hierarchy, consumption practices have become increasingly shaped by a status hierarchy. This yields the impression that living standards are declining even as wealth increases in real terms and creates a stagnation in satisfaction levels. Fourth, although globalization and technological change make it possible for industrialized economies to produce and market a hugely increased variety of goods, they also push certain industries to concentrate on middle-of-the-road outputs; these two tendencies create the simultaneous and contrasting impressions of greater variety and greater homogeneity. Finally, the differences between public and private consumption, which vary from place to place, give different local flavors to these global trends.

Many complex issues remain to be resolved. Most important, in discussions of globalization and inequality and of the contemporary experience, economists must avoid simplistic depictions of social behavior. Economic actors are not only wage earners, but also consumers, not to mention citizens (Inkeles 1983). Though the consumer society has been long in the making, I believe that it has entered a new and qualitatively different phase from the period prior to 1980. Within this deeper and wider consumer society, producer identities appear to be crumbling, especially in Western Europe where they have traditionally been stronger than in the United States. Scholars have yet to consider the implications of this transformation in identity for the economic effects of globalization and the feelings that people have about them, and hence the complex political and social processes they may set into motion.

NOTES

1 At the end of the 1980s, there was considerable opinion that middle-class incomes had actually fallen in the United States since the late 1970s. But the Boskin Commission's (Boskin 1996) reevaluation of the consumer price index showed that inflation had actually been considerably lower than had previously been thought. Though the details of the commission's findings provoked considerable controversy, there was little chal-

lenge to the overall conclusion. In the second half of this article, I will discuss one of the reasons for the inflation rate's reevaluation downward: the advent of higher product quality in many areas of the economy, so that prices reflect not inflation per se, but quality improvements.

2 See the special issue of the *Quarterly Journal of Economics,* February 1992, and Mishel, Bernstein, and Schmitt 1998.

3 In this regard, Wood (1995: 73) notes: "This heterogeneity of goods within statistically defined sectors is a major limitation of all the price data and one which has become worse over time. Manufactured imports from developing countries used to be concentrated on a few sectors, such as apparel and footwear, but are now spread across many sectors, partly because, for a wide range of goods, the production process has been split up, with the labor-intensive stages performed in developing countries, and the skill-intensive ones at home." See also Wright, in this volume.

4 Statistically speaking, North-South trade is a drop in the bucket compared with trade among the industrialized countries: The former is about 15 percent of the total, with the latter more than 80 percent.

5 This is predicted by trade and location theory. See Krugman 1995, which I review in Storper 1999.

6 The workers who are really being referred to in this argument are the population that corresponds with the postwar "middle class," or, in other words, semiskilled workers. The problem with most of the empirical and theoretical literature that has been reviewed in this article is its simplistic distinction between skilled and unskilled labor. Part of the reluctance to consider semiskilled workers must be attributed to the difficulty of defining them as a discrete category with the indicators available.

7 There is a voluminous literature on "comparative advanced capitalisms." For an interesting popularization, see Albert 1993.

8 But standard models do envisage the possibility that international migration of "technological capital" would affect relative prices: Richardson 1995: 44.

9 Although the accounts of some historians suggest that labor saving is the principal motivation of employers who adopted these technologies in the early days, many other accounts focus on the need to change practices of labor utilization in order to get the other benefits of the new techniques; in these studies, labor saving emerges as something like a secondary and opportunistic benefit of adoption, not its sole or primary purpose, as is often assumed (Abernathy, Clark, and Kantrow 1992; Utterback 1996). There is a lively debate over this. Some excellent analyses claim that managers are aware of, and are explicitly promoting, a declining technology-skill complementarity. See, for example, Lazonick and O'Sullivan 1997.

10 I have written more extensively about this issue in Storper 1999; Storper and Chen 1999.

11 Expressed more technically, there is considerable evidence that European producers are adjusting to globalization not only by becoming more specialized in what economists call "intrafirm trade" but also by making similar products and competing head to head, and that this is an important percentage of trade among the advanced countries (Storper and Chen 1999).

12 I translate this "back-and-forth movement" from Léon Walras's use of the French term *tâtonnement*—something like a back-and-forth method of finding one's way and adjusting to signals.

13 Some Western European countries reduced their poverty rates to less than 2 percent at that time, but the rates have since tended to rise. Poverty reduction proceeded in the United States with rapidity from 1955 until 1975. Since then, contrary to the popular impression, the rate has risen by only 1.5 percent. What this indicates is the presence in both Europe and the United States of a group that has remained mired in persistent poverty.

14 A classical version of this comes from locational or land-use economics, where Ricardian land rent is the result of a limited number of spots at a given location and at a given proximity to other locations. Although there is some possibility of expansion, through intensification of land use (higher buildings) or better transportation, the potential is not infinite and the user-attributes of the land change with expanding supply, often remaining inferior to the best locations, which are already used up and cannot be expanded.

15 Although total income distribution is not hugely different in the United States, because in other countries inherited wealth or income on property compensate for more egalitarian wage structures. Moreover, the low wage-dispersion rates of some countries reflect a pattern in which the bottom income brackets are brought closer to the middle while average wages are left low relative to the U.S. average. This is the case for France, for example, where the minimum wage, much higher than the U.S. one, is 60 percent of average wages, and the average is in turn a lot lower than that of the United States.

16 The state-of-the-art term is *contestable* markets, a form of competitive markets with a small number of producers (Baumol, Panzar, and Willig 1982).

REFERENCES

Abernathy, William J., Kim B. Clark, and Alan M. Kantrow. 1992. *Industrial renaissance: Producing a competitive future for America.* Cambridge: Harvard Business School Press.

Albert, Michel. 1993. *Capitalism versus capitalism.* New York: Four Walls Eight Windows Press.

Alessie, Rob, and Arie Kapteyn. 1991. Habit formation, interdependent preferences, and demographic effects in the almost ideal demand system. *Economic Journal* 101: 404–19.

Baumol, W., J. Panzar, and J. Willig. 1982. *Contestable markets and the theory of industry structure.* Cambridge: Harvard Business School Press.

Bearden, William O., and Michael J. Etzel. 1982. Reference group influence and product and brand purchase decisions. *Journal of Consumer Research* 9: 183–94.

Berman, Eli, John Bound, and Zvi Griliches. 1994. Changes in the demand for skilled labor within U.S. manufacturing industries: Evidence from the annual survey of manufactures. *Quarterly Journal of Economics* 109: 367–97.

Berman, Eli, John Bound, and Stephen Machin. 1997. Implications of skill-biased technological change: International evidence. Unpublished manuscript. Cambridge, Mass.: National Bureau of Economic Research (NBER).

Bernstein, J., and P. Mohnen. 1994. International R&D spillovers between U.S. and Japanese R&D Intensive Sectors. Working Paper no. 4682. Cambridge, Mass.: NBER.

Borjas, George, Richard Freeman, and Lawrence Katz. 1992. On the labor market effects of immigration and trade. In *Immigration and the work force,* edited by George Borjas and Richard Freeman. Chicago: University of Chicago Press.

Boskin, Michael, ed. 1996. Towards a more accurate measure of the cost of living. Final Report to the U.S. Senate Finance Committee.

Bound, John, and George Johnson. 1992. Changes in the structure of wages during the 1980s: An evaluation of alternative explanations. *American Economic Review* 82: 371–92.

Burtless, Gary. 1996. Trends in the level and distribution of U.S. living standards, 1973–1993. *Eastern Economic Journal* 22: 271–90.

Chao, Angela, and Juliet B. Schor. 1994. Empirical tests of status consumption: Evidence from women's cosmetics. Paper no. 96.01.007/2, Tilburg, The Netherlands: University of Tilburg, Work and Organization Research Centre.

Cline, William R. 1997. *Trade and income distribution.* Washington, D.C.: Institute for International Economics.

Crafts, N. F. R. 1998. The British economy: Missing out or catching up? In *European economies since World War II,* edited by Bernard Foley. New York: St. Martin's Press.

Cross, Gary. 1993. *Time and money: The making of consumer culture.* New York: Routledge.

Douglas, Mary, and Baron Isherwood. 1996. *The world of goods: Toward an anthropology of consumption.* London: Routledge.

Duesenberry, James S. 1949. *Income, saving, and the theory of consumer behavior.* Cambridge: Harvard University Press.

Duncan, Otis. 1975–76. Does money buy satisfaction? *Social Indicators Research* 2: 267–74.

Easterlin, Richard. 1995. Will raising the incomes of all increase the happiness of all? *Journal of Economic Behavior and Organization* 27: 35–47.

Eaton, Jonathan, and Samuel Kortum. 1995. Engines of growth: Domestic and foreign sources of innovation. Working paper no. 5207. Cambridge, Mass.: NBER.

Feenstra, Robert C. 1998. Integration of trade and disintegration of production in the global economy. *Journal of Economic Perspectives* 12, no. 4: 31–50.

Feenstra, Robert C., and Gordon Hanson. 1996. Foreign investment, outsourcing and relative wages. In *The political economy of trade policy: Papers in honor of Jagdish Bhagwat,* edited by Robert C. Feenstra, Gene Grossman, and Douglas Irwin. Cambridge: MIT Press.

Frank, Robert H. 1985. *Choosing the right pond: Human behavior and the quest for status.* New York: Oxford University Press.

———. 1999. *Luxury fever: Why money fails to satisfy in an age of excess.* New York: Free Press.

Frank, Robert H., and Phillip J. Cook. 1995. *The winner-take-all society*. New York: Free Press.

Frank, Thomas, and Matt Weiland, eds. 1997. *Commodify your dissent: The business of culture in the new gilded age (salvos from* The Baffler*)*. New York: Norton.

Freeman, Richard. 1995. Are your wages set in Beijing? *Journal of Economic Perspectives* 9, no. 3: 15–32.

Galbraith, John Kenneth. 1958. *The affluent society*. Boston: Houghton-Mifflin.

Goffman, Erving. 1956. *The presentation of self in everyday life*. Edinburgh: University of Edinburgh Press.

Gordon, Robert J. 1990. *The measurement of durable goods prices*. Chicago: University of Chicago Press.

Gottschalk, Peter, and Robert Moffitt. 1994. The growth of earnings instability in the U.S. labor market. *Brookings Papers on Economic Activity* 2: 217–72.

Hanson, Gordon H., and Ann Harrison. 1994. Rising wage inequality: The United States versus other advanced countries. In *Working under different rules*, edited by Richard Freeman. New York: Russell Sage Foundation.

Hirschman, Albert. 1973. An alternative explanation of contemporary harriedness. *Quarterly Journal of Economics* 87: 634–47.

Hochschild, Arlie. 1997. *The time bind*. New York: Metropolitan Books.

Hounshell, David. 1974. *From the American system to mass production*. Baltimore, Md.: Johns Hopkins University Press.

Hunt, Alan. 1996. *Governance of the consuming passions*. New York: St. Martin's Press.

Inkeles, A. 1983. *Exploring individual modernity*. New York: Columbia University Press.

Jencks, Christopher. 1992. *Rethinking social policy: Race, poverty, and the underclass*. Cambridge: Harvard University Press.

Johnson, P., and S. Webb. 1993. Explaining the growth in UK income inequality, 1979–1988. *Economic Journal* 103: 429–35.

Kahneman, Daniel. 1998. Assessments of individual well-being: A bottomup approach. In *Understanding well-being: Scientific perspectives on enjoyment and suffering*, edited by D. Kahneman, E. Diener, and N. Schwartz. New York: Russell Sage Foundation.

Kahneman, D., P. Slovic, and A. Tversky. 1979. *Judgement under uncertainty*. Cambridge: Cambridge University Press.

Katz, Lawrence F., Gary Loveman, and David Blanchflower. 1995. A comparison of changes in the structure of wages in four OECD countries. In *Difference and changes in wage structures*, edited by L. Katz and R. Freeman. Chicago: University of Chicago Press.

Katz, Lawrence F., and Kevin Murphy. 1992. Changes in relative wages, 1963–1987: Supply and demand factors. *Quarterly Journal of Economics* 107: 35–78.

Kramarz, F., S. Lolliver, and L. P. Pele. 1994. Wage inequalities and firm-specific compensation in France. Working paper. Paris: INSEE (Institut National des Statistiques et Études Économiques).

Krugman, Paul. 1992. The right, the rich, and the facts. *American Prospect* 11: 19–31.

———. 1995. *Development, geography, and economic theory*. Cambridge: MIT Press.

Krugman, Paul, and Robert Lawrence. 1993. Trade, jobs, and wages. Working paper no. 4478. Cambridge, Mass.: NBER.

Lawrence, Robert, and Matthew Slaughter. 1994. International trade and American wages in the 1980s: Giant sucking sound or small hiccup? *Brookings Papers on Economic Activity* 2: 161–226.

Lazonick, William, and Mary O'Sullivan. 1997. *Organizational learning and international competition: The skill-base hypothesis.* Annandale-on-Hudson, N.Y.: The Jerome Levy Economics Institute.

Leamer, Edward. 1994. Trade, wages, and revolving door ideas. Working paper no. 4716. Cambridge, Mass.: NBER.

———. 1995. A trade economist's view of U.S. wages and globalization. Los Angeles: UCLA Anderson Graduate School of Management. Photocopy.

Lebergott, Stanley. 1993. *Pursuing happiness: American consumers in the twentieth century.* Princeton, N.J.: Princeton University Press.

———. 1996. *Consumer expenditures: New measures and old motives.* Princeton, N.J.: Princeton University Press.

Lundvall, Bengt-Ake, ed. 1996. *National systems of innovation: Toward a theory of innovation and interactive learning.* London: Pinter.

Lury, Celia. 1996. *Consumer culture.* New Brunswick, N.J.: Rutgers University Press.

Lynn, Robert. 1971. *Personality and national character.* Oxford: Pergamon Press.

Madrick, Jeffrey. 1996. *The end of affluence: The causes and consequences of America's economic dilemma.* New York: Random House.

Maskell, P., H. Eskelinen, I. Hannibalsson, A. Malberg, and E. Vatne. 1998. *Competitiveness, localised learning, and regional development: Specialisation and prosperity in small economies.* London: Routledge.

Maslow, Abraham. 1954. *Motivation and personality.* New York: Harper & Row.

Miller, Daniel. 1998. *A theory of shopping.* Ithaca, N.Y.: Cornell University Press.

Mishel, Lawrence, Jared Bernstein, and John Schmitt, eds. 1998. *The state of working America, 1998–99.* Ithaca, N.Y.: Cornell University Press.

Nickell, Stephen, and Brian Bell. 1995. The collapse in demand for the unskilled and unemployment across the OECD. *Oxford Review of Economic Policy* 11: 40–62.

Park, W. G. 1995. International R&D spillovers and OECD economic growth. *Economic Inquiry* 33: 571–91.

Porter, Michael. 1990. *The competitive advantage of nations.* New York: Free Press.

Powell, Walter W., and Paul DiMaggio. 1992. *The new institutionalism in organizational analysis.* Chicago: University of Chicago Press.

Rauscher, Michael. 1993. Demand for social status and the dynamics of consumer behavior. *Journal of Socio-Economics* 22: 105–13.

Richardson, J. David. 1995. Income inequality and trade: How to think, what to conclude. *Journal of Economic Perspectives* 9, no. 3: 33–55.

Rosenberg, Stephanie. 1999. Survey of ethnic food markets in East Los Angeles. Client project. Los Angeles: UCLA Department of Urban Planning.

Sachs, Jeffrey, and Howard Schatz. 1994. Trade and jobs in U.S. manufacturing. *Brookings Papers on Economic Activity* 1: 1–84.

Schor, Juliet B. 1991. *The overworked American.* New York: Basic Books.

———. 1999. *The overspent American: Upscaling, downshifting, and the new consumer.* New York: HarperCollins.

Scitovsky, Tibor. 1976. *The joyless economy: An inquiry into human satisfaction and consumer dissatisfaction.* New York: Oxford University Press.

Scranton, Philip. 1997. *Endless novelty: Specialty production and American industrialization, 1865–1925.* Princeton, N.J.: Princeton University Press.

Sen, Amartya. 1987. *The standard of living.* New York: Cambridge University Press.

Slater, Don. 1997. *Consumer culture and modernity.* Oxford: Polity Press.

Storper, Michael. 1999. Globalization, localization, and trade. In *A handbook of economic geography,* edited by G. L. Clark, M. Feldman, and M. Gertler. Oxford: Oxford University Press.

Storper, Michael, and Yun-chung Chen. 1999. Globalization and localization in the OECD and the EU: An empirical analysis and search for alternative explanations. Paper presented at the DRUID Summer Research Conference, Rebild, Denmark, June.

Storper, Michael, and Robert Salais. 1997. *Worlds of production: The action frameworks of the economy.* Cambridge: Harvard University Press.

Tawney, R. H. 1952. *The acquisitive society.* London: G. Bell and Sons.

Tolliday, Stephen, and Jonathan Zeitlin, eds. 1992. *Between Fordism and flexibility: The automobile industry and its workers.* London: Berg.

Tomes, Nigel. 1986. Income distribution, happiness, and satisfaction: A direct test of the interdependent preferences model. *Journal of Economic Psychology* 7: 425–46.

Urry, J. 1995. *Consuming places.* London: Routledge.

Utterback, James. 1996. *Mastering the dynamics of innovation.* Boston: Harvard Business School Press.

Veblen, Thorstein. 1976 [1899]. *The theory of the leisure class.* New York: Penguin.

Veenhoven, Ruut. 1993. *Happiness in nations: Subjective appreciation of life in 56 nations.* Rotterdam: Erasmus University Press.

Wilson, William Julius. 1987. *The truly disadvantaged.* Chicago: University of Chicago Press.

Wood, Adrian. 1994. *North-South trade, employment, and inequality: Changing fortunes in a skill-driven world.* Oxford: Clarendon Press.

———. 1995. How trade hurts unskilled workers. *Journal of Economic Perspectives* 9: 57–80.

The Dialectics of Still Life:
Murder, Women, and Maquiladoras

Melissa W. Wright

> *Ambiguity is the pictorial image of dialectics, the law of dialectics seen at a stand-*
> *still. This standstill is utopia and the dialectical image therefore a dream image.*
> *Such an image is presented by the pure commodity: as fetish. Such an image are*
> *the arcades, which are both house and stars. Such an image is the prostitute, who*
> *is saleswoman and wares in one.* — Walter Benjamin, *Reflections*

Over a period of five years in the late 1990s, almost two hundred women were found murdered and dumped along the desert fringes of the Mexican industrial city of Ciudad Juárez.[1] On 21 March 1999, another young woman was found half-buried in the desert and bearing signs of rape and torture. Most of these women ranged in age from their teens to their thirties, and many worked in the export-processing maquila factories that have been operating in Mexico for more than three decades.[2] As international and national attention occasionally turned to these brutal murders, a number of stories emerged to explain the troubling phenomenon.

DIALECTICAL SUSPENSION

In this essay, I examine the image of the Mexican woman formed within these narratives with Walter Benjamin's notion of a dialectical image.[3] The dialectical image is one whose apparent stillness obscures the tensions that actually hold it in suspension. It is a cacsura forged by clashing forces. With this dialectical image in mind, I see the Mexican woman depicted in the murder narratives as a life stilled by the discord of value pitted against waste. I focus on the narrative image of her, rather than on the lives of the murder victims, to reveal the intimate connection binding these stilled lives to the reproduction of value in the maquiladoras located in Ciudad Juárez. Through a comparison of a maquiladora narrative of categorical disavowal of responsibility for the violence with another maquila narrative explaining the mundane problem of labor turnover, the Mexican woman freezes as a subject stilled by the tensions linking the two tales.

In the tale of turnover that is told by maquila administrators, the Mexican woman takes shape in the model of variable capital whose worth fluctuates from a status of value to one of waste. Variable capital refers to the labor power—what the worker provides in exchange for wages—that produces a value in excess to itself (see Harvey 1982). The excess coalesces into surplus value. Marx says that labor power is a form of variable capital since it is worth less than the value of what it produces. In the turnover story, the value of the Mexican woman's labor power declines over time even as her labor provides value to the firm. Furthermore, this deterioration produces its own kind of value as she furnishes a necessary flow of temporary labor. Her labor power is subsequently worth less than the value of her labor in a number of ways, given that her labor is valuable also for its inevitable absence from the labor process. Where the maquila spokespeople deny any similarity between the women described in the tale of turnover and those described in the stories absolving the maquilas of any responsibility in their murders, I endeavor here to locate the connections.

"Turnover" refers to the coming and going of workers into and out of jobs, and it often comes up during interviews in relation to the problem of worker unreliability. Industry analysts and administrators cite turnover as an impediment to a complete transformation of the maquila sector from a low-skilled and labor-intensive industry to one with more sophisticated procedures staffed by highly skilled workers (see Villalobos, Beruvides, and Hutchinson 1997). Workers who turn over, that is, who do not demonstrate job loyalty, are not good prospects for the training necessary for creating a skilled base. This form of variable capital is therefore the temporary kind. The turnover problem, however, has not completely inhibited the development of a higher technological base in the maquilas because some workers are not of the turnover variety. Training programs, combined with an emphasis on inculcating loyalty among workers, have created a two-tiered system within maquila firms for distinguishing between the "untrainable" and "trainable" workers. Gender is a critical marker for differentiating between these worker brands.

Benjamin (1969) provides a good point of departure for this feminist interrogation into one of Marx's (1977: 481) staple concerns: the dehumanizing process behind forming variable capital, which, he writes, "converts the worker into a crippled monstrosity." Through the image of dialectical stillness, Benjamin helps explain how this process involves not only the creation of value at the worker's expense but also a value that is valorized only insofar as it is counterposed to what it is not: waste. The kinship between discourse and materiality is key. In the maquilas, managers depict women as untrainable laborers; Mexican women represent the workers of declining value since their intrinsic value never appreciates into skill but instead dissipates over time. Their value is used up, not enhanced. Consequently, the Mexican woman personifies waste in the making, as the materials of her body gain shape through the discourses that explain how she is untrainable, unskillable, and always a temporary worker.[4]

Meanwhile, her antithesis — the masculine subject — emerges as the emblem of that other kind of variable capital whose value appreciates over time. He is the trainable and potentially skilled employee who will support the high-tech transformation of the maquila sector into the twenty-first century. He maintains his value as he changes and develops in a variety of ways. She, however, is stuck in the endless loop of her decline. Her life is stilled as her departure from the workplace represents the corporate death that results logically from her demise, since at some point the accumulation of the waste within her will offset the value of her labor. And after she leaves one factory, she typically enters another and begins anew the debilitating journey of labor turnover.

The wasting of the Mexican woman, therefore, represents a value in and of itself to capital in at least two respects. First, she establishes the standard for recognizing the production of value in people and in things: Value appreciates in what is not her. Second, she incorporates flexibility into the labor supply through her turnover. To use Judith Butler's formulation, this process reveals how discourses of the subject are not confined to the nonmaterial realm or easily shunted off as the "merely cultural" (Butler 1997). Rather, and as I endeavor to show here, the managerial discourses of noninvolvement in the serial murders of young female employees is indeed linked to the materialization of turnover as a culturally driven and waste-ridden phenomenon attached to Mexican femininity. The link is the value that the wasting of the Mexican woman — through both her literal and her corporate deaths — represents for those invested in the discourse of her as a cultural victim immune to any intervention.

In what follows, I begin by describing some of the stories commonly told to provide explanation for the murders. Then I present an analysis of the turnover narratives.

THE MURDER STORIES

Circulating through the media and by word of mouth — as onlookers try to determine if the murder victims were prostitutes, dutiful daughters, dedicated mothers, women leading "double lives," or responsible workers — is the question: "Was she a good girl?" The question points to the matter of her value as we wonder if she is really worthy of our concern.

When news of these murders first captured public attention in 1995, Francisco Barrio, then governor of the State of Chihuahua, raised this question when he advised parents to know where their daughters were at all times, especially at night. The implication was that "good girls" don't go out at night, and since most of these victims disappeared in the dark, they probably weren't good girls. The local police have regularly posed this issue when bereaved parties seek official assistance in locating their daughters, sisters, mothers, cousins, and family friends. The police frequently explain how common it is for women to lead "double lives" and ask the grieving and frightened family and friends to consider this possibility (Limas Hernández 1998). By day, she might appear the dutiful daughter, wife, mother, sister, and laborer, but by night she reveals her inner prostitute, slut, and barmaid. In other words, she might not be worth the worry.

Related to this story of excessive female heterosexuality is a "foreign serial killer" plot woven by the special prosecutor appointed to the case. In this tale, we hear of how these murders are far too brutal for a Mexican hand and resemble events more common to the country's northern neighbor. The idea here is that a suave foreigner appeals to a young woman's yen for sexual adventure, lures her into his car, and then murders her after having sex. On this theory, an Egyptian with U.S. resident status, working in the maquiladora industry, was arrested in 1996, but since then another hundred bodies have surfaced.

This version ties into the long-standing Mexican tradition of casting Ciudad Juárez as a city whose cultural values have been contaminated by greedy and liberal forces emanating from the United States (Tabuenca Córdoba 1995–96). Such was the narrative woven by a Spanish criminologist, José Parra Molina, contracted by Mexican officials in 1998 to examine the crimes. He surmised that Ciudad Juárez was experiencing a "social shock" due to an erosion of its "traditional values" resulting from contact with a "liberal" American society. Consequently, he concluded, you now "see in the maquiladora exits . . . the women workers seeking adventure without paying attention to the danger" (Orquiz 1998: 3C).[5] The logic internal to this narrative explains that exposure to the United States has eroded traditional Mexican values to such a degree that young women are offering themselves, through their impudent behavior, to their murderers. This criminologist, among others, suggested that these women and girls could also be walking into traps set by an international organ-harvesting ring that kills the victims for their organs, which are sold in the U.S. market. The problem here, according to this story, is a cultural one. In such a cultural climate, such murders are bound to happen, and thus, a cultural shift is required to "sanitize" the environment in which women along the border live and work. The cultural decline is found within the girls themselves. As the Spanish criminologist asked in reference to the discovery of a girl's body, "What was a thirteen-year-old girl doing out at night anyway?" Evidence of her presence outside her home in the nighttime does not prove her economic need or a city full of nighttime commuters. Rather, her presence in the night points toward a cultural decline within which her death, a form of absence, can be logically anticipated. Indeed, her absence ameliorates, to some degree, the cultural decline represented by her presence in the night since it takes her off the street for good. Her death is explained as a cultural corrective to the decimation of traditional values. As the Spanish criminologist said, these girls out at night are "like putting a caramel in the door of an elementary school." When somebody gobbles them up, like children with candy, at least the source of the tawdry temptation is destroyed.

I characterize this rendition as a "death by culture" narrative, which points to forces internal to a cultural system that are driving the deviant behavior. Death by culture is Uma Narayan's (1997) characterization of the global discourses for explaining women's death in the Third

World as somehow embedded in tradition, internally driven, and resulting from the distortion of "traditional" cultural values. The above murder narratives recreate the possibility that these women and girls are not only victims of a culture gone out of whack but also emblems of the loss of values. They represent cultural value in decline and in consequence are possibly not valuable enough in death to warrant much concern. When we find girls and women out on the streets at night, seeking adventure, dancing in clubs, and free from parental vigilance, we find evidence of diminished value in their wasted innocence, their wasted loyalty, and their wasted virginity. The logical conclusion is, therefore, not to seek the perpetrators of the crime as much as to restore the cultural values whose erosion these women and girls represent.

A number of *Juarense* activists and local women's groups have countered these murder narratives with a version of the victims as poor and hardworking members of the community who deserve more public attention than they are receiving. Through editorial writing and public appearances, these advocates warn that a "climate of violence against women" pervades the city. They identify male jealousy of wives'/girlfriends' economic independence and sexual and social liberty as motivating factors behind the crimes as well as behind police reluctance to treat the murders seriously. And they have met with the principal maquiladora trade association (AMAC) in the city to ask for assistance in curbing the violence. During one meeting, the director of AMAC explained that he saw no connection between the industry and the murders. The message was that, even though thousands of workers have to cross unlit, unpatrolled, and remote stretches of desert as they make their way to the buses that stop only on main thoroughfares, and even as many victims disappear while on such commutes, there is nothing that the industry can do to stop the violence. Rather, the industry's stance is that no degree of funding for security personnel, or outlays for improved streetlighting, or in-house self-defense workshops, or changes to production schedules will help.

This position has not changed noticeably even in light of more obvious connections linking maquiladora industrial activity with the murders. For instance, in March 1999, when the driver of a maquiladora bus raped, beat, and left a thirteen-year-old girl who worked in an American-owned maquiladora to die in the desert (she miraculously recovered and named her attacker), activists implored the maquiladoras to acknowledge some connection between the murders and the city's industrial activity. One activist, Esther Chavez Cano, who is also the director of the city's new rape crisis center, said, "This case is absolutely horrible. The maquilas should have as much trust in the bus drivers as they have in the managers. This is an example of how terrible things are in this city" (Stack and Valdez 1999). The maquiladoras have yet to respond to this indictment, and their position appears to be much the same as it was when the spokesperson for AMAC was interviewed in January 1999 by ABC.[6] He cited female sexuality and nighttime behavior as the principal issues. In making this point, he queried, "Where were these young ladies when they were seen last? Were they drinking? Were they partying? Were they on a dark street? Or were they in front of their plant when they went home?" The silent corollary to this statement is the understanding that "men will be men," especially macho men, and if a woman is out drinking or partying or dancing on Juárez Avenida, then she should be prepared for the risks.

The AMAC spokesperson is invoking a death by culture narrative to absolve the maquiladora industry of any implication in the violence. The maquila narrative depicts the murdered women as cultural victims of machismo combined with Third World female sexual drives and rural migrant naïveté. It gains purchase with the city's long-standing reputation as a cultural wasteland, where American contamination and loose women have led to moral decay (Sklair 1993; Tabuenca Córdoba 1995–96). And in such a cultural milieu, the murdering of women cannot be avoided. Their deaths are only symptoms of a wasting process that began before the violent snuffing-out of their lives. All the sorting through of the victims' lives illustrates the deep, cultural roots of waste; for, as we scrutinize the victims' sexual habits and sift through the skeletal and clothing remains, we are supposed to wonder all the while, "What was *she* doing there anyway?" What sort of culture devours its own?

My interest lies in the similarities linking this death by culture narrative with descriptions of labor turnover. In the story of turnover, the Mexican woman also plays a leading role. She is the culprit of extreme turnover as well as the reason some measure of turnover is necessary for profit. She emerges in this story as a dialectic image built of both waste and value. Her odd configuration has roots in the cultural construction of female sexuality, motherhood, and a fleeting work ethic. It also has roots in the physiognomy of the Mexican female form — in her nimble fingers and sharp eyes that eventually, and always eventually, stiffen and lose their focus. The manager of any maquila faces the challenge of having to monitor this wasting process, which, again, according to the turnover narrative, is a culturally driven cycle whose deleterious effects on women's working lives are inevitable. The maquila industry is helpless to divert this culturally driven, corporate death.

TURNOVER AND CORPORATE DEATH

To understand how, in the maquiladora context, the story of turnover produces a female Mexican subject around a continuum of declining value, we must examine it in relation to the value-enhancing process of training. As turnover refers to the coming and going of workers, "training" refers to the cultivation of worker longevity and firm loyalty. Both processes unfold through the materialization of their corresponding subjects: a temporary, unskilled labor force and trained, loyal employees, respectively. Trained workers are those whose intrinsic value has matured and developed into a more valuable substance, whereas temporary workers do not develop or transform over time. They simply leave when their value is spent.

Seeing turnover and training in this light adds another dimension to Marx's analysis of variable capital. The value of labor power varies not only because it produces value, as Marx urges us to consider: Labor power varies also because it produces waste. The laborer who is worth less than her labor is, in the story of turnover, eventually worthless even as she creates value. The trained subject, by contrast, is one whose intrinsic value increases over time and matures into a more valuable form of labor power, one that is skilled. As one American manager of a U.S. automobile manufacturer in Mexico put it, "Our goal is to take someone who just walked in the door and turn this person into a different kind of worker. Someone whose basic abilities have matured into something special."[7] Skilled labor power does not vary from the value that it produces to the extreme degree that unskilled labor does. Of course, there is some variation; otherwise profit would not be produced. At issue here is not the precise calculation of the dollar amount of profit that skilled labor creates but instead a sense that the more valuable the labor that goes into the production process, the more valuable the commodities emerging from it. The German general manager of a hi-fi sound systems manufacturer explained the situation to me this way: "To make quality goods, you need quality workers. . . . We still need some unskilled workers. Some of this work is still just assembly. But now we've got products that require people who are willing to learn something new."

Marx begins his analysis of capital with the commodity precisely to demonstrate that the products of capital cannot be understood without seeing their intimate relationship to the people who make them. He, too, was extremely concerned with subjectivity even though he over-determined the parameters for considering what sorts of subjects mattered in his analysis. My view of skill as a negotiated quality of value assigned to labor power takes its cues from feminist analyses of the valorization of workers and work and the formation of skill categories. Feminist scholars have demonstrated that we must consider how perceptions of the subject inform perceptions of the value promised by that subject's labor power and how skill is key for the differential valorization of the labor force (McDowell 1997; Cockburn 1985; Elson and Pearson 1981). This feminist contribution does not replace a Marxian analysis but rather, as I hope becomes clear in the following, reveals how poststructuralist theorizations of subjectivity are not necessarily at odds with a Marxian critique of capital (see Joseph 1998). Critical for Marx was an exploration of how value materializes as it does in capital, as we continually make abstract connections linking human energies with inanimate objects. Marx made this point clearly, but he failed to recognize how the many forms of labor abstraction that are categorized variably as degrees of skill complicate the relationship, linking the value perceived in laborers to the value perceived to be embodied in the commodities they make.

Events over the last decade reveal how maquiladora boosters and managers recognize the tight connection between perceptions of worker quality and recognition of the sorts of products workers can make. There are now about thirty-one hundred maquiladora facilities in Mexico, with a total employment of more than one million workers. Almost one-fourth of these workers are employed in maquiladoras located in Ciudad Juárez, and approximately 60 percent of these employees are women. Since the late 1980s, efforts to "skill up" the maquiladora labor force in the maquila industry have coincided with a concerted push by city developers and industry spokespeople to stress the labor market's ability to accommodate the global focus on product quality over quantity (Carillo 1990). Industry proponents, mindful of the heightened competition for foreign direct investment by Asian countries guaranteeing even lower minimum wage rates for an immense labor supply, have emphasized that the city offers not only vast amounts of unskilled labor but also a sizable labor force that is trainable in just-in-time organizational systems, computer technologies, and even research and design capabilities. "Our workers can do anything here with some training, make the best products in the world," the director of a Juárez development firm told me. Rarely is the claim made that this labor force *already* exists in the city. Instead, emphasis rests on the *potential* transformation of the existing labor market into one that will one day be brimming with skilled workers. In 1994, the administrator at one of the largest and most prestigious maquiladora development consultant firms explained the potential this way: "We know that if Juárez is going to prosper into the future, we have to adapt. And we already are. You don't find sweatshops opening here like before. Now we have high-technology companies, and they are looking for workers who can be trained. We are having more of these workers now, and they will help this city grow in the right direction." One highly lauded example of this sort of growth has been the General Motors Delphi Center, which opened its doors in 1995. In a *Twin Plant News Staff Report* article, "Brain School," the director of Chihuahua's Economic Development Office exclaimed, "The Delphi center will revolutionize industrial production in our area." His view was seconded by a maquila manager who explained: "Without a doubt the most significant change has been the high technology manufacturing. . . . It just proves how the Mexican worker has been able to assimilate the ways of American business" (1997: 39).

Sorting subjects into trainable and untrainable groups, then, is a first step toward upgrading that minority of the maquila labor force that will eventually assimilate to the demands of a dynamic global economy. Distinguishing between the trainable and the untrainable—the "quitters" and the "continuers" (Lucker and Alvarez 1985)—requires an evaluation of employees early in their careers in order to put them on the right track, either the unskilled or the skilled one. The Brazilian manager of a factory that manufactures automobile radios explained, "We can tell within one week if the operator is training material. It's obvious from the beginning." The principal marker of the untrainable subject is femininity. As feminist histories of industrialization have noted, the notion of women's untrainability has a genealogy far beyond the maquila industry (Fernández-Kelly 1983). The specificities of this untrainable condition vary depending upon how the relations of gender unfold within the matrices of other hierarchical relations found within the workplace: the family, heterosexuality, race, and age—to name but a few. In the maquilas, the discourse of female untrainability plays out through explanations that describe what women do well as "natural" (dexterity, etc.) and that explain the cultural constitution of Mexican femininity as adverse to training. "Most of the girls aren't interested in training. They aren't ambitious," the same manager of the automobile radio manufacturer told me. "I have tried to get these women interested in training," the American manager of an automobile firm explained, "but they don't want it. They get nervous if they think they will have to be someone else's boss. It's a cultural thing down here. And if they're not ambitious, we can't train them."

This culturally ingrained lack of ambition, nervousness with responsibility, and flagging job loyalty create the profile of an employee whose untrainable position cannot be shifted through training. When I asked the human resources manager of a television manufacturer how he could recognize those workers who were involved with in-house training programs, he said, "Well, most of the workers in the chassis assembly [all are women] aren't taking training. They're not as interested. Most of our trained workers come from the technical and materials handling [completely male-staffed] areas." The gendering of work positions in this particular firm, as in many others, also revealed a gendering of trainability and the skilling-up of the maquila labor force. There are no statistics calculating the percentage of women participating in the multitude of training programs offered throughout the city in addition to in-house training opportunities. However, my interviews with the managers of seven "high-tech" maquilas and with instructors who offer maquila training programs indicated that women represented fewer than 5 percent of those enrolled in any type of skills training. The rate of female promotion into positions defined as skilled in three high-tech firms was even less than that.

As a result, Mexican women are said to be the principal contributors to turnover, because untrainable workers are those who demonstrate the lowest degree of longevity on the job. "If you have a plant full of these girls," the Mexican general manager of a sewing operation explained, "then you're gonna have high turnover. And you can't train workers in that kind of environment." Although the trade journal literature rarely mentions gender as a variable in any maquiladora-related phenomena, managers are quick to mention sex difference as a key component of their "turnover problem." The Brazilian plant manager of a television manufacturer elaborated on this connection. "We have about 70 percent females here. That means high turnover. Sometimes 20 percent a month. Now the guys also sometimes leave but if they get into a technical position . . . they usually stay longer. Our turnover is high because we have so many girls." The American human resources manager of this same firm said, "You can't train workers if they won't stay around. That's the problem with these girls. You can't train them. They don't understand the meaning of job loyalty." The tautology described in this turnover narrative revolves around the following syllogism: Women are not trainable. Trained workers remain with the same firm longer than untrained ones. Therefore, women do not have any corporate loyalty.

Minimized, if not completely missing, from this narrative, and from the many articles dedicated to the "turnover problem" in the industry literature (see Beruvides, Villalobos, and Hutchinson 1997; Villalobos, Beruvides, and Hutchinson 1997) is a consideration of how the pigeonholing of women into the lowest-waged and dead-end jobs throughout the maquilas contributes to their high turnover rate. Instead, within the maquila narrative of female unreliability, we hear how her intrinsically untrainable condition cannot be altered through training. There is no remedy for her situation, at least none that the maquila industry can concoct. Even though trade journal articles abound that make the connection between training and enhancing worker loyalty, these lessons do not apply to her. Meanwhile, Mexican men who are relative newcomers to the industry are the ones climbing the ranks into skilled and higher-salaried positions, while Mexican women remain where they have been for more than three decades, in the positions with the least skill, least pay, and least authority. In fact, recent press attention to the skilling-up of the maquila labor force and renovation of the industry reveals the masculine image of the new maquila trained and trainable subject (Wright 1998). Things are changing in the maquilas, we know, not because women are changing but because Mexican men are. They have added a masculine and trainable dimension to the once only unskilled, feminine labor force. As the American human resources manager of a television manufacturer put it, "The men are more involved in the new technologies here. They are changing the industry." The women, meanwhile, in their status as "untrainable" employees, represent what does not change about the maquilas.

However, it is critical to bear in mind that the untrainable Mexican woman is not completely worthless to the firm, for if she were, she would not continue to be the most sought-after employee in the maquiladora industry. Local radio stations frequently air advertisements promising good jobs, the best benefits, and a fun social atmosphere for young women seeking employment. Some maquilas contract agencies to recruit women throughout the city's scattered neighborhoods and migrant squatter settlements. These agencies generally seek female employees and sometimes are often expected to recruit one hundred women for a particular firm in a single day. As an employee of one such agency explained in an interview with a local newspaper in July 1998 (Guzmán 1998: 5), "The agency offers jobs to both sexes, masculine and feminine, but for the moment, they are looking only for women to work in the second shift."

Women are so explicitly in demand for a number of reasons. Discourses that detail a blend of natural qualities combined with cultural proclivities establish the Mexican woman as one of the most sought-after industrial employees in the Western Hemisphere. For one thing, as throughout industrial history, Mexican women are still coveted for what are constructed to be the feminine qualities of dexterity, attention to detail, and patience with tedious work (Elson and Pearson 1989). They are, therefore, perfectly suited for the minute, repetitious tasks that still constitute much of contemporary manufacturing and information processing. Adding to the attractiveness of their supposedly natural abilities is the widespread perception of their cultural predisposition to docility and submissiveness to patriarchal figures. These discourses outline a figure who is not only aptly designed for assembly, sewing, and data entry but who, unlike her northern counterparts, is also seen to be thankful for the work, unlikely to cause trouble, and easily cowed by male figures should thoughts of unionization cross her mind. Discourses of this sort explain, in part, why, since the passage of NAFTA, maquilas have been setting up operations at an unprecedented pace and have continued to employ more women than men across the industry, even as they emphasize trainability.

Another property underlying the Mexican woman's popularity among maquiladora executives is the inevitability of her turnover. Her lack of corporate loyalty is, in the proper proportion, a valuable commodity since her tendency to move into and out of factory complexes reinforces her position as the temporary worker in a corporate climate that responds to a fickle global market. This need is well explained in a 1998 *Wall Street Journal* article (Simison and White 1998) about the General Motors Delphi operation: "Delphi says it relies on rapid turnover in border plants to allow it to cut employment in lean times and add workers in boom times." Part of what is so valuable about the Mexican woman is the promise that she will not stick around for the long haul. Her absence represents for the firm the value that flexibility affords it in a flexible market economy.

Turnover itself is, therefore, not necessarily a waste but the by-product of a process during which human beings turn into industrial waste. The trick facing maquila managers is to maintain turnover at the proper levels. Excessive turnover means that women are leaving at too high a rate for the firm to extract the value from their dexterous, attention-oriented, patient, and docile labor. An insufficient degree of turnover, however, represents another form of waste: an excessive productive capacity. For this reason, articles appear regularly in the principal industry journal, *Twin Plant News,* offering advice on how to manage the "very real problem" of *high* turnover (see Beruvides, Villalobos, and Hutchinson 1997; Villalobos, Beruvides, and Hutchinson 1997). Turnover that is too high (as opposed to turnover that is just right) means that unskilled workers are leaving before they have exhausted their value to the firm. The desired rate of turnover most often quoted to me was 7 percent annually, and that requires that most of the new workers remain at least one year. "If we could get these girls to stay here two years," the human resources manager of the automobile radio factory said, "then I would be happy . . . after that they always move on and try something new." The problem with turnover, therefore, is not that the women leave. Rather, the problem has to do with the timing of their departure in relation to the rate at which their value as workers declines with respect to the value of their turnover.

This task of monitoring the correct turnover rate requires a measurement of the amount of value residing in the labor of the Mexican woman who labors in unskilled work. Such measures are necessary in order to balance the value of her productive capacity as an active laborer with the value of her turnover. How does the value of her presence measure against the value of her absence? This is the question that maquila managers constantly pose, and they rely upon a cadre of supervisors and engineering assistants to figure it out. These lower-level managers track the march of repetitive tasks through the bodies of the female laborers who occupy the majority of such jobs through the industry. They watch for signs of slower work rates resulting from stiff fingers, repetitive stress disorders, headaches, or boredom (Wright forthcoming). And they note declining work performance in order to justify a dismissal without eligibility for severance pay. As the Brazilian manager of a television manufacturer told me, "This is not the kind of work you can do for years at a time. It wears you out. We don't want the girls here after they're tired of the work." In this, as in many other maquilas, an elaborate system of surveillance focuses on the work primarily performed by women workers on the assembly line (Salzinger 1997). Furthermore, according to my informants, any worker who reveals an interest in expressing grievances or organizing worker committees is routinely subject to harassment if not immediate dismissal. The Mexican human resources manager of an outboard motor company said, "We have a policy not to allow workers to organize. It's like that in all the factories. . . . These lawyers [the ones involved in union activities] are lying to the workers and trying to trick them. We try to protect them from this." Workers with feisty attitudes are thus not very valuable to the firm either. So if a Mexican woman loses her docility, one of her values has been spent.

Another method for monitoring the depletion of value in the bodies of women workers involves the surveillance of their reproductive cycles. Women seeking employment in a maquiladora commonly have to undergo pregnancy tests during the initial application process (U.S. Department of Labor 1998; Castañon 1998). The scrutiny of their reproductive cycles, however, does not end there. Also common is the continued monitoring of their cycles once they begin work. Reports vary depending upon the age of the employee and the particular factory, but a number of women have described to me and to others how on a monthly basis they are forced to demonstrate that they are menstruating to the company doctor or nurse. In several facilities, women have been pressured to show their soiled sanitary napkins. "They even make the *señoras* do it," one woman explained. "They treat us like trash." This pregnancy test is hardly fail-safe, and a number of women explained how they got around it. One who worked for a television manufacturer said, "I was pregnant, so I sprinkled liver's blood on the napkin. They never knew. But when I started to show, my supervisor got really mean." She was then moved into an area that required that she stand on her feet all day and lift heavy boxes. "I left because I was afraid for the baby." Harassment of pregnant women is common, although illegal, and demonstrates that once a woman displays a pregnancy, she is ripe for turnover. "This is not a place for pregnant women," one supervisor in a machine shop told me. "They take too many restroom breaks, and then they're gone for a month. It slows us down."

These procedures revolve around a dialectic determination of the female subject as one continuously suspended in the ambiguity separating value from waste. She is a subject always in need of sorting because eventually the value of her presence on the production floor will be spent while the value of her absence will have appreciated. The sorting must occur in order to maximize the extraction of her value before declaring her to be overcome with waste. This inevitability, according to the death by culture logic, is driven by a traditional Mexican culture whose intrinsic values are in conflict as women spend more time outside the home. The many characteristics that the managers attribute to Mexican women as a way to explain high turnover, such as a lack of ambition, overactive wombs, and flagging job loyalty, represent cultural traits that are designed to check her independence. She might be subverting some cultural traditions by working outside the home, but her culture will ensure that she not go too far afield by inculcating her with a disposition that makes her impossible to train, to promote, or to encourage as a long-term employee. The maquilas are helpless to divert the forces of a culture that, in effect, devours its own, as women's careers are subsumed to such ineluctable traditional pressures.

Her disposability, then, represents her value to the firm since her labor power eventually, as it is a cultural inevitability, will not be worth even the cost of her own social reproduction, which is the cost of her return to the workplace. And she, the individual who comes to life as this depleting subject, experiences a corporate death when her waste overrides her balance, because, as David Harvey (1982: 43) put it, "The laborer receives . . . the value of labour power, and that is that." Turnover is, therefore, this turning over of women from those offering value through their labor power to those offering value through the absence of their labor. And as they repeat their experiences on this continuum while occupying jobs for several-month stints in different maquilas, their own lives are stilled as they move from one maquiladora to the next in a career built of minimum-wage and dead-end jobs. These women experience a stilling of their corporate lives, their work futures, and their opportunities inside and outside the workplace that might emerge were they to receive training and promotions into jobs with higher pay and more prestige.

All the managers cited above agreed that the turnover rate could not be diminished by corporate measures such as higher salaries and benefits. The American human resources manager of the television manufacturer responded, "These girls aren't here for a career. If we raise the wages, that would have a negative effect on the economy and wouldn't produce any results. Turnover comes with the territory down here." The American general manager of the motorboat manufacturer said, "Turnover is a serious issue here, especially in the electronic work that the female operators do. But that's how they are. They're young and looking for experiences. You just have to get used to it down here. . . . I don't think wages would make any difference." The Mexican general manager of the television manufacturer replied, "Wages aren't the answer to everything, you know. Most of these girls are from other places in Mexico. They don't have much experience with American attitudes about work. And that's why we have problems with turnover." The German general manager of the electronic assembly plant explained, "We always try to cut down on turnover, but we don't expect to get rid of it. That wouldn't be realistic. Not in Juárez."

Within such interviews lurks a death by culture narrative, which absolves the maquila industry of any responsibility in the repeated corporate deaths experienced by most of their female workers. By spinning a tale full of vague referents to the obstinate turnover condition of Mexican women, they are explaining how turnover is part and parcel of a cultural system immune to maquiladora meddling. The specificities of that culture are not the issue. Instead, it is the exculpation of the maquila industry from any responsibility in guiding a turnover process that serves their purposes in some critical ways. Consequently, maquila preventive measures would be fruitless or even a further waste. Competitive wages, training programs for women workers, day care, flexible work schedules, attention to repetitive stress disorders, or a compassionate stance toward maternity would not, according to this narrative, make one whit of difference. These Mexican girls and women are going to turn over, as they always do, because of who they are. Turnover is part of their cultural constitution. And, as the women come and go, one after another, day after day, the managers exclaim their impotence against the wasting of women workers. These women, they maintain, are victims of their culture. Their eventual corporate deaths are evidence of death by culture.

DEATH BY CULTURE

In a March 1999 interview, a research psychiatrist from Texas Technical University who specializes in serial murders commented to the *El Paso Times* that these Juárez murderers "tend to 'discard' their victims once they get what they want from them" (Stack and Valdez 1999). Such a vision of the Mexican woman as inevitably disposable is common to both the murder and turnover narratives. At the heart of these seemingly disparate story lines is the crafting of the Mexican woman as a figure whose value can be extracted from her, whether it be in the form of her virtue, her organs, or her efficiency on the production floor. And once "they," her murderers or her supervisors, "get what they want" from her, she is discarded.

The vision of her disposability, the likelihood that this condition could exist in a human being, is what is so valuable to those who extract what they want from her. When she casts the shadow of the consummate disposable laborer whose labor power is not even worth the expense of its own social reproduction, she is a utopian image. In this particular manifestation, the Mexican woman is the utopian image of a culturally victimized variation of labor who guarantees her replacement — after being worn down by repetitive stress syndrome, migraines, or harassment over pregnancies — with fresh recruits who are, perhaps, leaving another place of employment for one of the same reasons. That the same women are turning over as they move from one place to another does not disrupt the utopian image of their constant decline as part of their continuum toward disposability. Quite the contrary, their value circulates through their continual flow from one factory to the next, since as a woman leaves one place of work, perhaps having been dismissed for missing a menstrual period, and then enters another once her menstrual flow resumes, she again represents value. Her fluctuation between value and waste is part of her appeal for her employer.

This image of the female worker as the subject formed in the flux between waste and value provides her contours as a variation of capital. With such a constitution, she can be nothing other than a temporary worker, one whose intrinsic value does not mature, grow, and increase over time. And therefore, as a group, Mexican women represent the permanent labor force of the temporarily employed. The individual instances of this subject come and go, as women deemed wasteful to a firm's project are replaced by new recruits. Her cultural constitution is internally driven and immune to any diversionary attempts by the industry to put Mexican women on a different path. Instead, she will repeat the pattern of women before her and perpetuate the problem of turnover so valuable to the maquilas.

Such a utopian image of the Mexican woman as a figure permanently and ineluctably headed toward decline, always promising that her labor power will be worth less than the cost of her own social reproduction, evokes Benjamin's elaboration of the fetish. Benjamin renovated Marx's analogy of the fetish as phantasmagoria to refer not only to the social relations of the market embedded in the commodity but also to the social relations of representation that were sustained in the commodity. According to Susan Buck-Morss (1989: 82), Benjamin's concern with "urban phantasmagoria was not so much the commodity-in-the-market as the commodity-on-display." Benjamin's point is that the mechanics of representation are as critical to the creation of value as the actual exchange of use values in the marketplace.

The fetish of the Mexican woman as waste in the making offers evidence for Benjamin's view of the fetish as an entity "on display." As a figure of waste, she represents the possibility of a human existence that is perhaps really worthless, and this representation is valuable in and of itself. If we really can see and believe in her wasted condition, then she opens up a number of valuable possibilities for numerous people. For the managers of the maquiladora industry, her worthlessness means they can count on the temporary labor force that they need in order to remain competitive in a global system of flexible production. The image of the murder victims—many of them former maquila employees abducted on their commutes between home and work—also represents value for the industry as cultural victims. Through the descriptions of Mexican cultural violence, jealous machismo, and female sexuality, maquiladora exculpation finds its backing. No degree of investment in public infrastructure to improve transportation routes, finance lighting on streets, boost public security, or hold safety seminars in the workplace will make any difference. Others can also benefit from the widespread and believable representation of the Mexican woman as waste in the making. The perpetrators of serial murders, domestic violence, and random violence against women can count on a lack of public outrage and official insouciance with regard to their capture. And the city and state officials in Chihuahua who are concerned about their political careers, under the public scrutiny of their effectiveness in curbing crime, can defer responsibility.

The stories of this wasting and wasted figure must always be told since, to adapt Butler's (1993: 8) calculation to my purposes, the naming of her as waste is also "the repeated inculcation of the norm." The repetitive telling of the wasting woman in the turnover and murder stories is requisite because of her ambiguity: the waste is never stable or complete. The possibility of her value—of fingers still flexible or of a murdered young woman who was cherished by many—lurks in the background, and so the sorting continues as we search for evidence of the wasted value. Her dialectic constitution is suspended through the pitting of the two antithetical conditions that she invariably embodies. We find this dialectic condition through the questions that ask: Is she worthy of our concern? Are her fingers nimble or stiff, her attitude pliant or angry, her habits chaste or wild? Through the posing of such questions, her ambiguity is sorted as if it were always present for the sorting. Meanwhile, she hangs in the balance.

NOTES

I would like to thank Rosalba Robles, Miranda Joseph, Esther Chavez Cano, Sarah Hill, Felicity Callard, Erica Schoenberger, David Harvey, David Kazanjian, Michael Denning, Alys Weinbaum, Brent Edwards, Neil Smith, Carol A. Breckenridge, the anonymous reviewers at *Public Culture,* and the participants at the University of Chicago Center for Gender Studies workshop for their comments on earlier versions of this essay, although any inconsistencies or lapses are mine alone. Research for this project was partially funded by the National Science Foundation.

1 The number of murders varies, depending upon the sources, from about one hundred forty to more than two hundred. Local activists in Ciudad Juárez have voiced a suspicion that not all of the murders are brought to public light, and for this reason I am persuaded that the larger number represents a more accurate assessment of the scope of the problem. My material for this essay derives from interviews and research conducted over a several-year period of ethnographic fieldwork in Ciudad Juárez, Chihuahua.

2 The word *maquila* is a shortened form of *maquiladora,* which refers to the export-processing factories located in Mexico that assemble appliances, electronics, and clothing; it also refers to data processing in high-technology operations.

3 Much of my discussion of Benjamin's theory of dialectics draws on Susan Buck-Morss's (1989) account.

4 My discussion of the woman as waste in the making is informed by the conceptualization of waste as a continual negotiation elaborated by Sarah Hill (1998).

5 All translations are provided by the author.

6 John Quinones interviewed Roberto Urrea, president of AMAC, on the 20/20 television program of 20 January 1999.

7 I conducted this and other interviews that I draw on throughout the text during a several-year period of ethnographic research within specific maquiladoras located in Ciudad Juárez. I specify the nationality of the managers in this text in order to demonstrate how a cultural explanation is widespread throughout the industry among managers of many nationalities. All the interviewees reported on here are men, with the exception of one human resources manager. I also use the problematic referent of "American" as it is used by my informants and commonly along the Mexico-U.S. border to identify residents and citizens of the United States who do not identify themselves as Mexican.

REFERENCES

Benjamin, Walter. 1969. *Reflections: Essays, aphorisms, autobiographical writings,* edited by Peter Demetz and translated by Edmund Jephcott. New York: Harcourt Brace Jovanovich.

Beruvides, M. G., J. R. Villalobos, and S. T. Hutchinson. 1997. High turnover: Reduce the impact. *Twin Plant News* 13 (3): 37–40.

Buck-Morss, Susan. 1989. *The dialectics of seeing: Walter Benjamin and the arcades project.* Cambridge: MIT Press.

Butler, Judith. 1993. *Bodies that matter: On the discursive limits of "sex."* New York: Routledge.

———. 1997. Merely cultural. *Social Text* 52–53: 265–77.

Carrillo, Jorge V., ed. 1990. La nueva era de la industria automotriz en México. Tijuana: COLEF.

Castañon, A. 1998. Buscan igualdad laboral. *El Diario de Ciudad Juárez,* 10 October, 3C.

Cockburn, Cynthia. 1985. *Machinery of dominance*. London: Pluto Press.

Elson, Diane, and Ruth Pearson. 1981. Nimble fingers make cheap workers: An analysis of women's employment in Third World export manufacturing. *Feminist Review* 8: 87–107.

———, eds. 1989. *Women's employment and multinationals in Europe*. Basingstoke, U.K.: Macmillan.

Fernández-Kelly, María Patricia. 1983. *For we are sold, I and my people: Women and industry in Mexico's frontier*. Albany: State University of New York Press.

Guzmán, R. 1998. Empresas maquiladoras buscan mano de obra en colonias. *El Diario de Ciudad Juárez*, 24 July, 5.

Harvey, David. 1982. *The limits to capital*. Oxford: Basil Blackwell.

Hill, Sarah. 1998. Purity and danger on the U.S.-Mexico border. Center for U.S.-Mexican Studies discussion paper, University of California, San Diego.

Joseph, Miranda. 1998. The performance of production and consumption. *Social Text*, no. 54: 25–62.

Limas Hernández, A. 1998. Desprotección ciudadana. *El Diario de Ciudad Juárez*, 16 July, 11A.

Lucker, G. William, and A. Alvarez. 1985. Controlling maquiladora turnover through personnel selection. *Southwest Journal of Business and Economics* 2 (3): 1–10.

Marx, Karl. 1977 [1867]. *Capital: A critique of political economy*. Vol. 1. New York: Vintage.

McDowell, Linda. 1997. *Capital culture: Gender at work in the city*. Oxford: Basil Blackwell.

Narayan, Uma. 1997. *Dis-locating cultures: Identities, traditions, and Third World feminism*. New York: Routledge.

Orquiz, M. 1998. Asesinatos de mujeres: "Como dejar un dulce en un colegio." *El Diario de Ciudad Juárez*, 2 August, 3C.

Salzinger, L. 1997. From high heels to swathed bodies: Gendered meanings under production in Mexico's export-processing industry. *Feminist Studies* 23: 549–74.

Simison, R., and G. White. 1998. Mexico's growth may explain GM buildup there. *Wall Street Journal*, 13 July.

Sklair, Leslie. 1993. *Assembling for development: The maquila industry in Mexico and the United States*. San Diego: Center for U.S.-Mexico Studies.

Stack, M., and D. W. Valdez. 1999. Juárez girl accuses driver in attack. *El Paso Times*, 19 March.

Tabuenca Córdoba, Maria-Socorro. 1995–96. Viewing the border: Perspectives from the "Open Wound." *Discourse* 18: 146–68.

Twin Plant News Staff Report. 1997. Brain school. 12 (8): 39–41.

U.S. Department of Labor. 1998. Public report of review of NAO submission no. 9701. 12 January.

Villalobos, J. R., M. G. Beruvides, and S. T. Hutchinson. 1997. High turnover: What it does to production. *Twin Plant News* 13 (2): 41–44.

Wright, Melissa W. 1998. Maquiladora mestizas, and a feminist border politics: Revisiting Anzaldúa. *Hypatia* 13 (3): 114–31.

———. 2001. Desire and the prosthetics of supervision. *Cultural Anthropology* 16.

Freeway to China (Version 2, for Liverpool)

Allan Sekula

Today the relationship between the sea and the land is increasingly the opposite of what it was in the nineteenth century. Sites of production become mobile, while paths of distribution become fixed and routinized. Factories are now like ships: They mutate strangely, masquerade, and sometimes sail away stealthily in the night in search of cheaper labor, leaving their former employees bewildered and jobless. And cargo ships now resemble buildings, giant floating warehouses shuttling back and forth between fixed points on an unrelenting schedule.

The contemporary maritime world offers little in the way of reassuring and nostalgic anthropomorphism, but surrenders instead to the serial discipline of the *box*. The cargo container, an American innovation of the mid-1950s, transforms the space and time of port cities and makes the globalization of manufacturing possible. The container is the very coffin of remote labor power, bearing the hidden evidence of exploitation in the far reaches of the world.

The adjacent ports of Los Angeles and Long Beach are the biggest in the Americas; taken together they now rank third or fourth in the world in container volume. Massive "public" investments in new rail lines, bridges, and container and coal-export terminals, costing more than three billion dollars, will more than triple the cargo capacity of the port of Los Angeles. These infrastructure projects are largely hidden from public scrutiny, and the port remains unrecognized and invisible. In this sense, the port of Los Angeles is the very exemplar of the postmodern port: vast functionalized tracts for container operations built upon ever expanding landfill, far from the metropolitan center. No one would describe Los Angeles as a maritime city. A port with a present and an optimistic future, but oddly indifferent to its own past.

Plans for Los Angeles port expansion were based on optimistic projections of continued manufacturing growth in East and South Asia. The recent Asian economic crisis has called these projections into question. Falling currencies may raise hopes of export-driven "recovery" on the backs of impoverished workers, but the complex global logistics of the system create new blockages and economic sinkholes. The balance of trade slips radically, with many containers returning to Asia from Los Angeles holding nothing but air.

Crisis or boom, with its low wages, south China is now a primary industrial hinterland for the port of Los Angeles. The delirious (or cynical) official claim that the sunken rail lines of the new Alameda corridor "promise to create 700,000 jobs" rings hollow and begs the question, Where?

As one Los Angeles dockworker put it, gazing out at the rising bulwark of Pier 400, dredged up from the bottom muck of the outer harbor, "Pretty soon they'll just drive the containers over from China."

It would be too easy to say, roughly borrowing an old idea from Auden about the differences between Europeans and Americans, that the port of Liverpool embodies a past without a present, while the port of Los Angeles embodies a present without a past (this being known to optimists and official boosters as the *future*).

Los Angeles holds its own pasts in the shadow-zones of official memory: evicted native coastal fishers converted into mission slaves for the early-nineteenth-century Spanish and Mexican hide trade, hooded Klansmen attacking anarcho-syndicalists outside the Wobbly hall in 1923, striking longshoremen shot and herded into pens by the Los Angeles police in 1934, Japanese immigrant fishermen sent packing to desert internment camps in 1942, most of these last never to fish again. Of this avaricious and often bloody coastal past, we have some souvenirs, including a large billboard looming over Hollywood, a phalanx of slim young models wearing "Dockers" trousers, a fitting counterpoint to Ronald Reagan's pseudomemories of a secret longshoremen's plot to take over the Hollywood studio unions in the name of international communism.

And Liverpool has its own version of a Los Angeles–style "invisible" maritime future: the headquarters of the Mersey Docks and Harbour Company retreats from the triumvirate of grand edifices at Pierhead, a modern corporation seeking coward's shelter in a glass bunker shielded behind the Seaforth gates. Inside, the company's officers refine an Orwellian discourse, erasing their own agency: workers "fire themselves."

But I would like to think that there are odder and more idiosyncratic connections between the ports of Los Angeles and Liverpool, less obvious than the intimate transatlantic links long established between Liverpool and New York.

Oceans apart, each port had its roster of remarkable working-class writers and intellectuals from the 1930s and 1940s: the Slovenian immigrant Louis Adamic, source of inspiration for a new generation of radical writers on Los Angeles, who wrote while clerking at the old pilot station at the mouth of the main channel in San Pedro, or the novelists John Fante and Chester Himes, all three ironists with senses of the absurd to match those refined by Liverpool's great working-class expressionist seafarer writers—James Hanley, George Garrett, and Jim Phelan.

And yet another link: halfway to the present, a junior-high-school student struggling in vain to imitate the accent of Ringo Starr, and later playing clumsy street football with the Music Machine, who practiced loudly down the street in a one-car stucco garage, unknown then to be the missing link between the British Sound and the future L.A. underground rock of the 1970s. Sean Bonniwell fading back as quarterback, lit cigarette dangling from his mouth, and telling us all to call radio stations and request "Talk Talk."

And despite the musically hipper neighbors, I harbored a secret fondness for Gerry and the Pacemakers, because, after all, the San Pedro ferry was about to be replaced by a suspension bridge I disliked and feared, especially after coming to school to learn that a cherished friend's father had been electrocuted while working on its looming green towers, so like the Golden Gate, but the color of seasickness and money rather than blood oranges. Ellen Rodriguez sitting there, stoically, in profile at her school desk, remembered all too vaguely as if she were an either studious or grieving figure in a Rivera mural, and my not knowing then and still not knowing what to say.

So here's the idea this time, no compensation for still not knowing. Trace a line of dockers' solidarity across the Pacific, from Freemantle and Sydney to Los Angeles. Set that line against the heavier line of transnational corporate intrigue, the line that seeks to strangle and divide and endlessly cheapen the cost of labor, the line that respects only the degradation of the "bottom line." Reverse the direction of the poet Charles Olson's reading of Melville's modernism: Melville's line tracing the American frontier's outward extension across the Pacific; his fore-knowledge, in 1850, of the "Pacific as sweatshop." Trace the thin line of resistance farther in reverse, crossing America and the Atlantic to Liverpool, great city of working-class toil, departure, refusal, and enjoyment.

The Liverpool dockers and their wives and families insist that theirs has been a "very modern" struggle, refuting the smug neoliberal dismissal of dock labor as an atavistic throwback to an earlier mercantile age. Postmodernists, who fantasize a world of purely electronic and instantaneous contacts, blind to the slow movement of heavy and necessary things, may indeed find this insistence on mere modernity quaint. (How *did* your tennis shoes get here from Indonesia, Mr. and Ms. Jogger?) But against the pernicious idealist abstraction termed "globalism," dockers enact an international solidarity based on intricate physical, intellectual, and above all *social* relationships to the flow of material goods. The dockers' line of contact extends outward from what is immediately at hand, to be lifted or stowed, and crosses the horizon to another space with similar immediacies. To sustain this solidarity, based on work, when work has been cravenly stolen away, is all the more admirable, sustaining hope for a future distinct from that fantasized by the engineers of a new world of wealth without workers. The dockers recognize this fantasy, and knowing full well that there can be no fully automated future, fathom its ugly secret motto: Everyone a Scab.

And ask Dave Sinclair to show his pictures, because he's been here in Liverpool all along the way, and has been thinking with the camera about the importance of the fence, and of grief.

Joan, Val, and Anne, three dockers' wives, in the pub the afternoon the docks dispute ended, January 1998. Photo © Dave Sinclair

The old American President Lines terminal, San Pedro, Port of Los Angeles, December 1992

Under the Hook (Triptych)

Offloading containers from the *President Adams,*
inbound from Hong Kong.

American President Lines terminal, Pier 300, Terminal Island, Port of Los Angeles, February 1997

Freeway to China 1

German engineer supervising the unloading of new
container cranes from the heavy-lift cargo ship *Teal*.
The cranes were manufactured for the German parent
company at a dockyard in Abu Dhabi, employing
Filipino and South Asian migrant laborers, then
loaded aboard the *Teal* for the long, top-heavy voyage
across the Indian and Pacific Oceans. Belgian owned,
the *Teal* is registered in the Netherlands Antilles, a
pervasive legal ruse that permits the hiring of a
cheaper — in this case Russian — foreign crew.

Freeway to China 2 (Portrait 1)

Mason Davis, welder and shipbuilders' union shop
steward on the *Teal–*Pier 300 project. Formerly
employed as a journeyman machinist at Los Angeles'
last remaining shipyard. Now most of the shipyard
work is gone: "This is my first real job in over a year."
When I try to track him down to give him a print
of this photograph, I'm told that he's left town for
New York, in search of work.

New Brighton, July 1999

Shipspotter

The Canadian container ship *Cast Performance* enters
the Mersey inbound from Montreal.

Late the next night I join a tug crew as they delicately
pull the same ship through the narrow Seaforth locks
and back out into the Mersey on its continuing
voyage. The work is difficult and as idiosyncratic as
the Mersey tides, and it seems evident that—despite
company threats to bring in replacement tugs from
Hamburg—had the tug crews felt empowered to stop
work in support of the dockers, the port of Liverpool
would have come to a standstill.

Liverpool, July 1999

Dockers Listening

Sacked Liverpool dockers listen to a radio call-in show responding to the Channel Four broadcast of *Dockers*, the film they cowrote.

CALLER #1: "Don't dockers know any other word but the F-word?"
CALLER #2: "We're becoming a Third World country."
CALLER #3: "A lot of factories have gone down in Liverpool because we weren't so militant."

Later that week I overhear two younger men discussing the film in furtive and embarrassed tones while they stand in line at McDonald's, grabbing a fast bite before they head off to their new jobs on the docks.

Capitalism and Autochthony:

The Seesaw of Mobility and Belonging

Peter Geschiere and Francis Nyamnjoh

A striking aspect of recent developments in Africa is that democratization seems to trigger a general obsession with autochthony and ethnic citizenship invariably defined against "strangers"—that is, against all those who "do not really belong." Thus political liberalization leads, somewhat paradoxically, to an intensification of the politics of belonging: fierce debates on who belongs where, violent exclusion of "strangers" (even if this refers to people with the same nationality who have lived for generations in the area), and a general affirmation of roots and origins as the basic criteria of citizenship and belonging.

Such obsessions are all the more striking since historians and anthropologists used to qualify African societies as highly inclusive, marked by an emphasis on "wealth-in-people" (in contrast to Europe's "wealth-in-things") and a wide array of institutional mechanisms for including people (adoption, fosterage, the broad range of classificatory kinship terminology). In many African political formations prior to liberalization, there was an important social distinction between *autochthons* and *allochthons,* but its implications were strikingly different from today. Often rulers came from allochthon clans who emphasized their origin from elsewhere, yet had privileged access to political positions. Since the late 1980s, in contrast, autochthony has become a powerful slogan to exclude the Other, the *allogène,* the stranger. Political liberalization seems to have strengthened a decidedly nonliberal tendency toward closure and exclusion (cf. Bayart 1996).

In certain respects, issues of autochthony and their violent impact on politics are a continuation of a much older preoccupation with ethnic differences: at least in some parts of Africa, the increasing currency of slogans about *autochtones* versus *allogènes* can be seen as marking a new form of ethnicity. In principle, ethnicity evokes the existence of a more or less clearly defined ethnic group with its own substance and a specific name and history. Precisely because of this specificity, ethnicity is open to debate and even to efforts toward deconstruction by alternative interpretations of history. Notions of autochthony have a similar effect of creating an us-them opposition, but they are less specific. They are equally capable of arousing strong emotions regarding the defense of home and of ancestral lands, but since their substance is not named, they are both more elusive and more easily subject to political manipulation. These notions can be applied at any level, from village to region to country. Autochthony seems to go together very well with globalization. It creates a feeling of belonging, yet goes beyond ethnicity's specificity. Precisely because of its lack of substance, it appears to be a tempting and therefore all the more dangerous reaction to seemingly open-ended global flows.

This emphasis on autochthony and belonging in politics is certainly not special to Africa: everywhere in our globalized world the increasing intensity of global flows seems to be accompanied by an affirmation of cultural differences and belonging. Unfortunately, eruptions of communal violence seem to be the flip side of globalization. For instance, there is a striking parallel between, on the one hand, attempts in Ivory Coast, Tanzania, and Zambia to disqualify eminent politicians—including Kenneth Kaunda, the father of the Zambian nation—on the grounds of foreign ancestry and, on the other hand, the strenuous efforts of politicians like Jean-Marie Le Pen in France or Jörg Haider in Austria to exclude "strangers" from citizenship (although both politicians run into great difficulties when they have to define who really belongs). In other modern democracies, and in Europe and North America as well, autochthony and roots have become major issues. They always were so in the Caribbean and other "plural societies" that can be considered products par excellence of globalization.

How is this upsurge of autochthony in very different parts of our globalized world to be explained? It may be reassuring to explain it away as the last flickering of some sort of traditionalist resistance against modern developments, but it is becoming ever more blatant that these movements are part and parcel of globalization processes as such. As many authors have stressed, the rapidly accelerating flows of people, goods, and images on a truly global scale not only lead to globalization, they trigger equally potent tendencies toward localization.[1] *Glocal-*

ization—to borrow an ugly but evocative shorthand for this ambiguity from Roland Robertson (1992)—seems to be a hotbed for preoccupations of belonging and autochthony. In such a perspective, cosmopolitanism and autochthony are like conjoined twins: a fascination with globalization's open horizons is accompanied by determined efforts toward boundary-making and closure, expressed in terms of belonging and exclusion (cf. Appadurai 1996).

There is some urgency in trying to gain more insight into such striking "paradoxes of flow and closure" (Meyer and Geschiere 1999), that is, into how globalization goes together with frantic attempts toward closure or how political liberalization in many parts of the world (and certainly in Africa) triggers an obsession with the exclusion of strangers and a highly nonliberal imaginary of autochthons versus allochthons as the basic political opposition. After all, millennial capitalism is marked not only by an accelerated opening of new peripheries for the world market, but even more strongly by frightening explosions of communal violence.[2]

It is tempting to analyze such paradoxes in terms of the tensions between, on the one hand, the increasing transnational character of capitalism that promotes an ever greater mobility of people, and on the other hand, the tenacity of the nation-state as a model that imposes boundaries and a tendency toward protectionism. Indeed, it is clear that Le Pen's and Haider's xenophobia is part of a desperate attempt to gain control over the nation-state, seen as the last defense of its citizens against the threat of globalization. In a somewhat different sense, it is quite striking that in Africa national regimes encourage people's obsession with belonging. Instead of promoting national citizenship, as implied by the idea of "nation-building" that dominated politics in the 1970s and 1980s, these regimes now seem to be more intent on producing "autochthons."

Yet it might be helpful to return globalization to history and to place its (or rather glocalization's) paradoxes in a longer historical perspective. In this respect, the focus of this volume on *capitalism*—a term that for some time seemed to go out of fashion among social scientists— is very relevant. In a longer time perspective, present-day dialectics of flow and closure in processes of globalization seem to be closely connected with certain contradictions in the unfolding of capitalism. Since the so-called victory of capitalism after the end of the Cold War, increasingly simplistic models of the market, with liberalization as its un-equivocal gospel, have become current (but cf. Bayart 1994 and Dilley 1992). For some, this victory is even supposed to bring "the end of his-tory." All the more important to emphasize in contrast that capitalism (or the market) still reproduces its own contradictions and therefore still produces history. One contradiction is of special importance to our theme of autochthony: Capitalism appears to be about the "free-ing" of labor as a necessary condition for creating a mobile mass of wage-laborers; yet in many instances it has also brought with it de-termined efforts to compartmentalize labor, imposing classifications — ever changing, but all the more powerful—in order to facilitate control over the labor market. Homogenization and exclusion are two sides of one coin in capitalist labor history, and this historical ambiguity seems to be a crucial factor in today's enigmatic intertwinement of globaliza-tion and autochthony.

In this essay we focus on Cameroon, and notably on its Southwest Province, which has recently become a hotbed of confrontations over autochthony and exclusion in direct relation to national politics. The southwest is one of the more economically developed parts of the coun-try. Already in the 1890s, the Germans (the first colonizers) had cre-ated a large-scale plantation complex here on the volcanic slopes of Mount Cameroon, near the coast. Throughout the twentieth century, these plantations attracted laborers from other parts of Cameroon and even from Nigeria. Capitalist agriculture did, therefore, lead to increas-ing mobility of labor in this region as much as elsewhere. To understand why autochthony has become such a fierce political issue in this par-ticular area, however, it is as important to emphasize that the specific ways in which labor was made available maintained and formalized dif-ferences within this labor force that would mark social relations in the region up until the present.

Southwest Cameroon certainly has its specificities, yet there are in-triguing (and quite worrying) parallels with developments elsewhere in Africa and in Europe. From a comparative perspective, this specific example may help to highlight the problems of a simplistic, but unfor-tunately prevalent, equation of capitalism with liberalization and ho-mogenizing notions of the individual. Historically, capitalist interests were as much involved in promoting the mobility of labor as in for-malizing cultural differences within the labor force (and thus freezing the boundaries of what used to be quite fluid communities). The example of southwest Cameroon illustrates this ambivalence particularly well. Closer attention to the seesaw in the evolution of capitalist relations between mobilizing and homogenizing the labor force on the one hand and formalizing difference on the other may help to explain the inherent link between globalization and communalism in its varying trajectories.

AUTOCHTHONY IN CAMEROON:
THE IMAGINARY AND THE LAW

On 14 February 1997, a train car full of gasoline capsized in the center of Yaoundé, the capital of Cameroon, spilling it onto a city square. This seemed to be a windfall for the many people who crowded the accident scene to fill tanks and bottles with the fuel. But when one man was so imprudent as to light a cigarette, there was a huge explosion that killed and wounded dozens of people. The same day *radio trottoir* (as the grapevine is called in Yaoundé) started to resonate with the rumor that "all victims were autochthons." According to our informant, this had a simple explanation: Local people had chased *les allogènes* from the spot of the accident, saying that it was their gasoline since it was their city. Consequently there were hardly any "strangers" left when the accident took place.[3] It is striking that radio trottoir considered even a horrible accident like this in terms of *autochtones* and *allogènes*.

The background to the increasing currency of these terms is the mounting tension in Yaoundé between the Beti people, who consider themselves locals, and the Bamileke people from western Cameroon, who are considered immigrants.[4] This tension is as old as the development of Yaoundé as the capital of the colony in the 1920s, when the city began to attract a growing number of people from the populous Grassfields area of western Cameroon. The exact numerical balance between the two groups within the city's present population is a subject of constant speculation, but the Beti fear that they have become a minority in their own city. Since 1990 this fear has attained new heights under political liberalization, because democratization evokes the specter of being outvoted by these strangers (many of whom have actually lived in the city for generations, some since 1918). It is in this context that notions like *autochtones* and *allogènes* have become so powerful in everyday life.

Indeed, the return of the country to multipartyism in 1990—in the context of the general wave of democratization in Africa and despite the tenacious resistance of President Paul Biya (who remains in power)—made the idea of autochthony a central political issue. Since then, there has been a constant proliferation of political parties. The most important parties are Biya's Cameroon Peoples' Democratic Movement (CPDM), the Social Democratic Front (SDF), with its main support among anglophones and francophones from the west; and the northern-supported Union Nationale pour le Développement et le Progrès (UNDP).[5] Democratization rapidly developed into a political stalemate between the CPDM, which remained in power (thanks to large-scale rigging of successive elections), and the SDF, as the main opposition party. More important than this proliferation of parties was the emergence of local and regional elite associations that were often actively supported by the Biya regime. These associations, although purportedly cultural and working for the development of the community, were usually more concerned with weakening the nationwide appeal of opposition parties like the SDF. Thus political liberalization was transformed into an effervescence of a new type of politics of belonging, often explicitly encouraged by the regime (see Nyamnjoh and Rowlands 1998; Geschiere and Gugler 1998).

This transition received pregnant expression in a series of new laws in the 1990s—not only in the successive electoral laws, but even in the 1996 constitution. A novel aspect of this constitution is that it mentions explicitly—in the preamble and in article 57, 3—the state's obligation "to protect minorities and preserve the rights of indigenous populations." Moreover, it requires that the chairperson of each regional council "shall be an indigene of the Region" while its "Bureau shall reflect the sociological components of the Region." There is a glaring contrast here with the preceding constitution (1972), which stated in the English version of its preamble:

> The people of Cameroon, proud of its cultural and linguistic diversity . . . profoundly aware of the imperative need to achieve complete unity, solemnly declares that it constitutes one and the same Nation, committed to the same destiny, and affirms its unshakeable determination to construct the Cameroonian Fatherland on the basis of the ideal of fraternity, justice and progress. . . . Everyone has the right

to settle in any place and to move about freely. . . . No one shall be harassed because of his origin.

The 1996 constitution replaced this emphasis on the rights of every national citizen with an emphatic respect for the rights of *minorities* and *indigenes*. These latter terms have a specific discursive background: they are borrowed from the discourse of the World Bank, which since the 1980s has increasingly stressed the need to protect "disappearing cultures." In the World Bank discourse, *minorities* and *indigenes* refer, for instance, to "Pygmees" and other hunter-gatherers, or to pastoralists. In Cameroon, however, these terms acquire a very different meaning and political impact (especially as the constitution makes no attempt to define them).

Striking illustrations are to be found in the successive electoral laws of the 1990s that seem to be intended mainly to protect locals from being outvoted by strangers. An elaborate set of rules and stipulations determines who may vote where. For presidential elections, section 8 of Law No. 92/010 (17 September 1992) requires that candidates be "Cameroonian citizens by birth and show proof of having resided in Cameroon for an uninterrupted period of at least 12 (twelve) months." One has to prove six months of continuous residence in a given locality to qualify to vote there, and to stand for elections in that locality one must be an indigene or a "long-staying resident" (this latter term is not further specified). Other requirements, not explicitly formulated in the law, are invoked by the Ministry of Territorial Administration (MINAT), which is both player and umpire.[6] During the consecutive presidential, parliamentary, and municipal elections of the 1990s, MINAT devised additional preconditions or used other diversionary tactics for determining who is allowed to stand candidate. The complicated electoral laws provide the government with precious opportunities to manipulate the electoral rolls in its favor while making matters extremely difficult for the opposition. For instance, it is common for opposition supporters to be told in the city where they live that they have to vote in their home area (village of origin), but once there they are informed by the local authorities that they have to vote where they live (in the city). In this way, many potential voters never make it to the polling station on election day. During every election, the newspapers carry stories about opposition voting lists that have been disqualified by MINAT, either for failure

place in the heart of Beti (that is, CPDM) country. In the fifties, Mongo Beti had gained international renown for his novels on life under colonial rule in Cameroon. But after independence he went into exile in France, fearing arrest by the authoritarian regime of Ahmadou Ahidjo, the country's first president. Nearly thirty years later, after political liberalization, he decided to return. Unfortunately, the scope for opposition still proved to be fairly limited. The idea that a prominent member of the Beti elite would stand candidate for the SDF was deeply shocking to most of the elite people of his own group, and Mongo Beti was subjected to a smear campaign as "traitor of his own people" (Nyamnjoh 1996: 14). As during the Sawa riots, this was the occasion for the government to intervene in a most drastic way: Invoking section 17 of the electoral code, it simply declared Mongo Beti's candidacy invalid since he had gained French nationality during his years in exile. Although many Cameroonians, politicians included, have a second nationality, this was not permitted for a Beti standing candidate against his own "brothers."

The "cultural associations" are clearly the government's alternative to opposition parties, but it would be too simple to see their flowering only as a product of manipulations by political elites in their quest for power. The omnipresence of the *autochtones-allogènes* opposition and the obviousness it has acquired in everyday life indicate that deeper issues are involved. Under democratization, questions such as "Who can vote where?" and even more important, "Who can stand candidate where?" acquired a pressing urgency and raised vital issues of belonging and citizenship. Cameroonians are acutely aware of what is at stake. The public debate, triggered by the new constitution and the subsequent Sawa demonstration, was joined by a broad scale of Cameroonian intellectuals, including academics and people abroad. At the end of 1996, for instance, CIREPE/Ethonet—a Cameroonian research bureau that includes academics from various universities—organized a large-scale survey in various regions of the country on issues of autochthony and belonging in politics. The researchers were happy—but apparently also quite surprised—to report that, at least according to the replies to their questions, the majority of Cameroonians did not support the growing emphasis on the tandem *autochtones-allogènes*. More than half the respondents said they opposed the use of such notions, and less than a fourth stated that such issues influenced their voting behavior (Zognong and Mouiche 1997a: 10). However, the authors themselves were clearly somewhat worried that the survey might have elicited normative replies rather than actual political practices. And indeed, the overall trend in the other contributions in the volume they edited indicates how difficult it is to escape from the conceptual tandem of *autochtones-allogènes* (Zognong and Mouiche 1997b).

Earlier, in May 1996, the Cameroonian journal *La Nouvelle Expression* had dedicated an entire issue to the topic of *Minorités, autochtones, allogènes, et démocratie* (1996). This issue offered a serious and consistent attempt to deconstruct these notions and to highlight their dangerous political implications. An essay by Professor Ngijol Ngijol of Yaoundé University provided a historical analysis of consecutive versions of autochthony and emphasized the dangers of including such an ambiguous notion in the very constitution of the country. Bertrand Toko showed how difficult it is to apply the notion of autochthony in cities that, like Douala and Yaoundé, from the very start of their urban development were populated by immigrants. He noted that it is all the more worrying that it is precisely in these cities that people invoke *autochtonie* as a self-evident basis for political and economic claims. Philippe Bissek raised the question as to why so many African regimes had recently seemed to bet on such primordial political slogans. These critical analyses were further enriched by relevant historical documents. However, the same issue of *La Nouvelle Expression* also contained other perspectives. For instance, in a long interview, Roger Gabriel Nlep, another academic from Yaoundé University, discussed his theory of *le village électoral*. To him "integration" was the central issue in Cameroonian politics. According to Nlep, people should be fully integrated in the place where they live, "but this supposes that there is not *un autre chez soi* (another home area)." Therefore, if somebody who was elected in Douala defended the interests of "his" village in another region, this should qualify as "political malversation" (*La Nouvelle Expression* 1996: 18).

In this interview with *La Nouvelle Expression*, Nlep was quite prudent in his discussion of *le village électoral*, but this very concept could be used quite differently. For instance, during the campaign for the municipal elections of 1996 and in subsequent interviews on Cameroonian television, Mola Njoh Litumbe, a politician from the southwest, interpreted the notion of *le village électoral* with more audacity, as meaning that urban migrants should go back to their village to vote—an interpretation reinforced by the regime's manipulations, discussed above, of electoral laws and voters' lists.[9] Others used even less prudent slogans in their defense of autochthony as a valid consideration in politics. For instance, Mono Ndjana (1997), a philosophy professor of the University of Yaoundé who was a very vocal supporter of the Biya regime, reproached "the" Bamileke for their *ethnofascisme* and denounced the arguments of his intellectual opponents as a *gauchissement du tribalisme* (leftist tribalism).

LAND AND FUNERALS AS CRUCIAL ISSUES OF BELONGING

Apart from the political issue—Who is to vote where?—two other issues are crucial for defenders of *autochtonie:* the access to land and, even more, the question of where someone is buried. In the 11 January 1993 *Le Patriote* (Yaoundé), Ava Jean painted a horror picture of Bamileke land hunger:

> The ideologists of western fascism in our country tell us that the Bamileke is a superior being . . . who has the right to settle anywhere in Cameroon. . . . They arrive somewhere, hands outstretched and mouth full of insults, begging for land in the name of national unity. Since it is common knowledge that Ewondo men cherish red wine, discussions take place in the bar nearby. Everything is settled. Then starts the shameful exploitation of Ewondo land. [Our translation]

The burial question is even more emotionally laden. For instance, Samuel Eboua, leader of the *Mouvement pour la Démocratie et le Progrès* and one of the grand old men of Cameroonian politics (former secretary-general at the president's office and former lecturer at the École Nationale d'Administration, the prestigious academy for civil servants) explained in an interview with Pascal Blaise that where one is buried is the crucial criterion of where one belongs: "Every Cameroonian is an *allogène* anywhere else in the country . . . apart from where his ancestors lived and . . . where his mortal remains will be buried. Everybody knows that only under exceptional circumstances will a Cameroonian be buried . . . elsewhere" (*Impact TribuUne*, 1995:14; our translation).

Indeed, the burial issue illustrates most vividly the extent to which these considerations permeate everyday life. In itself this is, again, not a new issue. In the 1970s, when President Ahidjo was still in power, radio trottoir spread the spectacular story of John Nganso, a Bamileke man from Kumba (the main town of the Southwest Province, so outside the Bamileke area) who aspired to become a government minister. Nicodemus Awasom (n.d.) summarizes the rumor thus:

> John Nganso was born circa 1940 in Kumba in British Cameroon [to] émigré parents from Dschang in the French Cameroons who had succeeded in escaping from the harshness of French colonial rule. . . . Nganso did his primary education in Kumba and proceeded to Nigeria and the United Kingdom for further studies. On his return to Cameroon, he joined the civil service and after the inauguration of the unitary state, he quickly rose to the rank of a Director in a government ministry, an achievement which was rare, if not impossible for an Anglophone. Nganso had acquired sufficient French and is alleged to have manipulated the ethnic card by identifying with Francophone Bamileke. Since he had the ambitions of rising beyond the rank of a Director, he had to integrate himself in the Bamileke caucus as a full-fledged Bamileke. He had to produce or show what did not exist: his late father's house and grave in Bamileke country as the supreme symbols of his Bamilekeness. Since his late father's compound and grave were found in Kumba, he could not convincingly pass for a Bamileke. The exigencies of his ambitions dictated that he had to acquire a compound in a Bamileke country he had never visited all his life and his father's corpse had to be exhumed and transported for reburial. Nganso had to undergo this ordeal to qualify as a Bamileke and a Francophone and renounce his disadvantaged Anglophone identity. Nganso's action provoked an uproar in Kumba where many Anglophones understood the political motives behind his act. The Ahidjo administration was so embarrassed by such sordid manoeuvres that Nganso was promptly dropped from his post. (12–13)

Nyamnjoh recorded another version of the story, according to which the Bamileke villagers told Nganso: "We do not know you. Show us your father's grave." At this, he had no other option than to disinter his father's body (buried in Kumba) and to bury it again in the ancestral village. The broad circulation of this story shows how convincing it is to people. Indeed, to many Cameroonians, burial location is *the* criterion for belonging. Some Bamileke migrants who had fled their home villages during the 1960s civil war and settled in the Southwest Province were said to have left explicit instructions with their children and grandchildren that they be properly buried (reburied) in their home villages once the situation had normalized.[10]

The issue in itself may not be new, but democratization and the renewed importance of the vote made such considerations all the more urgent in the 1990s. It is also against this background that slogans such as *le village électoral* were launched. Defenders of *autochtonie* never tire of repeating that immigrants, no matter how long they live in the city, still want to be buried in the village of their ancestors. And this—as the previous quotation from Eboua implies—shows where their basic loyalty is. As became clear with the Sawa movement, the conclusion to this line of thinking is that only autochthons should be allowed to stand candidates for important positions. It is also this logic of belonging that the government invokes to justify its endless manipulations of electoral lists. There is, indeed, a certain plausibility to the political logic of *autochtonie,* in view of the frequency with which urban migrants—even if they live for generations in the city, own land there, and build up their whole lives there—continue to bury their deceased in their village. Under political liberalization, such double commitments become all the more problematic.[11] Yet it is also clear that in practice notions of *autochtonie* lead to disturbing forms of exclusion.

The much discussed Association of the Elites of the Eleventh Province, founded in the Southwest Province, is a good example of how notions such as *autochtonie* or ethnic citizenship completely erode the ideal of national citizenship that had been central to former President Ahidjo's project of nation building in the 1960s and 1970s. As demonstrated above, issues of autochthony have been prominent in the Southwest Province, where the influx of plantation laborers since the 1890s has made the local population feel outnumbered and threatened. No wonder that democratization and the renewed importance of *belonging* in politics led to particularly fierce tensions in this area. It is in this context that the Association of the Elites of the Eleventh Province emerged. Already, the name is quite challenging, not to say enigmatic, since everybody knows that Cameroon has only ten provinces. Beltus I. Bejanga, the association's founding president, who teaches at the University of Yaoundé in the Central Province but considers himself an indigene of Kumba in the Southwest Province, explains the name in an interview with the *Herald* (Buea) (16 April 1997):

> The members of this association . . . are the children or grandchildren of our forefathers who came over from the former French Cameroon to the then Southern Cameroon (British). . . . These children or the grandchildren of these migrants had their education, training and everything in the British Cameroons and therefore they are members of what we call the Eleventh Province Association.

Asked why he chooses to call himself a member of this association instead of "identifying with where he was born," Bejanga continues with some heat:

> Exactly. We thought we belonged to where we were born—until recently SWELA [the South West Elites Association] was formed. In one of their meetings some of us attended but were driven out and called strangers who have no right to take part in the meeting. So we concluded that we didn't belong to English-speaking Cameroon, nor are we accepted in French-speaking Cameroon. . . . We want to draw the attention of the government to tell them that we are here, we are Cameroonians but have no statehood. The government should decide what to do with us.

Bejanga continues, emphasizing that "someone's home should be where you are born, where you went to school, where you live, where you have all your property." [12] But the *Herald* journalist quotes another elite from Kumba—probably a member of SWELA—who proposes to "refer to somebody's home as the place where he is buried when he dies." At this Bejanga gets really excited, apparently because he foresees that this criterion will make him a stranger in the area he considers to be his own:

> Will I claim my home when I am dead and buried? I think my home should not be where I will be buried, because I could die in the sea and my corpse never seen. . . . The government should step in and stop people from calling others "settlers" or "strangers." It is sometimes provocative. The government should say no to this.

This example vividly shows how vital an issue the place of burial has become. It shows also how the crucial role that regional and local elite associations came to play under political liberalization—a role that may affect political developments more than the proliferation of political parties—inevitably raises issues of autochthony and belonging. Encouraged by the government, SWELA became a major factor in regional politics, but one of the first things it did was to exclude so-called strangers like Bejanga—who until then considered himself a full-blown indigene of Kumba. Especially striking in the quotations above, therefore, is Bejanga's appeal to the government to set things right. This appeal can only be ironic, since Bejanga will know very well that the government is actively encouraging autochthony movements in the Southwest, if only to create a breach in the anglophone opposition. Indeed, with their ideology of autochthony, these elite associations are ideal remedies for the former one-party regime to contain the effects of multipartyism and remain in power (see also Konings and Nyamnjoh 1997).

PARALLELS IN AFRICA

This link between national regimes, autochthony, and elite associations seems to be a recurrent pattern in many African countries since the beginning of political liberalization. An issue of *Africa Today* (1998) on *Rethinking Citizenship in Africa* showed that in present-day Africa the theme of citizenship seems inevitably to raise issues of autochthony, minorities, and belonging. Bruce Heilman (*Africa Today* 1998: 371) noted that in Kenya, violence perpetrated by Kalenjin and Masai, as they defended "their" Rift Valley against "outsiders" such as the Kikuyu and the Luo, threatened to develop into true "ethnic cleansing" that was condoned by the national government. For Guinea-Conakry, Robert Groelsema (*Africa Today* 1998: 413) emphasized that the strong involvement of urbanized Guineans in hometown organizations created problems for democratization. The emphasis on belonging and autochthony seemed to be less divisive in countries where politicians succeed in depicting the whole nation as one unprivileged group vis-à-vis outsiders, as the articles in the same volume by Christopher Gray on Gabon or by Heilman on Tanzania suggested. This issue of *Africa Today* showed that although the question of autochthony is much older, it is especially since political liberalization in the late 1980s that issues of autochthony and belonging have penetrated into the very heart of national politics.

A striking example from Kenya was the famous—or notorious?—court case concerning SM's burial, discussed in the well-known book by D. W. Cohen and E. S. Atieno Odhiambo (1992). Upon the death of SM, an eminent Nairobi lawyer from the Luo clan, the question of where he should be buried became a fiercely contested issue between the elders of his Luo clan and his widow, who was a Gikuyu. Although his widow insisted on burying him in Nairobi, the Luo elders claimed that whatever his position in Nairobi and no matter how "modern" a figure he had been, SM was a Luo and therefore must be buried in the village. Interestingly enough, Oginga Odinga, the grand old man of Luo politics, sided with the Gikuyu widow and declared that this emphasis on burying at home was new. According to him, the Luo used to bury their dead in the area where they had migrated in order to confirm new claims. Even more striking was the national court of appeals reversal of the lower court verdict and its ruling in favor of the Luo elders. According to Cohen and Odhiambo, it was clear that the appeal court's decision was heavily influenced by a direct intervention from President Arap Moi himself. The Kenyan example shows again that authoritarian regimes often opt for supporting newfangled versions of autochthony as an effective means to contain the effects of multipartyism through subtle or not-so-subtle divide-and-rule tactics.

Of even more urgency is Mahmood Mamdani's (1998) study of the struggle of belonging in Kivu (East Congo) that led to an unprecedented degree of violence. By reconstructing the genealogy of the enigmatic Banyamulenge (who in the 1990s quite abruptly emerged as a major ethnic force in this area) and their changing role in the closely intertwined developments in Kivu and neighboring Rwanda, Mamdani analyzed both the long history of these tensions and the reasons they became explosive during the past decade. In this case, the Rwandan genocide and the subsequent movement of refugees acted as a catalyst. But this was further exacerbated by the opportunistic and fickle ways in which President Mobutu Sese Seko intervened in the conflict—especially after incipient political liberalization forced him to look for new points of support. Here again, the interaction between national politics and ideologies of *autochtonie* constituted a leitmotiv in these developments.

Parallel discourses on autochthony are certainly not limited to the African continent. It is striking, for instance, how much certain patterns in African discourses on *autochtonie* bring to mind the arguments of the New Right in Europe and its urgent summons to defend "ancestral lands" against threatening hordes of immigrants. Of the New Right prophets, one of the most vociferous and, until the late 1990s, most successful was Jean-Marie Le Pen, leader of the *Front National* (FN) in France. (Since the 1970s, he has regularly won 10 percent and more of the vote in various elections, and the majority vote in four municipalities in the southeast). The December 1998–January 1999 split in his party may have constituted a serious setback to his success. Nevertheless, because of his ideological fervor and also because relatively much has been written about him and the FN, Le Pen offers a convenient point of comparison with autochthony movements in Africa.[13] Precisely because there is an intricate mixture of differences and parallels, a comparison of the Le Penian discourse with that of the defenders of *autochtonie* in Cameroon might help to illuminate why such ideas seem to be so widespread and so appealing in the present configuration of our globalizing world.

A minor difference is that Le Pen consistently avoids — apparently because of possible problems with the law — terms like *étranger* and *autochtone;* yet the terms he uses instead (*immigré* and *Français*) have the same implications. Another difference is the emphasis in the French discourse on race and notably on color. Central to the FN's ideology is the fear of "wild immigration" and, since this refers notably to the threatening influx of Arabs and Blacks, color difference becomes a central obsession: The main danger is "a change in the nation's colour" (Taguieff 1985: 170). The emphasis on biological difference encourages the use of seductive biological metaphors: Le Penians like to describe the nation as an organism, for this enables them to argue that, as with any "healthy organism," it is only "natural" for the nation to defend itself against an invading illness (Taguieff 1996: 191). Such biological metaphors give the FN ideology a particularly slanderous tenor; for instance, when old colonial stereotypes about natives spreading contagious illnesses are raised: "[These immigrants] bring all sorts of illnesses with them into France . . . that constitute a heavy load on the French economic equilibrium . . . but endanger also the health situation of broad strata of the French population" (quoted in Taguieff 1985: 171; our translation of these and subsequent quotations from Taguieff).

In the Cameroonian version of autochthony, such biological connotations are largely absent, since there neither color nor other racial traits can serve as clear marks of distinction. Yet there is a similar emphasis on innate characteristics (for instance, the "greedy" Bamileke). At least as effective as the Le Penian emphasis on race in confirming the dangers of mixing with the Other are persistent rumors about different propensities toward witchcraft — for instance, that the Bamileke become rich only through their nefarious *famla* (witchcraft of wealth), while the Beti are forced to hand out the state's riches because of the jealous *evu* of their relatives.[14]

The biological emphasis in the discourse of Le Pen and his followers corresponds to a true phobia of *métissage* (mixing) in whatever form. This leads to urgent appeals to "purify" the nation in order to retrieve its "stolen identity" (*identité ravie*) (Lagrange and Perrineau 1996: 231). As Taguieff summarizes it, the "purification of the national body" demands a cleaning operation, since "clean France is supposed to be defiled by the presence of elements that are heterogeneous to its specific essence" (Taguieff 1985: 179, 188; see also Taguieff 1996: 180). Such metaphors of cleanliness and defilement inspire an ecological discourse — somewhat surprising in view of the FN's brutal environmental policies in the few communes where it has the majority — on the "beauty of France" that is threatened by *défiguration* (Taguieff 1985: 186–87). Although less explicit, there is an emphasis on purification in Cameroonian discourses as well. Persistent rumors accuse the Bamileke of making Yaoundé a dirty city with their organic refuse, but the latter are quick to put the blame on Emah Basile, the Beti government delegate. And Le Pen's celebration of the fields and forests of France, menaced by defilement (Taguieff 1996: 184), is reminiscent of Ava Jean's horror at how the Beti of Yaoundé, out of love for red wine, fritter away their ancestral lands to Bamileke strangers.

It is striking that important practical differences do not manifest themselves in the ideological discourse. In Cameroon, the main struggle is over the access of strangers to land, but in France the most direct source of tension is rather the idea that an increasing number of French people face unemployment because foreigners usurp jobs. In the ideology in France as much as in Cameroon, however, it is the notion of ancestral land that is of overriding importance. Indeed, despite these and many other practical differences that are no doubt of consequence, the similarities at the ideological level are striking. There is in both countries a strong emphasis on the "naturalness" of the autochthons' claims, backed up by what Taguieff (1985: 198) calls "the celebration of the natural community." Le Pen's urgent summons could be repeated by the Cameroonian autochthony advocates: "We have to act . . . and occupy our vital space, since nature abhors emptiness and if we do not occupy it, others will do so in our place. . . . All living beings are assigned vital areas by nature, in conformity with their dispositions and their affinities. It is the same for man and peoples" (Taguieff 1996: 186).

Such considerations are said to make the *défense identitaire* (defense of one's identity) not only perfectly legitimate but also urgent, and this then justifies the highly militant tone of the autochthony advocates both in Cameroon and in France. The FN journal *Le Militant* constantly repeats that time is pressing, since the French will soon be "minorities on the land of our forefathers. . . . Tomorrow it will be too late, tomorrow there will be no more French nation" (Taguieff 1985: 172). It is as if one is hearing the Sawa demonstrators shouting their slogans in the streets of Douala again.

Another common and crucial tendency is what Taguieff (1985: 181, 198) calls *la déréalisation* (the negation) of the individual by a *fétichisation* of belonging and origins: "The exaltation of the organic community imprisons . . . the individual . . . in the circle of its original belonging." Different patterns are possible here. In the Cameroonian theory of *le village électoral,* the emphasis on belonging is an attempt to exile nonautochthonous politicians from the city to their village and to remind them that they should strive to satisfy their ambitions there, in their own environment. In Le Pen's ideology the emphasis is rather on reminding the French that they are traitors if they do not respect their "belonging." We shall see below, however, that, in practice, there are quite surprising links between these seemingly opposite poles.

Cameroonian President Biya (with sword) refers to northwesterners who live in the south-west as "authoctones, settlers, political thorns in the flesh." Prime Minister Peter Mafany Musonge (in glasses), himself a southwesterner, calls them "strangers" and "Kam-no-Gos" and says to "Go No Kam Again." The Post (Yaoundé), 3 November 1997.

AUTOCHTHONY, GLOBALIZATION, AND THE PARADOXES OF CAPITALIST LABOR HISTORY

The major reason this comparison with the *Front National* in France is significant is that the upsurge of *autochtonie* in Cameroon (and in Africa in general) and Le Pen's success in France occurred at roughly the same time. In France, as in other European countries, the spectacu-lar electoral successes of the New Right in the 1980s came as a surprise. Even in the 1970s, few people had foreseen that these slogans would at-tract so much support. In Cameroon, it is only since the end of the 1980s that *autochtonie* became the overriding issue in national politics. What does it mean that parallel discourses emerge almost simultaneously and with such surprising force in highly different settings of our globaliz-ing world?

One tempting explanation for this simultaneity might be that such movements are a protest against accelerated globalization and the in-creased mobility of people it brings about. Indeed, proponents of these movements see immigration as a mortal threat to the *corps national* (Le Pen) and the safeguarding of the "ancestral land" (the Sawa movement in Douala). The influx of migrants evokes in both cases the specter of miscegenation and outside domination. Therefore complete closure of the borders—whether of the nation-state or the local community—is seen as an urgent necessity.

However, at closer inspection, the refusal of globalization by these movements is only partial. The Sawa movement or the Beti defense of the rights of the *originaires* (natives) are certainly not antimodern or antiglobal as such. On the contrary, the Sawa and Beti hatred of the "greedy" immigrants is strengthened by the idea that the immigrants profit more than the autochthons from new and highly coveted economic opportunities. Like these Cameroonian movements, Le Pen's FN is very eager to use the modern mass media to its advantage. Clearly these movements should be seen as part and parcel of globalization processes. They are the inevitable outcome of the ambivalence evoked by globalization's open-ended horizons that are both fascinating and frightening—or, as it was formulated above, the dialectics of flow and closure.

The case of southwest Cameroon is of special interest here because its tortuous labor history can help to place globalization's contradictions in a longer historical perspective. In this region it is particularly clear that present-day tensions between autochthons and strangers—the "kam-no-go" (came-no-go) referred to in the accompanying opposition newspaper cartoon—are directly related to the drastic ways in which, from the beginning of this century, capitalist interests tried to solve the pressing need for labor on the large plantations along the coast.[15] It became equally clear in this area that the imposition of capitalist labor relations required not only the freeing of labor that is always seen as necessary for capitalist development but at the same time its containment and compartmentalization. This tension between freeing and containing labor—between mobility and closure—seems to mark capitalist history elsewhere as well. With capitalism's supposedly definitive victory, there is no attention to such tensions in the neoliberal gospel that now seems to have attained such a stifling degree of self-evidence. Yet this seesaw of mobility and fixing has been crucial in setting the stage for the emergence of autochthony movements and communal violence in recent times.

In this respect, a crucial moment in the history of southwest Cameroon was the transition from German to British rule during the First World War.[16] Already in 1914, at the very beginning of that war, the

British had succeeded in conquering the extensive German plantations on the slopes of Mount Cameroon. Their reactions were somewhat mixed. On the one hand, they were clearly impressed by the whole complex, its infrastructure, and the concomitant provisions for the settlers. But soon they began to fear that this was something of a poisoned gift: for the next few years, the question of how to mobilize all the laborers needed for the maintenance of these huge plantations became an overriding problem. *Die Arbeiterfrage* (the labor problem) also had been a central issue in the German colony, leading to fierce clashes between the government and planters.[17] To the Germans, however, the solution was self-evident: Coercion was the only way to solve *die Arbeiterfrage*. There may have been constant debates about which forms of forced labor were the most opportune and about the extent to which the planters themselves should be allowed to apply force, but coercion was to be a fixed principle in the German version of "freeing labor."

To the first British officials on the spot after the conquest, it was equally self-evident that forced labor was against the very principles of British colonial policy. To them it was clearly unthinkable that the brutal and coercive German labor policies would be continued under British rule; however, this gave urgency to the question of how else sufficient labor could be mobilized. Several officials referred to the Gold Coast example of cash-crop production by local peasants as the obvious alternative: this implied that the plantations had to be divided into small holdings "to be leased to the natives of the country."[18] In 1917, however, they were in for a surprise when Sir F. D. Lugard, then governor of Nigeria, intervened. To him, there was clearly no question of dividing the valuable German plantation complex (which was, indeed, unique in West Africa). Moreover, he apparently felt that the district officers (DO's) were too sensitive in their objections to forced labor. Lugard's careful formulations are a masterpiece of keeping up appearances (the British cannot condone forced labor) and yet being practical (the German plantations have to be maintained at all costs). He felt that "we want to get to British methods, but to relax suddenly would be apt to encourage the natives in their naturally lazy ways." Furthermore, rather than a sudden policy switch, "the transition stage from being forced to go in and their going voluntarily must take some time," and to abruptly relax "iron discipline" might lead to chaos (BNA, Qd(a), Lugard, 11 October 1917). Accordingly, in the next few years the Resident in Buea ordered the various

DO's to deliver their contingent of laborers by whatever form of pressure they saw fit. The DO's were apparently appalled, as evidenced by Bamenda DO George Podevin's request for the Resident to send him the full text of Lugard's comments, not only the excerpt, "as it is somewhat difficult to understand his Honour's observations without these references." But the Resident refused this, using strong language to exhort his DO finally to take the recruiting of labor in his district seriously: "If you still persist in this passive resistance, it may be found necessary to remove you from Bamenda."[19] Apparently, even to the British, the desire to maintain the impressive plantation complex had priority over the official preference for the "peasant option."[20]

However, from 1920 on, the DO's in their annual reports announced triumphantly that labor was coming forth now "voluntarily" and that the controversial German recruiting methods no longer had to be followed. Did this mean that Lugard's prediction had been right and that the freeing of labor required coercion only during a short transitional period? It seems that more hidden forms of force did play a crucial role in this surprisingly rapid British solution to the labor problem. In the intervening years, the British system of "indirect rule" had been installed also in the populous Grassfields (the present-day Northwest Province). In their new role, the customary chiefs were made to mediate in the recruitment of labor, sending their contingents of "voluntary" laborers down to the coast. Even more important, at least initially, was the influx of laborers from the French part of Cameroon who were fleeing the wide array of forced labor imposed by the French. Thus pressures by customary chiefs and the French labor policies (notorious for their harshness throughout the interbellum period) made the transition to voluntary labor possible in the British area. However, this "solution" involved precisely the groups that are now at the heart of the autochthony issue in the southwest. Members of the Association of the Elites of the Eleventh Province, mentioned above, are the children and grandchildren of the refugee laborers from the French part of Cameroon who were never allowed to forget their external origin and now feel in danger of losing their citizenship because of the new politics of belonging triggered by political liberalization. And descendants of the immigrants from the Grassfields, sent by their chiefs to labor on the plantations, are the present-day "came-no-go" who are told to vote at home and not in the area where they live.

In southwest Cameroon, as elsewhere, the freeing of labor was a spasmodic process that was triggered by a complex interplay of mobilizing labor (largely through coercion) and compartmentalizing it (through preexisting labor controls).[21] In his path-breaking studies of labor relations on the plantations in southwest Cameroon, Piet Konings (1993, 1995) emphasizes the "high visibility of ethnic heterogeneity" on the plantations.[22] It is clear that the continuing role of particularistic networks in the recruitment of laborers played an important role in consolidating the divisions that have become so explosive in this area during the democratization process.

Indeed, this pattern has many parallels elsewhere in Africa. Throughout the continent, capitalist agencies tried to make "traditional authorities" play a role in the recruitment and control of laborers, often in an even more manifest way. As Konings emphasizes this in a more general article, "Two major prerequisites for capitalist development are (i) the procurement of a regular and adequate supply of labour and (ii) the establishment of managerial control over the labour process. . . . Chieftaincy in Africa has played a significant mediating role between capital and labour in the realization of capitalist objectives" (1996: 329). A. L. Epstein (1958), for instance, describes how for each ethnic group in the copper mines in Zambia, management imposed a separate system of "tribal elders" on the workers. Jeff Crisp (1984) and Carola Lentz and Veit Erlmann (1989) emphasize similarly the crucial role allotted to chiefs in the Ghanaian gold mines. In both cases, the efficacy of such impositions was limited, since laborers increasingly preferred to identify themselves as "workers" instead of "tribesmen."[23] Yet it is clear that management's reliance on "traditional authorities" (in reality, often neotraditional authorities) for controlling both the recruitment and the performance of the workers served to formalize and consolidate divisions within the labor force.

Konings (1996: 329) suggests that this pattern is especially characteristic of "areas where the capitalist mode of production has not yet deeply penetrated and . . . rural producers are still strongly rooted in non-capitalist forms of organization and value systems." Yet, in a more general perspective, such reliance on "traditional" demarcations might be reinforced by parallel efforts toward a compartmentalization of the labor force in order to facilitate control. For Europe as well, the long history of the freeing of labor seems to have been marked by a broad array of measures to classify the amorphous mass of potential labor, whether on the basis of its provenance or by dividing the work force through formal ranking. And throughout modern history, the paradox of both opening up and containing new labor reserves has been a crucial strand in capitalist policies all over the world. This is exactly the pattern that Le Pen evokes as some sort of specter. Indeed, there have been clear advantages in capitalist development, at least during certain periods, to tapping a reserve of cheap labor from outside the national borders and at the same time setting the outside laborers apart in order to play them off against the local workers. Similarly, there is a clear link in southwest Cameroon between the British solution to the labor problem on the plantations in the 1920s and the upsurge of autochthony as a particularly hot issue in this province more recently. The paradox that the "freeing" of labor as a crucial moment in capitalist development is intrinsically linked to the compartmentalization of the labor force provides the historical background to the spectacular re-creation of parochial identities today.

CONCLUSION: AUTOCHTHONY AND MILLENNIAL CAPITALISM

Why are autochthony and similar notions so appealing in the present-day constellation of our globalized world? The discussion above has shown that autochthony can best be studied as a trope without a substance of its own. It can be used for defining the Self against the Other on all sorts of levels and in all sorts of ways. Autochthony discourses tend to be so supple that they can even accommodate a switch from one Other to another. For the Bakweri of southwest Cameroon, for instance, the Other in the 1980s was primarily the francophones from eastern Cameroon, but in the 1990s it became (again) the Grassfielders of the Northwest Province. Yet this change could be accommodated within the same discourse. This suppleness may make such discourses better geared to the rapidly accelerating flows of peoples and images — and to the concomitant efforts toward closure — than more solid ethnicity discourses. If globalization is to be understood in terms of a continuing "dialectic of flow and closure," notions of autochthony, with their paradoxical combination of staggering plasticity and celebration of seemingly self-evident "natural givens," become an almost inevitable outcome of such dialectical tensions.[24] Their very plasticity keeps them geared to rapidly changing situations in which, indeed, even the Other is constantly becoming another.[25]

In this respect as well, however, globalization needs to be historicized. An obvious way to do this is to relate the kaleidoscopic metamorphosis of contemporary autochthony movements to longer-term contradictions in capitalist labor history. One of the dangers of the shallow models of capitalism that are increasingly current since the end of the Cold War is precisely that they can only interpret autochthony movements as tenacious forms of traditionalist resistance to modern developments. This may lead to a highly dangerous underestimation of the force of such movements.

The examples above have indicated the continuing relevance of the inherent contradictions in the development of capitalism to present-day issues. The paradoxes of capitalist labor history—the intrinsic relationship between the freeing of labor and countervailing tendencies toward its compartmentalization—set the stage for today's autochthony movements (and the concomitant threats of communal violence). This emphasis on inherent contradictions continues to be relevant for capitalism at the turn of the millennium as much as in earlier phases. Jean and John Comaroff (1999) show convincingly that such contradictions— for instance, between the heightened visibility of the capitalist consumer paradise and the more and more definitive exclusion of ever larger groups from it—become increasingly blatant. The same applies to the contradiction between the increasing mobility of people and more forceful forms of exclusion. Such a view of millennial capitalism as rife with contradictions (even if these are differently expressed from the Marxian ones) can help to historicize debates on globalization. Today's autochthony movements are more than simply a kaleidoscopic outcome of a play of flow and closure. In a longer time perspective they are intrinsically related to the contradictions of labor history in the earlier phases of capitalism.

NOTES

We owe special thanks to three Cameroonian colleagues, Margaret Niger-Thomas, Timothée Tabapssi, and Antoine Socpa, whose Ph.D. dissertations we supervised and whose research touches upon many of the issues discussed here. Pascal Perrineau gave valuable advice for the section on Le Pen and his *Front National* in France. Piet Konings helped us out with his great expertise on the labor history and recent political developments in southwest Cameroon. Moreover, we had the chance to profit from seminal comments by the participants of a Codesria conference on *Les Géographies de l'autochtonie* (organized by Mamadou Diouf and Peter Geschiere, Dakar, June 1999)—notably from Arjun Appadurai, Jean and John Comaroff, Mamadou Diouf, Mitzi Goheen, Achille Mbembe, Peter Pels, and Seteney Shami. Jean-François Bayart has been a true source of inspiration, as always.

1 For an overview of the literature, see Appadurai 1996 and Meyer and Geschiere 1999; see also Bayart, forthcoming, on globalization as "une combinatoire paradoxale de l'exacerbation des particularismes et de la prétention de l'universalité."

2 See Jean Comaroff and John Comaroff 1999 for a trenchant characterization of millennial capitalism; cf. Comaroff and Comaroff 1993.

3 Antoine Socpa, personal communication (June 1997).

4 Both ethnic names—like most ethnic names in Africa—are historical constructs subject to constant change. The Germans founded Yaoundé in 1889 in what for a long time was referred to as "Ewondo country" (*Yaund* is the German spelling of Ewondo), and the people of the area were referred to as *Ewondo*. The French, who conquered the main part of the colony during the First World War, made Yaoundé their capital in 1921. Lately, the term *Ewondo* has been superseded by the term *Beti*. This change is related to the crystallization of a larger ethnic bloc of forest peoples after President Biya, who is from the Bulu group, the southern neighbors of the Ewondo, came to power in 1982. Indeed, the present regime's ethnic policies have been highly instrumental in creating this wider sense of unity. The name *Bamileke* is purely colonial in origin: It seems to be a German corruption of a term by which their interpreters from the coast indicated "the people of the highlands." The highlands area in western Cameroon was (and still is) populated by a vast conglomerate of larger and smaller chieftaincies that were not united prior to colonial conquest.

5 The ethnic map of Cameroon is complicated by a distinction between anglophones and francophones that, especially since 1990, has become one of the major lines of opposition. After the First World War, the former German colony was divided between the French and British, with the result that cultural differences often fall along regional lines rather than the divide between anglophones and francophones. For instance the Bamileke—the francophone Grassfielders—have much in common culturally with the anglophone Grassfielders. The same is true for much of the anglophone Southwest Province, where people have more cultural similarities with francophones ("Sawa") of the Littoral Province than with the anglophone northwesterners.

6 The ruling CPDM party and government have consistently refused to establish an independent electoral commission.

7 A "Sawa" is "a man from the sea." Therefore, the notion of Sawa used to be evoked in order to express the unity of all "sea people." Indeed, there are close cultural, linguistic, and historical relations between the Batanga, the Douala, and some of the groups on the coast of the Southwest Province. Lately, however, the name "Sawa" has acquired such a broad meaning—somewhat parallel to the effort to create a larger Beti ethnic bloc—that it is supposed to include also the Bakweri, or even the Banyangi, still farther into the interior.

8 Cf. *Cameroun Tribune* (Yaoundé), 14 February 1996, 1; *Impact TribuUne,* April–June 1996. Cf. also Ava Jean in *Le Patriote* (Yaoundé), 11 January 1993.

9 In this context, politicians and authors often use the French distinction between *territoire* (territory, in a general sense) and *terroir* (area of belonging).

10 Dr. Stella Nana-Fabu, sociologist and third-generation migrant from Dschang, personal communication to Nyamnjoh, 25 May 1999.

11 Cf. Geschiere and Gugler 1998, especially the Introduction, on how the continuing importance of the village of origin for urban elites has led to a renewed vigor in many parts of Africa of "the politics of primary patriotism."

12 It is interesting that Bejanga does not refer here to the place where one works, since this would make him a person who belongs in Yaoundé.

13 For an overview of the literature on the FN, see Mayer and Perrineau 1996. It is important to emphasize that Le Pen and his successes are certainly not exceptional in Europe. In 1999, Jörg Haider in Austria became the most successful New Right leader in Europe in terms of the percentage of the national vote he won. Filip Dewinter in Belgium—whom journalists often describe (with some apparent surprise) as making a very civilized impression as "the perfect son-in-law"—has had similar electoral success in Antwerp. The most powerful New Right slogan comes from the arsenal of German-speaking ideologists who (especially in Switzerland) like to refer to the danger of *Ueberfremdung* (overstrangering).

14 In Le Pen's ideology, moreover, racial differences are equated with metaphors of genealogical distance (here he rejoins African ideas on autochthony): "J'aime mieux mes filles que mes nièces, mes nièces que mes voisines . . . j'aime mieux mes compatriotes, j'aime mieux la France et les Français . . . les Européens et les gens de l'Alliance atlantique" (interview by Alan Berger, *Figaro-Magazine* 5 April 1985: 113).

15 Note, in regard to the opposition cartoon, that, in real life, President Biya does not actually refer to northwesterners as *authoctones.* The cartoon seems to imply that he has given birth to an obsession with belonging that now haunts him and that he does not appear to have devised a convincing strategy for dealing with these contradictions.

16 On the labor history of southwest Cameroon in general, see Konings 1993 and 1995; Epale 1985. On changing labor policies during the transition from German to British rule, see Geschiere n.d.

17 For an overview of the literature on German Cameroon and the labor question, see Geschiere 1982; see also Wirz 1972.

18 See, for instance, Buea National Archives, CF 1913, Report Stobart, April/May 1916, under "Plantations" (henceforth cited as BNA).

19 BNA, Qd/a 1916, letters by DO Bamenda (Podevin) to Resident in Buea (Young), 22 August 1917; and Resident Buea to DO Bamenda, 22 September 1917; Qe, 1917, 2, letter by Resident in Buea to DO in Bamenda, 1 November 1917. Podevin was certainly not alone in his resistance to the new policy. In his 1918 annual report, Rutherford, then DO in Victoria, still sharply protested the new policy of forced recruitment (BNA, CF 1918, 31 December 1918).

20 This option involved developing the colonial economy through trade and small-

scale cash-crop production by supposedly autonomous peasants. Cf. Clarence-Smith 1993 and Phillips 1989 on British problems with the "peasant option." The southern Cameroonian example suggests that, if there seemed to be a more profitable alternative, even people like Lugard and Sir Hugh Clifford, his successor in Nigeria (both quoted by Phillips as great defenders of the peasant option—but see below), did not hesitate to go against the peasant option. Cf. also Fred Cooper's critique (1981: 31, 59 n. 36) of Wallerstein for suggesting, in line with his world-systems-theory approach, that to the colonial state in Africa, the peasant option was "the path of least resistance."

21 Cf., in general, Pierre-Philippe Rey's version of the "articulation of modes of production." In his view, the ongoing role of "pre-capitalist relations of exploitation" is everywhere crucial in forcing labor into capitalist relations of production (Rey 1973; see also Geschiere 1985).

22 Cf. also the early and seminal study by Ardener, Ardener, and Warmington (1960).

23 In contrast, for the Dagara laborers (from northern Ghana) in the southern gold mines, Lentz and Erlmann (1989) emphasize a continuing multiple identity as both workers and tribesmen.

24 Cf. Bayart (forthcoming): "l'illusion identitaire qui s'est refermée comme une piège sur l'histoire du monde au XIXème siècle . . . avec la conception ethnonationaliste de la cité."

25 Cf. a recent paper by the Comaroffs (1999) on the "zombification" of new immigrant laborers in South Africa. The interest of this occurrence is that this zombification is clearly linked to the quite abrupt opening of South Africa's borders.

REFERENCES

Africa Today. 1998. Special issue, *Rethinking citizenship in Africa,* edited by C. R. D. Halisi, Paul J. Kaiser, and Stephen N. Ndegwa, 45, no. 3/4.

Appadurai, Arjun. 1996. *Modernity at large: Cultural dimensions of globalization.* Minneapolis: University of Minnesota Press.

Ardener, Edwin, Shirley Ardener, and W. A. Warmington. 1960. *Plantation and village in the Cameroons: Some economic and social studies.* Oxford: Oxford University Press.

Awasom, Nicodemus F. n.d. Identity crises in a modern African nation-state: The case of bilingual Cameroon in historical perspective. Unpublished essay [1999].

Bayart, Jean-François, ed. 1994. *La Réinvention du capitalisme.* Paris: Karthala.

———. 1996. *L'Illusion identitaire.* Paris: Fayard.

———. Forthcoming. Sortir du XIXème siècle. In *L'État du monde.* Paris: La Découverte.

Clarence-Smith, Gervase. 1993. Plantation versus smallholder production of cocoa: The legacy of the German period in Cameroon. In *Itinéraires d'accumulation au Cameroun,* edited by Peter Geschiere and Piet Konings. Paris: Karthala.

Cohen, D. W., and E. S. Atieno Odhiambo. 1992. *Burying SM: The politics of knowledge and the sociology of power in Africa.* London: Currey/Heinemann.

Comaroff, Jean, and John Comaroff. 1999. Occult economies and the violence of abstraction: Notes from the South African postcolony. *American Ethnologist* 26: 279–301.

———. 1999. Alien-nation: Zombies, immigrants, and millennial capitalism.

CODESRIA Bulletin 3/4: 17–28. Also in *Forces of globalization,* edited by G. Schwab. New York: Columbia University Press (forthcoming).

Comaroff, Jean, and John Comaroff, eds. 1993. *Modernity and its malcontents: Ritual and power in postcolonial Africa.* Chicago: University of Chicago Press.

Cooper, Fred. 1981. Africa and the world economy. *African Studies Review* 24, no. 2/3: 1–87.

Crisp, Jeff. 1984. *The story of an African working class: Ghanaian miners' struggles, 1870–1980.* London: Zed Press.

Dilley, Roy, ed. 1992. *Contesting markets: Analyses of ideology, discourse, and practice.* Edinburgh: Edinburgh University Press.

Epale, Simon J. 1985. *Plantations and development in western Cameroon, 1885–1975.* New York: Vantage.

Epstein, A. L. 1958. *Politics in an urban African community.* Manchester: Manchester University Press.

Geschiere, Peter. 1982. *Village communities and the state: Changing relations among the Maka in southeast Cameroon.* London: Kegan Paul International.

———. 1985. Imposing capitalist dominance through the state: The multifarious role of the colonial state in Africa. In *Old modes of production and capitalist encroachment: Anthropological explorations in Africa,* edited by W. M. J. van Binsbergen and Peter Geschiere. London: Kegan Paul International.

———. n.d. Coercive labor or peasant production? The transition from German to British rule and its surprising outcome for the plantation economy of southwest Cameroon. In preparation.

Geschiere, Peter, and Joseph Gugler, eds. 1998. *The politics of primary patriotism.* Special issue, *Africa* 68, no. 3.

Jua, Nantang. 1997. Spatial politics and political stability in Cameroon. Keynote address presented at the Cameroon: Biography of a Nation workshop, Amherst College, Amherst, Mass., 20–23 November.

Konings, Piet. 1993. *Labour resistance in Cameroon: Managerial strategies and labour resistance in the agro-industrial plantations of the Cameroon Development Corporation.* London: Currey/Heinemann.

———. 1995. *Unilever estates in crisis and the power of organizations in Cameroon.* Hamburg: LIT Verlag.

———. 1996. Chieftaincy, labour control, and capitalist development in Cameroon. *Journal of Legal Pluralism* 37, no. 8: 329–46.

Konings, Piet, and Francis B. Nyamnjoh. 1997. The anglophone problem in Cameroon. *Journal of Modern African Studies* 35: 207–29.

Lagrange, Hugues, and Pascal Perrineau. 1996. Le syndrome lepéniste. In Mayer and Perrineau 1996.

Lentz, Carola, and Veit Erlmann. 1989. A working class in formation? Economic crisis and strategies of survival among Dagara mine workers in Ghana. *Cahiers D'Études africaines* 29, no. 1: 69–111.

Mamdani, Mahmood. 1998. *Understanding the crisis in Kivu: Report of Codesria mission to the Democratic Republic of Congo, September 1997.* Dakar: Codesria.

Mayer, Nonna, and Pascal Perrineau, eds. 1996. *Le Front National à découvert*. Paris: Presses de la fondation nationale des sciences politiques.

Meyer, Birgit, and Peter Geschiere. 1999. Introduction. In *Globalization and identity: Dialectics of flow and closure*, edited by Birgit Meyer and Peter Geschiere. Oxford: Blackwell.

Mono Ndjana, H. 1997. *Anti-Plaidoyer pour les ethnies*. In *La démocratie à l'épreuve du tribalisme*, edited by F. Eboussi Boulaga. Yaoundé: Friedrich-Ebert Stiftung.

La Nouvelle Expression. 1996. Special issue, *Minorités, autochtones, allogènes, et démocratie*, no. 1, 23 May.

Nyamnjoh, Francis B. 1996. *Mass media and democratisation in Cameroon*. Yaoundé: Friedrich-Ebert Stiftung.

Nyamnjoh, Francis B., and Michael Rowlands. 1998. Elite associations and the politics of belonging in Cameroon. In Geschiere and Gugler 1998: 320–37.

Phillips, Anne. 1989. The enigma of colonialism: British policy in West Africa. London: Currey.

Rey, Pierre-Philippe. 1973. *Les Alliances de classes*. Paris: Maspero.

Robertson, Roland. 1992. *Globalization: Social theory and global culture*. London: Sage.

Taguieff, Pierre André. 1985. L'Identité Française et ses enemis: Le Traitement de l'immigration dans le national-racisme français contemporain. *L'Homme et la société* 77, no. 8: 169–200.

———. 1996. La Métaphysique de Jean-Marie Le Pen. In *Le Front National à découvert*, edited by Nonna Mayer and Pascal Perrineau. Paris: Presses de la fondation nationale des sciences politiques.

Tatah Mentan, E. 1997. Colonial legacies, democratisation, and the ethnic question in Cameroon. In Zognong and Mouiche 1997b.

Wirz, Albert. 1972. *Vom Sklavenhandel zum kolonialen Handel: Wirtschaftsräume und Wirtschaftsformen in Kamerun vor 1914*. Zurich: Atlantis.

Yenshu, Emmanuel. 1999. The discourse and politics of indigenous/minority peoples rights in some metropolitan areas of Cameroon. *Journal of Applied Social Sciences* 1, no. 1: 59–76.

Zognong, D. 1997. La Question bamiléké pendant l'ouverture démocratique au Cameroun. In Zognong and Mouiche 1997b.

Zognong, D., and I. Mouiche. 1997a. Introduction générale. In Zognong and Mouiche 1997b.

Zognong, D., and I. Mouiche, eds. 1997b. *Démocratisation et rivalités ethniques au Cameroun*. Yaoundé: CIREPE/Ethonet.

Millennial Coal Face

Luiz Paulo Lima, Scott Bradwell, and Seamus Walsh

(Top) Charcoal worker, Campo Grande "Bom Despacho" Farm, Brazil, 1995. © Luiz Paulo Lima (Above) "Waste Management," San Salvador, 1997. © Scott Bradwell (Right) Production line E, garment factory, Sri Lanka, 1996. © Seamus Walsh

Modernity's Media and the End of Mediumship?

On the Aesthetic Economy of Transparency in Thailand

Rosalind C. Morris

A funny thing happened on the way to the STET (the Stock Exchange of Thailand). In November 1997, I had returned to Thailand amid a financial catastrophe that has since been labeled the Asian economic plague, to begin an ethnography of capitalist crisis. I imagined that it would be a project on the politics of transparency—that ideological pointing stick by which the market has appropriated for itself the function of regulating the state, where once it was the function of the state to regulate the market. I was, and am, interested in how capitalism in Thailand disguises itself as mere monetization, and how money's total and totalizing mediations have come to be experienced in the contrary idioms of immediacy and eternal present-being. I wanted to pursue the ways in which the rhetorics of transparency and visibility have been conceived in aesthetic domains where calls for the end of mimetic representation mirror and reiterate calls for disclosure and objectivity in the economic domain.

Before I got to the STET, however, a nationally renowned spirit medium named Chuchad appeared on a cable network talk show, hosted by a former academic, and confessed to twenty-six years of fakery. In a narcissistic act of tele-technic encompassment that Quesalid, the doubt-ridden sorcerer of Lévi-Strauss, could probably never have imagined, Chuchad not only theatricalized his newfound skepticism but also invited *all* mediums to join him in renouncing their dissimulating practice.[1] Ultimately, he called for an end to mediumship itself. This extraordinary event elicited newspaper coverage and cocktail party gossip even among the rationalists of Bangkok's elite. Nonetheless, the television broadcast was merely the anticipation of an even more spectacular disclosure that Chuchad would stage in a press conference: he would reveal everything, the tricks of his trade as well as the more scripturalist versions of Dhammic truth to which his recent reflections had led him. Having already devoted six years to the study of mediumship, I could not resist this strange and haunting invitation, which was directed as much at spectators as at mediums. Needless to say, I deferred the stock market and went in search of Chuchad and mediumship's end to Chantaburi, the city of Chuchad's residence, southeast of Bangkok.

Such flamboyant media savvy as Chuchad's is relatively recent but no longer exceptional among Thailand's contemporary spirit mediums. Thirty years ago, it was uncommon for spirit mediums to use or permit themselves to be represented via the mass media. Photography was implicitly forbidden, imagined in the terms that Balzac had once conceived of daguerreotypy: as a demonic receiving device that had the capacity to retain and thereby diminish the photographed subject's substance. More than most sites, mediumship seemed to retain a commitment to the etymology of the Thai words for photography, *kaan thaay ruup* (taking pictures). *Kaan thaay* can mean either taking or wasting, and even defecation. In combination with *ruup* (picture/s), it suggests not only taking pictures but also a concomitant transformation and discharge.[2] For mediums, the risk of photography was not only doubling, but transforming, substituting, and displacing. Television, for its part, was still available mainly in Bangkok. And cinema had not yet assumed the populist forms of home movies and videos. To the extent that spirit practices were brought into conversation with the mass media at all, it was as the auratic threshold of representation whose enframement as tradition had been precisely the result of mass mediatization. But then, thirty years ago, spirit mediumship was itself imagined as being on the verge of disappearance. Its "persistence," as folkloric and ethnographic texts expressed the matter, was conceptualized largely in terms of atavism and/or residue: as the repressed orgiastic impulse buried, along with Brahmanism, within Thailand's syncretized Theravada Buddhism.[3] It was also located on the periphery of the nation's geo body, a popular construed in opposition to the state's newly formed public.

Indeed, from the perspective of the self-consciously rationalist Buddhist orthodoxy that had been on the ascent since its founding during Rama IV's reign (1851–68), mediumship was imagined as a temporal interruption of the nation's modernity. Even in the 1970s, the mass media—still organized around the supremacy of radio—were instrumentalized in the interest of completing Thailand's modernist project and bringing that same putatively "ritualist" periphery into the national fold, calling it back from borders at which the demonic future history of communism was thought to be lying in wait.[4] In the national imaginary, there was no contradiction between ritualism and communism. To the contrary, one of the most potent ideological weapons of the period was one that attributed to communism occult practices and emasculating magic. Partly for this reason, the media began transmitting national culturalist messages in vernacular form, hoping to shore up or indeed to restore affiliation to the phantasmatic triad of "Nation, Religion, and Monarch" instituted under Rama VI's reign (1910–25).[5] As Walter Irvine has remarked, mediums themselves began to transmit the paranoiac messages prophesying boundary penetration that originated with the state, even though mediums had been imagined as the state's other.[6]

At that point, Thailand seemed to be on the verge of explosion. The class divisions that had first been transformed by the capitalization of rice production, and then deepened by industrially oriented development policies that favored the urban centers, were cast into particularly visible relief when agricultural workers joined forces with radical students. The military's bloody suppression of revolutionary efforts and the restoration of autocracy following the events of 6 October 1976 have left scars that are still liable to ache decades later, although Thailand is generally secure in its choice of market liberalism rather than social democracy. And efforts to compel identification with a racialized Thainess are increasingly impotent, as Thainess itself comes to connote less an essence than a consumer option in the marketplace of style.[7] Today, identifications between the local and the global, many of them facilitated by transnational communication systems, compete with those of nationalism. And revolution has all but disappeared, having been reduced to the status of mise-en-scène in which individuals perform their affiliation with bourgeois democracy and the market-based discourses of civic politics in the anticipation of being seen from afar by a multinational media audience.[8] In the simulacral space of the new mediascape, there are only representations — although the meaning of representation has itself changed. And this applies to mediumship as well. Having been imagined as the sign of pastness and as a representation of tradition in its abstract mode, having been denuded of its magicality, mediumship has been reborn. It circulates along with its own images, less the double of a lost original than part of an endlessly proliferating series in which it seeks merely to be legible as an image of its displaced self. In thirty years the population of mediums has multiplied more than 500 percent.[9] Now all mediums display photographs of themselves, and even television personalities have joined the ranks of the possessed.

It is in this newly mass-mediatized space that Chuchad lured audiences with the promise of authenticity. This would be the violent authenticity of an exposure in which mediumship's representations would be renounced, save those in which the techniques of performance themselves would become the object of performative inscription.

THE MEDIUM, THE MONK, AND THE MESSAGE

On November 29 at 10:00 AM I made my way to Chuchad's shrine, a semi-open structure located off a highway on Chantaburi's outskirts. From the highway the shrine is marked by a sign draped with costumes of Chuchad's possessing personae, loose two-colored satin bodysuits with patches sewn on them. To the extent that anyone recognizes these costumes as having historical reference, they are said to be of ancient Chinese style. Chantaburi's Chinese affiliations predate the formation of the modern Siamese state, and Chuchad himself is *luuk chin* (Sino-Thai). He is recognized in Chantaburi as a medium of a particular (local) kind, and the body piercings and feats of endurance for which he has become famous over the past two and a half decades are not the rupture of a local tradition so much as the instantiation of its ideal form—albeit one more associated in popular imaginings with the touristified festivals of Phuket than the daily life of Chantaburi.

Chuchad's renunciation was celebrated not at the shrine of everyday possession but in the enormous vacant lot adjacent to a strip mall and a new condominium development a few blocks away. Audience members were ferried to the alternative site on motorcycles driven by Chuchad's acolytes who were attired in flamboyant green and white satin. A small parade of trucks carrying billboards and broadcasting systems like those used at election time had driven through the city early in the morning and the previous day, announcing the event and inviting residents to attend. Their raucous, crackling messages and gaudy billboards competed with similar portable broadcasting systems that were inviting residents to an annual merit-making ceremony at the temple of the City Pillar on the other side of town. Despite the competition, more than a thousand residents arrived at Chuchad's site that morning and found places to sit on the hundreds of metal chairs that had been unfolded under tarpaulin canopies to make an enormous U-shaped grandstand. Food stalls embraced the rows of chairs, vendors selling the usual fare of sodas, distilled water, and dried cuttlefish. Behind them, and at each corner, were men in uniform, pacing in anticipation: several dozen military and city police, their eyes shielded by the visors of their tight helmets, along with the orange-clad personnel of the emergency services. Their agitation was dramatically countered by the laissez-faire demeanor of the audience members who chatted idly about family and recent events, and much less frequently about the man they had known as a medium. In the end, as the sun rose to unseasonable heat and the event proceeded, only the limp bodies of heat-stricken young women justified the mad scurrying of emergency workers.

Chuchad's revelation would not begin for another two hours. In the meantime, audience members heard a tape-recorded sermon by Phra Phyom, the renowned monk of Wat Suan Kaew. Phra Phyom's extraordinary reputation among lay Buddhists as a learned and politically outspoken monk was to authorize Chuchad's extraordinary confession. A year previously, Phra Phyom had publicly attacked then-Prime Minister Chawalit Yonchaiyudh and his wife for patronizing a temple devoted to the cult of Rahu, a figure of violent power associated with a kind of Brahmanic ritualism that, despite its recent popularity, has been implicitly excluded—along with mediumship—from legitimate religion since Rama IV's reign.

Phra Phyom himself has an interesting place in the history of religious legitimacies, having come under serious suspicion during the 1980s, when he introduced a new format of religious sermon into the radio programming of Thailand's national (military) radio station. That format was emphatically dialogic, using vernacular forms and local dialects to disseminate rather conservative interpretations of the Dhamma to rural audiences. It constituted a radical break from the format of Radio Thailand's Sunday sermon, the didactic *Phradhamma Tesana*. During a period of military retrenchment in the years immediately following the 1976 *hok tula* (October 6) massacre, nonconformist monks were permitted to deliver the Sunday sermon, an activity confined to high-ranked orthodox monks prior to the coup.[10] This was an effort to heal over the rift that had developed between conservative monks such as Kitthivudho, who had espoused the murder of communists, and more progressive monks who had joined the radical democratic students and agricultural laborers. Phra Phyom's new format was considered too radical even in this context. Though limited to formal interventions, his sermons were censored on the grounds that their populism constituted a form of commodification to which Buddhism ought not be subject.[11] This despite the fact that their content remained deeply orthodox in its valorization of the foundational texts and in its disavowal of ontology and its ritualist inscriptions.

The alliance between the populist conservative monk and the repentant medium rested on the medium's profession of epiphanic discovery —that he had received the Dhamma while listening to Phra Phyom. The medium required the monk to ensure the transmission of his own antiontological, antiritualist discovery. Yet in the end, on the stage of revelation, Chuchad delivered a message that openly contradicted Phra Phyom's earlier broadcast message. And the question of instrumentalization—of who was rendering whom the medium of his will—remains open to debate.

Phra Phyom's broadcast message consisted in a denial of the persistence of spiritual entities in this world. Of the spirits whom mediums serve as mounts (*maa*), he said: "They are dead. They have left this world. They cannot possess the bodies of human beings in this world when they have already moved on to others. The soul (*winyaan*) has no permanence."[12] For Phra Phyom, then, mediumship is fraudulent because there is nothing that could possess the body of the medium, merely the spectral illusion of something that has passed—irrevocably —from this plane of being. The medium who claims such a possession is therefore either deluded or, more threateningly, perpetrating a deception and confusing the minds of those common people who are in need of the real Dhamma.

Chuchad, on the other hand, would later insist on the existence of spirits but remark on the inadequacy of the human body to facilitate their descent into this realm. For him, the chasm that separates the materiality of the human form from the spirit that has passed into a realm of mitigated sensuousness is untraversable. At best, the appearance of possession could express a desire on the part of the medium for crossing this space. At worst, it could be the dissimulation of the one who knows how much others share this desire. This insistence on the bodily inadequacy of the medium inevitably opens onto a discussion of the techniques of seeming prosthetization: the means by which the appearance of possession is conjured. Chuchad referred to these techniques as *tekhnikaan,* combining the English term *technique* — from the Greek root *tekhne* (art) — and the Thai term *kaan* (action or operationalization). I will have more to say about technique, but for now we need only note that the opposition between Phra Phyom and Chuchad was one of the message versus the medium. Either there is nothing to transmit or there is no means of transmission. Silence or white noise.

WRITING ON THE TONGUE

The hours of waiting for Chuchad to mount the elevated stage were constantly interrupted by rumors of Phra Phyom's imminent arrival. The monk was coming. And then, he was not. He had sent his voice only. He would follow in body as well. We would hear a tape recording. We would receive a real sermon. Perhaps, someone remarked, we would hear a broadcast telephone conversation. At one point it was even said that he had arrived in a Mercedes limousine. He had not.

In fact, Phra Phyom had become not unlike the apparitions of deceased princes and Buddhist culture heroes whose descent into the bodies of mediums would normally be attended by clients seeking advice on love, health, and business. He was the embodiment of fame itself: a bastardized auratic presence that was always arriving, always imminent, but without specification. Chuchad paled as an object of conversation. As though anticipating this, the bus driver who had driven me to the event told me that he had never believed in Chuchad's performances, but that others did. The same combination of disavowal and attribution (or even accusation) circulated with generic regularity in the hours preceding the medium's performance, and only a few admitted to having been clients who has taken seriously the feats and knowledges that skeptics attributed to chicanery.

What drew these people to this performance? Why did they wait — so distractedly, and with growing professions of boredom — for a man they claimed never to have believed? Was it simply to have their own skepticism confirmed? Were they seeking the ambivalent pleasure (not without violence) of having a secret unmasked? The possibility of a merely triumphalist pleasure was quickly dissolved when Chuchad finally appeared on stage, accompanied by two other mediums who had decided to join him in his confession. The crowd strained to see the stage where Chuchad settled onto a throne, flanked by the flags of the *sangha* (the Buddhist clergy) and the nation. Their desire and agitation were assuaged only briefly, when the national anthem was broadcast and the spectators rose en masse with the police and emergency workers.

None of the spectators could indulge their desire for proximity. Only licensed journalists, photographers, and television news camerapeople were permitted an "immediate view." The spectators, myself included, were approximately twenty meters from the stage, behind the rows of media people and separated from them by empty space and props. Yet Chuchad's acolytes took great pains to ensure a line of vision between the medium and his audience, forcing the photographers to sit when their heads rose to intrude upon the scene. The medium narrated each moment of the unfolding events with a handheld microphone. For the most part, this broadcast narration placated the desire for actual nearness by substituting virtual proximity. But it also generated moments of crisis.

When static made of the space between us a chasm of unintelligibility, and when feedback spiked the air with the trace of that seemingly impossible fact—that broadcasting and recording devices are, essentially, the same thing—the promise of revelation was threatened by the emergence of opacity.[13] This opacity was not simply the failure of meaning. Rather, it was the sign of the transformation of mass mediatization itself: authorship (its emergence in Thailand traceable only to the nineteenth century) has been displaced by a logic in which representation and inscription have been reduced to the "tracking of 'traces without a subject.'"[14] Modern mediumship has come to occupy a place similar to that occupied by automatic writing in Western contexts.[15] Indeed, as I hope to make clear, the rapprochement between mediums and the media during the last three decades, and the consequent growth in mediumship, is understandable in terms of this development. Mediums now recognize themselves in technologies of mass mediatization. The consequences of that recognition have been twofold and contradictory. On one hand, mediums embrace technology, and mediumship proliferates in a cycle wherein mediums and the media provide each other with metaphors. This possibility is testified to in the language within which mediums now describe their practice: sacred sites are like "batteries"; the threads (*saisin*) within which ritual space is marked off, and which conduct spiritual power, are compared to "telephone wires"; mediums are said to be "like photographic negatives"; and the linkages between marked locations in the landscape are described in the idiom of "railway tracks." On the other hand, mediums seek to escape the relationship altogether in forms of ecstatic nonrepresentation or absolute renunciation. This latter possibility was, of course, manifest in Chuchad's confessional performance.

With the microphone next to his chin, Chuchad began his performance by cutting off his tongue. Opening his mouth wide for the cameras, he pinched his tongue between his fingers and drew a long rapier across it. The tongue fell into an opaque cup beneath his chin, and blood leaked from Chuchad's mouth. Another medium took the microphone and described the tongue that now lay in the cup, while Chuchad stood speechless before his assembled audience. In perpetrating such a displacement, it appeared that Chuchad had chosen to disavow disavowal, to repudiate his repudiation. He had rendered himself voiceless, and the only sounds he could make were those of exhalation and inhalation: sounds of the body as machine. We heard these sounds over the loudspeakers, and were unable to distinguish them from those other sounds emitted by the recording machine on which Phra Phyom had made his sermon. As Chuchad's breaths were broadcast, the crowd gasped and then repeated—in a manner that confused awe and automatism—the second medium's narration: "He's cut off his tongue!"

In fact, Chuchad did repudiate his repudiation, but only through a second gesture in which he reattached the severed organ. Chuchad placed the tongue on a piece of white paper, and the blood quickly diffused into the fibers. For a moment it appeared as though the tongue was writing a blunt, indecipherable hieroglyph. Chuchad then held the paper to his mouth so it was covering his face and pressed the tongue back into its original place. This time, he seemed to be rewriting, or rather, writing in reverse, and the glyph was inscribed on the tongue as though the tongue had been transformed into paper and the paper into pen. Thus did writing make speech possible. The medium pulled the paper away, folded it carefully, and then, with only a little blood reddening his lips, began speaking.

The restoration of Chuchad's tongue was the gesture that enabled his continued confession and thus his denunciation of possession performance. By effectively interrupting the voice — the instrument through which language and the presence of spirits articulate themselves — the tongue excision was already the performative repudiation of mediumship. Thus, repairing the tongue was the ironic subversion of the confession that it was supposed to facilitate. Yet Chuchad could not terminate his role as interlocutor until after the confession, and so the unmasking had to be masked, at least temporarily. It had to be demonstrated that the cutting and the healing of the tongue were simulated. With his tongue restored, Chuchad explained that it was an illusion, all a matter of technique (*tekhnikaan*). From the start, Chuchad explained, the cup contained a pig's tongue and a water and sugar mixture dyed red. After the simulated excision — when it looked as if he was spitting out his tongue — Chuchad had swiftly taken a mouthful of the mixture, which he then let seep from his mouth like blood.

Like all fables, this one staged risk in the form of a bad example. The object of transmission was the truth that the medium had discovered and recalled through remembering and reflecting on his childhood attraction to magic and its dissimulations. Here Chuchad made it seem as if voice was the vehicle of a simple exteriorization. As a result, much of mediumship seemed to be similarly organized. Yet, as the increasing frequency of untranslatable utterances and even glossolalia in contemporary spirit possession performances make clear, mediumship is increasingly concerned with the possibility that the truth of the spirits in the mass-mediatized world is not referential and certainly not universal, but rather centers on questions about the difference between noise and information.[16] Historically, in Thailand, mediums merely *transmit* the secrets of a reality thought to be populated by spirits. Mediums deny memory of their experience and their utterances during possession and repress themselves as agents of mediumship's discourse in every manner. Nonetheless, in the contemporary moment — the moment that Weber called secular — there is no guarantee of the truth of the message, no shared commitment to the real as the domain of spirits. In an era of visual hegemony, which is also, and always already, the era of the commodity form's generalization, only that which can be seen can be true. Indeed, it is this lack of guarantee that Chuchad seems to disavow as much as anything else. It is the possibility that mediumship has lost its identity with its message that leads him to claim that he has discovered the real truth of Dhamma — a truth incompatible with mediumship.

In Thai Theravada Buddhism, and especially in the Buddhism of premodern cosmologies, Dhamma (*tham*) denotes both law and nature and refers to a domain of natural signification where there is a pure identity between signifier and signified. The relationship is narrativized in the cosmological accounts of Yama in the chapter on "The Realm of Hell Beings"of the *Thraiphum Phra Ruang,* the Thai Buddhist cosmology.[17] The righteous adjudicator who presides over the realm of auxiliary hells, Yama receives almost everyone immediately after death and asks, "What merit or evil deeds have you done? Quickly now, think back and speak the truth!" Under the scrutiny of Yama, meritorious beings are "miraculously" equipped with memory and find themselves able to speak about all their good deeds. But those whose evil deeds outweigh the good find themselves in an amnesiac hell, unable to recall anything or to speak at all. In response to a mute evildoer, angels (*thewadaa*) who have recorded the deeds of meritorious beings on luminous jewel-encrusted gold tablets and the deeds of evil beings on dog hides read from the dog hide (itself vulnerable to rot and putrefaction). In response, the shamed evildoer is left only to confess. Confession is therefore a mode of accession or conformity to the message. And in this manner, the confession resembles a mediumship whose instrumentality and apparent immediacy are summoned only in the aftermath of a rupture and a failure of spirits to proceed in the cycle of rebirth.[18]

Few contemporary people treat the *Thraiphum Phra Ruang* as anything but quaint tradition, and the Buddhism to which Phra Phyom adheres has formally rejected the cosmology as a symptom of superstition and a relic of bygone times. But as recently as 1913, the image of Yama formed the centerpiece of the seal of the Thai judiciary, and the image still circulates widely in aesthetic and monumental productions, much as the blindfolded figure of justice does in Euro-American contexts.[19] If its referents are less widely known than they once were, the universal signified of justice nonetheless emanates from it. But ubiquity alone is inadequate to demonstrate relevance. It is because the logic of representation underlying the *Thraiphum Phra Ruang* recurs in mediumship — despite its repression by hegemonic Buddhism — that I invoke the chapter on "The Realm of Hell Beings" here. The story of Yama's adjudication imagines a righteous speech marked by the identity between deed and word. By contrast, the sinner's speech is one of deferral, and evil is figured as a gap between deed and word opened by the evildoer's forgetfulness. In the evildoer's case, speech is not the mere instrument of truth: it is both a symptom and a cause of sin. In the other case, speech corresponds to the actuality inscribed in gold—icon of purity and permanence in which the sign of value is its substance—and is aligned with the law. But where the law rules, there is no difference between the object and sign, nor between speech and voice. This, then, explains how it is that, according to the cosmology, the child who is born mute will learn "Pali, which is the language of truth" and which is imagined to precede the corruptions of human utterance.[20] Personified in the speechless child, a perfect unity binds the lawful world. For those who are its subject, writing serves to legitimate the utterance of the meritorious being and to supplement the failed speech of the sinner.

But the opposition between truth's silent ideality and sin's "overnaming," to use Walter Benjamin's term, is different from that which counterposes noise and information in the age of mass media.[21] In the latter instance, because inscription can only inscribe its own facticity, the message of mediumship becomes mediumship itself. Chuchad's performance was stretched taut between these two understandings of mediumship's representational function: the transmission of a referential truth and the repeated registration of the mere technique of its transmission. To restore the former, he had to make the latter visible. Chuchad was occupying a moment in which "writing" could only be instrumental and the object of representation was only itself. In other words, he was inhabiting the era of technique's fetishization, what Martin Heidegger would have simply called the era of technology.[22]

After the tongue cutting, Chuchad moved through what appeared to be an obstacle course of possession performance tricks. He climbed a ladder of swords and then showed the crowd how he distributed his weight across the dull blades. After traversing a bed of broken glass, he explained that it was made of bottles that were first frozen and then cracked, then spread in a box of sand where they shifted and so did not cut the bottoms of his feet. He beat his back with axes in a manner that only appeared to bring the full force of the blades onto his back. And he placed his hands in simmering oil while explaining the herbal ingredients that made the oil boil at a very low temperature.[23] The middle point of the obstacle course—an unexpectedly literal pièce de résistance—consisted in walking across a bed of coals that had been lit at the beginning of the confessional performance. Here, Chuchad encountered the day's only challenge: A barrier of rolled dried grasses on the perimeter of the coal bed was ignited by floating cinders during a sudden gust of wind. The flaming barrier grasses in turn blew onto the coals and re-heated them to higher than normal temperatures. Apparently immune to the heat, Chuchad walked across the coals with no visible adverse result. The two mediums accompanying him suffered minor burns.

Almost in spite of himself, Chuchad became the paragon of technical virtuosity. Indeed, at the point of the fire-walking, his technology of deceit was as impressive as any "real magic." The attribution of skill by audience members was cast in superlatives ("kaeng maak!" [he's very clever!]). Chuchad was so masterful, in fact, that his technique could almost be mistaken for the workings of spirits. This was science in its most magnificently theatrical form, and the medium had become its adept. The occult had returned in the guise of transparency. In this regard, Chuchad was reenacting his own life story. As a ten-year-old boy he had been awed by a medium's performance. Innately curious, he immediately set out to discover the principles underlying the tricks, and to his own amazement, he quickly discovered them. Soon he was a master magician, and indeed, he was so impressive that people began to attribute to him the power of spirits. Shortly thereafter he established himself as a medium. One can almost believe that he had read Claude Lévi-Strauss's account of Quesalid in "The Sorcerer and His Magic."

Even after his public confession, some of Chuchad's clients insisted that the claim of fakery was unconvincing: Chuchad had known things about them that would have been impossible without extrasensory powers. They seemed dismayed by the disavowal, and even disappointed. For them, no technical excellence was an adequate substitution for a relationship with spirits. But for most audience members, it was not only an adequate substitution, it was its own object of fascination. Men, in particular, spoke animatedly about how to perform the tricks, identifying with Chuchad who, as a young boy, had harbored such a natural propensity for chemistry, physics, and engineering. And it was as such a genius of science that Chuchad presented himself, describing each trick as an example not of magic but of science ("pen witthayasaat, mai chai sayasaat"). When he called upon the audience to exercise their individual powers of "objectivity" (using the idiom of *ruupatham* and *namatham*), he invoked a nationalized discourse of modernity whose oppositional terms are those of science versus magic, rationality versus supernatural belief, the visible versus the invisible, and mind versus body.[24] Indeed, the entire event was redolent of the rhetoric of another moment more than a century earlier that has since been emblematized in the image of the rationalist king, Rama IV, arguing with his Christian interlocutors for the superior and more rigorous rationality of Theravada Buddhism. It was this modernist reform Buddhism that Phra Phyom had attempted to popularize in his radically dialogic sermons.

Nonetheless, science could not explain why fascination was replaced by agitated disinterest as the afternoon proceeded. Halfway through the event, the visibly bored audience members were shifting in their seats and mopping their sweating brows. Many began to leave, or to talk about when it would all be over and other matters. "Naa bua," they said. "It's boring." In the violently climactic last moments of his revelation when Chuchad threaded his cheek with the same rapier that had cut off his pig's tongue—and which he then explained (away) as the result of bodily training—the audience was unable to summon itself to the task of observation. It was as though such observation had become a form of attention propelled by labor rather than desire. Chuchad had exhausted his audience, and its members glanced distractedly toward the stage as he began his verbal summary of a duplicitous life. Before he had completed his sermon, the space was almost entirely abandoned, and all that was left to signify the having-been-there of the audience was the tangle of discarded plastic water bottles and crumpled photocopies of statements distributed by his assistants during the course of the event.

It is helpful to recall here Friedrich Kittler's reading of the discourse network that overtook Europe in 1900 and that was articulated in the diverse writings of Sigmund Freud, Georg Simmel, and Rainer Maria Rilke. In that network "writing [became], rather than miniatures of meaning, an exhaustion that endlessly refused to end."[25] Kittler notes that, in this context, writing "is nothing beyond its materiality. The peculiar people who practice this act simply replace writing machines." And all that can be promised them is the "mystical union of writing and delirium." Either that or death, and death itself is not far from the face dissembled by boredom, decomposed in the stare that looks stupidly and sees nothing. Elsewhere, I have written about the relationship between mediumship and writing and noted the history of mediumship's transformation alongside a gradual shift away from a belief in the actual magicality of script to the representational capacity of inscription, to a deployment of writing in the mode of mathematics (such as in bureaucratic lists).[26] What we see in Chuchad's no longer scandalous renunciation is the next step in the process. That step occurs in a moment marked by the incorporation of technologies of mass mediatization into the language and performance of possession and by the discourses of lost tradition within which mediumship is now inscribed. Of course, when mediumship can no longer lay claim to truth, there is no choice but to either disavow truth or seek it elsewhere. And Chuchad chose the latter.

REPETITIONS UNDISCLOSED

What about this latter, putative truth to which Chuchad and Phra Phyom both directed us? Where does a medium go after having repudiated mediumship? What kind of mediation is not simply the inscription of its technique, but a renewed transmission of meaning? To consider this question, I returned to the lobby of my hotel where gem sellers were sitting in front of coffee cups and improbably large sacks of uncut rubies. Looking across the street as the sun went down and the neon signs turned the sky ghoulish, I watched the prostitutes who were buying food from the vendors before returning to the clubs where they could expect a couple of dollars for their labors. The five-story hotel was extravagant by Chantaburi standards. But the baht had slipped from 25 to 35 to 42 per dollar, so dollars were precious and the hotel was affordable. I retreated into the newspaper, to read stories of that day's economic news and to discover what new measures had been instituted by the government to meet the stringent requirements of the IMF loan package.

It is more than incidental that the baht had been floated the previous month in an effort to return it to a more adequate and natural representation of its worth (the worth of the nation's reserves). As though money could ever signify naturally! But Thailand seemed to be obsessed with the fantasy of a return to meaning and the possibility that the madness of its own economic excess could somehow be undone. The newspapers were full of stories about the new fetish of fiscal planning and market stabilization. And the transition from artificial stability to truer meaning seemed everywhere to incite dread and unease, but also the anticipation of relief. Indeed, when the prime minister fainted dramatically at a public event, he described his ordeal as one in which he "floated like the baht." The means for mitigating this awful uncertainty took the form of a stabilization strategy that, on some levels, can be reduced to a single demand—disclosure. If banks and lending institutions would reveal the true nature of their debt, it was repeatedly stated, then hopelessly overextended institutions could be closed, written off, and their assets centralized so as to permit the consolidation of national value and the restoration of the baht, as well as the nation's renown. More than sixty of Thailand's lending institutions were closed within six months of the IMF plan on the basis of this strategy. Foreclosures, downsizing, unemployment, and reruralization became the symptoms of rationalization via disclosure. The baht has stabilized, though inflation has not, and unemployment continues to rise. In the midst of all this, the most dramatic growth sector of the economy has been that of "direct marketing," known more colloquially as pyramid schemes.[27]

Pyramid schemes are, I would submit, the economic counterpart of mediumship, the mode of retailing in which the function of distribution and resale, and indeed the movement of capital, is masked in the rhetoric of directness. Directness itself is nothing but the withdrawal of an infrastructure of mediation into the person of the distributor, the occulting of technique in the very moment of display.

The end of this story can perhaps already be anticipated. Leaving the boredom of my grotesquely functionalized room, I went across town to the suburban house of Chuchad's cousin, whose niece happened to work at the hotel. There I met another relation of Chuchad's, a woman who had just returned from an Amway conference in Chicago. Chuchad has not only abandoned the ontology of mediumship for the putatively unmediated truth of Dhamma, but he has abandoned mediumship in order to be an Amway distributor. Or at least he has followed his career as a medium with a career as one of Amway's instruments. His assistants have, by and large, also become distributors, and they now constitute the base of his newly emergent power in the world of multilevel marketing. He has established telephone operators in three cities to field calls from the clients of his former profession and he uses the occasion of their contact—for advice and counsel—to recruit new consumers, and to convert an older form of repressed mediation into a new one. Like magic. And like all magic, Chuchad's metamorphosis entailed a repetition. Phra Phyom had been accused of sinful affiliation with commodification when he introduced direct sermons on the radio. Following his censorship, he began to record his sermons and to sell them on cassette tape because he no longer had access to the web of radio's audiences. Thus did the accusation become a prophesy and force him to be what he already was. So too, Chuchad's abandonment of mediumship was accompanied by an overt entry into the market economy, one in which he became what he already was: a middleman disavowing the mediations that he performed in order to produce the illusion of value, or meaning, or truth.

Mediumship works only in the repression of its own operations, of course. These operations are increasingly read as the limit and totality of its truth, and so, with a combination of nostalgia and contempt for belief, Chuchad risks boredom in order to claim what the economists promise: the market can substitute for magic, the media can be itself, the very nature of money—its abstractions and its generality—can compensate for the differences it effaces. Not the least of the disappearances in this process are those of capital itself. Amway Japan Ltd. and Amway Asia Pacific Ltd. had estimated assets of over U.S. $7 billion in 1996.[28] Growth has been fabulous during the past two years, slowing in many nations as a result of the fiscal crisis in 1997, but remaining strong in Thailand, where it achieved growth rates of more than 8 percent despite currency instability in the final quarter of that year.

The attraction of Asia for companies like Amway lies in the putative wealth of (at least some of) its citizens, its populousness, and the North American belief that Asian business is "conducted on the strength of personal, family, and ancestral relations."[29] Precisely because Asia is believed not to operate as an open economy, it offers the possibility for companies like Amway to establish competitive advantages by tapping into occult networks (that is, networks that are not publicly disclosed), in which conservative values can achieve the appearance of legitimacy and private relations can substitute for public ones. The notion that Asian economies are dominated not only by particular families but by the logic of family—by exclusive and unassailable ties between small communities of people—is, of course, the ideological foundation of much self-orientalizing discourse in the Asian and ASEAN (Association of South East Asian Nations) business community. Indeed, when Thai Foreign Minister Prachuab Chaiyasan addressed members of an Asia Society audience in September 1997, he mobilized precisely this rhetoric of Asian family values in his rejection of foreign demands for the total rationalization of local economies and the application of sanctions against states like Myanmar and Laos that had, at that point, resisted pressures to engage in market liberalization.[30] Prachuab has been by-passed, of course, and one could have prophesied as much given the degree to which he was prepared to admit the secret of new capital, namely that it operates on the basis of invisible power and affinities (like the return of an occult whose abolition had been the project but also the ironic effect of reform).

In its slippage between the individual families so idealized in the anachronistic imaginary of transnational capitalism and the racialized family of Asian nations, Prachuab's address revealed the metaphorical ruse of kinship's discourse and new capitalism's rhetoric. The language of small business became that of state protectionism for national interests. Amway plays upon this belief to extraordinary effect: The vast majority of its capital returns to the bizarre company town in Michigan where this behemoth of transnational capital is operated by two Christian men who still indulge in neocolonial fantasy concealed in the dream of immediacy. Holding tight to a theologically informed market liberalism, they pursue a noiseless world where feedback is impossible. And their recruits are eager mediums of this message.

Just as Chuchad remade himself as a magician by professing to display his technique, so the confessional disclosures of new capital and the rhetoric of transparency with which they cloak themselves effect the occulting of a system premised on secrecy. Siegfried Kracauer knew this well when he recalled Edgar Allan Poe's story of the purloined letter to explicate the process by which "the salaried masses" are made the media of a system in which they are denied knowledge and distracted with its entertaining simulacra.[31] It was to this realization that Chuchad returned me. And so I returned to the market after a detour through mediumship's enthralling dramaturgy of disclosure. The indirectness of the route was constantly and ironically haunted by the fact that it led through a fantasy of restored transparency. But then, what else is transparency in the massified world but a mediation so total that it has become invisible? It is this fact of total mediation that refuses the dream of meaning's unfolding and leaves all transmissions vulnerable to the resistant omnipresence of white noise. When white noise becomes audible, one hears the sound of a sleight of hand. The secrets of a new economy are being whisked away into the dream of another night.

NOTES

1 I take the term *tele-technic* from Jacques Derrida's *Specters of Marx: The state of the debt, the work of mourning, and the New International,* translated by Peggy Kamuf (New York: Routledge, 1994). Quesalid is the skeptical sorcerer described by Claude Lévi-Strauss in The sorcerer and his magic, in *Structural anthropology,* translated by John Russell (New York: Doubleday, 1967), 161–80.

2 Domnern Garden and Sathienpong Wannaprok, *Domnern-Sathienpong Thai-English Dictionary* (Bangkok: Amarin, 1994), 213.

3 Jacques Derrida discusses this notion of the encrypted orgiastic impulse and its tendency toward recurrence in *The gift of death,* translated by David Wills (Chicago: University of Chicago Press, 1995), esp. 8–9 and 20–21. I do not, however, mean to invoke the ethicized associations of "irresponsibility" that the Czech philosopher Jan Patočka mobilizes in his Christian philosophy. On the history of Buddhist modernization in Thailand, see Craig J. Reynolds, Buddhist cosmography in Thai history, with special reference to nineteenth century cultural change, *Journal of Asian Studies* 35, no. 2 (1976): 203–20, and, idem, The Buddhist monkhood in nineteenth century Thailand (Ph.D. diss., Cornell University, 1972); Stanley Tambiah, *World conqueror and world renouncer: A study of Buddhism and polity against a historical background* (Cambridge: Cambridge University Press, 1976); and Constance Wilson, State and society in the reign of Mongkut, 1851–1868: Thailand on the eve of modernization (Ph.D. diss., Cornell University, 1971).

4 See Katherine Bowie's excellent account of the Village Scouts and the statist efforts to counteract communism through organized forms of populist counterinsurgency: *Rituals of national loyalty: An anthropology of the state and the Village Scout movement in Thailand* (New York: Columbia University Press, 1997).

5 There are several fine treatments of nationalism during Vajiravudh's (Rama VI's) reign and in its immediate aftermath. Among them are Walter F. Vella, *Chaiyo! King Vajiravudh and the development of Thai nationalism* (Honolulu: University of Hawai'i Press, 1978); and Scot Barmé, *Luang Wichit Wathakan and the creation of a Thai identity* (Singapore: Institute of Southeast Asian Studies, 1993).

6 Irvine discusses the metaphor of boundary penetration, which originated in paranoid anticommunist discourses, as a "repeating image" in Northern Thai mediumship. See Walter Irvine, The Thai-Yuan "madman" and the modernizing, developing Thai nation as bounded entities under threat: A study in the replication of a single image (Ph.D. diss., University of London, 1982).

7 The terms within which that discourse has been cast, namely *ekkalak thai* (Thai identity) and *watthanatham thai* (Thai culture), were coined only in the 1930s and

1940s. Excellent accounts of the discursive development of nationalism can be found in *National identity and its defenders: Thailand, 1939–1989,* edited by Craig J. Reynolds (Chiang Mai: Silkworm, 1991). Prince Wan Waithayakon's original essay on "Thai culture" is reprinted as Thai culture: Lecture delivered before the Thailand Research Society [formerly the Royal Siam Society], 27 February 1944," in *The centennial of His Royal Highness Prince Wan Waithayakon Krommun Naradhop Bonsprabandh* (Bangkok: Office of the National Culture Commission, 1991; originally published in *Journal of the Thailand Research Society* 35, no. 2 (1944): 135–45).

8 Rosalind C. Morris, Returning the body without haunting in Thailand: The politics of revolution as mise-en-scène, in *Loss,* edited by David Eng and David Kasanjian (Berkeley: University of California Press, 2001).

9 Twenty years ago, Walter Irvine estimated that there were about three hundred mediums practicing in Chiang Mai, an increase of about 600 percent over a period of twenty years (Irvine, Thai-Yuan "madman"). The population continued to increase: in the early 1990s, when I asked mediums and monks to estimate the number of active practitioners, they guessed that there were between eight hundred and eleven hundred, although at roughly the same time Shigeharu Tanabe's informants led him to believe that the number was closer to five hundred. My own informal surveys at events suggested that the mediums and monks may have exaggerated their numbers and that Tanabe's more modest estimate was probably more accurate. See Shigeharu Tanabe, The person in transformation: Body, mind, and cultural appropriation (Special lecture, Sixth International Thai Studies Conference, Chiang Mai, 15 October 1996).

10 On the antidemocratic coup of 1976, Benedict Anderson's essay remains one of the most insightful. See Withdrawal symptoms: Social and cultural aspects of the October 6 coup, *Bulletin of Concerned Asian Scholars* 9, no. 3 (1977): 13–30. A recent memorial publication, under the title of *Rao mai lyym Hok Tula* [We haven't forgotten/won't forget October 6] (Bangkok: Committee for the Twentieth Anniversary of 6 October 1976), has begun the work of new critical and historical reflection on this event.

11 Ubonrat Siriyuvasak, Radio in a transitional society: The case of Thailand (Ph.D. diss., University of Leicester, 1989), 71–72.

12 Because this was a popular address and not a formal sermon, Phra Phyom omitted a philosophical discussion of the concept of "double-dependent origination," which would have actually insisted that it is not the selfsame soul that transmigrates.

13 The identity between recording and playback devices is a "discovery" of information science, particularly as formulated by Hans Magnus Enzensberger. For a discussion of this fact and its relationship to new discourse networks, see Friedrich A. Kittler, *Discourse networks, 1800/1900,* translated by Michael Metteer and Chris Cullens (Stanford, Calif.: Stanford University Press, 1990), 316.

14 Ibid., 316.

15 By "automatic writing" I mean that practice in which the writer seeks to merely transmit his or her unconscious thoughts and, in the process, to disavow the notion of authorial agency. The technique of automatic writing and, indeed, automatic writing's valorization of technique is perhaps most associated with surrealism, but it marks a more general transitional moment in the history of representation. That is the moment

in which the production of meaning ceases to be a function of writing, and actuality or facticity becomes the primary object of inscription.

16 This increasing performance of untranslatability takes the form of a marked discourse on translation by mediums and their attendants. Not only do mediums now remark that they speak extremely ancient and difficult dialects, but the performative elaboration of the translation has become part of the dialogue between clients and mediums: attendants whose sole function is translation have now begun to constitute a veritable type in the community of mediumship's supporting actors.

17 *Three worlds according to King Ruang: A Thai Buddhist cosmology* [translation of *Thraiphum Phra Ruang*], translated by Frank E. Reynolds and Mani B. Reynolds (Berkeley: University of California Press, 1982), 69–72.

18 Mediums and their clients explain that spirits must return to earth because of their incomplete *khammic* progress: Spirits generally were princes or other people who established moral law in their societies. As such, they were often, of necessity, perpetrators of violence at some point in their lives. The more violent of these beings must descend to earth to acquire the merit needed to complete their journey through the moral/cosmological universe. But even in instances where the returning spirit is a Thai Buddhist national hero such as King Ramkhamhaeng, no one describes the spirit as a *boddhisatta,* one who surrenders *khammic* progress for the benefit of others.

19 David Engel, *Code and custom in a Thai provincial town: The interaction of formal and informal systems of justice* (Tucson: University of Arizona Press, 1978), 4.

20 Reynolds and Reynolds, *Three worlds,* 122.

21 Walter Benjamin, On language as such and on the language of man, in *One-way street and other writings,* translated by Edmund Jephcott and Kingsley Shorter (London: Verso, 1979), 122.

22 Martin Heidegger, *The question concerning technology and other essays,* translated by William Lovitt (New York: Harper and Row, 1977).

23 Several years earlier a medium had plunged my hands into such a boiling oil. This medium was apparently less adept than Chuchad, for I received a rather severe scalding.

24 Thongchai Winichakul, *Siam mapped: A history of the geo-body of a nation* (Honolulu: University of Hawai'i Press, 1994).

25 Kittler, *Discourse networks,* 326.

26 Rosalind C. Morris, *In the place of origins: Modernity and its mediums in northern Thailand* (Durham, N.C.: Duke University Press, 2000).

27 By *pyramid schemes,* I mean to suggest structures in which retailers recruit more retailers. Although in many places a *pyramid scheme* is a legal category that is distinguished from other kinds of marketing by the fact that individuals can or cannot get their investment back in the event of failed sales, this distinction is one that mainly serves the interests of the multinational entities parading as local entrepreneurialism. Some retailers do prosper, but on a relatively small scale compared to that of the parent or more senior members of the structure.

28 James W. Robinson, *Empire of freedom: The Amway story and what it means to you* (Rocklin, Calif.: Prima, 1997), 129.

29 Ibid., 120.

30 Prachuab Chaiyasan, Foreign ministers from Southeast Asia: Thailand, speech delivered at the Asia Society, New York City, 29 September 1997.

31 Siegfried Kracauer, *The salaried masses: Duty and distraction in Weimar Germany*, translated by Quintin Hoare (London: Verso, 1998).

REFERENCES

Anderson, Benedict. 1977. Withdrawal symptoms: Social and cultural aspects of the October 6 coup. *Bulletin of Concerned Asian Scholars* 9, no. 3: 13–30.

Barmé, Scot. 1993. *Luang Wichit Wathakan and the creation of a Thai identity*. Singapore: Institute of Southeast Asian Studies.

Benjamin, Walter. 1979. On language as such and on the language of man. In *One-way street and other writings*, translated by Edmund Jephcott and Kingsley Shorter. London: Verso.

Bowie, Katherine. 1997. *Rituals of national loyalty: An anthropology of the state and the Village Scout movement in Thailand*. New York: Columbia University Press.

Chaiyasan, Prachuab. 1997. Foreign ministers from Southeast Asia: Thailand. Speech delivered at the Asia Society, New York City, 29 September.

Derrida, Jacques. 1994. *Specters of Marx: The state of the debt, the work of mourning, and the New International*, translated by Peggy Kamuf. New York: Routledge.

———. 1995. *The gift of death*, translated by David Wills. Chicago: University of Chicago Press.

Engel, David. 1978. *Code and custom in a Thai provincial town: The interaction of formal and informal systems of justice*. Tucson: University of Arizona Press.

Garden, Domnern, and Sathienpong Wannaprok. 1994. *Domnern-Sathienpong Thai-English Dictionary*. Bangkok: Amarin.

Heidegger, Martin. 1977. *The question concerning technology and other essays*, translated by William Lovitt. New York: Harper and Row.

Irvine, Walter. 1982. The Thai-Yuan "madman" and the modernizing, developing Thai nation as bounded entities under threat: A study in the replication of a single image. Ph.D. diss, University of London.

Kittler, Friedrich A. 1990. *Discourse networks, 1800/1900*, translated by Michael Metteer and Chris Cullens. Stanford, Calif.: Stanford University Press.

Kracauer, Siegfried. 1998. *The salaried masses: Duty and distraction in Weimar Germany*, translated by Quintin Hoare. London: Verso.

Lévi-Strauss, Claude. 1967. The sorcerer and his magic. In *Structural anthropology*, translated by John Russell. New York: Doubleday.

Morris, Rosalind C. 2000. *In the place of origins: Modernity and its mediums in northern Thailand*. Durham, N.C.: Duke University Press.

———. 2001. Returning the body without haunting in Thailand: The politics of revolution as mise-en-scène. In *Loss*, edited by David Eng and David Kasanjian. Berkeley: University of California Press.

Rao mai lyym Hok Tula [We haven't forgotten/won't forget October 6]. 1996. Bangkok: Committee for the Twentieth Anniversary of 6 October 1976.

Reynolds, Craig J. 1972. The Buddhist monkhood in nineteenth century Thailand. Ph.D. diss., Cornell University.

———. 1976. Buddhist cosmography in Thai history, with special reference to nineteenth century cultural change. *Journal of Asian Studies* 35, no. 2: 203–20.

———, ed. 1991. *National identity and its defenders: Thailand, 1939–1989.* Chiang Mai: Silkworm.

Reynolds, Frank E., and Mani B. Reynolds, trans. 1982. *Three worlds according to King Ruang: A Thai buddhist cosmology* [translation of *Thraiphum Phra Ruang*]. Berkeley: University of California Press.

Robinson, James W. 1997. *Empire of freedom: The Amway story and what it means to you.* Rocklin, Calif.: Prima.

Siriyuvasak, Ubonrat. 1989. Radio in a transitional society: The case of Thailand. Ph.D. diss., University of Leicester.

Tambiah, Stanley. 1976. *World conqueror and world renouncer: A study of Buddhism and polity against a historical background.* Cambridge: Cambridge University Press.

Tanabe, Shigeharu. 1996. The person in transformation: Body, mind, and cultural appropriation. Special lecture, Sixth International Thai Studies Conference, Chiang Mai, 15 October.

Vella, Walter F. 1978. *Chaiyo! King Vajiravudh and the development of Thai nationalism.* Honolulu: University of Hawai'i Press.

Waithayakon, Wan. 1991 [1944]. Thai culture: Lecture delivered before the Thailand Research Society, 27 February 1944. In *The centennial of His Royal Highness Prince Wan Waithayakon Krommun Naradhop Bonsprabandh.* Bangkok: Office of the National Culture Commission. (Originally published in *Journal of the Thailand Research Society* 35, no. 2 [1944]: 135–45.)

Wilson, Constance. 1971. State and society in the reign of Mongkut, 1851–1868: Thailand on the eve of modernization. Ph.D. diss., Cornell University.

Winichakul, Thongchai. 1994. *Siam mapped: A history of the geo-body of a nation.* Honolulu: University of Hawai'i Press.

Living at the Edge: Religion, Capitalism, and the End of the Nation-State in Taiwan

Robert P. Weller

Taiwan lies at the boundaries of the world. Economically it has flourished, but with hardly a company or brand name that would be recognized anywhere else. A late entry to world capitalism, it has skipped much of capitalism's high modernity of assembly lines and monopolies and thrives instead as a welter of networked little firms and subcontractors, both the site of global investment and a major global investor. Politically it has spent the last four hundred years as a backwater frontier of the Dutch, Chinese, and Japanese empires, until the cataclysm of 1949 cast it adrift. Culturally, its people wonder whether they are part of China or perhaps someplace else altogether. The island floats in limbo, not quite a nation and not quite a state, with no change in sight, but vibrant all the same with its economic success, its politics, and its people's arguments about who they really are.

This essay examines the religious side of how people live at these edges, shaping and making sensible their experience in distinct ways. Religious practices have developed in Taiwan that vary greatly in, among other things, the ambition of their social organization, their claims to universalizing moralities, and their conception of the relationship between self and society. At one extreme lies fee-for-service religion that caters to asocial individuals, grants any request without regard to morality, and celebrates shady deities through carnivalesque reversals and excesses. Its temples are postmodern celebrations of disorder and localization, a kind of feral religion. At the same time, temples to community gods that had long been the heart of Taiwanese religion beyond the household have grown in number and in scale, with new temples built and old temples reconstructed. These temples address individuals as embedded members of social networks. Although their orientation and organization is still primarily local, they also trace out new and old lines of migration and trade. At the other extreme are new pietistic Buddhist movements that proselytize for new social values and create new kinds of community—globalizing, encompassing, structuring, modern. Nearly all the new religious practices rework and transform cultural and social resources that were available to Taiwanese for centuries. The newness arises because of the complexities of Taiwan's place in the current world economic and political system.

ON THE EDGE

Taiwan's place at the literal edge of Asia—the island link between Japan, China, and southeast Asia—has shaped its political history. Most of its inhabitants before the seventeenth century were Austronesian speakers; the island was visited sometimes by Chinese or Japanese traders and occasionally used as a base by pirates. The Dutch took a kind of entrepôt-based control in the seventeenth century, only to be forcibly removed in 1661 by a Ming Dynasty loyalist using Taiwan as a last bastion against the new Qing government (a role Taiwan would later repeat). Chinese settlement increased drastically during this period, turning the island into the newest Chinese frontier and ultimately forcing the aboriginal population to sinicize or flee into the deep mountains.

The Qing Dynasty took over in 1683, but Taiwan was still very much a frontier, known for producing chronic rebellions the way other areas were known for producing scholars or silks. The Qing government had grave doubts about whether the island was really worth the investment, and Taiwan was not elevated to provincial status until 1884. Its new recognition lasted only eleven years, however. In 1895 China ceded Taiwan to Japan in the aftermath of the Sino-Japanese War. Fifty years of Japanese colonialism followed, bringing with it pacification of endemic violence, rationalization of bureaucracy and taxation, improvements in infrastructure, and the spread of basic education. On the other hand, the colonized population lost all political say above the local level, higher education was strictly limited, and major business positions were controlled by the Japanese.

The island reverted to Chinese control after World War II, but was still considered a backwater (worse yet, a backwater heavily influenced by Japanese language and values). Relations between local Taiwanese and the new government had already deteriorated when the Communist victories of 1949 forced the Nationalist government to flee to Taiwan, taking with it as much of its wealth and military might as it could muster. The Nationalists claimed to be the only legitimate government of China, just waiting to retake the mainland from its temporary occupation by Communist bandits. Taipei was proclaimed for the moment China's capital. The nationalists declared a temporary "state of emergency"—essentially martial law—that lasted roughly forty years. For the first time, Taiwan was not just the outer edge of empire. Taiwanese, however, were as much at the edge of political power as ever.

The Nationalists under Chiang Kai-shek learned their organizing techniques from the Soviet Union during an early alliance with the Communists. The Nationalist Party (*Guomindang*), organized along Leninist principles as a vanguard party, was present in every institution, including the military. The basic economic model was corporatist, although much of the technique of ideological control showed its common roots with the mainland. When I first visited in the late 1970s, walls were covered with slogans (Retake the Mainland!), television broadcasts offered quotes from President Chiang, and all media were tightly controlled.

This claim not to be at the edge had a weak point, of course—mainland China's alternative reading of the situation, which ultimately redefined Taiwan's position. The crucial blow came when the United States withdrew its diplomatic recognition of Taiwan in 1979. Diplomatically, Taiwan was fully in limbo from that point on. Removed from the United Nations, it has no voice in international treaties. Its claims to be a state are recognized by only a handful of the world's least powerful countries. Thoughts of giving up claims to China and becoming a new nation are immediately squelched by saber-rattling from the mainland. In addition, Taiwan was not part of China during the first half of the twentieth century, when ideas about Chinese nationalism developed most strongly. In a world organized by nation-states, Taiwan falls between all the boundaries.

The dilemmas this poses strengthened further after martial law was finally lifted in 1987. In the years that followed, local people could, for the first time in a century, speak explicitly about what it meant to be Taiwanese, in contrast to the Chinese they had been for the previous four decades, and the colonial Japanese they had been for the five decades before that. More than any other issue since 1987, the problem of identity has preoccupied Taiwan. When the government stepped back from its uncompromising paternalistic moralism, it left an empty field in which anything seemed possible. This new free space, added to Taiwan's irresolvable political position, has fostered the religious creativity we now see there.

Taiwan's economy is not so unusual as its current political situation, but the island's history has also fostered an economic edginess. Early on, Chinese settlers in Taiwan had been market oriented. By the nineteenth century, much of the island's agricultural production was directed toward the market rather than subsistence use. Taiwan was the major supplier of tea to the United States after the Civil War, and it exported its rice and sugarcane to mainland China and southeast Asia. The Japanese built up the agricultural base still further and invested heavily in infrastructure; Taiwan was to become a rice basket for Japan. When Chiang Kai-shek and his followers took over in 1949, they followed a developmental state model. They actively promoted key economic sectors through state-owned companies or the promotion of private industry, and their tight political control enforced docility in the labor force. Under a generally corporatist model, Taiwan's economy grew steadily. By the 1960s Taiwan was attracting the cheap labor industries that ride at the front of capitalism's advance. In Taiwan this included both textiles — the classic leading edge of the cheap labor frontier since textiles first moved from England to New England — and newer industrial manufacture such as cheap plastic toys and electronics.

This story of tough political rule and enlightened economic leadership could often be heard from Nationalist officials. The economy has another side, however. Quite unlike Japan or South Korea, the heart of Taiwan's economic growth has been very small-scale entrepreneurs, not the gigantic companies that work closely within state policy. Taiwanese bosses complain that workers stay around only long enough to learn the business, and then set themselves up in competition. There is a cliché in Taiwan that it is "better to be a chicken's beak than a bull's behind" (*ning wei jikou, bu wei niuhou*), and in fact, by some estimates, one of every eight adults in Taiwan is the boss of his or her own small business.[1] The government has not exactly hindered this growth, but has done very little to foster it directly. For example, tight banking policy has long made it almost impossible for small businesses to obtain credit. As a result, Taiwanese turn to the informal economy. Primary sources of credit thus include postdated checks and rotating credit associations.[2] None of these techniques have formal legal backing, and so all rely on informal networks of social trust to succeed. Entrepreneurs, potential entrepreneurs (which includes almost everyone), and even people working at household-based piecework production must develop and maintain ego-centered networks of connections to do well.

The 1980s brought economic transformations almost as great as Taiwan's political changes of the period. As the economy thrived, costs of labor increased until it made little sense to continue investing in the production of footwear, textiles, and injection-molded plastic. The source of the crisis was not so much that multinational companies left for greener pastures, but that Taiwanese entrepreneurs could no longer compete in these businesses, even despite the traditional advantages provided by household labor. Their small scale, however, meant that they did not usually have enough capital to move into high-technology and capital-intensive sectors. The logical solution would have been for them to invest overseas in the industries they already knew (and this has happened in the 1990s). At the time, however, government currency regulations and political fears of China—the most obvious source of cheap labor—prevented people from exporting their money. The result was a lot of unproductive investment, especially speculation in the stock and real estate markets (both of which crashed a few years later). Taiwan became a gambler's economy in which earlier values of hard work and savings no longer explained profits.

This changed again in the 1990s when barriers to overseas investment were largely removed and Taiwanese entrepreneurs rushed into the opportunities. Taiwan is the largest single investor in Vietnam and a very large investor in parts of China. This fosters a new mode of precariousness, with the constant specter of political or economic turmoil threatening to undermine investments. For all these political and economic reasons, and in spite of the wealth so much of the population has achieved, Taiwan is not an easy place in which to sit back and feel secure. All of these changes have intertwined with religious life in Taiwan, which has undergone several decades of creative expansion and seems to thrive on Taiwan's general uncertainty.

A number of previously obscure temples suddenly became prominent in Taiwan in the mid-1980s, just as the gambling economy thrived.
The most famous was the Eighteen Lords temple at the northern tip of
the island, rebuilt in the 1970s in the shadow of a nuclear power plant.[3]
There had been a small ghost shrine (which nobody could date) where
the plant was erected. Ghost shrines are usually small, but this was even
smaller than usual—too small to have been recorded—not much more
than a grave and an incense pot. According to most people who told
me the story, a fishing boat had washed ashore sometime in the past,
carrying seventeen unidentified dead bodies and one live dog. As is customary, locals buried the bodies in a mass grave, which they marked
with a shrine. The ceremony was disrupted when the dog, loyal to the
death (a value most associated with upright ministers, good business
partners, and powerful bandits), leaped into the grave after its dead
masters and was buried alive. Seventeen corpses and one suicidal dog:
the Eighteen Lords.

For years, soldiers on coastal sentry duty would on occasion worship
at the shrine, but not many others came there. When construction of
the nuclear power plant began in the 1970s, the land around the plant
was to be shored up, causing the new ground level to rise above the
existing shrine. Popular sentiment and eerie experience, however, persuaded the government to preserve the shrine in a room below ground.
A number of workers had died in construction accidents (often taken
as a sign of unhappy ghosts), and a backhoe mysteriously froze just as
it stood poised to destroy the original little shrine. These events helped
mobilize both workers and neighbors to lobby against destruction. The
government ultimately agreed "to respect local customs" by building a
new temple directly over the old shrine. This new temple is quite mag-
nificent by ghost-cult standards. On one side of the temple are images
of the Eighteen Lords, and on the other side is the grave, flanked by two
large bronze statues of the dog. This grave is a simulacrum of the original (both are mosaic tile–covered mounds), which is now preserved
in an underground room directly below its replica. The genuine grave,
reached through an unmarked basement staircase in the back of the
temple, is said to be the true center of power.

Ghosts symbolize improper deaths: They are the spirits of people who have no descendants to worship them because they died young or (like the Eighteen Lords) by means of violent death far from home. Unlike gods, ghosts will grant any request because, lacking descendants to worship them, they are starving in the underworld—this explains their fondness for any paying proposition. Their only condition is proper repayment (buying them gold medals, giving money to their temple, sponsoring operas for their pleasure), without which they will exact a nasty revenge. This is fee-for-service religion, something like cutting a deal with a local hoodlum. Ghosts have long had this greedy and individualistic streak, in contrast to the community-based and upright morality of gods. One of the most obvious ritual statements of this difference occurs in ritual offerings of incense. Gods receive incense in single pots that combine the smoky offerings of entire worshiping communities. At their annual propitiation ritual, ghosts receive instead separate, single sticks of incense (often marked with the name of the donor) stuck into plates of food. Worshipers are individualized, and any sense of community is minimized.

The Eighteen Lords temple differs from this normally shadowy corner of Taiwanese religion only in having suddenly jumped into the open. By the late 1980s, the Eighteen Lords temple may have been the most popular one on the island. Thousands of people visited every night, knotting up traffic on the north coastal highway. People said it was especially popular with prostitutes, gamblers, and petty criminals. Visitors were warned to watch out for pickpockets who came both to worship and to steal. In fact, all kinds of people made offerings, and talismans from the temple could be seen everywhere—in rearview mirrors, in fish restaurants, in fancy hotels.[4] Bending the government to its will accounted for the initial fame of this temple. But its boom really began in the mid-1980s with the rise in popularity of temples like this to shady characters who offered ritual efficacy for morally suspect fees.

The Eighteen Lords emphasized the departure from community and conventional morality that their worship encouraged through a series of reversals. People worshiped there at night, and the center of power was underground at the original grave. Instead of offering sticks of incense at the grave, they erected lit cigarettes. A wall now blocks access to the grave from the front (where the incense pot stands), so the cigarettes must be offered from behind. The trip from parking lot to temple was equally carnivalesque: unorganized crowds made their way toward the temple amid rows of carnival games (shoot the balloons, knock over the ducks, and all the rest). And as a reminder of the driving force behind it all, everyone asked for cash. Even the toilets were fee-for-service.

The temple spawned more than its share of commercial offshoots. These included souvenir dogs (I saw one on an altar in a small business, smoking a lit cigarette), but more significantly, a movie, a television soap opera, and even a fake temple a bit closer to town on the same highway.[5] One subplot from the movie—it was postmodern itself, all subplots and no plot—was particularly striking. The heroine of the moment was a beautiful prostitute, stuck in debt-bondage to her pimp. Her handsome boyfriend was a gambler who could not win enough money to buy her freedom. The boyfriend's clownish sidekick came to the rescue by worshiping the Eighteen Lords. As he was leaving the temple, a book blew open to disclose a formula for successful gambling. To follow the formula the gambler needed a talisman made from the umbilical cord of a newborn baby, although the book also warns that the fate of the baby will be endangered. By happy coincidence, the sidekick's wife had just given birth: the father ripped the cord off the wailing baby in the hospital, and soon everyone's problems were solved (except, I imagine, the baby's, whose story the film drops). The film itself looks like a quick attempt to profit from the temple's popularity, but its greed and its plots align well with the principles at play in worship of the Eighteen Lords.

This image of ghosts is not new in Taiwanese (or, more generally, Chinese) culture, but its sudden surge in popularity by the late 1980s was a significant change. In part, this temple and others like it—one to a murdered thief, another to an executed bank robber—thrived by revealing winning numbers for an illegal lottery that also grew in popularity during this period. As a form of the numbers game, this lottery gave fairly high odds of success for a temple that could ambiguously suggest three or four digits. With thousands of worshipers looking for signs in the incense smoke or through divination techniques, the odds on any given day that a devotee would win were not bad. People said that standard community gods were unwilling to help people gamble. But lottery numbers were only part of the explanation for the new prominence of these temples. The sudden flowering of the illegal lottery during these years also demands explanation—a state-run lottery had existed for many years without such competition.

What the illegal lottery and these newly popular fee-for-service temples had in common was the prospect of unearned wealth. Their popularity increased in the late 1980s because of the specific economic and political conditions of the period. First, the suspension of martial law opened a moral free space for new social practices, including worship of the Eighteen Lords. Second, although people had achieved the standard of living that is usually associated with developed countries, they were also caught in a momentary economic vise: with surplus money and nowhere productive to put it, unproductive investments that might lead to unearned wealth seemed to make sense. When this situation changed in the 1990s, especially as Taiwanese were then increasingly able to invest in mainland China, both the Eighteen Lords and the illegal lottery faded in importance.

The Eighteen Lords and similar temples seem playfully postmodern. Who could better symbolize the apparent loss of shared values than a pile of unrecognized dead bodies? They inflict no set morality. They do not even suggest a morality by favoring an immorality; they just do not care about such issues. Their space is restless and chaotic, always filled with masses of people, but never the same people. No one has the authority to impose a unified interpretation on this, nor do interpretive social mechanisms exist that might order it. Even the movie made no attempt at a unified reading of the temple. These ghosts are radically individualistic, serving people's selfish ends without regard for older social ties such as family or community, and without any effective means to foster a unified, authoritative meaning.

GODS AND NETWORKS

These ghost temples stood out partly because, for the first time, they began to rival community god temples. Most gods, like ghosts, are the spirits of dead people. But unlike ghosts, gods are known for their upright acts before or after death, or both. Many people worship ancestral spirits and nonancestral gods at home altars. The most important god temples, however, are run by local community committees. There is no priesthood affiliated with these temples, although Daoist or Buddhist priests may be hired to conduct rituals. Nor is there any institutional organization beyond individual temples. Some nearby temples are connected historically through "incense division," in which a branch temple starts up by bringing incense from the mother temple and usually reaffirms the tie annually by making a pilgrimage to the mother temple. Maintenance of such ties is evidence of historical roots and ongoing economic or social connections. Overseas communities often maintain ties to their home communities through incense-division networks.

In many respects, worship of community gods is contrary to Western conceptions of religion. For example, one of my earliest impressions in Taiwan was that my anthropological instincts about sacred and profane were defied. This was not just the observation that religion and daily life were inextricably intertwined; I was much more struck by the absence of sacred space in rituals. Early in my first extended field research, I observed a Buddhist altar that had been set up to feed the lonely ghosts during the seventh lunar month. During the ceremony people walked up to the monk conducting the ritual, surrounded the altar, and even grabbed objects from the altar. Temple altars are normally very approachable, and gods, when they physically appear through spirit mediums, are so approachable that people just sit around and have ordinary conversations with them. This sense reflects popular attitudes, though it is not a priestly view of things — the Buddhist monk had busily created a meditational mandala around himself, and a glance at temple architecture shows a division of sacred space. Furthermore, there was not even a clear translation of the term "religion" into Chinese before the twentieth century, when China borrowed the term from Japan, which got it in turn from Western philosophy. A number of older informants still do not recognize the term today, and among those who do, many deny that they have any religion (meaning something institutionalized, textual, priestly) and will say only that they "carry incense" (*gia: hiu:*).

The distinction between the worlds of commerce and religion also was never very applicable in Taiwan. Any act of worship beyond a minimal lighting of incense requires burning "spirit money." The most common forms of spirit money in Taiwan are cheap squares of paper decorated with gold or silver foil. (In Hong Kong some look like secular currency inscribed with the English words "Bank of Hell.") In contrast to the fee-for-service ghosts, however, people do not talk about money for gods as fixing a contractual relationship or as bribery. Instead, the image is of the reciprocity through which people build community and personal networks. For instance, in her book on Chinese ritual and politics, anthropologist Emily Martin Ahern quotes a Taiwanese worshiper as follows: "Police act one way to people who give them red envelopes [bribes] and another way to those who do not. But gods are not like that. It is not that the more things you give them the more they will help you. It is only necessary to do good deeds and burn three sticks of incense and they will be enormously happy. A god is a being with a very upright heart."[6] This is a very different conceptualization from the repayment to ghosts, but it also shows the general comfort with commerce beyond the marketplace in Taiwan. The standard wedding or funeral gift, for example, is cash.

God temples in Taiwan have also thrived over the last few decades, although they have not enjoyed the spectacular spurt of growth that ghost temples briefly did. They have increased in both quantity (the number of temples per capita has been rising since about 1972) and quality (as older temples are rebuilt on larger scales and at great expense).[7] Some of these temples are entrepreneurial, especially those associated with spirit mediums. A contractual relationship between the client and the human spirit medium (but not the deity) is also involved. This sector has grown like any other petty capitalist product—mediums have multiplied the number of deities on their altars because different gods fit different market niches, and mediums innovate new techniques in competition with each other.[8] The appeal to market segmentation in religion corresponds to the general fracturing of marketing to fit the disunities of the population.

The most important temples are still those dedicated to community gods. These temples are uncompromisingly local in orientation. Other towns may have temples to the same deities, and some deities are nationally recognized, but each god in his or her temple primarily looks after just that locality. Many of these temples have recently been rebuilt at great expense. Lists of contributors and their financial gifts are typically posted outside temples, and these donors are often featured in videos of major rituals produced by the temples. Giving money to a temple claims a relationship of reciprocity simultaneously with both the gods and the local community, declaring community membership and asserting the right to future social and supernatural support (often by wealthy people who no longer live there). Rebuilding a local temple or contributing money to its ritual life are in part ways of solidifying the social networks that are so crucial to Taiwan's mom-and-pop capitalism. Gods and patrons are intertwined in these obligations, which are concretized in the increasingly ornate forms of the temples themselves.

The networks that trace historical connections among temples remain as important as ever, because, above all, Taiwan's current rage for investment in China encourages entrepreneurs to revivify temple ties to their ancestral homelands, where they plan to invest. Mainland China relaxes its usual glare at popular religious practice in these areas, recognizing that Taiwanese investment in local temples also eases the flow of capital for other purposes. Temples are thriving on both sides of the Taiwan Strait as symbols and mediators of new economic ties. Anthropologist Brigitte Baptandier provides an example of the ironies that can result. Back when representatives of Taiwanese temples could not visit the mainland, she took a Taiwanese version of a temple text concerning the goddess Linshui Furen to the mother temple in Fujian Province. A few years later the mother temple held a conference on the goddess, and the organizers were able to invite their Taiwanese counterparts. They reprinted the text and gave it to the Taiwanese, who happily brought it back as evidence of their own renewed authenticity.[9] On the other hand, Taiwanese feel a new kind of power in these relationships — they are now returning as magnates, not prodigal sons — and this sometimes shows up in claims that Taiwanese images are more authentic than those from the mainland.[10]

Taiwan's odd political position also plays out through temples. Two of Taiwan's most famous temples are dedicated to the goddess Mazu. The temple in Beigang is considered senior to the temple in Dajia, which hosted a famous pilgrimage to Beigang every year. When travel to the mainland became possible, members of the Beigang temple initially refused to go, in what amounted to a claim of their temple's own ultimate authenticity. On the other hand, jumping at the chance to go to the original mother temple, members of the Dajia temple brought back incense and then claimed seniority to the Beigang temple. These events were islandwide gossip for a while, and were widely interpreted as Beigang support for Taiwan independence and Dajia support for reunification. Temples have thrived as the nodes of economic and political networks but remain subject to the intricate particularities of Taiwan's unusual economy and unique politics.

Yet another religious growth area in Taiwan comes from the rise of several indigenous pietistic sects, loosely related to earlier Chinese traditions such as the White Lotus.[11] A wide range of such groups now exists, making it difficult to generalize about them. The largest and most influential pietistic sect in Taiwan today is the Way of Unity (*Yiguan Dao*), which claims over a million followers. Its members run most of the vegetarian restaurants in Taiwan and include one of the wealthiest men in the world, the shipping magnate Zhang Rongfa. The sect is currently planning to build a university.

Many of the sects are millenarian. Their temples often have large statues of Maitreya, the Buddha of the next age, whom members say is (or will soon be) on earth. Many sects also worship a goddess, the Eternal Venerable Mother (*Wusheng Laomu*), who created the world but is now saddened and disappointed by her children's lack of morality. Nearly all these sects give a prominent place to spirit writing, in which a deity writes commentaries in sand through a possessed medium using a planchette. Most sectarians are also self-consciously syncretic, drawing on Buddhism, Daoism, and Confucianism and sometimes crossing the globe for their religious resources. For instance, in a spirit-writing text published by one of these groups there is a transcript of a panel discussion involving the "founders of the five religions": the Primordial Heavenly Worthy (central to Daoism), Sakyamuni, Confucius, Mohammed, and Jehovah. The moderator is Guan Gong, the popular Chinese god of war, business, and loyalty.[12] The message is that all the religions of the world share the same basic message of morality.

The sects claim to be moral revivals in an era of moral crisis. They unite large numbers of followers around clear leaders and clear sets of ideas. They come together as ordered groups—the word *congregation* is tempting. This is very different from the relatively disorganized and disaggregated popular worship of gods and especially of ghosts. Many of the sects emphasize this orderliness through the body. For example, pietistic sectarians typically wear blue or white robes over their clothing when they worship or conduct spirit-writing sessions, a significant departure from usual ritual practice. They tend to worship in neat rows with coordinated movements and segregation by gender (men on the left in standard Confucian order); this contrasts with the unorganized worship typical at community god temples, and even more with the total chaos at the Eighteen Lords. Unlike popular temples where anyone can walk in and worship, sect membership is voluntary and strongly marked in dress and behavior. Distinctions between sacred and profane are now relevant, as the select are distinguished from others. Having become accustomed to the nonsacred nature of much ritual space, when I first visited sectarian temples I was surprised that I was not allowed to approach the altars, or sometimes even to see the god. As part of this delineation of sacred space, money has also been removed from the ritual—there is no spirit money in any form.

This is not to say that sectarians oppose either the market economy or Taiwan's modernist state. Their new morality is anything but revolutionary. In the sectarian panel discussion I mentioned above, for instance, the Primordial Heavenly Worthy—perhaps conscious of the political "state of emergency" at the time—offers a summary of the panel's conclusions: "Those who cultivate the Dao should respect the Constitution, be faithful to the nation, be faithful to human plans, not abandon the laws, and behave as good citizens. . . . [They] should be filial to their parents, carefully attend to their funeral rites, and make sacrifices to them."[13] Most of the groups in fact trumpet the market success of their members, arguing in Weberian fashion that sect members make good business connections because of the understanding that comes from sharing the same moral position, even with strangers. Some sects also make a calculation of the profit and loss of the self—each convert is supposed to accumulate enough merit to achieve individual salvation.[14]

These sects offer an overarching morality that is comfortable with the market, but uncomfortable with what is seen as the moral failing of society. Like revived god temples, but even more powerful, they help establish networks of like-minded people that have been crucial to Taiwan's economic expansion. Like the ghost cults, they celebrate the market but with a very different moral message. While ghosts enjoy exactly the loss of a shared sense of morality and revel in the reduction of all relationships to commodity exchange, the sects attempt to rebuild moralities and to construct communities on a new basis. Ghosts relish living at the edge—quite appropriate for liminal beings—but the sects react against it. These sects remain very important in Taiwan, but they have been overshadowed by another form of organized religion, more purely based in Buddhism.

Roughly simultaneous with the beginning of the Eighteen Lords enthusiasm and the increased popularity of sectarian religion in the 1970s, Taiwan also saw a resurgence in various sorts of Buddhism. I will concentrate here on the largest of these groups, the Compassionate Relief Merit Association (*Ciji Gongde Hui*). Claiming about 4 million members, it is the only social association in Taiwan larger than the Nationalist Party.[15] It gives away over U.S. $20 million each year in charity, and many followers also volunteer large amounts of time visiting the poor or working in the Compassionate Relief Hospital in Hualian, where the movement began. Compassionate Relief is led by a frail but charismatic Buddhist nun named Zhengyan. The vast majority of followers are lay people, and the group does not emphasize joining the *sangha*, the order of Buddhist monks and nuns.

Zhengyan began her movement on Taiwan's poor east coast in 1966 with five disciples and thirty housewives who contributed a few cents a day and sewed children's shoes to support medical charity. Now the group has branches around the world, runs a university, and is building its second cutting-edge hospital. Like the Eighteen Lords and some other Buddhist groups, it grew slowly and steadily through the 1970s and expanded very rapidly in the 1980s. Its popularity has outlasted that of ghost temples. Compassionate Relief is almost matched in scale by a few other Buddhist groups such as Buddha Light Mountain (*Fuoguang Shan*) and Dharma Drum Mountain (*Fagu Shan*).

Compassionate Relief is notable for its concern with secular action. It downplays many traditional aspects of Buddhism in Taiwan such as sutra singing and philosophical discussion. The emphasis is consistently on changing this world and creating a Pure Land on earth by bringing the Buddhist message of simplicity and compassion into all aspects of people's lives. Of the followers about 80 percent are women, who until recently wore identical conservative dresses (the dresses are now differentiated by rank). Followers gather periodically in small groups to carry out charitable works, and in larger groups to listen to Zhengyan's sermons (either in person or on video) or to member testimonials about their new lives.[16] The sermons are light on Buddhist text and heavy on action in the world. Zhengyan is known for her terse advice on how to live with problems, not how to transcend them. She urges people to cut down on conspicuous consumption and to devote their resources and energy to helping the poor and sick.

Member testimonials, like their Protestant counterparts, tend to contrast current happiness with former lives of dissolution and dissatisfaction. At a testimonial in 1995, one woman said, "I used to have closets full of clothes. None of them ever seemed beautiful enough to satisfy me. But now I have found that most beautiful dress. It is the one I am wearing [the Compassionate Relief uniform]." A few even relate tales of changing loyalties from the Eighteen Lords to Zhengyan—feral religion tamed again. A consistent theme in discussions about conversion to Compassionate Relief is the first viewing of Zhengyan, when visitors are often lost in uncontrollable weeping in the presence of their frail leader. I have seen families prostrate themselves at her feet with tears flowing down their cheeks.

Much of the movement is about the remaking of the self—the charismatic transition through tears in the presence of Zhengyan, the messages of the testimonials, the instruction to volunteer among the poor and sick. The new self is molded just as much in the bodily practices of daily life. Serious followers keep a vegetarian diet and are required to abstain from alcohol—a primary lubricant for much business in Taiwan. Followers are even instructed to wear their seatbelts. The uniforms, like those of the pietistic sects, help mark group membership; they contrast as much with individualistic daily dress as their carefully constructed group ceremonies contrast with the disorganized daily worship at temples.[17] Compassionate Relief uniforms also carry their own specific meanings. Worn over everyday clothing, sectarian robes emphasize distinctions between the sacred and profane and highlight the necessity of purity when dealing with deities. Their traditional design also promotes the general feeling in those groups of a revival of Confucian tradition. Compassionate Relief uniforms, on the other hand, are more like everyday dress. The emphasis is thus on the secular world, rather than the sacred world of sectarian temples.

Compassionate Relief is not an antimarket movement by any means, but it does look to heal the moral problems of the market-based universe. Like many moral revivals, it discourages consumption and encourages social relations outside of contract and commerce. Charity, after all, is a fundamentally nonmarket way of redistributing wealth, although its money often comes initially from the market. Historically in China this combination of Buddhism and charity is new (even begging by monks was downplayed there), but popularizing Buddhist groups and private charitable organizations have long histories of and close ties to the rise of the commodity economy in China. For example, the rise in philanthropic associations in the late Ming Dynasty (sixteenth century) was a response to an influx of Spanish silver. By joining with local Confucian elites in philanthropic ventures that addressed social problems, newly rich merchants were able to justify their new wealth.[18] Compassionate Relief gave the practice a Buddhist form and assigned women the leading role, but it also helps answer the old moral problems of new wealth. That is why this group — unlike, for instance, many of the Japanese "new religions" — appeals particularly to the wealthy. Many of the other new pietistic and Buddhist movements now also command enormous followings and huge pots of money, and philanthropy serves similar functions for them. Two have opened or are planning universities, and Buddha Light Mountain was involved in the U.S. presidential campaign contribution scandal of 1996.

Buddhist groups and pietistic sects promise a moral compass at a time when people feel that their older moralities are crumbling under the economic and political pressures of current Taiwanese life. They refocus market profits into nonmarket activities, cleansing the cash in good causes. Among the new religious movements, Compassionate Relief is the most worldly and also the most popular with women. These aspects are probably related: the movement offers a way of maintaining the conservative image of women as nurturing mothers and the valuation of a "simple" life, while breaking down the related social barriers that had limited women's activities to the family. The pietistic sects lean instead more toward revitalized Confucianism, which is clearly less appealing to women.[19]

Compassionate Relief also thrived at this particular moment for political reasons. Another Buddhist reformer, a monk named Yinshun, had been silenced by the Buddhist establishment (with government support) in the 1950s because his work seemed too close to leftist agitation. However, by the 1970s, when Compassionate Relief began to grow,

Taiwan's authoritarian government had become staunchly laissez-faire on social issues. Swayed largely by neoclassical economics (in spite of their large state-owned sector), they kept taxation low in exchange for providing little welfare, unemployment, or health benefits. This began to change only after 1987, when democratization changed the political dynamics of offering social services. Given Taiwan's economic direction at the time, it was convenient for the government that Compassionate Relief met genuine social needs without government involvement. Zhengyan has never offered direct political support to the government and is generally seen as independent, but there is, no doubt, a happy coincidence of purpose.

WHY THIS? WHY NOW?

Anthropologists in Taiwan in the early 1970s tended to think indigenous forms of religion were fading away. This notion may in part have been a remnant of modernization theory assumptions that secularization was inevitable, but it was also supported by crude statistical measures for religion, like registered temples per capita.[20] Growth in indigenous forms of religion began in the early 1970s and has generally continued unabated, although individual movements can ebb and flow over just a few years. This growth coincides roughly with the period when Taiwan moved firmly into an export-oriented economic policy with minimal state support of society beyond education and infrastructure — the kind of model that has more recently become the general liberal economic prescription for the entire world. Taiwan did very well under these policies, but its success also encouraged the economic worries of the 1980s (as cheap labor gradually dried up) and the political worries of the 1990s (as democratization has pushed the issue of independence or reunification to the point of ongoing identity crisis).

It is not enough to point out that modernization theorists misunderstood the relationship between secularization and capitalism. Taiwan is hardly unique in casting doubt on that theory, or in experiencing the kinds of moral doubts that religion can address. Nor is it enough to point out that these religious developments respond roughly to market pressures that are not unusual around the world — an uneasy combination of growing individualism in a Hobbesian world of competition and contract, combined with an attempt to create new forms of community. Instead, it seems worth exploring why Taiwan's animated, vigorous, and diverse set of religious possibilities takes the particular forms it has at this historical moment. At one side, the Eighteen Lords wildly celebrate the moral freedoms of the individual in the market. At the same time, resurgent god cults help solidify business networks, and organized religious movements offer entirely new moral communities. One can move from the chaotic midnight mass of self-interested worshipers to neat congregations of identical followers; we see fads for nameless and homeless ghosts, for gods with communitarian loyalties, for charismatic and saintly leaders. Some people, in fact, switched almost overnight from ardent followers of ghosts and gambling to loyal welfare workers for Compassionate Relief. As Taiwan has thrived in the new capitalist world, it has simultaneously become more localizing and more universalizing, pushed market competition and charitable redistribution, celebrated individualism and constructed social values, wallowed in disorderly ghosts and crafted new kinds of order. It is both postmodern and modern, together and inseparable.

Part of the answer to the particularities of Taiwan's current religious vigor lies in its long history of involvement in global trade, market economies, and borderland politics. While the configuration of the world economy in the late twentieth century was of course new, China—and especially Taiwan—already had an intimate familiarity with things like cash and contracts. Neither the political tension of Taiwan's current limbo nor the economic edginess of life in a changeable commodity economy are new for the Chinese. In China's history political edges abound: There are international and domestic regional boundaries where communication and political control have been difficult and where the strength of non-Chinese ethnic groups made social interactions more complex. Taiwan nearly always fit this category, although the events of the last few decades have made its position even more anomalous. Especially during periods of political weakness in China, these edgy places have sprouted unusual religious growths. Peripheral Guangxi in the 1840s, for example, was just such a place, and one of its main deities at the time was King Gan, who had achieved high office by murdering his mother and burying her in a grave whose geomancy was said to guarantee his future success. Other deities in the area included a sexually licentious couple and a dung-throwing vagrant. Speaking through possessed spirit mediums, several deities extorted money from innocent passers-by.[21] This was distant indeed from the image of the upright bureaucratic gods promoted in most areas.

China's earlier surges of market and commodity dominance also had religious interactions. In addition to the rise of philanthropic associations and popularizing Buddhism in the late Ming, another episode that resonates today was the 1768 wave of soulstealing in China. A strand of a victim's hair, or a victim's written name, was allegedly used for someone else's personal gain; the victim—often a child—was robbed of his spiritual essence and would soon waste away and die.[22] This was a period of economic prosperity in China (after the British began to buy Chinese tea but before they wreaked their opium revenge), and the accusations occurred in China's wealthiest region. In this area, where recently there had been a rapid population increase, the new wealth led to a general freeing of peasant labor, but only to enter a buyer's labor market. This was not capitalism, but it was a form of market culture based in rapid commercialization and its social effects.

Even the great variety of religious options in Taiwan today is not new. Devotion has not been strongly institutionalized in China since the Song Dynasty dropped the earlier idea of adopting Buddhism or Daoism as a state religion. Correspondingly, for centuries most religion in China and Taiwan has been either strictly locally controlled in community temples or only loosely centralized through rival centers of Buddhist and Daoist ordination. Most worship has been performed within the home, overseen by no higher authority. Under these circumstances, China and Taiwan have long brewed a wide variety of local religious options, and there is little institutional obstacle to change when compared to Christianity or Islam.

These historical precedents in part explain Taiwan's reaction to millennial capitalism. But the movements I have discussed are not simple continuations of earlier religious ideas, even though each one has direct precursors. Rather, they differ from earlier movements because they are integral parts of Taiwan's recent economic and political transformations, which are not just a reiteration of earlier bouts of commercialization or political weakness. One aspect of this change in the global context is communication, including both through the media and transportation. The new ease of movement has allowed people and temples to act on larger scales than ever before, including the international stage for Compassionate Relief (it has branches in nineteen countries), the new levels of interaction between Taiwanese and mainland temples, and even the islandwide popularity of the Eighteen Lords temple. New media play just as strong a role: the Eighteen Lords spawned a movie and a television soap opera, community temples hawk souvenir videos of major rituals, and, like Zhengyan, important clergy frequently preach on television.

The specific forms of religion today in Taiwan are unique, both in comparison to their historical antecedents and to comparable religious resurgences in other parts of the world. The Eighteen Lords cult, for example, aggrandizes ghosts beyond anything documented earlier in China or Taiwan. As a ghost temple, it differs fundamentally from the unruly god cults of 1840s Guangxi. In some ways it is more similar to the recent growth in many parts of the world of what Jean and John Comaroff call "occult economies," which generally paint a Hobbesian world of all against all, with individualism run rampant and amoral self-interest the only goal.[23] There is rarely any institutional structure beyond the locality, and while the themes draw on indigenous traditions, they also reflect a rapid transnational flow in the cultural capital of evil.

These religions are all feral in a sense, but Taiwan's Eighteen Lords is also quite different from the others, including the South African instance the Comaroffs document in detail. South Africa has seen an epidemic of witchcraft accusations, sometimes culminating in the murder of the "witch" by the old revolutionary means of "necklacing," that is, being garlanded with a rubber tire that is then set alight. The accused witches are said to be wealthy, old, and infertile. One common theme is that they murder people and revive their bodies to work as agricultural slaves at night. During the day the zombified bodies are stored in metal oil drums. Other tales tell of the harvest of human body parts, ideally from freshly slaughtered children, to make magic potions for personal gain. The epidemic of witchcraft accusations, and the very real violence that results from it, has been serious enough to spawn government commissions of enquiry. In great contrast to this grim portrait, Taiwan's version of fee-for-service religion is essentially playful, not evil. The difference reflects the very different experiences of capitalism so far by the Taiwanese, and especially the great success of Taiwan's particular form of networked mom-and-pop entrepreneurs. Rampant self-interest does not seem quite so evil when most people have clearly thrived on it. Indeed, the Taiwanese Eighteen Lords is as much a celebration of capitalist greed as a damnation of it.

Community god temples in Taiwan are the closest thing to a simple revival of what was already there. Even they, however, are caught up in the new systems. They are part of the rapid cross-strait expansion of personal networks as economic investment opportunities have grown over the last decade. Partly for this reason, they have also become crucial to the new local and international politics of identity. This is evidenced by arguments about relative "authenticity" of ritual and iconography and about independence and reunification versions of a goddess. More locally, the new role of community temple religion appears when political candidates behead a cock in front of the community god to prove the seriousness of their promises, or when temples help organize local environmental demonstrations. Temples and local political power have long had an intimate relationship, but democratization has helped change its nature. At still larger scales, the pietistic sects claim a relation to market success that is new in their history, and the Buddhist moralizing of Compassionate Relief is part of a transformation in women's social position.

These changes correlate to Taiwan's complex and weakly institutionalized religious history and to Taiwan's specific adaptations to its unusual economics and politics. In part, Taiwan's current identity crisis is the result of the growth of networked capitalism during its decades along the global cheap-labor frontier that has now moved farther west into China and southeast Asia. In part, the identity crisis is also the creation of its anomalous political world. Identity in Taiwan is in so much flux both because the island has no place in a world of nation-states and because of its market experience. Were it not for the political loosening after martial law, the consequent explosion of worry about what it means to be Taiwanese, and the international (or intranational—that confusion itself is the problem) conundrums it has created, religious culture in Taiwan would look rather different. Taiwan's wide range of indigenous alternatives reflects its fragmented identities as a postmodern economy in a nonnation-nonstate, less certain of its religious certainties than in other places and other times. Its rich religious cultures evolved around the tensions of modernity in its particular historical context, but their specific realizations require us to look to the forms of life that characterize the edges of the economic and political worlds, shaped by the convergence of their histories and a new world system.

NOTES

1 Gary G. Hamilton, Culture and organization in Taiwan's market economy, in *Market cultures: Society and morality in the new Asian capitalisms*, edited by Robert W. Hefner (Boulder, Colo.: Westview Press, 1998), 48.

2 See Jane Kaufman Winn, Not by rule of law: Mediating state-society relations in Taiwan through the underground economy," in *The other Taiwan: 1945 to the present*, edited by Murray A. Rubenstein (New York: M. E. Sharpe, 1994).

3 For a longer description, see Robert P. Weller, *Resistance, chaos, and control in China: Taiping rebels, Taiwanese ghosts, and Tiananmen* (London: Macmillan, 1994), 124–43.

4 Temple employees, who help worshipers read the poetic talismans that are part of standard temple divination, see a wide range of people and listen to their personal situations. These employees invariably told me that the people who came to this temple seemed no different from those at any other temple. The Eighteen Lords temple allows visitors the frisson of thinking they are rubbing elbows with gangsters and prostitutes, without actually forcing them to do so.

5 The movie was *Shiba Wanggong* [The Eighteen Lords] (1985), and the soap opera was *Shiba Wanggong chuanqi* [The strange tale of the Eighteen Lords] (China Television Service, 1985).

6 Emily Martin Ahern, *Chinese ritual and politics* (New York: Cambridge University Press, 1981), 99.

7 See Chiu Heiyuan and Yao Lixiang, Taiwan diqu zongjiao bianqian zhi tantao [Discussion of religious changes in the Taiwan area], *Bulletin of the Institute of Ethnology, Academia Sinica* 75 (1986): 657.

8 See Donald Sutton, Transmission in popular religion: The Jiajiang troupe in southern Taiwan, in *Unruly gods: Divinity and society in China*, edited by Meir Shahar and Robert P. Weller (Honolulu: University of Hawaii Press, 1996), for an example of how a ritual performance style changed during the twentieth century in response to the market.

9 Brigitte Baptandier, The Lady Linshui: How a woman became a goddess, in Shahar and Weller, *Unruly gods*.

10 See P. Steven Sangren, Anthropology and identity politics in Taiwan: The relevance of local religion (paper presented at the Taiwan Studies Workshop, Fairbank Center for East Asian Research, Harvard University, 1995).

11 See David K. Jordan and Daniel L. Overmyer, *The flying phoenix: Aspects of Chinese sectarianism in Taiwan* (Princeton, N.J.: Princeton University Press, 1986).

12 Shengxian Tang, *Xiudao zhinan* [Compass for the cultivation of the Dao] (Taizhong: Dajiang Press, 1978).

13 Ibid., 10.

14 See Joseph Bosco, *Yiguan Dao:* "Heterodoxy" and popular religion in Taiwan, in *Taiwan, 1945–1991: Responses to directed political and socio-economic change*, edited by Murray R. Rubenstein (Armonk, N.Y.: M. E. Sharpe, 1992).

15 See Lu Hwei-syin, Women's self-growth groups and empowerment of the "uterine family" in Taiwan, *Bulletin of the Institute of Ethnology, Academia Sinica* 71 (1991): 29–62; Zhang Wei'an, Fuojiao Ciji Gongde Hui yu Ziyuan Huishou [The Buddhist Compassion Merit Society and recycling] (paper presented at the Workshop on Culture, Media, and Society in Contemporary Taiwan, Harvard University, 12 June 1996); and Chien-yu Julia Huang and Robert P. Weller, Merit and mothering: Women and social welfare in Taiwanese Buddhism, *Journal of Asian Studies* 57 (1998): 379–96.

16 Many of these practices sound Protestant, although there is no evidence of borrowing. The general social message, however, is said to stem in part from Zhengyan's early contact with several Catholic nuns, who compared Buddhism unfavorably to Catholicism for its lack of social action.

17 When a Taiwanese graduate student of mine who had been doing research in Namibia first walked into Compassionate Relief's Taipei headquarters, she saw all the uniforms and exclaimed, "Zionists!"

18 Joanna F. Handlin Smith, Benevolent societies: The reshaping of charity during the Late Ming and Early Ch'ing, *Journal of Asian Studies* 46 (1987): 309–37.

19 For more on the gender issue, see Huang and Weller, Merit and mothering.

20 See Chiu and Yao, Taiwan diqu zongjiao, 655–85.

21 See Robert P. Weller, Matricidal magistrates and gambling gods: Weak states and strong spirits in China, *Australian Journal of Chinese Affairs* 33 (1995): 107–24.

22 Philip A. Kuhn, *Soulstealers: The Chinese sorcery scare of 1768* (Cambridge: Harvard University Press, 1990).

23 Jean Comaroff and John L. Comaroff, Occult economies and the violence of abstraction: Notes from the South African postcolony, *American Ethnologist* 26 (1999): 279–301.

REFERENCES

Ahern, Emily Martin. 1981. *Chinese ritual and politics.* New York: Cambridge University Press.

Baptandier, Brigitte. 1996. The Lady Linshui: How a woman became a goddess. In Shahar and Weller.

Bosco, Joseph. 1992. *Yiguan Dao:* "Heterodoxy" and popular religion in Taiwan. In *Taiwan, 1945–1991: Responses to directed political and socio-economic change*, edited by Murray R. Rubenstein. Armonk, N.Y.: M. E. Sharpe.

Chiu Heiyuan, and Yao Lixiang. 1986. Taiwan diqu zongjiao bianqian zhi tantao [Discussion of religious changes in the Taiwan area]. *Bulletin of the Institute of Ethnology, Academia Sinica* 75: 655–85.

Comaroff, Jean, and John L. Comaroff. 1999. Occult Economies and the violence of abstraction: Notes from the South African postcolony. *American Ethnologist* 26: 279–301.

Hamilton, Gary G. 1998. Culture and organization in Taiwan's market economy. In *Mar-

ket cultures: Society and morality in the new Asian capitalisms, edited by Robert W. Hefner. Boulder, Colo.: Westview Press.

Huang, Chien-yu Julia, and Robert P. Weller. 1998. Merit and mothering: Women and social welfare in Taiwanese Buddhism, *Journal of Asian Studies* 57: 379–96.

Hwei-syin, Lu. 1991. Women's self-growth groups and empowerment of the "uterine family" in Taiwan. *Bulletin of the Institute of Ethnology, Academia Sinica* 71: 29–62.

Jordan, David K., and Daniel L. Overmyer. 1986. *The flying phoenix: Aspects of Chinese sectarianism in Taiwan.* Princeton, N.J.: Princeton University Press.

Kuhn, Philip A. 1990. *Soulstealers: The Chinese sorcery scare of 1768.* Cambridge: Harvard University Press.

Sangren, Steven P. 1995. Anthropology and identity politics in Taiwan: The relevance of local religion. Paper presented at the Taiwan Studies Workshop, Fairbank Center for East Asian Research, Harvard University.

Shahar, Meir, and Robert P. Weller, eds. 1996. *Unruly gods: Divinity and society in China.* Honolulu: University of Hawaii Press.

Shengxian Tang. *Xiudao zhinan* [Compass for the cultivation of the Dao]. 1978. Taizhong: Dajiang Press.

Shiba Wanggong [The Eighteen Lords]. 1985.

Shiba Wanggong chuangi [The strange tale of the Eighteen Lords]. 1985. China Television Service.

Smith, Joanna F. Handlin. 1987. Benevolent societies: The reshaping of charity during the Late Ming and Early Ch'ing. *Journal of Asian Studies* 46: 309–37.

Sutton, Donald. 1996. Transmission in popular religion: The Jiajiang troupe in southern Taiwan. In Shahar and Weller.

Weller, Robert P. 1994. *Resistance, chaos, and control in China: Taiping rebels, Taiwanese ghosts, and Tiananmen.* London: Macmillan.

———. 1995. Matricidal magistrates and gambling gods: Weak states and strong spirits in China. *Australian Journal of Chinese Affairs* 33: 107–24.

Winn, Jane Kaufman. 1994. Not by rule of law: Mediating state-society relations in Taiwan through the underground economy. In *The other Taiwan: 1945 to the present,* edited by Murray A. Rubenstein. New York: M. E. Sharpe.

Zhang Wei'an. 1996. Fuojiao Ciji Gongde Hui yu Ziyuan Huishou [The Buddhist Compassion Merit Society and recycling]. Paper presented at the Workshop on Culture, Media, and Society in Contemporary Taiwan, Harvard University, 12 June.

Millenniums Past, Cuba's Future?

Paul Ryer

Book cover photo by Jeremy Wolff

Photo by Paul Ryer

Socialism or Death

Both this commercial North American representation of a Cuban appropriation of a U.S. symbol and the image of a decaying revolutionary slogan too easily map onto Western complacencies regarding the inevitability of capitalism and the futility of alternative ideologies or resistant practices. Image consumption of this sort not only naturalizes a not–New World Order, it also implicates the consumer: the star-spangled woman pictured is not actually waiting for Fidel, but for a dollar-rich foreign client—one of the very persons most likely to find a comfortable irony, eroticism, or pathos in such photographs.

Consuming *Geist*: Popontology and the Spirit of Capital in Indigenous Australia

Elizabeth A. Povinelli

On 16 August 1998, several people from Belyuen and I drove to Wadeye (Port Keats) and ran into the ark of a covenant, a building underway aimed at housing an indigenous spirituality. This building has several aspects, modalities, and scales — physical, subjective, textual. It is dispersed across multiple social fields — law, business, and public life — and the purpose it serves goes by several names: cultural tourism, ecotourism. In this essay, I seek to understand the sources and limits of this built environment and its social, subjective, and economic implications for indigenous Australians.

David Harvey (1989: 339) has noted that post-Fordist capitalism seems to be dominated by "fiction, fantasy, the immaterial (particularly money), fictitious capital, images, ephemerality"; the stock market and various financial instruments are well cited examples. Herein, I examine a related market — the market in the uncanny, the mystery (rather than the mysterious), the fourfold (*morphe*) as it operates in northern Australia. I will propose that one of the operations of this market is to hold certain groups of people accountable for manifesting for certain other groups a Heideggerian form (morphe). It will also emerge that the market itself relies upon a complex set of textual mediations generating both an object for and a limit to capital forms of commodification. What might these particular modalities of capital and textuality tell us about the dynamic relation among text, subject, and economic practice at the beginning of the new millennium? More specifically: How do we understand the textual sources of the indigenous Spirit that capital commodifies? Note: I will seek the answer to these questions not in analysis of the representation of the Spirit of commodity capital, but rather in an interrogation of how the building of various sorts of capital infrastructures is mediated by various sorts of textual architectures and by the subjective inhabitation of both. In short, the logic and timing of the subject are not equivalent to the logic and timing of capital.

REGIMES OF THE SPIRITUAL

We had not gone to Wadeye to chase the market of the Spirit. We had planned to spend the week mapping the coastal region historically associated with the Marriamu and Marritjaben Aborginal people with other men and women living at Wadeye in preparation for a sea claim to be lodged under the Native Title Act of 1993. The map would help demonstrate the continuing existence of the traditional laws, customs, beliefs, and practices of the Marriamu and Marritjaben. It is such traditional customs that give their native title its legal efficacy in Australian statutory and common law. Most jurists loosely agree with Justice Olney's understanding of traditional customs as a set of laws, customs, practices, and traditions that are "integral to a distinctive culture" rather than a mere "description of how people live" or a description of how their ancestors once lived (*Hayes v. Northern Territory* 1999: 20). It is not required by the national law that these customary laws be demonstrated to be "spiritual" in nature, although in the common sense and common parlance of national courts, parliaments (federal, state, and territory), and public spheres, Aboriginal customary law is considered to be saturated and fully comprehended by the cosmogonic myth-ritual of the Dreamtime. What *is* required of applicants—before their native title claim can be registered—is that they acknowledge their native title rights and interests to be subject to all valid and current laws of the Commonwealth and the Northern Territory. According to the current phrasing of native title applications in the Northern Territory, they also must further acknowledge that the exercise of these rights and interests might be regulated, controlled, curtailed, restricted, suspended, or postponed by reason of the existence of valid concurrent rights and interests by or under such laws. This acknowledgment is a formal textual act: the statutorily mandated form and content of a native title application. Because applications are usually prepared by non-Aboriginal lawyers and anthropologists, most claimants never know they have been represented as acquiescing in this hierarchy of legal power and authority.

But it was neither the expanse of the Dreaming nor the conceit of national law that initially caught my breath. Instead, I was taken aback by the expansion of the local airstrip. Wadeye, also known as Port Keats, is the sixth-largest town in the Northern Territory, a fact often obscured by its remote location, situated as it is off the main highway that runs south from Darwin to Alice Springs. Of these towns, Wadeye is the poorest, with all the health and social problems that attend poverty: low life-expectancies and high childhood mortality, substance abuse, suicide, and depression. My companions and I had driven the long dirt track to the community many times and knew well the actual physical relief of reaching the airfield at the other side. Exhausted by the dusty road, the jarring and seemingly endless potholes, the heat, the racket, we would always wonder aloud why we had not flown. The answer was the cost. And, this time, instead of a dirt landing strip, we were greeted by enormous earthmovers paving and lengthening what was emerging as an airport. *Where the Green Ants Dream* came to my mind, but no one from Belyuen had seen Werner Herzog's 1985 film, with its dramatic exploration of Aboriginal spirituality through the tropic re-figuration of Aboriginal ceremonial grounds and actors as airstrip and plane. Responding to my surprise, my classificatory mother Gracie Bin-bin described the renovations as an Aboriginal countermovement to the movement of non-Aboriginal desires. "Tourists coming," she said. "Ansett coming to Port Keats. Drop them tourist off. Maybe they look museum. Listen to bush stories. Might be bush food. Fly back. Berra-gut [white people] like that kind a business. Lot a money gana be this Port Keats."

We never did finish mapping the coast on that trip. Our exercise was interrupted when, on the third day of the field trip, senior Marriamu and Marritjaben men and women were called to witness the ritual pun-ishment of a young male family member. The night before, this young man and several of his friends had stolen and wrecked a car belong-ing to a non-Aboriginal man living in the community. As punishment, the young men were flogged by their elders, a ritual overseen by white Northern Territory police. A similar practice in a small Aboriginal com-munity just north of Wadeye had made headlines several years before. Several men from Peppimenarti went on trial for, and were eventu-ally found guilty of, manslaughter. As public spectacle, coverage of the Peppimenarti trial focused primarily on the defense argument that the death was an accidental result of indigenous men's customary ritual business and thus not subject to the Australian penal code (Watt 1992a, 1992b). The defendants lost their case. Practices that provide robust evidence of the existence of traditional laws so vital to native title and land-rights cases may still not be efficacious grounds for an argument in criminal courts.

During the public flogging at Wadeye (which is how people there describe the practice—evoking, in the process, older British codes of colonial discipline), I walked to the newly opened carpeted and air-conditioned Wadeye Art Gallery with one of my classificatory husbands, Timothy Dumu. Some of his award-winning work was featured there. Orienting visitors to the artworks were numerous brochures describing what made Wadeye art culturally distinctive (read: culturally valuable). The brochures drew attention to specific aesthetic forms and represented them as spiritual traditions that visitors could "see" in the art hanging on the walls. What visitors could also see were prices far below those found in regional and national cities.

Local art brochures and prices are simply local nodes of a regional, national, and international supertext generated by the semicoordinated and uncoordinated (indeed competitive) activities of other dealers and art houses. This supertext provisionally coordinates the aesthetic and economic values of Aboriginal art, crafts, music, and culture. The very notion of getting art at a "deal"—and thus of this art instantiating such a deal—depends upon a larger circulation of art and people (Myers 1998). In fact, Wadeye was connected to this circulatory system even before the expansion of the airport and the creation of the art gallery. Wadeye barks painted during the 1960s were featured in the most recent Sotheby's indigenous art catalogue, listed for between $500 and $5,000 (all dollar figures in Australian dollars). The head of Sotheby's Aboriginal art collection, Tim Klingender (whose sister acted as the solicitor for some of the men and women I was working with on a previous land claim) has worked with local Wadeye people and anthropologists to trace the barks' meanings, their painters, and the period in which they were painted in order to convey to potential buyers the cultural values that inform the economic value of the artworks. Both Timothys have their own notions about what motivates a tourist to buy or bid on a piece of art. That day at the Wadeye Art Gallery, Timothy Dumu described consumer desire in the following way.

If that thing im Dreaming, Berragut look.
Like this one I been paint,
  Im dreaming.
  Im got that story.
I been ask.
  Im right.
  I can paint this one.
Wulman im been say.

Whites are interested if it's about the Dreaming.
Like this one I painted.
  It's Dreaming.
  It's got that story.
I asked.
  It's alright.
  I can paint this Dreaming.
Old man said.

White collectors desire nothing more than the consumption of Aboriginal spirituality, their Dreamings, and they are willing to pay good money for it. But my husband linguistically enacts a limit to his compliance with this desire, textually inverting the hierarchy mandated by the statutory requirements for registering a native title claim. The form of his utterance, its poetic parallelism, encloses this spectral interest of whites in the social dynamic of local cultural authority: "Wulman im been say."

But there might be something else to listen for here, something more than a subaltern inversion of discursive hierarchies of desires and authorities: the subjective embodiment of contrasting deontic mandates. What can be made of Dumu's statement, "I can paint this one"? Is it simply a recitation of local customary social norms? Or a performative enactment of the self as a proper Aboriginal subject qua abider of the customary? Or could this quotidian statement—as much and as little considered as any of the remarks that passed in the long conversation we had—be considered the linguistic precipitate of subjectivity in a field of competing capital and cultural obligations and desires? In other words, is Dumu saying something that would appear in its negative form as "I should not or must not paint this design" or as "I cannot paint this design—I literally cannot make my hands move in such a way as to materialize this *thing*"? Likewise, is his art valuable because he iterates and follows the iterative trail of "the customary," or because this iteration is also a marker of the subjective strain of obligation in a particular form of national and global life? What matter, politically and analytically, to how these questions are answered? I begin by interrogating the specific spatial economy of the Spirit at Wadeye.

CARGO CULTS

It is hard not to think of the Wadeye airstrip as evidence of the existence of a local cargo cult. But the airport is not the materialization of any purely local scheme. Rather it is the physical unfurling of Commonwealth and Northern Territory government efforts to build national space in such a way as to produce surplus values for national citizen/subjects. This is increasingly the represented function of government in late liberal democracies like Australia. The idea of marketing the spiritual nature of Aboriginal culture and economy has been tested throughout Aboriginal Australia for at least half a century. And not just Aboriginal Australia: as numerous scholars have demonstrated, economies and governments on the local, regional, and national levels are increasingly dependent on tourism, particularly spiritual-cultural tourism (see Smith 1989; Urry 1997; for the Australian case, see Craik 1991; Jacobs and Gale 1994; Frow 1997; Thomas 1999).

But at the core of the question of why such a place as Wadeye has its new airstrip is a systematic textual misunderstanding regarding the scale, temporality, and spatiality of tourist capital. In daily papers, on radio and television, public analysts continually refer to a quantity of capital associated with the tourism industry. For instance, the *Northern Territory News* reported that "The Territory's $700 million-plus tourism industry would be hit hard by trade-offs negotiated as part of the new goods and service tax" ("GST 'to hit NT tourism,'" 31 May 1999). But what is this "$700 million" that is at risk? On the one hand, it is a sign figuring, in the process of referring to, the sum total of all movements and modalities of capital associated with a delimited domain of economic practice. But on the other hand, "700 million" is a singular nominal form that indexes Singularity, Quantity, and Objectness, a singular, objective quantity of *some thing*. Situated within the grammatical present imperfect, this nominal form figures particular movements and particularized moments of capital as an aggregated thing: an *it* existing in toto, out there, right now, at continual risk of being "hit hard" — that is, abused unfairly. Lest this seem no more than the unfortunate slip of an overworked copyeditor, note what a tourist outfitter in Darwin quipped to me and, in so quipping, suggested might be the relationship between the public circulation of textual figurations of tourism capital and subjective understandings of the goal of business: "There's 700 million dollars out there. The question is how we get it here."

A grammatical and textual figuration is misapprehended as a real condition: Speakers follow their own projections of semantically and pragmatically entailed conceptual space into the world of socially mediated things instead of examining why and how these figured spaces might be used and useful (for the grammatical and metapragmatic unconscious, see Wittgenstein 1998 [1953]; Whorf 1956; Silverstein 1981). The conceptualization of tourism capital as a unified, flowing mass presents businesses with questions of how to freeze, halt, or impede the "flow," "circulation," and "migration" of capital. That is, businesses face not only the problem of how to compress space-time to decrease cost and increase profit, but also how to decompress space in order to localize surplus value. At both of these moments of capital, Commonwealth, State, and Territory governments actively assist Australian businesses. Various state agencies and private consumer organizations conduct consumer surveys, support community development schemes, employ consultants to model culturally sensitive approaches to development, and modify physical and regulatory space to ease access for developers and their clients. Indeed, it can be said that built physical environments — airstrips and other physical infrastructures — are articulated within no less built statutory and regulatory environments. For example, in a step designed to facilitate the traffic of tourists, the governments of the United States and Australia have modified immigration regulations in such a way as to permit services such as the issuing of visas — once the province of government agencies — to be provided by corporations such as Qantas Airlines. Meanwhile, the Australian Department of Arts, Sports, Environment, Tourism, and Territories struggles to regulate the transnational movement of Aboriginal cultural heritage and artifacts in the face of studies emphasizing the role played in the Aboriginal art trade by overseas investors who are driven as much by an interest in speculating on an art market as by connoisseurship. It is such loosely coordinated and uncoordinated physical, legal, and regulatory spaces that constitute the "scaffolding" within which are built the infrastructure of airports and art galleries in such places as Wadeye. Furthermore, these physical and regulatory spaces themselves emerge in a field of textually mediated consumer desires, an emergence that depends at every step on textual projections similar to those informing the presentation of tourism capital. For a germane example: a widely cited 1990 survey conducted by the Australian Council found that 49 percent of international visitors were interested in seeing and learning about Aboriginal arts and culture, 30 percent purchased Aboriginal art or items related to Aboriginal culture, and $30 million per annum was generated by this tourism (see Finlayson 1991). Likewise, in her study of cultural tourism in northern Queensland, Julie Finlayson found that most tourists wished to speak or live with Aborigines in order to learn about their way of life and the spiritual-cultural attitudes underlying their use of the environment. But she also found that most visitors to the Queensland city of Cairns did not visit the neighboring Aboriginal community of Kuranda, because its proximity made it seem inauthentic, tourist-oriented, crime-ridden, and socially maladapted. Forty-nine percent, 30 percent: Even though no superordinate Being of type "Tourist" exists, Dumu and the Australian Council model their practices on this textually figurated and projected thing. Once textualized as part of a homogenous type — Tourists — the thing can be indexed to other things across social space that in theory permits of infinite expansion, the congruencies and differences among individual things built up from variations of type (this/that type of Tourism, Tourist) and dimensionality (this/that aspect of this/that type of Tourism, Tourist). These textual creatures underpin government and business representations of how and why Aboriginal communities such as Wadeye should develop.

And yet when the production of space is viewed with a focus on the generation of surplus value, it can be seen that building pathways for tourists to Aboriginal communities initiates the movement of capital out of the community. More precisely, the community becomes a site in which surplus values are generated for those outside the community (see Loveday and Cooke 1983; Altman 1988; Knapman, Stanley, and Lea 1991). Even if no tourists ever fly to Wadeye, considerable private capital has been generated by the thought that Wadeye is the type of place they would wish to go to. By convincing local leaders that a certain type of tourism might provide a significant influx of capital ("tourism is a $700-million-dollar industry") and jobs ("tourism employs x number of persons") and by linking social and mental health to capital and jobs ("this will help cut down on juvenile violence by giving young people jobs"), multimillion-dollar contracts can be tendered and awarded for building airfields, art galleries, and hotels, generating revenue and jobs for regional non-Aboriginal people. And deciding how to structure a culturally sensitive form of spiritual consumption generates work for anthropologists, linguists, and social workers. It is true that some public funds and resources are reallocated to local Aboriginal men and women through government programs such as Community Development and Employment Project (CDEP), a work-for-welfare scheme meant to provide training to the locally employed. But private building companies do not hire local labor, and anthropologists' informants are usually not paid. Instead, the local unemployed, who suffer a degree of economic immiserization unimaginable to most Australians, usually stand as silent witnesses to this consumptive building of their Spirit. Such space as has been structured for them can be seen unfolding in the barbed-wire halos some communities have been erecting on electrical poles to curb youth suicide.

If tourists do arrive in Wadeye in any significant number, their economic value to the local community depends on their consumption of something—a hunt, a piece of art or craft, a story, an experience. Ironically, perhaps, in buying any such commodity, tourists are likely to stimulate rather than prevent the exploitation of the community for the generation of surplus value to the benefit of people outside the community. Most indigenous people living along the northwest coastal region do not produce paintings whose value lies in the $5,000 range. Rather they produce raw materials for the arts-and-crafts market. Take, as an example, the ubiquitous didjeridoo. Aboriginal men and women are most likely to find, cut, strip, and hollow out the tree trunks from which didjeridoos are made. They then sell these semifinished products to local middlemen, usually non-Aboriginal men and women, who do the painting or employ others to do it. (Many didjeridoos, bark paintings, canvas paintings, and boomerangs are produced entirely by non-Aboriginal people.) Middlemen then sell the finished products to stores in regional cities such as Darwin, or to other middlemen who ship them in turn to southern ports. Finding, cutting, stripping, and hollowing out ten didjeridoos consumes, at an average, three days labor for one skilled person; at this stage, the value of each hollowed pipe is about $15. As the product makes its way to the consumer, the price may be radically increased ($50, $100, $200). This price hike is replicated across product categories in the market for cultural artifacts. At the bottom of the chain are the kinfolk of those preparing the object for sale, who are relied upon to be on the lookout for the raw materials to pick up or chop down—seashells, tortoise shells, trees—while otherwise engaged in the bush. These original suppliers receive their remuneration in the form of smoke, drinks, or small change.

But what is the value of these hollow sticks to those who purchase them? One way of finding an answer is to return to Timothy Dumu's assessment of white consumer desire. Before saying what his comment demonstrates, let me first say what I don't think it demonstrates: I don't think that Dumu presents us with an example of a cynical subject deploying identity strategically (though I could present numerous more or less pure instances of such a deployment). Nor, for that matter, do I think that this would be an instance of what Gayatri Spivak (1989) calls "strategic essentialism." Instead, I would suggest that the poetic form and content of Dumu's comment encodes his subjective experience of discursively embodied scales and levels of obligation—culture's embodiment. If so, the very moment of the utterance bears witness to the subjective limit of culture's objectification and transformation into capital and the object-destination of capital consumption. At bottom, the question of whether to regard Dumu's statement as a strategic deployment of customary identity or as an instance of the subjective limit to the commodification of Being-in-culture is a question about where to locate the subject in our reading of the text. Is the subject to be read off the text? Or is the subject outside the text commenting on it? Or should the text be read as the product of a socially mediated subject?

I cite a second example that can clarify what is at stake in these questions and the choice of models we can use to answer them. In a conversation with me in 1993, the late Betty Bilawag described the feelings of panic she experienced when she attended a meeting to discuss whether mining should be allowed in Marriamu country. When she realized younger family members were about to vote en masse in favor of mining near a particularly dangerous Dreaming site, she described her actions in this way:

> I been panic. I been have to get up. I been have to get up, talk now. "No. No. You're not going to forget them Dreaming. You can't forget. They still there. They still going. They dangerous, that mob. You say 'No.'"

Panic made Bilawag get up, but this panic can be understood as a corporeal index—a discursive depth charge of sorts—of the embodiment of various orders and levels of obligation. Because the modality and timing of subjectivity is not equivalent to that of commodification, this type of embodied obligation, or modal subjectivity, impedes capital's spatial expansion, throws its timing off, if it does not halt it.

It is not necessary to conceptualize a coherent subject in order to conceptualize the vital sociological consequences of moments in which subjects experience contrasting yet compulsory obligations. At risk in these moments are not simply discursive norms and legal codes, but the subject him- or herself. The psychic experience of numerous people throughout the northwest coastal region provides examples of the personal consequences of acting wrongly. These are people identified as *piya wedjirr* (literally "head-rotten"), who might be said to have been traumatized by their inability to reconcile competing obligations and desires. Others point to them as evidence of the hard power of "Aboriginal law." Even so, I am not suggesting we think of these subject limits as *the* limit of capital. Nor would I suggest that true resistance to capital must be affective in nature and form. But Bilawag's panic does suggest a type of moment that marks *a* limit to capital internal to the subject. As Bilawag's reminiscences suggest, this subjective embodiment of culture varies, often significantly, across age and social groups within an Aboriginal community—her younger family members were poised to vote "yes," after all. And what surprise is this, that culture's embodiment reflects the variations, slippages, dispersions, and ambivalences of discursive formations across the terrain of indigenous social life?

But it is, in fact, the subjective strain of inhabiting these fields of embodied obligation, I am suggesting, that tourists, lawyers, and other visitors mistake as a sign of the distinctive spiritual nature of Aboriginal society. Witnessing the throes of her panic, non-Aboriginal people experience Bilawag's "spirituality" rather than her travail within ideologies of capital and culture. A subjective grinding in the midst of contrasting social and cultural fields is misapprehended as the movement of the Spirit. While capital might find its limit in moments in which subjects experience the trauma of navigating contrasting social and cultural mandates, such moments are quickly fetishized as authentic culture — as the valuable "real stuff" of culture (and law). It is this trauma that tourists of the Spirit seek to purchase.

Why then do tourists mediate their purchase through objects — drone pipes, postcards, and bark paintings — rather than paying Aboriginal people directly for their acts of alienation, their reformation as a Heideggerian bridge for another? An answer seems to lie in the object of purchase itself, which is not an Aboriginal person or an Aboriginal way of Being in any particular place, but an experience that Aboriginal people manifest when they inhabit particular kinds of placing themselves, or being placed, in a limit — when they straddle the cliffs of contrasting discursive orders. Hollow drone pipes and other cultural memorabilia act as mnemonics for this nomenic experience.

There is no great evil master plan that pushes indigenous subjects like Timothy Dumu toward the variously configured limits of their subjective well-being. Many boosters of Aboriginal spirituality support local cultural practices against other market forces. But it is precisely this support that continually forces Aboriginal subjects to inhabit — to embody — the throes of being in the middle of contrasting and competing deontic mandates. A September 1999 issue of *The Weekend Australian* furnished a good case in point. In an article about the production of Aboriginal art in the Kimberlies, the survival of Aboriginal art — and through this art its culture — was pitted against the economic interests of pastoralists (McCulloch-Uehlin 1999: 5). While such an argument provides a useful reminder of the fragmented nature of capital, it also cites and actually increases the pressure on Aboriginal persons to tarry in spaces of contrasting normative injunctions — to inhabit not only sites of competing Aboriginal and non-Aboriginal deontic orders, but also of competing non-Aboriginal political and economic values.

> Aborigines have a limited statutory right under two sections of the Western Australian Land Act of 1993 to access their traditional lands without permission from lessees, which may not be relevant in the case of the Texas Downs refusal. "It's a common experience for Ab-

original people right across the Kimberley," said Kimberley Land Council deputy director June Oscar. Many people hope Aborigines will simply walk on to a pastoral lease unannounced. (McCulloch-Uehlin 1999: 5)

As the example suggests, the art market is hardly the only national social field that generates stress on indigenous subjects while purporting to support their spiritually imbued customary law, encouraging them to occupy complex sites of negation while leaving unexamined why many people within the nation might desire they do so. Recall that the reason we went to Wadeye on 16 August 1998 in the first place was to produce a body of legally efficacious evidence demonstrating the survival of traditional Marriamu and Marritjaben customary law. In the shadow of the police-supervised flogging, we were quickly reminded that this law is not a recognized part of the Australian common law today, any more than it was in 1936, 1896, or 1789. But this legal fact did not dissuade the state of Queensland in 1996 from proposing "a radical scheme" that would make "customary law — including the use of corporal punishment — compulsory in isolated black communities" (Emerson 1996: 4). The legislation was intended to police juvenile crime in remote communities through the policed agency of traditional culture.

Viewed as a means of unburdening state resources, this state-backed, compulsory return of customary law would be mediated by majoritarian, commonsense standards of corporeality (standards that are, in fact, never described, lest in the description the imaginary of a shared majoritarian intuition about this corporeality be punctured). The Minister of Aboriginal and Islander Affairs, Mr. Lingard, reassured an (imagined) jittery constituency that "extreme punishments such as spearing would be ruled out," though "other forms of corporal punishment would be acceptable but would have to be monitored" (Emerson 1996: 4). Far from inciting the public to consider their own commonsense intuitions about corporeality — to interrogate their underlying assumptions critically — Lingard merely cites the ever-bracketed force of liberalism: "There is no doubt that some people might say that customary law might go too far and that some time we might have to look at that but I think the elders would have enough common sense not to go too far" (Emerson 1996: 4).

As I mentioned above, in 1992 some Peppimenarti men did go too far and were found guilty of manslaughter. Curiously, this very case was cited to me by a Belyuen resident some years later, on 18 September 1999, as evidence of the national legal support of customary law. As vice president of the Belyuen Community Council and as a participant in the CDEP program, Marjorie Bilbil had attended two meetings within the span of a week, one a regional meeting of local governments with territory officials, the other a meeting of senior Aboriginal participants in CDEP. In both meetings, non-Aboriginal persons urged senior Aboriginal men and women to revive customary laws — physical sanctions and rituals — as a method of "settling down the young people." When she discussed these meetings with me, Bilbil referred to the Peppimenarti case, saying that the young men had not been punished "much" because their actions had been traditional: "They [berragut, whites] don't do much when they look that traditional law." Marjorie Bilbil did not stop her analysis there. Instead she noted that the uneven landscape of national and local power had led to a pattern of Aboriginal male dispersion across the Top End. "Like desert way, they got that hard law. But you look, that man he might be Arnhem way, or Roper way, or anywhere, Bagot, Tiwi. They marry into that other family, find that women, stay with her family now. 'Too hard because, my law. I had to go.' They say that." In other conversations with other senior women from Belyuen, the difficulty of reviving "hard law" is discussed from another perspective: that women simply cannot bring themselves to "kill" their daughters ("kill," in this case, referring to the use of physical force in a way now considered by them to be "too rough").

To stop the story here would be to end with the following conclusion: Jurists and businesses are producing space to meet their needs, though impeded in their quest by the subjective limits of commodification and the internal dynamic of the relatively autonomous fields of national social life. (What criminal law might prohibit, land-claim processes encourage; what statutory legislation might outlaw, capital might fetishize and commodify.) If subjectivity is viewed as a built internal dynamic, its architecture can in this case be considered to be under a constant state of pressure, as Aboriginal subjects are encouraged to tarry in fields of competing deontic orders.

But I want to go on to argue that the entextualization of the Spirit — the generic production of indigenous spirituality at the millennium —

mediates the building of physical and subjective space in such a way as to impede this simple narrative of gradual homogenization and domination by capital. Thus, I return to the question of why capital is building and chasing this particular phantasmatic form. I focus on a specific genre that I call *popontology* and examine how its figuration of Being articulates with the commercialization of spirituality. To suggest how a genre of the Spirit soils every dwelling built for it, this analysis will range far afield from Port Keats and Belyuen.

Before examining this generic space, let me pause over the simple fact that most Australian citizens and most citizens of other nation-states—judges, writers, tourists—will never encounter face-to-face the special spiritual relationship that Australian indigenous persons are said to have with the landscape. No actually existing Aboriginal subject will describe to them the content, contours, or modalities of her own personal beliefs or understanding of local community beliefs: what she might believe; what must, or should, be believed; or on what evidentiary grounds she might base these judgments insofar as can be said or known. Most people will never smell, taste, or otherwise corporeally inhabit the real space-time of her social life or that of any other indigenous person in any of the variegated global spaces where she or other indigenous people are thought to be found. Whatever understandings observers have of an indigenous modernity, they will never encounter the resistant or compliant, but in either case dialogical, space of an actively listening indigenous subject. Nevertheless, many people throughout the world will come to believe that indigenous persons like those living at Wadeye have a unique ontotheological relationship to their land. That is, knowing nothing of the Wadeye community, they will come to believe they know quite a lot about the spiritual Being of people living there and will feel confident enough about this knowledge to formulate judgments about indigenous spirituality. An inquiry into the source of this self-certainty would reveal that it lies for the most part in cinematic and print texts. As Aboriginal scholar and activist Marcia Langton has written, "The most dense relationship" informing Australian understandings of Aboriginal people "is not between actual people, but between white Australian and the symbols created by their predecessors"—and, it might be added, contemporaries (Langton 1993: 33; see also Michaels 1994; Ginsberg 1991).

The term *popontology,* shorthand for "popularized ontotheological novels and films," will here refer to a wide range of fictional and quasi-fictional texts that describe an encounter with an unalienated form of spiritual Being by specific types of human beings and social lives. These textual forms and types, modes and modalities share certain characteristics. They are marked by and marketed to class, gender, sexuality, race/ethnicity, and religious groupings; gradable into high-, middle-, and lowbrow types; and manifested in film, print, and musical forms. Indigenous popontology is a subgenre of this form, situating the spiritual encounter with an indigenous person, group, or spirit-Being, usually from Australia or the Americas, less so from Asia, Africa, and Europe. Some sense of the range of indigenous popontology texts can be conveyed by these examples: classic and contemporary New Age texts such as *The Teachings of Don Juan* (Castaneda 1968), *Mutant Message Down Under* (Morgan 1994), and *Crystal Woman* (Andrews 1987); travelogue accounts such as *The Songlines* (Chatwin 1987); high-, middle-, and lowbrow films such as Nicholas Roeg's *Walkabout* (1970), Herzog's *Where the Green Ants Dream,* and Stephen Elliot's *The Adventures of Priscilla, Queen of the Desert* (1994); and televisual public service programming such as the series of animated Dreamtime stories shown by the Australian Broadcast Corporation (ABC) in 1997.

Mikhail Bakhtin observed long ago that "there is not a single new phenomenon (phonetic, lexical or grammatical) that can enter the system of language without having traversed the long and complicated path of generic-stylistic testing and modification" (Bakhtin 1986: 65). Though many of the texts I draw on will have little long-lasting commodity or literary value, they are valuable insofar as they index and entail emergent public anxieties about human Being in particular human cultural, social, and technological formations. They present the voicings and legibilities of the present only insofar as they import terms, phraseology, and scenes from other already generically organized social and textual spaces.

The delicate but nevertheless sociologically meaningful nature of the discursive emergences captured in these popontological texts is suggested by two recent films, *The Matrix* (the Wachowski brothers, 1999) and *eXistenZ* (David Cronenberg, 1999). In both, an insidious form of irrealis Being, made possible by advances in corpo-perceptual technology, threatens the attachment of humans to reality—or, rather, threatens the continuing relevance of a certain framing of "reality." In the tradition of such futuristic cyborg fantasies as *Blade Runner* (Ridley Scott, 1982) and *Robocop* (Paul Verhoeven, 1987), *eXistenZ* catches viewers up in a play of placement (where the characters *are* in relation to a referentially ungroundable cyborgian virtual-reality) as opposed to a morality play (how one should be fully or properly in any given reality). Although the freedom fighters of *eXistenZ* do fight for a technologically unalienated and unmediated form of reality, the moral question—what it is to be truly, properly, and fully human—is displaced, or at least continually deferred, by the placement question: Where (in what reality) are we now? Not that *eXistenZ* marks an epistemic displacement of older discursive forms of Being-proper. *The Matrix* continues this older anxiety about proper Being, presenting a struggle on behalf of one form of referentially grounded Being as more proper to *human* being than another. But *eXistenZ* suggests the emergence of a new set of questions regarding Being in the context of a discursively as of yet undigested corpo-technology.

Likewise, popontological narratives are not in themselves captivating, boring, or upsetting. They are transformed into these qualities and moods—are produced as sites of success or failure—not simply by the internal logic of their narrative form or artistic style, nor by the inherent allure of their topic (spiritual Being), but by subtler, narratively figurated experiences. People feel spiritually addressed because the text has been shaped by the generic shape of the world they inhabit. Even from a purely intertextual perspective, such sites as Australia and the Aboriginal Dreamtime or Peru and its Mayan initiations find their "footing" in previous representations of India and its Hindu gods, Nepal and its Sherpa shamans, Theosophy, Krishna Consciousness, and Transcendental Meditation.[1] But the textual field that provides legibility to indigenous popontology is not limited to the indigenous and subaltern, their gods and enchanted realms. John Sayles's *Secret of Roan Inish* (1995) occupies a space opened by Robin Hardy's earlier film, *Wicker Man* (1973), itself grounded in a faux-Freudian matrix of primitive (Celtic) and degenerate (aristocratic) sexuality. Independent films such as *Safe* (Todd Haynes, 1995) and *The Rapture* (Michael Tolkin,

1991), mass-market films and television shows such as *Contact* (Robert Zemeckis, 1997), *The Sweet Hereafter* (Atom Egoyan, 1997), and *The X-Files* likewise invaginate and prey on conversations circulating about secular and modern, enchanted and disenchanted Being.

Far from constituting a revolutionary move, therefore, situating the fantasy of real Being in a phantasmatic indigenous scene may be little more than another dispersion of types of bodies that will bear the interrogatory pressure currently exerted on Being-in-general in specific social formations. The indigenous is merely another—perhaps not even the latest—identity to provide a provisional structure to speculations about the state of Being in Western (post)modernity. Indigenous popontology as a distinct form reached a certain public attention in 1968 with the publication of Carlos Castaneda's *The Teachings of Don Juan: A Yaqui Way of Knowledge*. Indeed, the evolving contours and content of the "nonordinary reality" of Castaneda's three-decade-long career provide a case study of how popontological figurations of indigenous being simply construct a site that registers and figures the shifting terrain of public debates.[2]

What voicings are being caught and figured in popontological accounts of indigenous spirituality? And in what way do the specific media of this figuration—print and film media—contribute to how these voicings are figured and, subsequently, extended as the expectations of visitors regarding actually existing indigenous people? Some voicings should not surprise us. For example, many texts explicitly discuss the epistemological dilemma of staking truth claims while acknowledging that all knowledge is the product of particularizing cultures. That is, the texts voice current academic and public debates about multiculturalism, colonialism, morality, truth, and tolerance. So, for example, if Castaneda's writings mark the emergence of indigenous popontology, they also register the constantly evolving provisional textual resolutions of these cross-fertilizing and contested social fields: activist liberation movements, academic and public debates, and nationalisms and citizenship forms. More recently, Castaneda (1998) has described "the role of culture" as "that of restricting the perceptual capacity of its members." He credits indigenous people with the discovery of this prison-house of culture. In his commentary on the thirtieth anniversary of the publication of *The Teachings of Don Juan,* he writes:

Don Juan Matus and the shamans of their lineage regarded *aware-ness* as the act of being deliberately conscious of all the perceptual possibilities of man, not merely the perceptual possibilities dictated by any given culture whose role seems to be that of restricting the perceptual capacity of its members.

Fortunately for indigenized *Geist,* if the intention of culture is to imprison us, it would seem that the intent of the universe is to be continually testing our awareness.

> [The shamans] *saw* that the universe creates zillions of *organic beings* and zillions of *inorganic beings.* By exerting pressure on all of them, the universe forces them to enhance their awareness, and in this fashion, the universe attempts to become aware of itself. In the *cognitive world* of shamans, therefore, awareness is the final issue. (Castaneda 1998: xix; emphasis added)

If popular narrative accounts of real Being propose that humans can overcome the blinding restrictions of cultural knowing and thereby experience the wholeness proper to *human* Being, in so arguing they turn away from a simple cultural relativist position (a strain of the culturalism Castaneda would have encountered in anthropology courses taught in the University of California system during the 1960s). Instead, in his and in others' accounts, the actual parallel world in which true, unalienated Being resides is not located *in* any one cultural world, nor the composite of all cultural worlds à la Ruth Benedict's "great arc of culture" or Charles Taylor's "final horizon." The task of wisdom seekers is not to develop a theory or understanding of the actual nature of actual cultural worlds, but to draw on local cultural knowledges to experience what is beyond them, us, everyone — the possibility of reaching beyond every actual cultural form into a subtending energy matrix. It is this matrix of Being — a Being that dwells within some social locations more than others — that is the desired object of these texts. No matter the valorization by right-thinking scholars of *entre nous* as the proper position of cosmopolitan consociality, these texts turn toward *au-delà,* or more accurately, *couper.* The between-us is here merely a provisional aural and visual structure that acts as a conduit for a getting-beyond. In other words, it is neither the self nor the other sought in these scenes, but rather a passageway or a transition. As Vincanne Adams (1996) writes with regard to New Age representations of Sherpas, the sort of spiritual authenticity imputed to them is accessible only *through* intimate bonds with the Sherpas themselves. This *au-delà,* this desire to be liberated from culture (a state now standing in for the travails of contemporary national life), accounts in part for the particular allure of indigenous spirituality. *Indigenous* is nothing less than the name used to designate the state of Being prior to modernity and its concomitant identity formation, nationalism (Povinelli 1999).

The conservative implications of this strain of popontology have been clear to Native American activists such as Vine Deloria for quite a long time, and to many Internet writers and surfers. There were similar cultural critiques in 1998 on the Web site "Wanting to Be an Indian": "When this ritual is brought into a New Age context, its meaning and power are altered. The focus shifts to White people's needs and visions, which in most New Age venues are about individual growth and prosperity. There is no accountability to a community, particularly any Native community."

The divergent politics of indigenized popontology and indigenous social struggles are well expressed by a statement in Marlo Morgan's *Mutant Message Down Under:* "Real Aboriginal People [are] not concerned with racism, but concerned only with other people and the environment" (Morgan 1994: xiii–xiv). Across this literature, narrative plots reinscribe racial hierarchies as they purport to be leveling cultural hierarchies. In plot after plot, a nonindigenous person just happens to be the designated spiritual heir apparent of a dying indigenous group. Castaneda just happened to be the person chosen by the last living members of Don Juan's group, a spiritual selection Don Juan cannot explain. Morgan (1994: 3, 15) was called to her spiritual journey from "two thousand miles" away, an "extreme honor" the Aborigines "cannot explain." Two *National Geographic* reporters just happened to be the "ones chosen" to become the "spirit-journeyers on the path of the Wisdom-keepers" by "the Grandfathers" of a Native American tribe (Arden and Wall 1998: 17, 21).

The discursive voicings that popontological texts register and mediate are not only concerned with the dilemma of maintaining racial and cultural hierarchies in the shadow of late liberal forms of multiculturalism and postcoloniality. Many of these texts compel readers with their treatment of what might be termed the anxieties and aspirations of little Being, and the exhaustions of ordinary Being—at least those anxieties, aspirations, and exhaustions that writers and market researchers associate with their readership, largely middle-class white women. Prominent themes in these texts thus include: the body (fat, deformation, aging, disease), liberal social issues (racial, gender, economic inequality, environmental depletion), and relationships (divorce, isolation, intimacy, the ethics of care). Popontology is often not framed by big people, big issues, or big Being, but rather by the little dramas of everyday life—a message made explicit in Carlos Castaneda's most recent writings. Even the works of indigenous authors and filmmakers tend to frame narratives about spiritual and cultural rebirth in the quotidian, familiar scenes of social exhaustion. The New Zealand film *Once Were Warriors* (Lee Tamahori, 1995), for instance, opens with the exhausted spaces of industrialization and the subject-destroying effects of structural unemployment and underemployment on indigenous communities.

Setting these themes aside for a moment, let me ask what, then, are the means by which specific textual media voice the Spirit? Put another way, what critical purchase does understanding the linguistic technology of the popontological Spirit provide toward an understanding of its material entailments? Lest such questions seem too heady for a body of work that amounts to cultural flotsam, let me propose that what is foregrounded in many of these texts is nothing less than the problem posed by the linguistic vehicularization of Being to the description and experience of Being. In *Mutant Message,* for instance, Morgan reflects on the difference between language and "the system of interpretation proper to human beings." She and other authors urge readers to decenter language as the primary semiotic vehicle of Being, emphasizing instead music, movement, rhythm—or, more accurately, the vibrations from which music, movement, and rhythm are composed (see, for instance, Rael and Sutton 1993).

The dilemma is this: If popontological spirituality positions itself against any and every particular language and cultural system, it nevertheless relies on the semiotic nature of language to signal the provisionality of any and every linguistic proposition. That is, even in negating language, popontological texts rely on metalinguistic framings. They use language to transpose, or map, one set of conventional schemata ("this is language") against another ("I am referring to a domain outside language"). Popontology, as all metalinguistic texts, is trapped in the language it seeks to escape. Popontological Being is not located at either end, so to speak, of a transposition-translation process, but in the transitional moments of this movement into form, in mapping rather than the map or, more exactly, in the sense of a tending toward an incipient mapping. Popontology relies on a procedural rather than substantive Spirit. The proceduralisms of Spirit are braced by repeated explicit dismissals of substantive Being. *Don't focus on the content of the words,* readers are told. Rather, experience (in the movement of semantic, pragmatic, and metapragmatic processes) the Spirit. In putting it this way, these texts once again reveal their delicate ideological sinews, how they incorporate political debates about the proceduralism and substantive nature of liberal citizenship and multiculturalism within their spiritual quests. Different popontology media draw on different semiotic functions to convey the experience of this movement. But all cinematic, television, and print media rely on a set of visual or verbal cross-references that locate Being not in the nominalized scenes being cross-referenced, but in the metasemiotic experience of crossing from, over, and into.

Where the Green Ants Dream (1985) presents a useful example of these textual enactments of the indigenous Spirit. The film begins with two sets of desert mounds: one is composed of the debris of industrial mining, the other is the home of green ants. At its simplest, the film uses a series of cuts between these two types of mound not to encourage the adoption of one perspective or another, or even of their contrastive nature, but rather to incite an interpretive movement, the creation of a new sign from their juxtaposition. Though the film may encourage the sense that the new interpretation arises purely from the juxtaposition of the two images, the movement of interpretation among viewers involves a more complex lamination and delamination of multiple mounds and deserts. The Temptation of Christ and other tropes of prophetic lamentation crowd into the scene, as do Native American images, such as those cited in *Koyaanisqatsi* (Godfrey Reggio, 1983), itself cited in *The Adventures of Priscilla, Queen of the Desert.*

The film's depiction of moments of translation (or, more accurately, partial mistranslations) likewise figures the experience of semiosis and interpretation as a glimpse of unalienated Being. Take, for instance, a conversation among the film's three central characters: Tribal Elder,

Spokesperson, and the white protagonist, Hackett. Throughout the film, Tribal Elder speaks in an uncaptioned Aboriginal language, and Spokesperson translates Tribal Elder's words for Hackett and the listening public. Spokesperson's translations are never smooth. He falters, speaks haltingly, starts over, repeats. Rather than diminishing the authority of Tribal Elder's and Spokesperson's utterances, the semantic opacity of the Aboriginal language spoken and its halting translation intensifies it. It does so by indexing the realm the filmic narrative seeks—meaning beyond language, an impenetrable other world-Being. This untranslatable meaning, beyond the perceptual possibilities dictated by any given culture, is in the film mapped into other interactional spaces, for example onto disputes about capitalism's frustration in culturally inscribed spiritual space—that is, a frustration with the type of embodied obligations discussed above.

> TRIBAL ELDER: [Aboriginal language]
> HACKETT: What's he saying?
> SPOKESPERSON: There'll be no digging, and there'll be no blasting.
> HACKETT: Ah, I see. And may I ever so politely ask why?
> SPOKESPERSON: This the place where the green ants dream.
> KOL (a mining engineer): Ants, green ants, dreaming here. Why the fuck can't they dream somewhere else?

These mappings, remappings, and unmappings across conventionalized and invaginated semiotic spaces cannot be followed to their fullest, not for lack of time and space, but because they are theoretically infinite in their play. And it is, I would suggest, the unconscious experience of the movement of this generic play, its infinite invaginations, its provisionalities, that is experienced as Being's unfurling. In experiencing this movement as spirit, readers and viewers are not mistaking semiosis for Being, but recognizing the conventional signs by which non-Aboriginal EuroAmericans and Australians know Spirituality, experience it as such, and calibrate its presence in particular human beings.

Though films such as *Where the Green Ants Dream* critique forms of commodification and capital extraction, popontological texts are clearly not divorced from the workings of capital. Some of the texts that make up this genre are honest attempts to rethink the nature of Being in the historical conditions of the late twentieth century. But—in a case analogous to consumer support of Aboriginal art—good intentions often result in increasing the value of these texts as commodities. In trying to appeal to an audience, the authors of socially conscious texts strive to voice compelling critiques of the dehumanizing aspects of capital. Paradoxically, the better they achieve their task, the more successful a commodity form the text becomes.

Take, for instance, Morgan's *Mutant Message Down Under*. The book is an impassioned plea for humanity to take seriously the question of Being, "to understand that pulse [of] being human and human being-ness" that alone can begin the "human progress toward *being*" and "stop" the human "destruction of the earth and of each other" (Morgan 1994: xiv, 8, 177). The Real People, a central Australian Aboriginal tribe, lead her on a spiritual journey into the dual interior of the continent and of her self. Morgan recounts her insights as she gradually heals the divisions within herself, and between herself and the world, and learns to understand the artificiality of all social and natural separations, all physical discomforts, and all social and cultural conflicts. The Real People teach her *to Be,* truly and fully, by teaching her to understand all forms of having — including a formal language — as being had by false classification, being possessed by possessions, being alienated from her own and global oneness. Modernity, she discovers, has made mutants of mankind. Though herself a mutant, Morgan is chosen to relay the Real from down under, to denounce the distorting encrustations of contemporary global social conflict.

Morgan financed the original print run herself. But after her book sold more than 350,000 copies, HarperCollins bought the rights for U.S. $1.7 million, and United Artists began discussions about a possible movie venture. Outraged at what Robert Egginton, coordinator of the Dumbartung Aboriginal Corporation, called the book's "cultural genocide of the spirit" (Egginton 1997), a delegation of central Australian Aboriginal men and women traveled to the United States and Great Britain to protest the book's representation of traditional Aboriginal culture. In response, HarperCollins added a preface describing the book as a work of fiction, and sales continued briskly.

Bracketing for a moment the question of authorial exploitation, one thing this short market history clearly shows is that the more fully certain texts capture the feeling of modern alienation and anomie, the better they serve consumptive capital. Every time consumers buy or urge someone else to buy *Mutant Message* or any other example of a myriad of indigenously marked books, films, tapes, and CDs, they position themselves in the divine drama the text describes. They become mutant messengers of hope and open a potential passageway between reader and divine healing—even as they become part of the circuit of capital.

PRACTICAL MATTERS

Many writers of popontology insist that their purpose is not to enrich themselves through the exploitation of the Spirit, but to make unalienated spirituality practical. On its dust jacket, the publishers of *Master Dharma Drum: The Life and Heart of Ch'an Practices* tell readers that it "offers us fresh insights into the ways we can bring Ch'an study and practice into our daily lives" (Sheng-Yen 1996). I do not speak as a Ch'an practitioner, but I would not be surprised if such a book did indeed make spirituality practical, for a characteristic feature of popontology texts is that they are articulated within other social fields in such a way as to allow their narratives to be practiced. Understanding the nature of this practice necessitates displacing the concept of "genre" from a purely literary domain into its broader interactional environment—right back, in fact, to Wadeye and Belyuen. In other words, we need to keep in mind Mikhail Bakhtin's understanding of the dialectical nature of dialogical genres—"the long and complicated path of generic-stylistic testing and modification"—and their embeddedness in the multidimensional and multimediated space that Michael Silverstein (1993) has called "interactional textuality."

Though not obviously a part of the popontological genre, Blanche McCrary Boyd's *Revolution of Little Girls* nevertheless neatly captures the sociological nature of textual articulations. Toward the end of the novel, the protagonist describes her recent initiation by a shaman: "I'd gone to Peru to be initiated by a shaman, and, in the three months since my return, I'd been pursued by a group of imaginary girls. 'Some people get in touch with their inner child,' Meg said. 'You have to get a crowd' " (Boyd 1991: 182).

With light irony, Boyd uses various "voicings" to gain a foothold in a range of sociological spaces, speaking to readers who might have had flirtations with or still be committed to the New Age, cultural feminism, psychological self-help, or self-empowerment. But Boyd also potentially incites some of her readers to follow her character's track, to click on the Internet and find a Web page like "Return of the Galactic Maya." As of 15 January 1998, this "Mayan initiation journey" promised "a chance to tap into the true power of Mayan culture," which would provide a setting for "contemplating the beauty of the Great Spirit as being of light," a "destiny . . . encoded in our genes." It advertised a summer solstice tour and initiation led by Elder Hunbatz Men, Mayan shaman Quetza-Sha, and Dr. Carlos Warter, and provided fax and phone numbers where reservation-takers would be standing by, along with state functionaries, their regulatory environments, and the local communities fashioned to receive them. Obviously, *The Revolution of Little Girls* and "Return of Galactic Maya" are just isolated nodes in an unmapped—unmappable because emergent—global track of New Age travel, massage schools, and the casual surfers, chat rooms, and communities of the Internet.

The semiotic mediation of indigenous spirituality presents travelers with a set of expectations about what they might, and have a right to, expect from the people and places to which they travel. At the heart of these textual mediations is the expectation of an experience of Being in the presence of the Spirit. And this expectation is manifested spatially—it interprets physical space and is extended into social interactional space. Compare, for example, Belyuen and Wadeye. Belyuen lies on the Cox Peninsula across the Darwin harbor. Ever since the British settlement of Darwin, the proximity of indigenous camps on the peninsula has provided visiting dignitaries, international celebrities, filmmakers, writers, and academics with access to Aboriginal culture. Periodically between the 1930s and 1950s, it served as a base for national radio programs, films, and anthropological studies, and traveling dignitaries, scholars, and celebrities who desired and were provided with a variety of cultural performances, productions, and artifacts gathered there. However, as the transportation infrastructure between the Cox Peninsula and Darwin improved, Belyuen has gotten closer to Darwin and, in the process, lost its aura of distinctiveness. In 1984, when I first arrived at Belyuen, the ferry ride between Darwin and the Cox Peninsula took upward of an hour. Nowadays, it takes fifteen minutes. Likewise, the drive from Darwin to Belyuen now takes roughly seventy minutes, rather than the two to three hours it previously took, depending on the condition of the dirt road.

The legal status of Cox Peninsula lands has also contributed to a sense that the culture of the area has whitened. Under a land claim unresolved for the last twenty years, most of the peninsula remains Commonwealth land, a no-man's land of economic and political practice. Capital investment for large- and small-scale business ventures continues largely to be unavailable until the claim is resolved. And no Aboriginal group has any clear legally sanctioned mandate for excluding non-Aboriginal people from the country or restricting their activities in certain places. In late September 1999, non-Aboriginal campers defiled a women's ceremonial ground. Several residents of a small residential development nearby responded by saying that, as Commonwealth land, the area was open to everyone for any type of use. It was considered "white land" as much as "black land." The lack of legally enforced Aboriginal title encourages and discourages particular types of visitors. Middle-class families on package tours are not likely to visit. But self-described freaks, New Age travelers, ferals, or sportspersons camp on beaches or in the scrub by themselves or alongside Belyuen men and women. These forms of interactions have their own economy of scale, resulting in small-scale exchanges: beer, food, shirts, or smoke for small informal conversations, song performances, tours to sacred sites.

If physical and regulatory space have fashioned Belyuen as a place too close to white society to profit from the commodification of the Spirit, Wadeye has been too isolated. Located off the Stuart Highway and in the middle of a large Aboriginal reserve, Wadeye is physically hard to reach. Several Aboriginal communities lying closer to the main highways profit from the tourist trade. The regulatory environment likewise impedes tourism. Wadeye lies within the Daly River Aboriginal Land Trust, as designated under the Aboriginal Land Rights (Northern Territory) Act of 1976. The community can and does require that nonresidents obtain permits before visiting; and, indeed, all non-Aboriginal people traveling within the land trust are supposed to have a permit issued for some designated community. Even as they impede travel to Wadeye, the difficulty these physical and regulatory environments present travelers functions as an interpretant of that space as more authentically Aboriginal.

The question facing those building regulatory and physical environments at Wadeye is how to capture the tourism market now serviced by other Aboriginal communities without, in the very process, deauthorizing space. Put it this way: As Wadeye becomes a bridge to *Geist* — as it forms material space in the Spirit of consumer capitalism — it risks installing the deauthorizing signs of Western commerce.

If popontology, law, and economy provide critical texts by which space and thus its capital manifestations are formed and interpreted, they also orient visitors' expectations of what will be found in these spaces. These expectations include an understanding that a visit to an Aboriginal community is not about: (1) the horror, exhaustion, and anxiety of being in the world of capital space-time, but rather the experience of *Geist* in the midst of this space-time; (2) Aboriginal people or their lives, but rather an experience only Aboriginal people can afford; (3) the aporia of truth, ethics, or moral action in the face of fundamental alterity, but rather the experience of a shared movement of human spirituality in spite of this alterity. Law and capital, publics and politicians do not need to be colluding in some way — to be engaged in a concerted mass conspiracy — to be seen to be producing in different forms and for different purposes certain human beings as valuable insofar as they afford passageway to an enchanted spiritual Being and away from the conditions of the Spirit of capital. Indeed, these various discursive contexts and practices disperse commonsense understandings of indigenous spirituality and themselves constitute the dispersed sites in which this spirituality is produced.

And yet the people who are charged with transporting visitors to this enchanted realm, to an experience of Being-in-dwelling, themselves dwell within the legal and economic debris of advanced capital. They inhabit a form of poverty that makes well-intentioned visitors afraid, physically ill, subject to panic. It is a type of poverty that can place such visitors in limits similar to those in which Timothy Dumu and Betty Bilawag found themselves. Tourism in these limits risks (and promises) opening experience not to the Spirit that capital commodifies, but to the overwhelming presence of liberal capitalism's bad faith, its dirty corners, its broken covenants.

NOTES

1 For the concept of "footing," see Goffman 1979.

2 By 1998 Castaneda no longer considered near-death experiences with psychotropic substances to be the necessary entryways into nonordinary Being; rather, body weight,

flexibility, and stress are diagnosed as what constrains the manifestation of desire under commodity capital, and thus are means by which the practitioner of a new yoga inflected by indigenous knowledge ("magical passes") can enter extant actual worlds (Castaneda 1998; see also Harner 1990).

REFERENCES

Adams, Vincanne. 1996. *Tigers of the snow and other virtual Sherpas: An ethnography of Himalayan encounters.* Princeton, N.J.: Princeton University Press.

Altman, J. C. 1998. *Aborigines, tourism, and development: The Northern Territory experience.* Darwin: NARU (Northern Australian Research Unit).

Andrews, Lynn. 1987. *Crystal woman: Sisters of the Dreamtime.* New York: Warner Brothers Books.

Arden, Harvey, and Steve Wall. 1998. *Travels in a stone canoe: The return to the Wisdom-keepers.* New York: Simon & Schuster.

Bakhtin, Mikhail. 1986. *Speech genres and other late essays,* edited by Caryl Emerson. Austin: University of Texas Press.

Boyd, Blanche McCrary. 1991. *The revolution of little girls.* New York: Random House.

Castaneda, Carlos. 1968. *The teachings of Don Juan: A Yaqui way of knowledge.* New York: Washington Square Press.

———. 1998. *Magical passes: The practical wisdom of the shamans of ancient Mexico.* New York: Harper Perennial.

Chatwin, Bruce. 1987. *The songlines.* New York: Viking.

Craik, Jennifer. 1991. *Resorting to tourism: Cultural policies for tourism development in Australia.* Sydney: Allen & Unwin.

Egginton, Robert. 1997. A report on *Mutant Message Down Under. Bounah Wongee, Message Stick Online,* no. 2, 31 October.

Emerson, Scott. 1996. Tribal law plan for black youth. *Australian,* 8 August, 4.

Finlayson, Julie. 1991. Australian Aborigines and cultural tourism: Case studies of Aboriginal involvement in the tourism industry. Working paper no. 15, Centre for Multicultural Studies, University of Wollongong, NSW.

Frow, John. 1997. *Time and commodity culture: Essays in cultural theory and postmodernity.* Oxford: Oxford University Press.

Ginsberg, Faye. 1991. Indigenous media: Faustian contract or global village. *Cultural Anthropology* 6, no. 1: 91–112.

Goffman, Erving. 1979. Footing. *Semiotica* 25: 1–29.

Harner, Michael. 1990. *The way of the shaman.* New York: HarperCollins.

Harvey, David. 1989. *The condition of postmodernity: An enquiry into the origins of cultural change.* Cambridge: Basil Blackwell.

Hayes v. Northern Territory. 1999. FCA (9 September).

Jacobs, Jane M., and Fay Gale, eds. 1994. *Tourism and the protection of Aboriginal cultural sites.* Canberra: AGPS.

Knapman, Bruce, Owen Stanley, and John Lea. 1991. *Tourism and gold in Kakadu: The impact of current and potential natural resource use on the Northern Territory economy.* Darwin: NARU.

Langton, Marcia. 1993. *"Well, I heard it on the radio and I saw it on the television": An essay for the Australian Film Commission on the politics and aesthetics of filmmaking by and about Aboriginal people and things.* Sydney: Australian Film Commission.

Loveday, P., and P. Cooke. 1983. *Aboriginal arts and crafts and the market.* Darwin: NARU.

McCulloch-Uehlin, Susan. 1999. Gate slams shut on artists' dreaming land. *Weekend Australian,* 18–19 September, 5.

Michaels, Eric. 1994. *Bad Aboriginal art: Tradition, media, and technological horizons.* Sydney: Allen & Unwin.

Morgan, Marlo. 1994. *Mutant message down under.* New York: HarperCollins.

Myers, Fred. 1998. Uncertain regard: An exhibition of Aboriginal art in France. *Ethos* 63, no. 1: 7–47.

Povinelli, Elizabeth A. 1999. Settler modernity and the quest for indigenous traditions. *Alter/native modernities,* edited by Dilip Gaonkar, special issue, *Public Culture* 11: 19–47.

Rael, Joseph, and Lindsay Sutton. 1993. *Tracks of dancing light: A Native American approach to understanding your name.* Dorset, U.K.: Element Books.

Sheng-Yen, Ch'an. 1996. *Master Dharma Drum: The life and heart of Ch'an practices.* Elmhurst, N.Y.: Dharma Drum Publications.

Silverstein, Michael. 1981. The limits of awareness. Sociological working paper no. 84, Southwest Educational Development Laboratory, Austin, Tex.

———. 1993. Metapragmatic discourse and metapragmatic function. In *Reflexive language,* edited by John Lucy. Cambridge: Cambridge University Press.

Smith, Valene, ed. 1989. *Hosts and guests: The anthropology of tourism.* Philadelphia: University of Pennsylvania Press.

Spivak, Gayatri. 1989. In a word: Interview with Ellen Rooney. *differences: A Journal of Feminist Cultural Studies* 1, no. 2: 124–56.

Thomas, Nicholas. 1999. *Possessions: Indigenous art/colonial culture.* London: Thames and Hudson.

Urry, John. 1997. *Consuming places.* New York: Routledge.

Watt, Bob. 1992a. Flogging a custom, a court told. *Northern Territory News,* 28 July, 3.

———. 1992b. Flogging outside law. *Northern Territory News,* 6 August, 3.

Whorf, Benjamin. 1956. Grammatical categories. In *Language, thought, and reality: Selected writings of Benjamin Lee Whorf,* edited by John B. Carroll. Cambridge: MIT Press.

Wittgenstein, Ludwig. 1998 [1953]. *Philosophical investigations,* translated by G. E. M. Anscombe. Oxford: Blackwell.

Cosmopolitanism and the
Banality of Geographical Evils

David Harvey

The revival of the science of geography . . . should create that unity of knowledge without which all learning remains only piece-work. — Immanuel Kant

Without a knowledge of geography gentlemen could not understand a [newspaper]. — John Locke

Cosmopolitanism is back. For some that is the good news. Shaking off the negative connotations of its past (when Jews, communists, and cosmopolitans were so frequently cast as traitors to national solidarities), it is now portrayed by many (most eloquently by Held [1995]) as a unifying vision for democracy and governance in a world so dominated by a globalizing capitalism that it seems there is no viable political-economic alternative for the new millennium. The bad news is that cosmopolitanism has acquired so many nuances and meanings as to negate its putative role as a unifying ethic around which to build the requisite international regulatory institutions that would ensure global economic, ecological, and political security in the face of an out-of-control, free-market liberalism.

Some broad-brush divisions of opinion immediately stand out. There are those, like Nussbaum (1996, 1997), whose vision is constructed in opposition to local loyalties in general and nationalism in particular. Inspired by the Stoics and Kant, Nussbaum presents cosmopolitanism as an ethos, "a habit of mind," a set of loyalties to humanity as a whole, to be inculcated through a distinctive educational program emphasizing the commonalities and responsibilities of global citizenship. Against this are ranged all manner of hyphenated versions of cosmopolitanism, variously described as rooted, situated, vernacular, Christian, bourgeois, discrepant, actually existing, postcolonial, feminist, ecological, socialist, and so on and so forth. Cosmopolitanism here gets particularized and pluralized in the belief that detached loyalty to the abstract category of "the human" is incapable in theory, let alone in practice, of providing any kind of political purchase even in the face of the strong currents of globalization that swirl around us.

Some of these "countercosmopolitanisms" were formulated in reaction to Nussbaum's claims. She was accused by some of her respondents (see Nussbaum 1996), for example, of merely articulating an appropriate ideology for the "global village" of the new liberal managerial class. The famous line in the *Manifesto*—"the bourgeoisie has through its exploitation of the world market given a cosmopolitan character to production and consumption in every country" (Marx and Engels 1952: 42)—could easily be used to undermine her stance of neutrality. And it is indeed hard to differentiate her arguments from those rooted in Adam Smith's neoliberal moral subject cheerfully riding market forces wherever they go or, worse still, those embedded in the globalizing geopolitics of U.S. national and international interests (Brennan 1997: 25). There is, in any case, something oppressive, her respondents noted, about the ethereal and abstracted universalism that lies at the heart of her cosmopolitan discourse. How can it account for, let alone be sympathetic to, a world characterized by multiculturalism, movements for national or ethnic liberation, and all manner of other differences? What Cheah and Robbins (1998) call "cosmopolitics" then emerges as a quest "to introduce intellectual order and accountability into this newly dynamic space . . . for which no adequately discriminating lexicon has had time to develop."

The widely held belief that such a new lexicon is needed may well propel us onto new intellectual terrain in the new millennium. The material conditions that give rise to the need are also widely understood to be those of "globalization" (see Held 1995: 267). These same forces have led other commentators such as Readings (1996) and Miyoshi (1997, 1998) to question prevailing structures of knowledge entirely and to ask what kinds of scholarly knowledge production will be necessary to sustain or transform a world in which millennial capitalism seemingly reigns triumphant. Readings, for example, argues compellingly that the traditional university has outlived its purpose. In Europe, the kind of university founded by Wilhelm von Humboldt in Berlin two centuries ago helped guard and solidify national cultures. In the United States, the university helped create tradition, found mythologies, and form a "republican subject" able to combine rationality and sentiment and to exercise judgment within a system of consensual democratic governance. But globalization (of culture as well as of economies), the rise of transnational powers, and the partial "hollowing out" of the nation-state (themes all advanced by Held) have undermined this traditional role. So what happens, Readings asks, when the knowledge structure that the university was meant to preserve goes global and transnational along with everything else? Multiculturalism as a seeming antidote does not help, as Miyoshi (1997: 202) observes. Rather, multiculturalism and cultural studies "conceal [the] liberal self-deception" of academics by providing "an alibi for their complicity in the TNC [transnational corporation] version of neocolonialism." These followers of postcolonial or post-Marxist discourse, he argues, are merely "collaborating with the hegemonic ideology, which looks, as usual, as if it were no ideology at all." Mere reform of knowledge structures, says Readings (1996: 169), risks "blinding us to the dimensions of the task that faces us—in the humanities, the social sciences, and the natural sciences—the task of rethinking the categories that have governed intellectual life for over two hundred years."

Nussbaum likewise calls for an entirely different educational structure (and pedagogy) appropriate to the task of rational political deliberation in a globalizing world. On this point both she and her critics, as well as a variety of other commentators such as Held, Readings, Miyoshi, Brennan, and Cheah and Robbins, would agree. But what kind of educational structure and what kind of pedagogy? "Our nation," complains Nussbaum (1996: 11–12), "is appallingly ignorant of most of the rest of the world. The United States is unable to look at itself through the lens of the other and, as a consequence, [is] equally ignorant of itself." In particular, she argues, "To conduct this sort of global dialogue, we need knowledge not only of the geography and ecology of other nations—*something that would already entail much revision in our curricula*—but also a great deal about their people, so that in talking with them we may be capable of respecting their traditions and commitments. Cosmopolitan education would supply the background necessary for this type of deliberation" (my emphasis). This appeal to adequate and appropriate geographical and anthropological understandings parallels, perhaps not by accident, a more general revival of interest in geographical knowledges in recent times. But Nussbaum merely follows Kant (without acknowledging it). For Kant held that adequate geographical and anthropological knowledges provide the necessary conditions of all practical application of knowledge to the material world.

In what follows, therefore, I shall take a closer look at the potential positioning of geographical and anthropological knowledges in any new intellectual order designed to build a more cosmopolitan ethic as a foundation for democratic governance within a globalizing capitalism. In the course of our inquiry, we will find that geographical and anthropological knowledges play a crucial, though often hidden, role in defining what any cosmopolitan project might be about in theory as well as in practice.

KANT'S GEOGRAPHY

I begin with Kant because his inspiration for the contemporary approach to cosmopolitanism is impossible to ignore. (I have even heard it said that the European Union is the Kantian dream of a cosmopolitan republicanism come true.) I cite perhaps the most famous passage from his essay on "Perpetual Peace": "The peoples of the earth have entered in varying degrees into a universal community, and it is developed to the point where a violation of laws in *one* part of the world is felt *everywhere.* The idea of a cosmopolitan law is therefore not fantastic and overstrained; it is a necessary complement to the unwritten code of political and international law, transforming it into a universal law of humanity" (Kant 1991: 107–8). Now consider Kant's *Geography,* a little-known work. Whenever I have questioned Kantian scholars about it, their response has invariably been the same: it is "irrelevant," "not to be taken seriously," or it "lacks interest." There is no published English edition (though there is a translation of Part I as a master's thesis by Bolin [1968]), and a French version appeared only in 1999. There is no serious study of Kant's *Geography* in the English language other than May's (1970), though there are occasional forays into understanding his role in the history of geographical thought in the works of Hartshorne (1939), Tatham (1951), Glacken (1967), and Livingstone (1992). The introduction to the French edition provides materials for an assessment.

In one sense the lack of interest is understandable, since the content of Kant's *Geography* is nothing short of an intellectual and political embarrassment. As Droit (1999: v) remarks, reading it "comes as a real shock" because it appears as "an unbelievable hodge-podge of heterogeneous remarks, of knowledges without system, of disconnected curiosities." To be sure, Kant seeks to sift the sillier and obviously false tales from those that have some factual credibility, but we are still left with an incredible mix of materials more likely to generate hilarity than scientific credibility. But there is a more sinister side to it. While most of the text is given over to often bizarre facts of physical geography (indeed *Physiche Geographie* was the title of his lectures), his remarks on "man" within the system of nature are deeply troubling. Kant repeats without critical examination all manner of prejudicial remarks concerning the customs and habits of different populations. Thus we find:

> In hot countries men mature more quickly in every respect but they do not attain the perfection of the temperate zones. Humanity achieves its greatest perfection with the white race. The yellow Indians have somewhat less talent. The negroes are much inferior and some of the peoples of the Americas are well below them. (Kant 1999: 223; my translation from the French)

> All inhabitants of hot lands are exceptionally lazy; they are also timid and the same two traits characterize also folk living in the far north. Timidity engenders superstition and in lands ruled by Kings leads to slavery. Ostoyaks, Samoyeds, Lapps, Greenlanders, etc. resemble people of hot lands in their timidity, laziness, superstition and desire for strong drink, but lack the jealousy characteristic of the latter since their climate does not stimulate their passion greatly. (Cited in May 1970: 66)

> Too little and also too much perspiration makes the blood thick and viscous. . . . In mountain lands men are persevering, merry, brave, lovers of freedom and of their country. Animals and men which migrate to another country are gradually changed by their environment. . . . The northern folk who moved southward to Spain have left progeny neither so big nor so strong as they, and which is also dissimilar to Norwegians and Danes in temperament. (Cited in May 1970: 66)

As Kant writes elsewhere as well, Burmese women wear indecent clothing and take pride in getting pregnant by Europeans; the Hottentots are
dirty and you can smell them from far away; the Javanese are thieving,
conniving, and servile, sometimes full of rage and at other times craven
with fear, . . . and so it goes (as Vonnegut might say).

Of course, it is possible to excuse such thoughts as mere echoes of
Montesquieu and other scholars such as Buffon (to say nothing of merchants, missionaries, and sailors). Many of the fervent defenders of universal reason and of universal rights at that time, Droit (1999: v) notes,
cheerfully peddled all manner of similarly prejudicial materials, making
it seem as if racial superiorities and ethnic cleansings might easily be
reconciled with universal rights and ethics (though Kant, to his credit,
did go out of his way to condemn colonialism). And all manner of other
excuses can be manufactured: Kant's geographical information was limited, the course in geography was introductory, meant to inform and
raise issues rather than solve them, and Kant never revised the materials for publication (the text that comes down to us was compiled from
Kant's notes, supplemented by those of his students).

But the fact that Kant's *Geography* is such an embarrassment is no
justification for ignoring it. Indeed, this is precisely what makes it so
interesting, particularly when set against his much-vaunted universal
ethics and cosmopolitanism. Dismissal in any case does not accord with
Kant's own thoughts and practices. He went out of his way to gain
an exemption from university regulations in order to teach geography,
and he taught the course no less than forty-nine times (compared to
the fifty-four occasions he taught logic and metaphysics—his most important course—and the forty-six and twenty-eight times he taught
ethics and anthropology, respectively). Furthermore, Kant considered
that geography (together with anthropology) defined the conditions of
possibility of all knowledge and that such knowledge was a necessary
preparation—a "propaedeutic" as he termed it—for everything else.
Although, therefore, geography was obviously in a "precritical" or "pre-
scientific" state, its foundational role required that it be paid close attention. It was presumably one of Kant's aims to bring it into a more
critical and scientific condition.

The fact that he failed to do so, Kant later hinted, was significant: He
simply could not make his ideas about final causes work on the terrain
of geographical knowledge. "Strictly speaking," he wrote (in a passage

that Glacken [1967: 532] regards as key), "the organization of nature has nothing analogous to any causality known to us." Presumably Kant deeply sensed this problem of analogy as he sought to construct geographical understandings.

It is possible, May (1970) argues, to reconstruct some of the putative principles of geographical knowledge from the general corpus of Kant's writings. Geography was not only a precursor but also, together with anthropology (see Kant 1974), destined to be the synthetic endpoint of all of our knowledge of the world (understood as the surface of the earth, as "man's" habitation). The distinction between geography and anthropology largely rested on a distinction between the "outer knowledge" given by observation of "man's" place in nature (geography) and the "inner knowledge" of subjectivities (anthropology). Geography organizes knowledge synthetically through the ordering of space, as opposed to history, which provides a narration in time. Geography is an empirical form of knowledge that is marked as much by contingency and particularity as by the universality that can be derived from first principles. Spatial ordering, therefore, produces, according to May, regional and local truths and laws rather than universals.

May does not tell us how Kant proposed to relate such local truths and laws to the universals of reason. But if his account is right, then geographical knowledge is potentially in conflict with or disruptive of Kant's universal ethics and cosmopolitan principles. Even if it is accepted, as Kant himself held, that the universality of ethics is immune to any challenge from empirical science, the problem of the application of such ethical principles to historical-geographical conditions remains. What happens when normative ideals get inserted as a principle of political action into a world in which some people are considered inferior and others are thought indolent, smelly, or just plain ugly? Some of Kant's more temporizing remarks on the principles of "perpetual peace" arise precisely when such actual geographical cases present themselves. But it boils down to this: either the smelly Hottentots and the lazy Samoyeds have to reform themselves to qualify for consideration under the universal ethical code (thereby flattening out all geographical differences), or the universal principles operate as an intensely discriminatory code masquerading as the universal good.

This contrast between the universality of Kant's cosmopolitanism and ethics and the awkward and intractable particularities of his geography is important. If (as Kant himself held) knowledge of geography defines the conditions of possibility of all other forms of practical knowledge of the world, and if his geographical groundings are so suspect, then on what grounds can we trust Kant's cosmopolitanism? Yet there is one way to see this as a fruitful starting point for discussion. For while it is possible to complain endlessly of "the damage done by faction and intense local loyalties to our political lives" (Nussbaum 1997: 8, citing the Stoics), it is also important to recognize how "human passions" (which Kant believed to be inherently aggressive and capable of evil) so often acquire a local and disruptive expression. The nether side of Kant's cosmopolitanism is his clear recognition that "everything as a whole is made up of folly and childish vanity, and often of childish malice and destructiveness" (cited in Nussbaum 1997: 10). If this assertion is true of the geographical/anthropological world that we inhabit and that cosmopolitanism has to confront and defeat, then we might understand certain recent events in its light — for instance, the sight of NATO bombs (orchestrated through that newfound cosmopolitan republicanism that characterizes the European Union backed by the United States) raining down on Yugoslavia as ethnic cleansing and rape warfare proceed on the ground in Kosovo. This kind of cosmopolitanism coming to ground geographically is not a very pretty sight. Nor are its justifications — like Ulrich Beck's widely reported supportive comment on the bombing of Kosovo as an example of "NATO's new military humanism" — very convincing (see Cohen 1999: 10).

As several commentators (for example, Beck 1982; Shapiro 1998) have observed, there is a startling gap between Kant's philosophical and practical geographies. It is, I want to suggest, imperative in the current conjuncture, when Kant's universalism and cosmopolitanism have the purchase they do, to find means to bridge the gap. That task is even more compelling given that popular geographical knowledge (as opposed to politically corrected academic wisdom) has not advanced much beyond the disorganized and prejudicial state in which Kant left it. Indeed, the general state of geographical knowledge among students at elite universities is even worse than what we find in Kant's *Geography* (prejudicial content included). The nobility of Kant's (and our) ethical vision needs to be tempered by reference to the banality of his (our) geographical knowledges and prejudices.

In *The Order of Things* (1970), Foucault records his irrepressible laughter upon reading a passage in Borges concerning a Chinese encyclopedia with a wild taxonomy dividing animals into such disparate categories as "embalmed," "frenzied," "belonging to the Emperor," "painted with a very fine camelhair brush," and so on. It is a pity that Foucault reserved his laughter for the humorous Borges rather than for the deadly serious Kant. For Kant's *Geography* is almost as bizarre as any Borges story.

The disruption of meaning signaled in the Borges story led Foucault to reflect upon the "enigmatic multiplicity" and the fundamental disorder to which language could so easily lend itself. There is, he observed, "a worse kind of disorder than the *incongruous,* the linking together of things that are inappropriate; I mean the disorder in which fragments of a large number of possible orders glitter separately in the dimension, without law or geometry, of the *heteroclite.*" This led him to formulate the concept of "heterotopias," which are "disturbing, probably because they secretly undermine language, because they shatter or tangle common names, because they make it impossible to name this *and* that. . . . Heterotopias (such as those to be found so often in Borges) desiccate speech, stop words in their tracks, contest the very possibility of grammar at its source; they dissolve our myths and sterilize the lyricism of our sentences" (Foucault 1970: xvii–xviii). Kant's *Geography,* by this definition, is heterotopic. Cosmopolitanism cast upon that terrain shatters into fragments. Geography undermines cosmopolitan sense.

In a lecture given to architects in 1967 (shortly after *The Order of Things* was published), Foucault sought to give heterotopia a more tangible referent, to take it beyond a mere effect of language and into the realm of material practices. The lecture was never revised for publication, though he did permit its publication shortly before he died. In this detail, it resembles Kant's unpublished *Geography* (of which Foucault, as translator of Kant's *Anthropology,* may well have been aware). But there the resemblance ends. Extracted by his acolytes as a hidden gem from within his extensive oeuvre, the essay on heterotopia, unlike Kant's *Geography,* has become an important means—particularly within postmodernism—of simultaneously resurrecting and disrupting the problem of utopia.

Foucault appealed to heterotopia in order to escape from the "no place" that is a "placeful" utopia into sites where things are "laid, placed and arranged" in ways "so very different from one another that it is impossible to define . . . a common locus beneath them all" (Foucault 1970: xvii). This was, of course, a direct challenge to rational planning practices as understood in the 1960s and the utopianism that infused much of the movement of 1968. Heterotopia seemed set fair to provide a privileged means to escape the norms and structures that imprisoned the human imagination (including, incidentally, Foucault's own anti-humanism). Through a study of the history of spaces and an understanding of their heterogeneity, it became possible to identify spaces in which difference, alterity, and "the other" might flourish or (as in architecture) actually be constructed. Hetherington (1997: viii) summarizes the concept of heterotopia as "spaces of alternate ordering. Heterotopia organize a bit of the social world in a way different to that which surrounds them. That alternate ordering marks them out as Other and allows them to be seen as an example of an alternative way of doing things."

The formulation is surficially attractive. It allows us to think of the potential for coexistence in the multiple utopian schemes—feminist, anarchist, ecological, and socialist—that have come down to us through history. It encourages the idea of what Marin (1984) calls "spatial plays" to highlight choice, diversity, difference, incongruity, and incommensurability. It enables us to look upon the multiple forms of transgressive behaviors (usually normalized as "deviant") in urban spaces as important and productive. Foucault includes in his list of heterotopic spaces such places as cemeteries, colonies, brothels, and prisons. There are, Foucault assures us, abundant spaces in which "otherness" and, hence, alternatives might be experienced and explored not as mere figments of the imagination but through contact with social processes already in motion.

But Foucault assumes that such spaces are somehow outside the dominant social order or that their positioning within that order can be severed, attenuated, or, as in the prison, inverted. The presumption is that power/knowledge is or can be dispersed into spaces of difference. This idea is tacitly reneged upon in *Discipline and Punish* and given an entirely different reading in his 1978 interview on "Space, Knowledge, and Power" (Foucault 1984: 239–56). Furthermore, heterotopias presume that whatever happens in such spaces of otherness is in principle of interest and even in some sense acceptable or appropriate. The cemetery and the concentration camp, the factory and the shopping malls, the Disneylands, Jonestown, the militia camps, the open-plan office, New Harmony, and gated communities are all sites of "alternative way[s] of doing things" and therefore in some sense heterotopic. What appears at first sight as so open by virtue of its multiplicity suddenly appears as banal: an eclectic mess of heterogeneous and different spaces within which anything "different"—however defined—might go on.

Ultimately, the whole essay on heterotopia reduces itself to the theme of escape. "The ship is the heterotopia par excellence," wrote Foucault (1986: 28). "In civilizations without boats, dreams dry up, espionage takes the place of adventure and police take the place of pirates." I keep expecting these words to appear on commercials for a Caribbean cruise. But here the banality of the idea of heterotopia becomes all too plain, because the commercialized cruise ship is indeed a heterotopic site if ever there was one; and what is the critical, liberatory, and emancipatory point of that? Foucault's heterotopic excursion ends up being every bit as banal as Kant's *Geography*. I am not surprised that he left the essay unpublished.

Yet he must have sensed that something was important in the essay; indeed, he could not let it die. He later worried, perhaps with a critique of Kant in mind, at the way "space was treated as the dead, the fixed, the undialectical, the immobile," while "time, on the contrary, was richness, fecundity, life, dialectic" (Foucault 1984: 70). If "space is fundamental in any form of communal life," then space must also be "fundamental in any exercise of power," he argued. The implication is that spaces outside of power, heterotopia, are impossible to achieve. But, like Kant with respect to geography, he lets the idea of heterotopia remain in circulation but does not take responsibility for its content, leaving it to others to pick up the pieces. And when asked in 1976 by the editors of the newly founded radical geography journal *Herodote* to clarify his arguments, Foucault gave evasive and seemingly uncomprehending answers to what, on the whole, were quite reasonable probing questions (Foucault 1980). By refusing again and again to elaborate on the material grounding for his incredible arsenal of spatial metaphors, he evades the issue of a geographical knowledge proper to his understandings (even in the face of his use of actual spatial forms such as panopticons and prisons to illustrate his themes) and fails to give tangible meaning to the way space is "fundamental to the exercise of power." And his final admission that a proper understanding of geography is a condition of possibility for his arguments — the Kantian propaedeutic once more — seems like a tactic to get his geographer interlocutors off his back. In any case, he never elaborated on his final recognition that "geography must indeed necessarily lie at the heart of [his] concerns." Nor, interestingly, have any of his followers taken up this challenge.

GEOGRAPHICUS INTERRUPTUS

So what, then, are we to make of these two cases of great philosophical figures who failed to pin down geographical knowledge and spatial understandings in any systematic or organized way, but who explicitly acknowledged the importance of that knowledge to their more general philosophical and political concerns? There is one simple answer. If heterotopias are disturbing and undermining of received forms of sense and meaning, and if geographical knowledge is inherently heterotopic (or, as Kant had it, always local, regional, and contingent), then geographical and spatial understandings undermine and disturb other forms of rational understanding. Those committed to traditional rationality (in governance, democracy, or anything else) then have a vested interest in suppressing or evading geographical questions (in exactly the way that Foucault did in his 1976 interview). The seeming banality of geographical knowledge makes it an easy enough target for dismissal.

Yet there is also something troubling about geographies. I have long espoused the view that the insertion of space (let alone of tangible geographies) into *any* social theory (including that of Marx) is always deeply disruptive of its central propositions and derivations (see Harvey 1984). I see no reason to renege on that view now. This disruptive effect makes space a favored metaphor in the postmodernist attack — inspired, for example, by Foucault's *The Order of Things* — upon all forms of universality. Consider an example that predates the more familiar postmodernist positions. In the field of economics — which is, after all, the most complete of all the social sciences as a "rationalized" form of knowledge/power working from first principles — the problem of spatial ordering produces some deep and seemingly unresolvable paradoxes. In 1957 Koopmans and Beckman published an article that threw "serious doubt on the possibility of sustaining an efficient locational distribution of activities through a price system." The "decisive difficulty," Koopmans (1957: 154) reported, is that the "dependence of one man's (locational) decision criterion on other men's decisions appears to leave no room for efficient price-guided allocation." Throw spatiality into the hopper of economic reasoning and the whole logic falls apart because prices can never do their proper work. This is not an unusual result, as Webber and Rigby (1996) have recently confirmed. Koopmans and Beckman (1957: 74) reported they were so distressed by the result that they delayed publication for several years (though, unlike Foucault and Kant, they did at least directly acknowledge the fundamental nature of the difficulty).

But now that the issues of spatiality (and to some degree of geography) have been rediscovered and partially reinserted into mainstream theories and practices, what exactly gets done with them? Consider, first, how a disruptive spatiality worms its way into critical examination of cosmopolitanism. Connolly (1995: 137), for example, argues (correctly, in my view) for "a more cosmopolitan, multidimensional imagination of democracy that distributes democratic energies and identifications across multiple sites." But when faced with the obvious next step of identifying what "a more multiplicitous spatialization of democratic energies" might mean, he reviews other political theorists only to conclude that "through the optic of political nostalgia" (and by implication through the optic of political theory), it is impossible to identify "the *place* that might, if not supplant loyalty to the state, compete with it so that sometimes a new 'we' finds itself bestowing allegiance on constituencies and aspirations in ways that contest the state's monopoly over political allegiance" (Connolly 1995: 159). Connolly (1998) later accepts the disruptive consequences for political theory in general (and Kant's cosmopolitanism in particular) of rapidly shifting spatialities (appealing to Virilio's concept of speed), but seeks this time to interpret time-space compression as an ambivalent opportunity for a new kind of "rhizomatic" and "fragmented" cosmopolitanism in which the Internet figures large as a vehicle for democratic possibility.

What Connolly needs to complete his project is some sense of how spatialities and geographies (the actual places he is looking for) are actively produced and with what consequences. He fails to register, for example, that "speedup" in modern culture has been produced by a capitalist-military alliance as a means to preserve and enhance specific class and territorial powers, and that the Internet has no liberatory potential whatsoever for the billion or so wageworkers who, according to the World Bank (1995: 1–2), are struggling to eke out an existence on less than a dollar a day. Tangible geographical knowledge is essential at just the point where political theorizing breaks off. Key concepts of "site," "spatiality," "speed," and "place" provide only convenient metaphors to disrupt received political wisdoms. Such concepts remain untheorized even though Connolly's is preeminently a sophisticated theoretical work. The disruptions of spatialities provide merely a means to argue for a broad-based political pluralism and a multidimensionalism of difference. In the tracks of Foucault, Connolly evades questions of real geography and even the production of space.

Shapiro (1998), to take another example, sets out to explore the Kantian ethics of global hospitality in the midst of global difference. He points out that Kant "envisioned a world in which an enlarged ethic of hospitality would diminish the significance of the bordered world," but that he did so in a way that "effaces much of the difference that the Kantian ethics of global hospitality is designed to appreciate." Kant was not sensitive to "peoples and nations that were not organized in the form of states." His notion of peace, it follows, depended upon relationships between states, and "his notion of war did not recognize contested terrains—for example, the struggles between settlers and indigenous peoples—within states" (Shapiro 1998: 701). Faced with the dilemma of how to reconcile Kant's philosophical and practical geographies, however, Shapiro merely resorts to a self-referential study of the variety of spatial, geographical, and territorial metaphors deployed by the usual suspects (Derrida, Foucault, and Lyotard—though, interestingly, Deleuze and Guattari get passed over), ignoring the active terrain of the production of space and of geographies—as if the only thing that matters is getting the metaphors right rather than investigating the material geographical and social processes whereby human populations get disaggregated and differentiated. Had Shapiro read Kant's *Geography*, he might have worried more about Kant's recorded "sensitivities" to people and places. As it is, the study is interestingly learned, but sadly deficient in its understanding of the contingencies that arise "from the

284 * DAVID HARVEY

interactions of space and discourse" within the contemporary political economy of globalization.

And it is not too helpful, either, simply to dismantle Kantian universals into local and contingent meanings as, for example, Walzer (1983: 314) does in formulating a "radically particularist" theory of justice in which "every substantive account of distributive justice is a local account." Like Foucault's heterotopia, this all sounds very noble until confronted with the realities of conflicting senses of justice between different groups, which pit, for example, the militia movement and the KKK against immigrants and non-Caucasians (whoever they are). The sense of justice varies from neighborhood to neighborhood in most cities (I know a neighborhood where incest and homophobia are strongly accepted as social norms), and such differences often become a manifest source of serious political and juridical conflict. What Elster (1992) calls "local justice" is a fact of geographical as well as of institutional life and a fact that deserves close attention. Theoretically, this seems to pose an intractable dilemma. We are caught between a relativism that suggests that for each cultural group there is some theory of justice that captures its ethical intuitions and moral universals that may be just as unpalatable even if they can be defined. But because justice, as Walzer (1983: 314) argues, may be "rooted in the distinct understandings of places, honors, jobs, things of all sorts, that constitute a shared way of life," it does not follow that "to override those understandings is (always) to act unjustly." The cosmopolitan temptation is, of course, to revert to Zeno's dream of a "well-ordered and philosophical community" where we should not be "divided from one another by local schemes of justice," but regard all human beings as "fellow citizens" (cited in Nussbaum 1997: 6).

Such arguments ignore how places and localized ways of life are relationally constructed by a variety of intersecting socioecological processes occurring at quite different spatiotemporal scales (see Harvey 1996: 350–52). They do not pay attention to historical-geographical processes of place and community construction. To ignore these processes and build a particularist theory of local justice with respect to places and cultures as embodied *things* is to advocate a fetishistic politics that would try (fortunately, against all odds) to freeze existing geographical structures of places and norms forever. The effect would be as dysfunctional as it would be oppressive. Compared to that, Kant's cosmopolitanism as a norm for intervention in an unsatisfactory and violent world of geographical difference appears positively liberatory.

Consider, now, this same problem from a different disciplinary direction. Kant, recall, saw anthropology and history as necessary complements to geography as the basis for a holistic and synthetic understanding of the world. While Kant's formal distinctions have been rendered somewhat porous with the passing of time, it is stunning to contemplate the purchase they still have upon professional disciplinary distinctions. The focus on subjectivities (identities) in anthropology still contrasts with the object stance often taken in geography. Though we have been urged again and again to see the world in more unified spatiotemporal terms, history and geography still define themselves, respectively, through narrative and spatial ordering.

The subaltern studies group in South Asia seems to have succeeded in blurring the boundaries between anthropology and history, but how does it treat geography? Deshpande (1998) provides one example. He investigates the relations between globalization, conceptions of the Indian nation, and the construction of "Hindu-ness" (or *hindutva*) as a locus of distinctive identity and meaning. He sees the history of these relations as "closely and crucially intertwined with a geography" (255). Nehru's secular developmental model depended, for example, upon a "privileged pan-Indian elite that could, by and large, afford to cut loose its regional moorings" (261). It entailed a distinctive spatial logic (the history of which "has yet to be written") of "multi-dimensional relations of domination established along the inter-regional, rural-urban, and city-megacity axes" (260). The effect was to construct a distinctive social geography within the Indian national space. But its corollary was to spawn a variety of regional-ethnic movements. *Hindutva,* as an oppositional movement, exploits "the ideological vulnerability of the placeless universalism of the Nehruvian nation-space" and seeks "to rekindle a personalised commitment to particular places that are nevertheless embedded within the abstract social space of hindutva" (263). *Hindutva* appeals to "the sedimented banalities of neighbourliness — the long-term, live-in intimacy of residential relationships among persons and families and between them and their local environment" (270).

The terms are interesting; it is the *banality* of mundane everyday local experiences that defines truths that acquire the status of "self-evident common sense." This forms the basis for a politics (including pathological expressions of intercommunal violence) that is far removed from Kant's cosmopolitanism. The "banalities" of local geographical loyalties disrupt the cosmopolitan ideal of Nehruvian developmentalism. This seems a productive line of enquiry until Deshpande turns to Foucault for enlightenment: "One way of understanding spatial strategies is to think of them as ideological practices involved in the construction of heterotopias. This is the sense in which spatial strategies attempt to tie an imagined space to a real place in such a way that these ties also bind people to particular identities and to the political/practical consequences they entail" (251). The formulation is, as usual, surficially attractive. It also has theoretical cachet. But it ends up flattening an otherwise interesting argument into a conceptual world that is no less banal than the "sedimented banalities of neighbourliness" that it interprets. Deshpande soon discovers that the full implications of heterotopia crucially depend upon "the context of its mobilisation for some larger than everyday activity or campaign" (272) (i.e., it is dependent upon some nonlocal source of power). Nehru had his steel mills and *hindutva* has its symbolic centers. Both are equally heterotopic sites. And so what?[1]

THE BANALITY OF GEOGRAPHICAL EVILS

How, then, are we to understand the geographical racisms and ethnic prejudices of Kant's *Geography*, the eclectic and amoral heterotopia of Foucault, and the tendency of theorists of all stripes to simply delight (as Smith and Katz [1993] point out) in the conveniently disruptive metaphors of spatialities, cartographic metaphors, and the like, rather than to confront the banal problematics of materialist geographies? It is exactly at this conjuncture that the imposing figure of Heidegger looms so large. For, if there is any theorist of rootedness in locality who really takes it all the way, then surely Heidegger is it. His attachment to "dwelling" and "place," coupled with his thorough rejection of all forms of cosmopolitanism (capitalist, socialist, modernist), seems to place him in polar opposition to Kantian ethics. And Heidegger attracts as much, if not more, attention among the scholarly elite as does Kant. The battle between those two philosophical titans and the traditions they have spawned will doubtless rage for the next millennium in much the same way that the founders of Greek philosophy (both Kant and Heidegger drew heavily for inspiration on different strains of pre-Socratic thought) defined major intellectual schisms in the past.

There is one aspect to this debate that strikes me as odd. For Heidegger, it is the phenomenological experience of objects, places, spaces, time, and cultures (languages and myths) that counts. But these are largely deployed as metaphysical concepts. He avoids the world of actual time-deepened material geographical experiences (though his affiliations to the Germanic cultural and linguistic tradition are evident). Like Foucault, he fails to connect to the material circumstances of a lived geography. The most famous exception is Heidegger's (1971) invocation of the traditional Black Forest farmstead as a site of "dwelling" and "being" in the world. But his presentation is romanticized. Heidegger accepts that the conditions he describes are not material qualities of the contemporary world and that this particular *heimat* is not something to which he or we can return. This has left his followers struggling with the question of how to define the "authentic" qualities of "real places" and what the "rootedness" of a work of art might mean — in short, how to give more tangible meaning to Heidegger's abstractions. We also have to struggle to comprehend Heidegger's support for National Socialist ideology (and its active political practices). What do such cultural and political attachments have to do with his philosophical arguments about "dwelling" in "place"?

It was Hannah Arendt (1977), whose longtime and abiding attachments to Heidegger have also proved a puzzle, who coined the phrase "the banality of evil" as she watched the Eichmann trial in Israel. The connections here may seem farfetched or even bizarre (though no more so than the intimacy of the Arendt-Heidegger relationship). For what if Arendt's characterization of evil has some subterranean connection to the banalities of "dwelling," of "place," and of "heimat" as social constructs essential to the human condition? What if Deshpande's "sedimented banalities of neighbourliness" are so fundamental to the human condition (as even Foucault ended up acknowledging of space) that they form the preconditions — the Kantian propaedeutic — for all knowledge of and action in the world (including those of Eichmann)? From this perspective, would it not be true that Heidegger gives a metaphysical foundation, a philosophical voice, to Kant's *Geography*?

Such a possibility gets evaded in contemporary discussions. Heidegger rates only one entry, for example, in Cheah and Robbins's

Cosmopolitics (1998), even though the frequent appeals to some sort of "rooted" cosmopolitanism are loud and recurrent throughout the book. But the one entry for Heidegger is telling: The citation reads, "Nationalism is not overcome through mere internationalism; it is rather expanded and elevated thereby into a system." It is that thought that leads Jonathan Ree (1998: 78) to comment on the way that Kant's transition from the idea of cosmopolitanism to the idea of perpetual peace involved the reduction of "the shining ideal of world citizenship" to "a grudging concession that we ought always to allow foreigners to travel among us unmolested, provided they do not stay around too long." *Perpetual Peace,* Ree contends, "allows cosmopolitan rights to be swallowed up again by the old patriotisms they were originally meant to supplant." The argument is exactly the opposite of Shapiro's. The rootedness of peoples in place (the geographical rootedness of the nation-state in particular) draws us rather awkwardly back to Kant's actual geographical world characterized by folly and aggression, childish vanity and destructiveness, the world of prejudice that cosmopolitanism must counteract or actively suppress in the name of human progress. It takes but a small step then to see geographies and spatialities (and local loyalties) not only as disrupters of order and of rational discourse, but as undermining universal morality and goodness. They become, as with Kant's *Geography,* the fount of all prejudice, aggression, and evil. Even the knowledge of that geography (as with that of Kant) must be suppressed. Heidegger's uncompromising honesty takes us precisely to the metaphysical root of what that particular "evil" (both intellectually and politically) might be about. East Timor, Rwanda-Burundi, and Kosovo tell us what it might mean on the ground.

But what if this is only half of the story? Heidegger certainly did not believe himself to be peddling the metaphysics of inherent evil. His acolytes would find the equation of the banality of evil with his metaphysics unacceptable. In their view, the evil (if such it is) arises out of the dreadful cosmopolitan habit of demonizing spaces, places, and whole populations as somehow "outside the project" (of market freedoms, of the rule of law, of modernity, of a certain vision of democracy, of civilized values, of international socialism, or whatever). What if Heidegger is right in insisting that Kant's cosmopolitanism inevitably slips into an internationalism rooted in nationalism? Isaiah Berlin (1997), for one, was also prepared to see Kant as "an unfamiliar source of nationalism";

the Kantian ideal of autonomy of the will, he remarked, when blended with the doctrines of Herder and Rousseau, "led to terrible explosions" and "pathological" forms of nationalism. In this light, the peculiar version of U.S. cosmopolitanism makes sense: It is based on "an Americanism distinct from patriotism" that idealizes America as a beacon to humanity and that exports Americanism as a "portable ethos" and as an object of universal desire (Brennan 1997: 308). But the myth cannot be sustained without emphatic denunciations and demonizations of "evil empires" (one of Reagan's favorite phrases) and resistant spaces — Cuba, Iran, Libya, Serbia or, for respectable suburbanites, "the inner city" (with all its racial codings).

This tension points to an intellectual impasse in our dominant representations (the collection of commentaries in Nussbaum 1996 reeks of it). An awful symmetry defines the two positions. And the symmetry is secured because we cannot deal with "the banality of evil" (as manifest in East Timor, Rwanda-Burundi, Yugoslavia, in intercommunal violence in South and Southeast Asia [see Das 1990, 1995], and even in the periodic eruptions of disorder in our own cities) — because, in turn, we cannot deal with geographical difference itself. Nussbaum (1997: 23) inveighs against the collapse of values and the indifference to cosmopolitan goals, which she finds are "in grave jeopardy" even outside the United States. A world in which religious, ethnic, and racial conflict are so rife provides "reason for pessimism," as does the fact that "the very values of equality, personhood and human rights that Kant defended, and indeed the Enlightenment itself, are derided in some quarters as mere ethnocentric vestiges of Western imperialism."

But what kind of geographical knowledge is presupposed here? How easy it is to justify (as Beck apparently does) those NATO bombs on Serbia as a grand effort to eradicate a particular geographical evil in the name of Kantian ethics? It is even possible to support State Department threats against Serb authorities for crimes against humanity while supporting the U.S. refusal to sign the international convention against such crimes in order to protect Henry Kissinger and his innumerable colleagues from indictment. Failure to specify or investigate the anthropological and geographical conditions makes such double positions entirely feasible, all in the name of universal ethics.

It is precisely at this point that Nussbaum needs to follow Kant into the nether regions of his *Geography* and there, perhaps, confront the metaphysical foundation given to that *Geography* by Heidegger. The only way out of the impasse, to break the awful symmetry around which politics has rotated so fearfully for two centuries or more, is to press for that "revival of the science of geography" that will not only "create that unity of knowledge without which all learning remains only piece-work," but will also better equip us to deal with the palpable but seemingly intractable problem of the banality of geographical evils on the ground (Kant, cited in May 1970: v).

But within that project lurks another: What kind of geographical knowledge is adequate to what kind of cosmopolitan ethic? Failure to answer that deeper question condemns cosmopolitanism of any sort to remain an abstracted discourse with no tangible meaning other than the ad hoc, pragmatic, and often opportunistic application of universal principles to particular geographical instances (the devastating hallmark of foreign policy habits in the United States). So what kind of geographical knowledge do we now possess, and is it adequate to Nussbaum's cosmopolitanism? To answer these questions requires a brief consideration of the status and role of geographical knowledges in our intellectual and political constructions.

A SHORT HISTORY OF MODERN GEOGRAPHY AS A DISCIPLINE

Kant's teaching on the relevance of geography was not without immediate effects. Perhaps the most interesting way to look at this is through the careers of the brothers Humboldt, both of whom were directly and deeply affected by Kant. Wilhelm von Humboldt was drawn to the inner life. He became a logician, linguist, and historian, and founded the University of Berlin as a model for the modern university. As Wilhelm's cosmopolitanism became diluted by ethnic influences and allegiances, so he became more closely identified with the state apparatus, taking on state functions. In parallel fashion, knowledge production within the university he founded became more and more subservient to state and ethnic interests (Readings 1996). This was the model that was carried elsewhere — to the United States, for example, where the Johns Hopkins University was founded as that country's first research university. This is the model that Readings regards as now defunct.

Alexander von Humboldt was inspired by Kant's *Geography*. Unlike Kant, who never left Königsberg, he took to an outer life of exploration, of travel and scientific observation, culminating in a glorious attempt at Kantian-style synthesis of geographical understandings. This massive scientific work was entitled, appropriately enough, *Cosmos* (Humboldt 1847). Alexander — whose intellectual center of gravity was Paris rather than Berlin — drew heavily upon an older tradition that, beginning with the Renaissance, produced a massive explosion in geographical knowledge and geographical sensibilities, exercising some of the finest mathematical minds (Mercator, Gauss) and some of the most powerful of the Enlightenment and political thinkers (Montesquieu, Rousseau, and Adam Smith, as well as Kant). No matter how oddly and bizarrely formulated, geographical knowledge during this period was implicated in the construction of all manner of other knowledges (see Glacken 1967).

Alexander was enamored of this tradition and reveled in its excitements. He was, Zeldin (1994: 198–202) argues, "a pioneer of global thinking, without concealing that his purpose was not merely to understand the universe in its entirety, but no less to avoid the pain caused by the tragedies it constantly produces. His *Views of Nature* (1808) is dedicated to 'minds oppressed with care . . . [needing] to escape from the storm of life.' " In order to grapple with such evils, Alexander had to do something else with the encyclopedic knowledge he had amassed.

> [He] tried to extract a new way of life from his researches, abstract though some of them might seem. This is rare, because it conflicts with the rules of specialisation, which require one to keep one's mouth shut on subjects on which one is not a trained expert; and since nobody can be an expert on the art of life, it has become dangerous to speak about it. Intellectuals have increasingly been limiting themselves to lamenting the lack of values in modern times. The importance of Humboldt is that he dared to make a link between knowledge and feeling, between what people believed and do in public and what obsesses them in private. (Zeldin 1994: 198)

There is, in this, a peculiar irony. Alexander moves closer to being the real and thoroughly informed cosmopolitan, an interdisciplinarian sensitive to the pain of the world by virtue of his geographical understandings, while his brother, who began as the ethical cosmopolitan, succumbs to national interests elevated into internationalism (cf. Heidegger's complaint cited above). Wilhelm became more and more directly embroiled in German politics, while Alexander became a more and more isolated monadic figure in Paris until his expulsion from France as a potentially dangerous radical free thinker in the revolutions of 1848. "We have diverged like two opposite poles," wrote Wilhelm (May 1970: 78).

Not everything was well with Alexander's geography, of course. It retained its Eurocentrism (and much of the prejudice that went with it), it documented resources and populations that were open to commercial exploitation, and it adeptly shaped geographical knowledge toward the interests of patrons (locating the gold mines of Mexico for the King of Spain in return for research funding, for example). But it also managed to transcend these interests and give a more systematic and scientific as well as humanistic grounding to the materials that Kant had left so disordered. It pointed the way to a thorough geographical foundation for Kant's cosmopolitanism. But *Cosmos,* as May remarks, "fell still born from the press," and that for two compelling reasons.

First, there was little space or place for Alexander's exertions in the kind of university structure that Wilhelm had pioneered. Knowledge got carved up and fragmented into distinctive, professionally organized disciplines as the nineteenth century wore on. This "disciplinary carve up" produced a pattern of knowledge that served the pursuit of national interests, such as empire and military power, national identity and solidarities, internal administration, and so on. This was precisely the allure that Daniel Coit Gilman, a geographer, gave to the Johns Hopkins University as its founding president in 1876. He paid lip service to Alexander's achievements, but another geographer, Arnold Guyot, was his true mentor. Guyot argued that geography "provided 'scientific' justification for the EuroAmerican domination of the world," and that racial superiorities were innate; he argued that "the people of the temperate continents will always be the men of intelligence, of activity, the brain of humanity," while "the people of the tropical continents will always be the hands, the workmen, the sons of toil" (cited in Heyman forthcoming). Gilman therefore appropriated the ethnicized version of the Berlin University model and designed the system of knowledge production at Hopkins with the geopolitical interests of the United States specifically in mind. He did not find it necessary, however, to set up a geography department; the whole university was construed as a geopolitical agent.

Furthermore, as the word "discipline" announces only too directly, knowledge production was increasingly policed and put under surveillance by a whole apparatus of group identifications and evaluations that seem to have set themselves more firmly in concrete with the passing of time. The Renaissance tradition of geography as everything understood in terms of space, of *Cosmos,* got squeezed out. It was forced to buckle down, administer empire, map and plan land uses and territorial rights, and gather and analyze useful data for purposes of business and state administration. The founding of geographical societies throughout Europe exactly mirrored the rise of administrative concerns about empire (Capel 1981; Livingstone 1992, chap. 7). Caught between Durkheimian sociology and the historians, for example, the French geographers were left with hardly anything of substance to chew upon, even as the historians appropriated ideas from geographers like Vidal de la Blache to found the celebrated Annales School (which laudably retains its geographical groundings to this day). Caught, in the United States, between geology and the social sciences, geography as a discipline either battled for a niche through concepts of landscape and the particularities of region or, as with Isaiah Bowman, sought a role as geopolitical adviser to the U.S. national interest (Smith 1984; Godlewska and Smith 1994). Bowman, as president of Johns Hopkins University, finally established a geography department "in the national interest" in 1948 (see Smith n.d.).

But there was another deeper intellectual problem with Alexander's work. He accepted the Kantian distinction between history as narration and geography as spatial ordering, and displayed little interest in dynamics. He argued in *Cosmos* that "the mysterious and unsolved problems of development do not belong to the empirical region of objective observation, to the description of the developed, the actual state of our planet" (cited in May 1970: 78). This proved a fatal error. Alexander's work could be celebrated as a product of one of the last great Renaissance thinkers. But it was destined to be swept aside by the Darwinian revolution, in which evolution and process (and by implication time and history) took precedence over pattern and form (space and geography) in every branch of knowledge production including, of course, the social sciences.

Geographers of various stripes struggled toward the century's end to give their geography a more evolutionary and emancipatory twist. The social anarchists — geographers like Élisée Reclus and Peter Kropotkin — invented a version of the geography of freedom (Fleming 1988) that has remained influential as a subversive strain of thought to this day, but for obvious reasons suffered marginalization from the mainstream (except in the refracted versions in the urban and regional planning of Patrick Geddes and Lewis Mumford). At the turn of the century, Friedrich Ratzel took the innovative step of collapsing Kant's inner and outer distinctions into something called "Anthropogeographie," but unfortunately got so lost in organic metaphors (of the state in particular) and social Darwinism that he was later regarded, unfairly as it turns out, as the founder of Nazi geopolitical thought. This kind of Darwinian geopolitical and imperialist geography (which had its Anglo and French counterparts in Guyot, Halford Mackinder, and Albert Demangeon), along with environmental determinism (the other major strain of independent geographical thinking), lost respectability even as it struggled to retain some semblance of Humboldtian synthesis. When *Reader's Digest* condemned "the hundred geographers behind Hitler" (Dorpalen 1942) in the midst of World War II, professional geographers suffered all the indignities that Heidegger was later to experience, but without any of the deeper intellectual resources needed to defend themselves. Professional geographers for the most part retreated into the safety of mere description of spatial orderings (Smith 1999).

Attempts to treat as porous the borders between geography and anthropology (in the work of Daryll Forde, Carl Sauer, and Alfred Kroeber, for example) or between history and geography (Arnold Toynbee, Paul Wheatley, and Donald Meinig, for example) indicated the possibility of cross-disciplinary fertilization, but remained isolated endeavors in an increasingly segmented and professionalized world of knowledge production. Even today, when the grounds for separation between anthropology and geography as intellectual traditions appear shakier and shakier (and with a good deal of interaction between the disciplines occurring in practice), the disciplinary police forces attached to tradition seem hell-bent on keeping the professional identities separate and sacrosanct. From time to time, geographers of a more academic persuasion have tried to resurrect the power of their Renaissance origins by waving the flag of "synthesis" (usually with a little help from Kant). But the disciplinary carve-up of the late nineteenth century remains powerfully with us, entrenching itself ever more deeply as it becomes less and less relevant. Geography as a formal discipline lost its appetite for synthesis. The Humboldtian inspiration was largely lost. Geography as a discipline largely stuck to static descriptions of spatial orders and hoped for the best.

The marginalization of the discipline of geography did not diminish the significance or power of geographical understandings. No society, after all, can do without a working knowledge of the distribution and organization of those conditions (both naturally occurring and humanly created) that provide the material basis for the reproduction of social life. No social group can subsist without a working knowledge of the definition and qualities of its territory, of its environment, of its "situated identity" in the world, of the spatial configurations of actually existing and potential uses (including symbolic and aesthetic as well as economic values) essential to its existence. No social order can afford to turn its back upon the powers to produce space, place, and environments according to its own vital needs, desires, and interests. No society dare ignore the untoward and unintended consequences of the environmental and geographical transformations it has wrought. Every individual and every social group possesses, therefore, a distinctive "geographical lore" and "geographical praxis," some loosely structured body of knowledge and experience about matters geographical. The social transmission of that knowledge is vital to the perpetuation or transformation of any social order. It is a vital aspect of power and an object of political and social struggle.

Geographical knowledges have therefore often flourished in subterranean environments not open to critical scrutiny: To begin with, the United States, the Pentagon, the State Department, and the CIA are good examples. A wide array of geographical technologies, such as Geographical Information Systems and remote sensing for espionage and missile targeting, have been devised to secure military and tactical advantages. But it is only a certain kind of geographical knowledge and praxis that flourishes in these environments. Organized from the standpoint of the geopolitical survival of the United States, geographical knowledge is oriented to military, economic, and cultural control of the world (it was mobilized as a tool of Cold War politics, as was anthropology, part of which became involved—with fractious disciplinary consequences—in counterinsurgency work in Asia and Latin America).

This kind of geography exhibits a deliberate and brutal ignorance of and deep lack of respect for local traditions, meanings, and commitments—except and insofar as such knowledge provides means to manipulate and deceive. It demonizes spaces and places for political purposes. This geography was and is every bit as "evil" as that constructed by the hundred geographers behind Hitler, but it is protected from critical and ethical judgment by an aura of benevolently conceived national and global security interests. When this knowledge leaks out into fields such as international relations or strategic studies, its role is well understood. Academic think tanks (appropriately financed) and even whole university departments flourish with clear signs that read: "No admittance except on the business of the national interest." This geography reflects a distinctively U.S.-based cosmopolitanism (cf. Brennan's characterization cited above). Free-spirited critics are kept out or actively repressed, as happened most spectacularly during the McCarthy years in the United States.[2]

These are not the only places where geographical knowledges flourish. In all of the major institutions engaged in the geopolitics of political-economic development (from the World Bank and the OECD to the boardrooms of large corporations and into the proliferating mass of NGOs working toward a variety of ends), certain kinds of geographical understandings have operated as critical undergirdings for policy formulation and political-economic strategizing. From time to time, these understandings get explicitly formulated or rendered more sophisticated (as, for example, at the 1998 World Bank Conference on Development Economics, which devoted considerable space to the theme "Is Geography Destiny?" [Pleskovic and Stiglitz 1999]). Each nation-state, each revolutionary movement, and every institution (from the Vatican to the Iranian Mullahs) possesses its own distinctive version of geographical and geopolitical knowledge, tailored to its distinctive interests.

Developers and real estate interests, financiers and supermarket chains, marketing organizations and the tourist industry, all produce geographical knowledges through their pursuit of commercial advantage and political-economic power. Popular magazines (such as *National Geographic*), the producers of commercial travelogues and brochures, films and television programs, the nightly news and documentaries transmit geographical information in ways that give a powerful ideological cast (in which the interests of the dominant classes and the nation-state brook large) to our understanding of the world. Beset by interminable banalities and thoroughly filtered through the media (even sometimes with a benevolent aim, as for famine relief), the aggregate effect of such diverse activities occurring at multiple sites is to produce ideological representations and images of the world that harbor all manner of tacit—or in some cases explicit—expressions of geographical, racial, ethnic, cultural, or political difference with more than a hint of class or ethnic superiority attached. When assembled as a collective power, these multiplicitous geographical visions produce what Smith (1997) calls "the satanic geographies" of contemporary globalization. This is not, presumably, the kind of geographical knowledge Nussbaum has in mind as basic preparation for her cosmopolitan ethic.

When cast as a pragmatic handmaiden to the pursuit and maintenance of political-economic power, the subversive and potentially emancipatory side of geographical science (of the sort that Alexander von Humboldt pioneered and the social anarchists tried to perpetuate) gets lost. But the need for better and more systematic geographical understandings has welled up from the political-economic base to permeate other zones of knowledge production where it has been less easy to control. It suffuses international relations, certain areas of sociology, planning, and economics (most particularly through a concern with what is called "the new economic geography"—see Krugman 1999; Storper 1997). It appears, above all, in history and anthropology (the other half of the Kantian propaedeutic, with its emphasis upon localities, cultures, inner identifications, symbolic meanings, local knowledges, and "thick" descriptions of a fragmented and unevenly developed world). Geographical systems of representation have, mainly courtesy of cultural studies, become common grist for discussion in the humanities. Postcolonial writings, most notably of the sort pioneered by Guha (1983, 1997) and others, coupled with the prominence of Said's (1978) work, have opened a vital door to a broad-based critical geographical sense in several disciplines. Environmental and ecological contradictions have similarly opened up a massive terrain of debate about matters geographical (of the sort that both Kant and Alexander von Humboldt would have appreciated) that demand close attention across multiple fields of ecology, zoology, hydrology, epidemiology, and the like. All of this has been paralleled by the vigorous growth of critical perspectives within the hitherto marginalized discipline of geography itself.

Nussbaum's appeal for more adequate geographical and anthropological understandings occurs, therefore, in the context of a general revival of interest in geographical knowledges. The current interest in issues such as the role of spatiality in social and political life, attachments to place, and the possibilities and pitfalls of cartography and mapping signal this revival; so, too, does the extraordinary proliferation of spatial, cartographic, and geographical metaphors as tools for understanding the fragmentations and fractures evident within a globalizing world. Geographical knowledges are vaster, more sophisticated, and more multiplicitous than ever in their detailed and specialized manifestations. But they remain fragmented, undertheorized, and often beyond systematic consideration. Even though its multiple parts constituted across many disciplines are more vigorous than ever, geography as a whole is still declared dead (for who could possibly be interested in, let alone place their emancipatory hopes in, "dead" space, given the fecundity and richness of everything temporal?).

But if Nussbaum's cosmopolitanism is to become anything other than a pious hope, nothing short of a modern-day (Alexander) Humboldtian synthesis will do. The fragmented pieces of geographical knowledge cannot fit the bill because they collectively fail to match the universality of the cosmopolitan ideal. Cosmopolitanism, in short, is empty without its cosmos. But Alexander's *Cosmos,* while it may inspire, is not a model to be followed. Its acceptance of the Kantian prescription to construe geographical knowledge as mere spatial ordering, kept apart from the narratives of history, must be transcended. A revolutionary transformation of historicogeographical knowledges suited to the times can be accomplished through the dynamic unification of "dead" spatiality with "live" narrative (the conversion of concepts of space and time into a more unified field of thought defined by *space-time*), and through the unification of historical and geographical perspectives. If capitalism produces its own distinctive geography — replete with competing geopolitical power plays for competitive advantage — within an increasingly cosmopolitan system of production for the world market, then the dynamics of that process, including its unintended consequences, must be in the forefront of both theoretical and political concerns. A revolution in knowledge-structures that lays out, as Kant demanded, the common preconditions for practical intervention in the world by unifying geographical, historical, and anthropological understandings is both necessary and possible.[3]

GEOGRAPHICAL KNOWLEDGES AND MILLENNIAL NEEDS

A slow revolution in the role of geographical knowledge has been long gestating in the subversive interstices of thought and action. In part this must be attributed to the demand for improved knowledge structures to encompass capitalism's millennial problems and needs (environmental transformations and uneven geographical developments that call for far better global management). But opposition to the bland homogeneities of globalization (with all of its power inequalities) increasingly focuses on geographical differences, on regional resistances, on place-bound ethics and identifications (nationalisms, "critical" regionalisms, and even localisms). Deshpande's "sedimented banalities of neighbourliness" are called upon to do duty in political lines of fire. Time-space compressions engineered through the mechanics of capital accumulation have helped produce localized reactions at a variety of scales that fetishize places and spaces, even threatening to turn them into exclusionary and separatist zones of radicalized resistance and difference (see Harvey 1989: 303–6). Local resistances and separatisms proliferate as an antidote to neoliberal globalization. The result is a chronically unstable dialectics of space and place that brings geographical elements into the center of politics. New forms of geographical knowledge arise in response to such tensions.

From such a perspective, in which history and dynamics cannot be evaded, geographical knowledges turn out not to be so banal as they seem. Historical-geographical concepts of space, speed, site, place, region, motion, mobility, environment, and the like are rich in possibilities. As many geographers have argued, they can be integrated theoretically with social, literary, and ecological theory, albeit in a transformative way (see, for example, Gregory 1994; Harvey 1996; and the recent survey by Brenner 1997). Static spatial and geographical concepts can and must be rendered dynamic. They can be admitted into theory as active aspects or "moments" in social processes (see Giddens 1981, 1984). Topics such as "the production of space" (Harvey 1973; Lefebvre 1991); the shifting geographical mobilities of capital and labor; deterritorialization and reterritorialization (the production of regionality in human affairs); massive urbanization and migratory movements; the degradation and production of resource complexes or even of whole ecosystems; and the radical transformations in time-space relations and of geographical scales occurring in social, political, and cultural life can all be built into understandings of the temporal dynamics of capitalism with advantage.

Spatiality and geography, taken dynamically, do not necessarily betoken the total disruption of all received wisdoms. But they do challenge and transform meanings and modes of expression in important and sometimes unexpected ways. Nor are regional, local, and geographical loyalties necessarily to be perceived as the inherent locus of all political evils. However, the cultivation or even the invention of such loyalties is so often such a vital aspect of brutalizing geopolitical power that it is all too often deliberately held apart from critical interrogation (often by appeal to an unshakable and unquestioned originary or founding "myth" of nationhood that supports otherwise naked state power as some kind of "manifest destiny"). The depiction of others' geographical loyalties as banal or irrational (as in the case of intercommunal violence) helps foster ignorance of and disinterest in the lives of those others; meanwhile, space after space is opportunistically demonized or sanctified by some dominant power as a justification for political action. Such biased geographical knowledges, deliberately maintained, provide a license to pursue narrow interests in the name of universal goodness and reason. The last two centuries have seen plenty of that.

But the result of such deliberate distortions of geographical understandings, as Henri Bergson long ago complained, is to permit a hidden spatiality and geography to control our lives. As this "hidden control" is increasingly recognized for what it is, the need to refound a more unified critical geographical understanding of the world to parallel the contemporary striving for a cosmopolitan ethic becomes even stronger. For geographical dynamics pervade everything we do, no matter how emphatically they may be ignored or dismissed as analytical categories open to question. Retrospectively we see how geographical dynamics have proven central in the quest to dominate nature and other peoples, to build and perpetuate distinctive power structures (such as a capitalist class or imperialist systems) or social identities (such as the nation-state). Like maps, the preeminent form of representation in geography, what Harley (1988: 300) calls "the ideological arrows have tended to fly largely in one direction, from the powerful to the weaker in society." The social history of geographical knowledge, like that of maps, exhibits "few genuinely popular, alternative, or subversive modes of expression"; hitherto, geographical knowledges and maps have preeminently been "a language of power not of protest."

A critical understanding of such dynamics can become a force for the construction of alternative social orderings. Radical reconstructions of received representations and meanings of geographical information are possible: if geography has been imagined and made a part of capitalism's historical geography, then it can be reimagined and remade in an image other than that of capital in the future. The transformation of physical and social environments, the production of new kinds of space relations, the free proliferation of uneven geographical developments, and the reconfiguration of regional configurations can be seen as part of a liberatory political praxis (see Harvey 2000). In remaking our geographies, we can remake our social and political world. The relations are both reciprocal and dialectical.

So what kind of geographical knowledge will fit with what kind of cosmopolitanism? The two issues are, in the final instance, mutually determining, dialectically intertwined. Some form of geographical knowledge is presumed in every form of cosmopolitanism. "Almost any use of 'cosmopolitanism' implies some embedded geopolitical allegory," writes Wilson (1998: 352). The reluctance to reveal or even acknowledge what that knowledge or allegory might be about (signaled at the very outset by the refusal within the academy to bring Kant's cosmopolitanism into dialogue with his *Geography*) is both a moral failing and a political liability. Cosmopolitanism bereft of geographical specificity remains abstracted and alienated reason, liable, when it comes to earth, to produce all manner of unintended and sometimes explosively evil consequences. Geography uninspired by any cosmopolitan vision is either mere heterotopic description or a passive tool of power for dominating the weak. Liberating the dialectic between cosmopolitanism and geography seems a critical propaedeutic to the formation of any radically different way of thinking and acting in the world.

If the frozen structures of knowledge production desperately need to be reformed (Nussbaum) or revolutionized (Readings) to cope with contemporary conditions and needs, then the reconstitution of geographical knowledges in a dialectical relation to cosmopolitanism must be central to that effort. The need is plainly there. One does not have to accept the more hyperbolic statements about globalization (including those of Readings) to know that there are multiple confusions over how spaces and places are being constituted, how whole ecologies of life are being overturned and displaced, how social relations are being sustained or transformed, how new geographies are daily being produced. The hidden spatialities and containers of our thinking, being, and acting in the world have been breaking down. Our geography is being remade to constitute an entirely new kind of amoral order of capitalist power.

Abundant resources and opportunities to reconstitute geographical knowledges now exist. Some of those resources lie within the discipline of geography itself, as it increasingly escapes its ghettoized marginalization through the rise of a powerfully articulated critical geography (see, for example, Peet 1998; Gregory 1994; Harvey 1996). But geographical knowledge is too broad and too important to be left to geographers. Its reconstruction as a preparation for a civilized life and its synthesis as an endpoint of human understandings depends on overcoming the old Kantian distinctions between history (narration) and geography (spatial ordering) and between geography (the outer world of objective material conditions) and anthropology (the inner world of subjectivities). That would probably require the reconstitution of some new structure of knowledge (perhaps the anthropogeography that Ratzel prematurely sought to establish). Imagine powerful institutes dedicated to getting the conditions of all knowledge—the Kantian propaedeutic—exactly right! The "rethinking" of "the categories that have governed intellectual life for the last two hundred years," which Readings deems essential, is possible because it is necessary. Kant and Alexander von Humboldt may not have gotten it right, but in their presumption that full and appropriate geographical knowledge was a necessary condition for cosmopolitan being in the world, they set a goal that has never yet been met. A hefty dose of geographical enlightenment, from whatever source, now as then, continues to be a necessary condition for any kind of peace, perpetual or otherwise, in the millennium to come. It must be central to the reconstructions that Nussbaum and Readings have in mind.

But to argue for opening up the dialectic between the cosmopolitan tradition and geographical knowledge and thereby getting the Kantian propaedeutic right is far too vague. The unfolding of that dialectic depends on the underlying nature of the political project and is bound to be penetrated by political power as much in the future as it has been in the past. The revolutionary tradition of geographical thought (Reclus and Kropotkin), with its emphasis upon the geography of freedom, is open to reconstruction. The workers of the world (whom Marx and Engels erroneously thought of as ideal cosmopolitan subjects because they "had no country") can still seek to unite and overthrow global bourgeois power, with its distinctive form of cosmopolitanism, though this time they too must be far more mindful of uneven geographical developments (the dialectic between socialist internationalism and geography has never functioned freely, if it has functioned at all). Environmentalists may likewise seek to challenge bourgeois power for other reasons, and in so doing construct a new ecological cosmopolitanism — one that is articulated through appropriate bioregional structures and sustainable communities, and one that is organized across the surface of the world according to thoroughly grounded geo-ecological principles.

This brings us back to all those hyphenated cosmopolitanisms with which we began. But now we see them differently. Many of them disappear as irrelevant because to open the dialectic between cosmopolitanism and geography is immediately to see that there can be no universality without particularity and vice versa, that both are always implicated in (an "internal relation of") the other (Ollman 1993; Harvey 2000). To pretend, then, that we have to make some choice between "universal" and "rooted" cosmopolitanism (or even, in the end, between Kant and Heidegger) is a false characterization of the problem. Learning to see cosmopolitanism and geography as internal relations of each other radically reconstitutes our framework for knowledge of the world.

But some of the hyphenated versions of cosmopolitanism still stand. For a critical history shows that "Western" cosmopolitanism these last two hundred years has either been infected by religious power (the Catholic cosmopolitanism of which Antonio Gramsci complained) or by bourgeois sensibilities, pieties, and "feel-good" justifications for their hegemonic project of global domination of the world market. It is either that or being held captive (as in American political life) to local interests proclaiming noble universal values (this habit began most emphatically

when revolutionaries in Paris proclaimed the universal rights of man).
Modern versions of cosmopolitanism cannot evade such connections.
Thus Held's (1995) eloquent plea for a new form of cosmopolitan governance and democracy has as much to do with making the world safe for
capitalism, market freedoms, and social democracy as it has to do with
any other conception of the good life. Political connections of this sort
are both inevitable and necessary, even though, for obvious reasons, the
promulgators of such universalisms often take as many pains to fudge
or obscure their political underpinnings as to hide their geographical
presuppositions and implications.

A meaningful cosmopolitanism does not entail some passive con-
templation of global citizenship. It is, as Kant himself insisted, a principle of intervention to try to make the world (and its geography) something other than what it is. It entails a political project that strives to
transform living, being, and becoming in the world. This obviously requires a deep knowledge of what kind of geographical world we are
intervening in and producing, for new geographies get constructed
through political projects, and the production of space is as much a
political and moral as a physical fact. The way life gets lived in spaces,
places, and environments is, like the Kantian propaedeutic itself, the beginning and the end of political action. The cosmopolitan point is, then,
not to flee geography but to integrate and socialize it. The geographical
point is not to reject cosmopolitanism but to ground it in a dynamics of historical-geographical transformations. The political point is not
only to change our understanding of the world by getting the Kantian
propaedeutic right, but to remake the world's geography in emancipatory and practical ways.

END GAME

"I have enjoyed this discussion with you because I've changed my
mind since we started. . . . Now I can see that the problems you put to me
about geography are crucial ones for me. Geography acted as the support, the condition of possibility for the passage between a series of factors I tried to relate. Where geography itself was concerned, I either left
the question hanging or established a series of arbitrary connections. . . .
Geography must indeed necessarily lie at the heart of my concerns."

Many thanks to Elke Heckner and particularly to Eliot Tretter, who both supplied me with thoughts and references.

1 Deshpande's is not, unfortunately, an isolated instance of potentially insightful analysis gone awry in Foucauldian trendiness. Azoulay (1999), to cite one other recent example, wrecks a potentially sensitive analysis of the conflict between Palestinians and Jews in Jerusalem by navigating straight into the abyss of Foucault's heterotopic theory. To her credit, she recognizes that something is lacking in the whole idea, but once within its thrall she never manages to reemerge from its banality to deliver the cogent insights of which she seems so capable. Is there no better theoretical handle to deal with geography and spatiality in such situations?

2 See, for example, Newman's 1992 account of the life and times of the geographer/historian Owen Lattimore, appointed by the geographer Isaiah Bowman to the Johns Hopkins University faculty and denounced as a traitor to McCarthy by another Bowman appointee, the conservative geographer George Carter.

3 But here there is an irony, neatly symbolized within, of all places, the University of Chicago itself, where the Kantian identifications and dualisms evidently still exert their hidden powers. A professor of law and ethics in that university, drawing (like Wilhelm von Humboldt) upon all the resources of the inner life fueled by deep studies of ancient and modern texts, can only complain helplessly about the collapse of cosmopolitan values and the banality of all those geographical evils that beset the outer world, while the tradition of Alexander von Humboldt is laid to rest through the university's decision to close down rather than revolutionize its geography program.

REFERENCES

Arendt, H. 1977 [1963]. *Eichmann in Jerusalem: A report on the banality of evil.* Harmondsworth, U.K.: Penguin.

Azoulay, A. 1999. Save as Jerusalems. In *Giving ground: The politics of propinquity,* edited by J. Copjec and M. Sorkin. London: Verso.

Beck, U. 1982. *Risk society: Towards a new modernity.* London: Polity Press.

Berlin, I. 1997. *The sense of reality: Studies in ideas and their history.* London: Chatto and Windus.

Bolin, R. 1968. Immanuel Kant's *Physical Geography,* translated by Ronald L. Bolin. M.A. thesis, University of Indiana.

Brennan, T. 1997. *At home in the world: Cosmopolitanism now.* Cambridge: Harvard University Press.

Brenner, N. 1997. Global, fragmented, hierarchical: Henri Lefebvre's geographies of globalization. *Public Culture* 10: 135–67.

Capel, H. 1981. Institutionalization of geography and strategies of change. In *Geography, ideology, and social concern,* edited by D. Stoddart. Oxford: Blackwell.

Cheah, P., and B. Robbins, eds. 1998. *Cosmopolitics: Thinking and feeling beyond the nation.* Minneapolis: University of Minnesota Press.

Cohen, R. 1999. A generation of German pacifists at odds over war. *New York Times,* 6 May, A10.

Connolly, W. 1995. *The ethos of pluralization*. Minneapolis: University of Minnesota Press.

————. 1998. Speed, transcendentalism, and cosmopolitanism. Manuscript, Department of Political Science, Johns Hopkins University, Baltimore, Md.

Das, V. 1990. *Mirrors of violence: Communities, riots, and survivors in South Asia*. Oxford: Oxford University Press.

————. 1995. *Critical events: An anthropological perspective on contemporary India*. New Delhi: Oxford University Press.

Deshpande, S. 1998. Hegemonic spatial strategies: The nation-space and Hindu communalism in twentieth-century India. *Public Culture* 10: 249–83.

Dorpalen, A. 1942. *The world of General Haushofer: Geopolitics in action*. Port Washington, N.Y.: Kennikat Press.

Droit, R.-P. 1999. Kant et les fourmis du Congo. *Le Monde,* 5 February.

Elster, J. 1992. *Local justice: How institutions allocate scarce goods and necessary burdens*. New York: Russell Sage Foundation.

Fleming, M. 1988. *The geography of freedom: The odyssey of Élisée Reclus*. Montreal: Black Rose Books.

Foucault, M. 1970 [1966]. *The order of things*. New York: Vintage Books.

————. 1980. Questions on geography. In *Power/Knowledge,* edited by Colin Gordon. London: Harvester Press.

————. 1984. *The Foucault reader*. Harmondsworth, U.K.: Penguin.

————. 1986. Heterotopias. *Diacritics* 16, no. 1 (spring): 22–28.

Giddens, A. 1981. *A contemporary critique of historical materialism*. London: Macmillan.

————. 1984. *The constitution of society*. Cambridge: Polity Press.

Glacken, C. 1967. *Traces on the Rhodian shore: Nature and culture in Western thought from ancient times to the end of the eighteenth century*. Berkeley: University of California Press.

Godlewska, A., and N. Smith, eds. 1994. *Geography and empire*. Oxford: Blackwell.

Gregory, D. 1994. *Geographical imaginations*. Oxford: Blackwell.

Guha, R. 1983. *Elementary aspects of peasant insurgency in colonial India*. New Delhi: Oxford University Press.

————, ed. 1997. *A subaltern studies reader*. Minneapolis: University of Minnesota Press.

Harley, J. B. 1988. Maps, knowledge, and power. In *The iconography of landscape,* edited by D. Cosgrove and S. Daniels. Cambridge: Cambridge University Press.

Hartshorne, R. 1939. *The nature of geography: A critical survey of current thought in the light of the past*. Lancaster, Pa.: Association of American Geographers.

Harvey, D. 1973. *Social justice and the city*. London: Edward Arnold.

————. 1984. On the history and present condition of geography: An historical materialist manifesto. *Professional Geographer* 36: 1–11.

————. 1989. *The condition of postmodernity*. Oxford: Blackwell.

————. 1996. *Justice, nature, and the geography of difference*. Oxford: Blackwell.

————. 2000. *Spaces of hope*. Edinburgh: Edinburgh University Press.

Heidegger, M. 1971. *Poetry, language, thought,* translated by Albert Hofstadter. New York: Harper and Row.

Held, D. 1995. *Democracy and the global order: From the modern state to cosmopolitan governance.* Stanford, Calif.: Stanford University Press.

Hetherington, K. 1997. *The badlands of modernity: Heterotopia and social ordering.* London: Routledge.

Heyman, R. Forthcoming. The geography of university history: The "corporatization" of the university and the Berlin-Baltimore narrative. *Antipode.*

Humboldt, A. von. 1847. *Cosmos: Sketch of the physical description of the universe.* London: Longman, Brown, Green, and Longman.

Kant, I. 1974 [1798]. *Anthropology from a pragmatic point of view,* translated by V. L. Dowell. The Hague: Martinus Nijhoff.

———. 1991. *Kant: Political writings,* edited by H. Reiss, translated by H. Nisbet. Cambridge: Cambridge University Press.

———. 1999. *Géographie [Physique Geographie],* translated by M. Cohen-Halimi, M. Marcuzzi, and V. Seroussi. Paris: Bibliothèque Philosophique.

Koopmans, T. 1957. *Three essays on the state of economic science.* New York: McGraw Hill.

Koopmans, T., and M. Beckman. 1957. Assignment problems and the location of economic activities. *Econometrica* 25: 53–76.

Krugman, P. 1999. The role of geography in development. In Pleskovic and Stiglitz 1999, 89–125.

Lefebvre, H. 1991. *The production of space.* Oxford: Blackwell.

Livingstone, D. 1992. *The geographical tradition.* Oxford: Blackwell.

Marin, L. 1984. *Utopics: Spatial play,* translated by Robert A. Vollrath. London: Macmillan.

Marx, K., and F. Engels. 1952 [1848]. *The manifesto of the Communist Party,* translated by S. Moore. Moscow: Progress Publishers.

May, J. 1970. *Kant's concept of geography and its relation to recent geographical thought.* Toronto: Toronto University Press.

Miyoshi, M. 1997. A borderless world? In *Politics, poetics: Documenta X, the book,* edited by Documenta and Museum Fridericianum Veranstaltungs-GmbH. Kassel, Germany: Cantz.

———. 1998. "Globalization," culture, and the university. In *The cultures of globalization,* edited by F. Jameson and M. Miyoshi. Durham, N.C.: Duke University Press.

Newman, R. 1992. *Owen Lattimore and the "loss" of China.* Berkeley: University of California Press.

Nussbaum, M., with respondents. 1996. *For love of country: Debating the limits of patriotism.* Boston: Beacon Press.

———. 1997. Kant and stoic cosmopolitanism. *Journal of Political Philosophy* 5: 1–25.

Ollman, B. 1993. *Dialectical investigations.* New York: Routledge.

Peet, R. 1998. *Modern geographical thought.* Oxford: Blackwell.

Pleskovic, B., and J. Stiglitz, eds. 1999. *Annual World Bank conference on development economics.* Washington, D.C.: World Bank.

Readings, B. 1996. *The university in ruins.* Cambridge: Harvard University Press.

Ree, J. 1998. Cosmopolitanism and the experience of nationality. In Cheah and Robbins 1998.

Said, E. 1978. *Orientalism: Western conceptions of the Orient.* London: Routledge and Kegan Paul.

Shapiro, M. 1998. The events of discourse and the ethics of global hospitality. *Millennium* 27: 695–713.

Smith, N. 1984. Isaiah Bowman: Political geography and geopolitics. *Political Geography Quarterly* 3: 69–76.

———. 1997. Satanic geographies of globalization. *Public Culture* 10: 169–89.

———. 1999. The lost geography of the American century. *Scottish Geographical Journal* 115: 1–18.

———. n.d. *The geographical pivot of history: Isaiah Bowman and the geography of the American century.* Manuscript.

Smith, N., and C. Katz. 1993. Grounding metaphor: Towards a spatialized politics. In *Place and the politics of identity,* edited by M. Keith and S. Pile. London: Routledge.

Storper, M. 1997. *The regional world: Territorial development in a global economy.* New York: Guilford Press.

Tatham, G. 1951. Geography in the nineteenth century. In *Geography in the twentieth century,* edited by G. Taylor. London: Methuen.

Walzer, M. 1983. *Spheres of justice.* Oxford: Blackwell.

Webber, M., and D. Rigby. 1996. *The golden age illusion: Rethinking postwar capitalism.* New York: Guilford Press.

Wilson, R. 1998. A new cosmopolitanism is in the air: Some dialectical twists and turns. In Cheah and Robbins 1998.

World Bank. 1995. *World development report: Workers in an integrating world.* New York: Oxford University Press.

Zeldin, T. 1994. *An intimate history of humanity.* New York: HarperCollins.

Contributors

Scott Bradwell is a doctoral candidate in anthropology at the University of Chicago who recently completed fieldwork in Nejapa, El Salvador.

Jean Comaroff is Bernard E. and Ellen C. Sunny Distinguished Service Professor in the Department of Anthropology at the University of Chicago. *John L. Comaroff* is Harold H. Swift Distinguished Service Professor in the Department of Anthropology at the University of Chicago and senior research fellow at the American Bar Foundation in Chicago. Their publications include *Of Revelation and Revolution,* vol. 1 (1991) and vol. 2 (1997), as well as the edited collection, *Civil Society and the Political Imagination in Africa: Critical Perspectives* (1999).

Fernando Coronil teaches anthropology and history at the University of Michigan. His publications include *The Magical State: Nature, Money, and Modernity in Venezuela* (1997), "Beyond Occidentalism: Towards Non-Imperialist Geohistorical Categories," in *Cultural Anthropology* (1996), and (with Julie Skurski) "Dismembering and Remembering the Nation: The Semantics of Political Violence in Venezuela," in *Comparative Studies in Society and History* (1991).

Peter Geschiere teaches African anthropology at Leiden University, the Netherlands. He is the author of *The Modernity of Witchcraft: Politics and the Occult in Postcolonial Africa* (1997) and is editor (with Birgit Meyer) of *Globalization and Identity: Dialectics of Flow and Closure* (1999).

David Harvey teaches geography at Johns Hopkins University. He is the author of *Justice, Nature, and the Geography of Difference* (1996), *The Limits to Capital* (rev. ed., 1999), and *Spaces of Hope* (2000).

Luiz Paulo Lima is an award-winning photographer with the Brazilian newspaper *O Estado de São Paulo*. His material has been widely published and exhibited.

Caitrin Lynch received her Ph.D. in anthropology at the University of Chicago and is a former managing editor of *Public Culture*. She is the author of "The 'Good Girls' of Sri Lankan Modernity: Moral Orders of Nationalism and Capitalism" (*Identities*, summer 1999).

Rosalind C. Morris teaches anthropology at Columbia University, where she is also the director of the Institute for Research on Women and Gender. She is the author of "Educating Desire: Thailand, Transnationalism, Transgression" (*Social Text*, 1998) and *In the Place of Origins: Modernity and Its Mediums in Northern Thailand* (Duke, 2000).

Francis Nyamnjoh is the former head of the Department of Sociology and Anthropology at the University of Buea, Cameroon. He now teaches sociology at the University of Botswana in Gaborone, Botswana, and is completing a study on media and democratization in Africa in the 1990s. He is also a playwright and the author of the novel *The Disillusioned African* (1995).

Elizabeth A. Povinelli teaches anthropology at the University of Chicago. She is author of the forthcoming book *The Cunning of Recognition* and the editor (with George Chauncey) of a special issue of *GLQ* entitled *Thinking Sexuality Transnationally* (1999).

Paul Ryer, a graduate student at the University of Chicago, conducted fieldwork in Cuba from 1995 to 1997.

Allan Sekula's text and color photographs are excerpted from his exhibition of the same title, shown in the 1999 Liverpool Biennial. Sekula's previous work on the maritime world and global class relations can be found in *Fish Story* (1995). His most recent book is *Dismal Science: Photo Works, 1972–1976* (1999).

Dave Sinclair's photographs of the Liverpool dock struggle can be found in *Dockers* (1999), the film script written by the Liverpool dockers and their wives in collaboration with Jimmy McGovern and Irvine Welsh.

Irene Stengs is a graduate student in anthropology at the University of Amsterdam, working on a dissertation entitled "Worshipping the Great

Modernizer: King Chulalongkorn, Patron Saint of the Thai Middle Class."

Michael Storper teaches in the School of Public Policy and Social Research at the University of California at Los Angeles. He also teaches at the University of Paris/Marne-la-Vallée. He is the author of *The Regional World: Territorial Development in a Global Economy* (1997) and (with Robert Salais) *Worlds of Production: The Action Frameworks of the Economy* (1997).

Seamus Walsh is a San Francisco–based photographer and traditional boatbuilder who lived in Sri Lanka in 1995 and 1996.

Robert P. Weller teaches anthropology at Boston University. He is the author of *Alternate Civilities: Chinese Culture and the Prospects for Democracy* (1999) and *Resistance, Chaos, and Control in China: Taiping Rebels, Taiwanese Ghosts, and Tiananmen* (1994).

Hylton White is a graduate student in anthropology at the University of Chicago, working on sacrifice, social value, and problems of domestic reproduction in Kwazulu-Naral, South Africa.

Melissa W. Wright teaches geography and women's studies at the University of Georgia. Her recent publications include "Maquilador Mestizas and a Feminist Border Politics: Revisiting Anzaldúa," in *Hypatia* (summer 1998) and "The Politics of Relocation: Gender, Nationality, and Value in a Mexican Maquiladora," in *Environment and Planning* (fall 1999).

Jeffrey A. Zimmermann is an artist in Chicago. He has painted numerous murals, many of which address Latino influences and experiences in the city. His work can be viewed at *http://jazim.com/.*

Index

Langton, Marcia, 255
Language and linguistics, 200, 261–62, 263, 279
Lash, Scott, 9, 10, 12
Law, 30, 38–39, 242–44, 253, 285
Lawrence, Robert, 89, 93
Lea, John, 248
Leamer, Edward, 94, 96, 99
Lebergott, Stanley, 103, 108
Lefebvre, Henry, 67
Lentz, Carola, 183
Le Pen, Jean-Marie, 160–61, 176–77, 187 nn.13 and 14
Lewis, Tom, 11
Limas Hernández, A., 128
Litumbe, Mola Njoh, 169
Liverpool, port of, 148–49
Livingstone, D., 274, 294
Lolliver, S., 95
Los Angeles, port of, 147–48
Lottery, 6–7, 46 n.7, 59–62, 222–23
Loveday, P., 248
Loveman, Gary, 89, 93
Lucker, G. William, 134
Lugard, F. D., 181
Lukacs, John, 29
Lundvall, Bengt-Ake, 114
Lury, Celia, 104, 106, 113
Lynn, Robert, 104

Machin, Stephen, 100
Macpherson, Crawford, 42
Madrick, Jeffrey, 105, 109
Mamdani, Mahmood, 174
Maquiladoras: job training and turn-over in, 126, 131–37, 138–40; women in, 126–29, 139–40, 142–44
Maquiladora trade association (AMAC), 130–31
Marcos, Subcomandante: and Fourth World War, 71–73
Marin, L., 280
Marx, Karl: on cosmopolitanism, 272; on labor, 9–10, 126, 127, 133, 143; land/rent, 67, 83 n.3; on nature, 67, 68; on the state, 32; on wealth, 68
Maskell, P. H., 98
Maslow, Abraham, 110
Master Dharma Drum: The Life and Heart of Ch'an Practices, 265
The Matrix, 256, 257
May, J., 274, 277
McCulloch-Uehlin, Susan, 252–53
McDowell, Linda, 133
McMichael, Philip, 10, 33
Media: electronic media, 22, 193–94, 199–200; movies, 256–58, 262–63; newspapers, 30, 38, 166, 169; radio, 38, 196–97; television, 24, 38, 192–93, 210 n.3. *See also* Technology
Mediumship: occult economy and, 19–27, 36, 46 n.7, 57–62, 235; in Taiwan, 22, 211 n.9, 225; theatricality of, 198–201, 203–5, 212 nn.16 and 18; use of electronic media by, 193–94, 199–200; writing and, 199–200, 211 n.15, 227, 237 n.4
Mexico. *See* Maquiladoras
Meyer, Brigit, 160
Michaels, Eric, 255
Middle class, 70, 90, 109–11, 115, 118 n.1, 119 n.6
Miliband, Ralph, 32
Miller, Daniel, 4, 47 n.18, 105, 113
Mishel, Lawrence, 99, 109
Miyoshi, M., 272, 273
Mobutu Sese Seko, 174
Moffitt, Robert, 95
Mohnen, P., 102
Moore, Sally Falk, 30
Morgan, Marlo, 256, 260, 261, 264
Morris, Rosalind C., 21
Mouiche, I., 168–69
Moulian, Tomás, 75
Mouvement pour la Démocratie el le Progrés, 170
Mouvement Progressiste, 167
Movies, 256–58, 262–63
Murphy, Kevin, 93

Readings, B., 272, 273, 291, 302

Reclus, Élisée, 294–95

Ree, Jonathan, 289

Reggio, Godfrey, 262

Religion: Buddhism, 202–5, 212 n.18, 224, 229–32, 235; commercialism, 205, 208, 224–25; fee-for-service religion, 6, 23–24, 221–22, 232–36; *hindutva*, 286; in Taiwan, 227–28, 232–35; temples, 220–26, 228–29, 233–36, 237 n.4; use of media, 192–93, 196–97, 208

Revolution of Little Girls, 265–66

Ricardo, David, 67, 91

Richardson, J. David, 92, 96, 100

Ries, Nancy, 35

Rigby, D., 283

Rilke, Rainer Maria, 205

Risk, 5–7, 20, 46 n.7, 57–62, 78–80, 222–23

Robbins, B., 272, 273, 288

Robertson, Roland, 161

Roeg, Nicholas, 256

Roitman, Janet, 18, 34

Rongfa, Zhang, 227

Rosenberg, Stephanie, 115

Ross, Robert, 28–29

Rowlands, Michael, 164

Rupnik, Jacques, 43

Sachs, Jeffrey, 93

Safe, 257

Said, Edward, 298

Salacuse, Jeswald W., 39

Salais, Robert, 97

Salzinger, Leslie, 139

Sanford, Charles, 79, 80

Sassen, Sakia, 12, 28, 33, 82

Sawa, 166–68, 172, 179–80, 186 n.7

Sayer, Derek, 32

Sayles, John, 257

Schatz, Howard, 93

Scheper-Hughes, Nancy, 21

Schmitt, John, 99, 109

Schneider, Jane, 23

Schor, Juliet, 103, 105, 106–7, 110, 111

Scitovsky, Tibor, 106, 114

Scott, Ridley, 257

Scranton, Philip, 100

Secret of Roan Inish, 257

Seekings, Jeremy, 17

Sen, Amartya, 110

Sennett, Richard, 4

Shapiro, M., 278, 284, 289

Shapiro, Martin, 39

Sheng-Yen, Cha'an, 265

Silbey, Susan S., 30

Silverstein, Michael, 247

Simison, R., 138

Simmel, Georg, 205

Simons, Marlene, 74

Sklair, Leslie, 13, 131

Skurski, Julie, 73

Slater, Don, 104, 106

Slaughter, Matthew, 93

Slovic, P., 107

Smith, Adam, 42, 44, 67, 272

Smith, N., 287, 294, 297

Smith, Valene, 246

Social Democratic Front (SDF), 164, 166–68

Socialism, 71, 240

The Songlines, 256

Sontag, Susan, 3

South Africa, 20–21, 34, 40

South West Elites Association (SWELA), 173–74

Space: cosmopolitanism and, 282–83; heterotopias, 280–81; national, 246, 266–67, 286, 289–90; sacred space, 224–25; tourism and, 246–52, 267–68

Spirituality, aboriginal, 242–45, 251–55, 267

Spivak, Gayatri, 250

Stack, M., 131, 142

Stanislaw, Joseph, 28

Stanley, Owen, 248

Stiglitz, J., 297

Stolper-Samuelson model, 91, 94, 98

Storper, Michael, 11, 12, 97, 298

Wealth: distribution of, 7, 70, 72–73, 89–90; human resources as source of, 67–69, 76–77; occult economy, 19–27, 36, 46 n.7, 57–62, 235; philanthropy and, 22, 231

Webb, S., 89

Webber, M., 283

Weber, Max, 25, 32, 201

Weiland, Matt, 113

Weiss, Linda, 70, 75

Weller, Robert P., 6

Where the Green Ants Dream, 256, 262, 263

White, G., 138, 139

Whorf, Benjamin, 247

Wicker Man, 257

Will, George, 7

Wilson, R., 302

Wilson, William Julius, 90

Wittgenstein, Ludwig, 247

Women: in Buddhism, 231; death by culture, 129–31, 140, 141; feminization of workforce, 9, 12, 17, 135; job training and turnover of, 126, 131–37; in maquiladoras, 126–29, 139–40, 142–44; value of labor, 58, 69, 126–27, 143–44

Wood, Adrian, 93, 94, 96, 100, 119 n.3

Woods, Dwayne, 42

Worby, Eric, 38

Workforce: for Aboriginal art production, 249–50; dockworkers, 149–51, 157; exploitation of, 2, 28, 48 n.35, 181–83, 191; feminization of, 9, 12, 17, 135; gender

stereotypes in, 127, 134–37; job security, 4–5, 71; job training and turnover in, 126, 131–37, 138–40; labor-saving techniques, 102–3, 119 n.9; production/consumption distance and, 9–13, 78, 103–4, 147; skill levels in, 89–95, 97–99, 119 n.6, 134–38; standards of living, 76–77, 107–9, 118; technologies and, 96, 100–101; unionism, 45, 155; women in, 58, 69, 126–29, 131–40, 142–44; youth in, 6, 26, 249

World Bank, 76, 77, 165, 284, 297

World War IV. *See* Marcos, Subcomandante

Worsley, Peter M., 24

Worsthorne, Peregrine, 30

Wright, Melissa W., 15, 136

The X-Files, 258

Yergin, Daniel, 28

Yinshun, 231–32

Young, Crawford, 43

Youth generation, 6, 16–19, 26, 47 n.20, 249

Yúdice, George, 2

Zeitlin, Jonathan, 101, 102

Zeldin, T., 292

Zemeckis, Robert, 258

Zhengyan, 229–30, 232, 235

Žižek, Slavoj, 13

Zognong, D., 166, 168–69

Library of Congress Cataloging-in-Publication Data
Millennial capitalism and the culture of neoliberalism /
edited by Jean Comaroff and John L. Comaroff.
p. cm. — (Public culture (Durham, N.C.))
"The text of this book originally was published, without
the essay by Melissa W. Wright or the index, as vol. 12,
no. 2 of Public culture. . . . Wright's essay originally
appeared in vol. 11, no. 3 . . . , pages 453–474" — P. .
Includes bibliographical references and index.
ISBN 0-8223-2704-x (cloth : alk. paper) —
ISBN 0-8223-2715-5 (pbk. : alk. paper)
1. Free enterprise. 2. Liberalism. 3. Capitalism.
I. Comaroff, Jean. II. Comaroff, John L., 1945– III. Series.
HB95 .M55 2001   330.12'2—dc21   00-046658